SCOTTY BOWMAN

A Life in Hockey

DOUGLAS HUNTER

VIKING

VIKING

Published by the Penguin Group

Penguin Books Canada Ltd, 10 Alcorn Avenue, Toronto, Ontario, Canada M4V 3B2

Penguin Books Ltd, 27 Wrights Lane, London W8 5TZ, England

Penguin Putnam Inc., 375 Hudson Street, New York, New York 10014, U.S.A.

Penguin Books Australia Ltd, Ringwood, Victoria, Australia

Penguin Books (NZ) Ltd, cnr Rosedale and Airborne Roads, Albany

Auckland 1310, New Zealand

Penguin Books Ltd Registered Offices: Harmondsworth, Middlesex, England

First published 1998

10 9 8 7 6 5 4 3 2 1

Printed and bound in Canada on acid free paper ∞

CANADIAN CATALOGUING IN PUBLICATION DATA

Hunter, Douglas, 1959–
    Scotty Bowman: a life in hockey

ISBN 0-670-87990-8

1. Bowman, Scotty. 2. Hockey coaches – Canada – Biography. 3. Hockey players – Canada – Biography. I. Title

GV848.5.B68H86 1998   796.962'092   C98-931374-3

Visit Penguin Canada's website at www.penguin.ca

For Drew

1

✧ THERE IS A MARVELLOUS piece of raw footage in the archives of the National Film Board of Canada. Unedited and without sound, it captures in black and white the final minutes of game five of the 1950/51 Stanley Cup final series between the Toronto Maple Leafs and the Montreal Canadiens. After Bill Barilko's overtime goal wins Toronto its fourth Cup in five years, the exultant Leafs gather on the ice of Maple Leaf Gardens to collect the Stanley Cup from league president Clarence Campbell. The Canadiens have retired from the scene, and the frame is filled with Leaf players. Team captain Ted Kennedy looks off-camera and mutely shouts, "Joe!" The next scene features a grinning "Gentleman Joe" Primeau, former Leaf captain and now winner of the Stanley Cup in his first season as the team's coach. Joe is dressed in a dark suit and fedora, as out of place amid the throng of celebratory players as a civilian on a battlefield.

It has ever been thus in hockey: coaches shuffling cautiously onto the rink in their Sunday best and gleaming dress shoes, alien to the terrain. Sometimes their feet do not even touch the ice. Move forward five springs from Gentleman Joe's triumph and you'll find another rookie NHL coach, another former team captain, captured in the bliss of victory. Toe Blake is supported on the shoulders of Dickie Moore and Bernie Geoffrion, steadied by the hand of Jacques Plante. You can see his shoes in the photograph; Moore has a grip on Blake's leg, just above the ankle, revealing a stylish pair of argyle socks beneath the wool trousers. He waves his trademark fedora like a politician swept up in an election landslide. Blake is so divorced from the melee of the rink that Moore and Geoffrion might have retrieved him from an office on Ste-Catherine Street.

The ice has long been the exclusive domain of the player and the on-ice officials; anyone else who steps onto it and makes their precarious way across its slick and sometimes bloodied surface has to admit that they don't belong. Hockey physically isolates the coach from the game he directs like no other professional sport. He stands behind his players on the bench, more like a spectator than a participant. When the buzzer sounds, when the final whistle blows, when the final pitch is thrown, the masterminds of basketball, football and baseball can stride confidently onto the playing surface without a hint of negotiating a strange landscape. Yet whenever it is time for the Stanley Cup to be presented, a carpet is rolled out to give the men in suits safe passage, corralling them in a plush extension of the world on the other side of the boards.

Hockey reminds the coach that he is not a part of the game, and in some cases reminds him that he never was a part of it. Many coaches are former NHL players, as Primeau and Blake were, but many others, like Scotty Bowman, have come to coach in the league without ever having participated in the fray they strive to choreograph. Bowman played as a teenager, but a professional career eluded him, and he would never know how it felt to skate a shift against a Beliveau, to shoot for the top-right corner against a Sawchuk, to take a punch to the temple from a Schultz. Despite appearing to be at the heart of every contest, Bowman, on the eve of his seventh Stanley Cup coaching win, had long existed on the periphery of a game he understood probably better than anyone else alive.

Which is why he brought his skates to Detroit's Joe Louis Arena for game four of the 1996/97 Stanley Cup finals between his Red Wings and the Philadelphia Flyers. Should the Red Wings win the game and sweep the Flyers, Scotty Bowman was not going to be content simply to do the time-honoured cross-ice shuffle like Primeau did, or be hoisted aloft as Blake was. He was going to enter the players' world through the only available portal: the celebration of victory. He was going to strap on the blades, take to the ice, grasp the glittering barrel of Lord Stanley's prize, and experience the rare sensation of gliding before a euphoric crowd with more than a century of glory, some of it his own, hoisted above his head.

When Scotty Bowman coached the Detroit Red Wings to their 1996/97 Stanley Cup win on the evening of Saturday, June 7, at Joe Louis Arena, the franchise's first since 1954/55, those forty-two gaping seasons inspired many headlines and commentaries. It was less what the team had accomplished—sweeping Philadelphia in four—than what it had undone—nearly half a century of disappointment. Five trips by Detroit to the finals from 1955/56 to 1965/66 ended in losses; the most bone-wearying period ran from 1962/63 to 1965/66, when three Cups out of four featured the Red Wings as losers. Then came the great wilderness adventure, when the team missed the playoffs in all but two of sixteen seasons. And then the years of increasing promise, which suddenly turned grim: swept in the 1994/95 finals, eliminated in the 1995/96 conference championships.

The 1996/97 playoffs finally delivered the team from its four-decade purgatory with an almost sobering efficiency. It was not quite the tour de force the Red Wings had performed in 1951/52, when they'd crushed all playoff opposition with eight straight wins, but it was nonetheless impressive. There were none of the stuttering misfires of a great machine that cannot get all cylinders working together, as had happened in the previous two seasons. After a close series with St. Louis, which the Red Wings won 4–2 but in which they'd outscored the Blues only 13–12, the Wings took flight, winning sixteen and losing two against Anaheim, Colorado and finally Philadelphia, a team that had nothing to deflect Bowman's arsenal. The Red Wings had figured out not just how to win, but how to win convincingly. They had lost in four to New Jersey in the 1994/95 finals, outscored 17–6. In 1996/97, they defeated in four the Flyers, outscoring them 16–6.

A long time, forty-two seasons: in Detroit, the general manager's position had changed hands eight times, the coach's job twenty-one times. The arena had changed, from the Olympia to Joe Louis. Ownership had changed, from the Norris family to the Ilitch family, from a grain shipper and boxing mogul's son to a pizza purveyor. The league had changed, from six to twenty-six teams, with more to come. A rival league, the World Hockey Association, had come and gone. The rules had gone through endless permutations: changes in the dimensions of the goal crease, in the distance from the goal line to the end boards, in offside rules, in rules to restrict brawling, in dimensions for equipment. The curved stick had shown up. The goal mask had shown up. The Russians had shown up. The Red Wings of 1996/97 had enough Russians to fill an entire shift: Viacheslav Fetisov and Vladimir Konstantinov on defence, Sergei Fedorov, Igor Larionov, Vyacheslav Kozlov up front. All but Kozlov (who was too young) had won Olympic gold with the Soviet national team in 1988. When Detroit had last won the Stanley Cup, the Soviets had never iced a hockey team at the Olympics; in fact, the Soviets had never participated in any Olympics, in any sport. In 1956, the Soviets won the hockey gold medal on their first try, and Detroit lost the Stanley Cup finals to the Montreal Canadiens to begin the forty-two-season drought. The entire Soviet hockey programme had happened in the lull between Red Wing victories; indeed, much of the history of the Cold War and the Evil Empire, from the Hungary uprising of 1956 to glasnost and perestroika in 1989, had unfolded, with eight years to spare. By the time Detroit won in 1996/97, there wasn't even a Soviet Union any more.

Forty-two years is a long time in the twentieth century.

At sixty-three years of age, his retirement rumoured to be looming, Scotty Bowman's hockey career spanned those forty-two years and then some. His career not only figured prominently in the end to the Red Wings' drought, it had begun before there was a Red Wings Cup-winning streak to give way to a drought. His years as an NHL coach are unique in providing a guided tour of the highlights of post-expansion hockey, the thirty NHL seasons from 1967/68 forward. But the run-up to his NHL career consumed another twenty-six years of hockey. Bowman's life, in short, encapsulates the postwar game. The native Montrealer had embarked on his life in the game when the idea of a Canadiens dynasty was scarcely formed. The Canadiens had eighteen Stanley Cup victories ahead of them when he came along. He would guide them to five of them before getting around to helping the Wings reclaim that elusive trophy. By doing so, he set himself apart from all fellow coaches. He now had seven Stanley Cup rings—eight if you counted the 1990/91 championship with Pittsburgh, in which he served as director of player development. No one else in the legion of active NHL head coaches could boast of more than one Cup title.

That Scotty Bowman won his one-thousandth NHL game as a coach, in January 1997, is truly impressive. The milestone also underscores the nature of the modern NHL and Bowman's role in it. Thirty seasons after beginning his career in the league, he alone was still on the job, barking orders to players, castigating officials, juggling lines, baiting opponents. Not one of the eleven other men who were coaching NHL teams when he made his league debut with the St. Louis Blues in 1967/68 was still behind the bench. And none of the eighteen-member Class of 1978/79, the season Bowman won his last of five Stanley Cups for Montreal, held head coaching jobs in 1996/97.

Some former adversaries had fallen by the wayside simply because time had caught up with them. Toe Blake, Montreal's coach in 1967/68 when the Canadiens defeated Bowman's Blues in the Cup finals, had retired after that season. Fred Shero, who had lost the 1975/76 and 1978/79 finals to Bowman, first as coach of the Philadelphia Flyers, then as coach as the New York Rangers, was fired by the Rangers in 1980/81. Both Blake and Shero died in 1990. Many others, however, were gone from the bench because they had done everything in their power to become something other than coaches as quickly as possible. Coaching is a junior management job, a front-line posting that delivers no more job security than actually playing the game, and lately perhaps even less.

In days not so long ago, when one man could legitimately try to hold down the jobs of both coach and general manager, many tried to do so. A coach who was also the general manager could do far more than pencil in starting lineups and discipline players. He could trade them, demote them, draft them—in short, control them the way a coach never could. When the league expanded in 1967/68, half the six new clubs attempted to operate with a coach/general manager, but the complexity of the new game's business side soon made it clear that, with rare exceptions, the two roles were best kept separate. At the start of his second NHL season, Bowman was St. Louis's coach and general manager, and his desire to be more than a coach, at times to put coaching completely behind him, would mark his entire career. However, it was in Buffalo in the 1980s, when he attempted do both jobs with the Sabres, and then could find no one who satisfied him as a coach while he concentrated on managing, that he experienced his one true career failure. In the end, it was his coaching that most endeared him to team owners and senior management, although it did not provide his initial return to the game after the humiliation of Buffalo.

The skill for which Scotty Bowman is best known—coaching teams to Stanley Cup victories—has not always been the skill he has most ardently striven to practise. Everyone around him, it seemed, was either being fired as a coach or moving up the corporate ranks. Though he was eager to put coaching behind him in pursuit of job security, the least secure job in management ended up delivering him that very security—a security enjoyed by scarcely anyone else.

The coaching turnover between the 1996/97 and 1997/98 seasons underscored the uncertainty now attached to the assignment. As general managers increasingly lost their job security, coaches became even more vulnerable. The comings and goings above them in the ranks cost them their positions, as new managers arrived with their own coaches. Bowman was one of sixteen coaches returning to work with their old teams in the twenty-six-team league in the fall of 1997. The ten off-season casualties included Terry Murray, coach of the Stanley Cup finalist Flyers, and coach of the year Ted Nolan in Buffalo, replaced by former team captain Lindy Ruff after he turned down what he considered a low-ball, one-year contract. The surviving coaches were soon down to thirteen as three more fell in rapid succession: Terry Crisp in Tampa Bay on October 26, Tom Renney in Vancouver on November 13, and Doug MacLean in Florida on November 24. Counting these early-season dismissals, coaching jobs between 1996/97 and 1997/98 had a 50 percent casualty rate.

The casualties began mounting again in the new year, as teams prepared to take a run at a playoff spot, or worried about the ability of their coaching staff to shape a Cup winner. In February 1998, during the league Olympic break, Colin Campbell was dismissed by the Rangers as the 1993/94 Stanley Cup champions continued to struggle. He was replaced by John Muckler, who had been sacked as Buffalo's general manager the previous summer. In March came two more firings. Philadelphia general manager Bobby Clarke reinforced his reputation as hockey's most ruthless executive by axing his second coach in less than a year; Wayne Cashman was demoted to assistant coach and replaced by Roger Neilson. Soon thereafter, New York Islanders general manager Mike Milbury added another chapter to his long association with Rick Bowness by dropping him as his coach and returning to the bench himself.

The vagaries of the profession have caused Scotty Bowman minimal distress. In thirty-one NHL seasons, Bowman has changed jobs only four times, and he has been steadily employed in the league for all but three seasons. By the 1990s, Bowman had been around so long that players who had once done his bidding were now his peers in coaching and management. Bob Gainey, his star defensive forward of the 1970s in Montreal, coached a little more than five seasons before settling exclusively into the role of general manager and vice-president in Dallas in 1995. Ken Dryden, his goaltender for five Montreal Stanley Cups, had never coached or managed at all in the NHL (or anywhere else) when he secured the presidency of the Toronto Maple Leafs in 1997. Wayne Thomas, who had helped mind the Canadiens' net when Ken Dryden departed for a year of law articling, became assistant general manager of San Jose in 1997. The most impressive former Bowman players were Glen Sather and Al Arbour. A journeyman Canadien in 1974/75, in a few short seasons Sather was coach, then general manager, then president of the Edmonton Oilers, then the impresario of the Oilers' five Stanley Cup wins of the 1980s. Arbour, who drew his first coaching assignment under Bowman in St. Louis in 1970/71, went on to lead the Islanders to four Stanley Cup wins in the early 1980s.

Serge Savard, who was on defence for all five of Bowman's Canadiens victories, came and went as Montreal's general manager; now Rejean Houle, who had left Bowman's authority in 1973 to play in the WHA (and returned to play for Bowman in 1976), was running the Canadiens in Savard's stead. Larry Pleau, who had played Junior hockey for Bowman and had jumped from Montreal to the WHA in 1972, was named general manager of St. Louis for 1997/98, after spending eight years in the Rangers' management, most recently as vice-president of player personnel. Jacques Lemaire, another five-Cup Bowman veteran, was a Stanley Cup winning coach in New Jersey, and seemed to be as secure in his job as any coach could be, but after an early playoff exit in 1997/98 he tendered his resignation. Lemaire's old teammate and assistant in New Jersey, Larry Robinson, was coaching Los Angeles. Other players from Bowman's Montreal years were working as assistant coaches around the league: Doug Jarvis, Rick Wilson, Rod Langway, Jacques Laperriere, Guy Lapointe, Jimmy

Roberts. Still others—Peter Mahovlich and Pierre Mondou—were scouting for NHL clubs. From the rosters of his Buffalo years there was Jim Schoenfeld, coach of the Phoenix Coyotes; Don Luce, Buffalo's director of player personnel; Craig Ramsay, assistant coach of the Ottawa Senators; Andre Savard, chief scout in Ottawa; and Don Edwards, goaltending coach in Los Angeles. Mike Ramsey, who played for Bowman in Buffalo, Pittsburgh and Detroit, was an assistant coach in Buffalo. Phil Myre, a goaltending backup for Bowman in Montreal and Buffalo, was Ottawa's pro scout. Jacques Caron, who had played goal for Bowman in Junior hockey, was the goaltending coach in New Jersey. And Bob Plager, who had played for Bowman in St. Louis, was the Blues' director of pro scouting.

Scotty Bowman is more than just an experienced practitioner of the game; he is the very experience of the modern game. When you look at where he has been, what he has done, you see the game. Your first glimpse of him comes as a dynasty is emerging (by the measure of this century's breakneck timeline) like some brilliant star coalescing from a cloud of cosmic gases. A bright light is waxing, and Scotty is charting a far-flung orbit.

2

❖ THE GLORY YEARS of Les Canadiens known to modern fans
began in wartime. These were the brief but critical Tommy Gorman
years in Montreal, years that were later overshadowed by the decades
of success that followed under two storied general managers, Frank
Selke and his protege, Sam Pollock. But Gorman, a professional
chameleon who had gotten in with the National Hockey League on
the ground floor by becoming a part owner of the Ottawa Senators in
1917, brought respectability to a teetering Canadiens franchise, something his successors could build upon. By the time Gorman assumed
command of the Canadiens as general manager in 1940, he had won
three Stanley Cups as part-owner of the Ottawa Senators, run the
New York Americans NHL franchise for bootlegger Bill Dwyer, bailed
out of Dwyer's operation to manage the Agua Caliente race-track in
Mexico, plotted his fortune by bringing the thoroughbred phenomenon Phar Lap from Australia for a North American tour, watched his
dream of riches evaporate when the horse died under mysterious circumstances, landed on his feet in Chicago, where he coached the Blackhawks to their 1934 Stanley Cup win, and switched to the Montreal
Maroons, with whom he won another Cup in 1935. When the
Maroons franchise was shut down in 1938 in favour of the Canadiens as the sole Montreal NHL club, Gorman stayed in the picture as

manager of the Montreal Forum. With the Canadiens on the skids in 1940, Gorman was given the general manager's job by the franchise's owner, Senator M. Donat Raymond.

"Colourful" barely does justice to the character of Thomas M. Gorman. He would boast of perpetrating an outrageous fraud while running the Agua Caliente thoroughbred track from 1929 to 1932. He brought in a top American racehorse named Westy Hogan, painted him brown, called him Little Boy, and set him running in a race that dinged bookies for an estimated $500,000. With that sort of nerve and ingenuity in his background, the allegation that he was dumped by Senator Raymond in 1946 over ticket sale irregularities, while un-substantiated, does not seem implausible.

Whatever the reason Gorman left the Canadiens, his six seasons in command through the war years reversed the franchise's decline and paved the way for the successes that lay ahead in the 1950s, 1960s and 1970s. When he arrived in 1940, Gorman placed the entire Montreal team on waivers, except for star left-winger Toe Blake, a former Maroons property. He then brought in a young play-making centre, Elmer Lach, from Saskatchewan, and secured Dick Irvin from the Maple Leafs as his coach. He beefed up the franchise's connections and influence in the Quebec amateur leagues and made sure players had off-ice jobs in vital war industries that kept them clear of the Canadian home-defence draft. By 1943 he had a club that could completely dominate the competition—competition that was, however, greatly weakened by the loss of players to compulsory military service in Canada and the United States.

However inflated the Canadiens' accomplishments were during the war years—the team lost only five of fifty games in 1943/44 on the way to winning the Stanley Cup, and eight of fifty in 1944/45, and hoarded five of the six first-team All Star positions in 1944/45—the strengths of the organization Gorman revamped were genuine and would survive the return to peacetime. Only Gorman himself, it appeared, was vulnerable. When Frank Selke became available as general manager in the summer of 1946 after a falling out with the Leafs' leading shareholder, Conn Smythe, Gorman was let go; he bought into the Ottawa Auditorium, and later he reinvented himself again, this time as the manager of figure skating sensation Barbara Ann Scott.

Frank Selke was the man who was running the Canadiens and its development empire when Scotty Bowman came to the organization, first as a player and then at various times as a coach, a scout and an assistant manager. Selke was a refugee of the Toronto Maple Leafs, as was Irvin, the Canadiens' coach. All through Irvin's years in Toronto, which began in 1931, he had worked with Selke, an often unheralded architect of the Maple Leafs franchise. Selke had coached the Toronto Marlboros to victory in the 1929 Memorial Cup, the national Junior championship. His 1927/28 Marlies gave the Leafs Eddie Convey, and the 1928/29 team produced Alex Levinsky, Red Horner, Charlie Conacher and Busher Jackson. Conn Smythe, the Leafs' managing director and principal force, hired Selke as his assistant, and Selke lent a big assist in creating the Maple Leaf dynasty.

When war broke out in 1939, Conn Smythe turned his attention to forming his own anti-aircraft battery and left Selke to run the Leafs as he went off to war. Under Selke, and with Hap Day coaching, the Leafs reversed more than a decade of frustration by winning the 1941/42 Stanley Cup, then played giant-killer in 1944/45 by upsetting Gorman's Canadiens in the semifinals and defeating the Detroit Red Wings in the finals. Smythe returned home wounded in September 1944, and was convinced that Selke was scheming with board members to have him ousted from Maple Leaf Gardens. In the spring of 1946, Smythe informed Selke that he intended to make a run at the presidency, and he made it clear that if Selke wasn't prepared to vote his shares in his favour, there would be no place for him in the new organization. Smythe wouldn't achieve his power play until November 1947, but Selke could see the Leafs' future clearly after the 1945/46 season, and he left the club.

That summer, Senator Raymond was in Toronto on business, learned

Selke was available and offered him the general manager's job with the Canadiens. Gorman was firmly instructed to move aside. Almost twenty years would pass before Selke, too, felt the pressure from management to make way for a newcomer, this time exerted in a more kindly way. In the meantime, he would take up the job Gorman had begun and build a sports operation that would rival anything in any professional league.

Selke arrived at a watershed in the history of the NHL. The 1946/47 NHL season was the first to be played free of the exigencies of wartime: well into the 1945/46 season, players were still trickling back into team lineups as they were demobilized. Red Dutton, the league's interim president, was about to give way to a new hiring, Clarence Campbell, who would run the league (according to the owners' wishes) until 1977. The league, which had reached a high of ten franchises in 1926, had seen its numbers dwindle steadily through the Depression. The demise of the Brooklyn Americans in 1942 had left the league at six. When the war ended, franchise applications were received from half a dozen American cities, but the league under Campbell resolved to remain in its compact configuration for the next two decades. With only about one hundred full-time NHL starting positions available, and wave upon wave of new talent pushing its way up, the Original Six era would see some of the finest hockey the game will ever witness.

Montreal had won the 1945/46 Stanley Cup, defeating Boston 4–1 in the finals after finishing first overall for the third straight season. The Canadiens made it four straight in 1946/47, but lost the Cup finals 4–2 to Toronto as the Leafs won their first of four Cups in five seasons. The Canadiens missed the playoffs altogether in 1947/48, a season that had already reached its nadir on January 11, when a double ankle fracture ended the career of captain Toe Blake, thus disbanding the celebrated Punch Line of Blake, Elmer Lach and Maurice Richard.

The Canadiens created by Gorman had one season's grace under Selke before the overhaul began. The team that had won the Cup for

Gorman in 1945/46 was much the same team that had won in 1943/44. Then came the beginning of steady and sweeping changes, particularly after the failure to make the playoffs in 1947/48. Only five players—Elmer Lach, Butch Bouchard, Ken Mosdell, Maurice Richard and Billy Reay—would still be around when the Canadiens next won the Cup, in 1952/53. Selke was securing a new generation of amateur talent and ushering them into the Canadiens' lineup. Over the course of those six seasons, from 1947/48 to 1952/53, sixteen new faces who would have their names affixed to the Stanley Cup in 1952/53 made their debuts, and another two, Jean Beliveau and Don Marshall, put in appearances while still amateurs. Of these eighteen, only three arrived from outside the Montreal development system: Calum MacKay, picked up from the Detroit minor pro system, Bert Olmstead, acquired in a trade from Chicago, and Johnny McCormack, a postwar refugee of the Leaf development system. Everyone else was a product of Montreal's own prodigious efforts to scout, sign and develop teenage amateur talent.

The list was a testament to Selke's determination to create a farm system that would rival and even exceed any other in the league. He clearly eclipsed the impressive Toronto network, and only Jack Adams in Detroit fashioned a talent pipeline that delivered comparable results. As the 1940s gave way to the 1950s, the list of home-grown talent the Canadiens managed to ice was astounding: Doug Harvey, Tom Johnson, Bud McPherson and Dollard St. Laurent on defence; Gerry McNeil and Jacques Plante in goal (with Charlie Hodge in reserve); Busher Curry, Bernie Geoffrion and Lorne Davis on right wing; and Dick Gamble, Dickie Moore, Don Marshall and Ed Mazur on left wing.

For a young left-winger like William Scott Bowman, entering the Canadiens' talent system at such an auspicious time in franchise history must have been both exhilarating and daunting. Montreal was creating a hockey powerhouse, and it would have been most any local teenager's dream to be part of it. But this powerhouse had such vast resources of talent that the number of young players who would one day crack the starting lineup of the parent NHL club would be dwarfed by the number of prospects who would prove to have no prospect at all with any club in a six-team league. The greatest teams in Canadian Junior hockey rarely saw more than a couple of players from any given season reach the NHL ranks. In 1948/49, the Montreal Royals (not part of the Canadiens system) won the Memorial Cup, but only one player, Dickie Moore, was destined to find an NHL starting job.

The success Montreal experienced in building a postwar talent network was due not only to Selke's personal commitment to building a development system, but also to his recognition that he was not going to be able to do it single-handedly. Two men played front-line roles in Selke's efforts to tap into and develop the best amateur talent from around the country. One was Ken Reardon, who retired from the Canadiens blueline after 1949/50. Reardon (who married a daughter of team owner Senator Raymond) was vital to developing the Montreal talent pool in western Canada. A native of Edmonton, Reardon rose to a team vice-presidency as he cultivated the west.

The other key figure in Selke's ambitions was an organizer of minor baseball and hockey in Montreal, Sam Pollock. Pollock was one of Selke's first hirings when he arrived to run the Canadiens, and he would become Selke's successor as general manager, nosing out Reardon for the post. Reardon would bear Pollock no ill will. "He's the most intelligent man I've ever met," Reardon says. "Not just in hockey. In life."

Pollock's role was in the trenches of the talent battle. In 1947, Pollock was hired to run the Montreal Junior Canadiens and oversee player development. He faced what seemed an uphill battle. In the Memorial Cup eastern playdowns of 1946/47, before Pollock's arrival, the Junior Canadiens, reduced at times to ten skaters by injuries, lost 11–3 and 21–0 to the St. Michael's College Majors, a team packed with future Maple Leafs. Pollock would coach and manage at the Junior and minor pro level, building the strength of the development system along with the playing strengths of the young men under his influence. His job was to shape the Canadiens teams of the future. Early in Pollock's long career with Montreal, Scotty Bowman, a teenager in the development system's second wave, which would produce star Canadiens in the mid- to late-1950s, fell under his tutelage.

Pollock would become revered as one of the sharpest front-office minds in professional sport. He entered the business as a short, stocky bull of a man with a head for business, a love of sport and a pyrotechnic temper. He had no pretensions, and no desire to become any sort of star himself. He worked superhuman hours, always paying attention to the bottom line, yet never losing sight of the unique human element of his business. He showed an almost unerring sense for quality in people, and he cultivated subordinates carefully, bringing them along over many years. Virtually all of Pollock's career with the Montreal Canadiens was spent in some association with Scotty Bowman, and almost all of Scotty Bowman's long career with the Montreal Canadiens was spent in close association with Sam Pollock.

Pollock's first coaching success came with the 1949/50 Memorial Cup. Dickie Moore had crossed over to Pollock's Junior Canadiens, and Moore's teammates that season included fellow future Canadiens Bucky Hollingworth, Charlie Hodge and Don Marshall. With Pollock managing and Canadiens star Billy Reay helping Pollock with the coaching (after Montreal made a quick playoff exit), the Junior Canadiens defeated the Regina Pats, another Montreal farm team, which graduated to the Canadiens Eddie Litzenberger, Paul Masnick and Lorne Davis.

As Pollock brought along his prospects, Selke's Canadiens searched for Stanley Cup success. After missing the playoffs in 1947/48, when Toe Blake's career was cut short, Montreal had lost the 1948/49 semifinal to Detroit 4–3. In 1949/50, Montreal was upset 4–1 in the semifinals by the underdog New York Rangers, who went on to lose in double-overtime in game seven to the Red Wings in the Cup finals.

While the parent club struggled through one fruitless playoff quest after another, the farm system gathered momentum. In 1951/52, Pollock's Junior Canadiens were back in serious contention for the

Memorial Cup. The team did not have the depth of his 1949/50 squad, but Pollock's 1951/52 lineup nonetheless comfortably dominated play in the Quebec Junior league. While Dickie Moore had left the Junior Canadiens to play his first thirty-three games as a full-fledged Canadien, Pollock still had his big scorer, nineteen-year-old Don Marshall, who received a one-game call-up from Montreal; goaltender Charlie Hodge, who'd been only sixteen when he'd won the Memorial Cup under Pollock in 1949/50; and Bucky Hollingworth, Dave McCready, Bill Sinnett and Herb English.

Marshall and Hodge were the team's greatest talents. Marshall joined the Montreal Canadiens at centre in 1954/55, the beginning of an eighteen-season NHL career that would see him participate in all five of the Stanley Cup wins Montreal amassed in the late 1950s before moving on to New York, Buffalo, and Toronto. Charlie Hodge would spend a seeming eternity as a Canadiens goaltending understudy before gaining a starting job in 1960/61; he would win two Vezina trophies and four Stanley Cups with Montreal before concluding his NHL career in Vancouver in 1970/71. Bucky Hollingworth went on to play defence with Chicago and Detroit from 1954/55 to 1957/58. One addition to the Junior Canadiens after the 1949/50 win was Connie Broden, who would fill in at centre for the parent team for six regular season games in 1955/56 and 1957/58. Six games in the 1956/57 playoffs and one game in the 1957/58 playoffs would put his name on the Stanley Cup.

From the perspective of Stanley Cup history, perhaps the most noteworthy member of Pollock's 1951/52 Junior Canadiens team was one of its most unheralded: an eighteen-year-old graduate of the Verdun minor system, Scotty Bowman, who had been in the local Canadiens development regime since he was a fourteen-year-old Midget player in 1947. Bowman had been used by Pollock for twenty-seven games in 1950/51, contributing two goals, no assists, and sixteen penalty minutes. He had also participated in nine playoff games, with no points or penalty minutes, as the Junior Canadiens were eliminated in the Memorial Cup playdowns by the Quebec Citadels, who featured Jean

Beliveau and Camille Henry. The Junior Canadiens did not begin the 1951/52 season in mid-October with Bowman; his first appearance back with the club came on December 19, in a 7–2 defeat of the Granby Royals. It was the last game before the Junior Canadiens departed on their annual exhibition tour of western Canada, playing other Junior teams in Montreal's amateur system. Pollock was sufficiently pleased with the performance of the checking left-winger that he took Bowman west with him, and Bowman showed enough mettle to secure a starting position as the team returned home for the second half of the Quebec Junior schedule.

Like Bowman, most of the Junior Canadiens were home-grown talents—Bowman came from the Verdun neighbourhood that had produced, among others, Hollingworth and, a decade earlier, Buddy O'Connor and Maurice Richard. He grew up on a tenement block, one of four children born to John and Jean Bowman. Freda, the daughter, was the eldest, followed by three boys. Scotty was born September 18, 1931; three years later came Jack, and about seven years after Jack came Martin. Scotty and Jack shared a room and were the sports enthusiasts. Although bronchial ailments held him back, Jack managed to play football and hockey as a youth before pursuing an accounting career. He was almost fifty when he switched careers and became an NHL scout. Martin chose a much different career path than his brothers, becoming an English professor at Champlain College in St. Lambert, Quebec, translating French plays for Scottish theatres in his spare time.

Scotty Bowman's father was a sheet metal worker with Canadian National Railways, his mother a ferocious euchre player who supplied him with a motivating query: "If you like the game, why lose at it?" His parents were Scottish immigrants who arrived in 1929, but Bowman was fluently bilingual, raised in a working-class neighbourhood in which hockey served as a common language.

The Junior Canadiens for whom he came to play were overwhelmingly an anglophone team. The francophone talent in the Quebec Junior league was found on teams such as the Quebec Citadels, the Three

Rivers (Trois Rivieres) Reds and Montreal's own Nationales, who had Henri Richard, younger brother of Maurice. Henri, the "Pocket Rocket," would switch to the Junior Canadiens in 1952/53 before beginning his Montreal Canadiens career in 1955/56, and he would play a leading role in the management drama that would see Bowman become the coach of the Canadiens in 1971. While the 1951/52 Junior Citadels were without Beliveau, who had graduated to the Senior Citadels, they still featured Camille Henry, who would star at centre with the New York Rangers for twelve seasons before joining Bowman's St. Louis Blues. Finally, the Three Rivers Reds boasted the Quebec Junior league's stand-out defenceman, Jean-Guy Talbot, who would also play for Bowman in St. Louis, but first would play the villain's role in the signature moment of Bowman's brief playing career.

The professional hockey world was crowded with characters who would figure in Bowman's future. Emile Francis, who would give him plenty of playoff trouble as coach and general manager of the Rangers in the 1970s, was sparkling in the Rangers' net on a call-up from Cincinnati to fill in for an injured Chuck Rayner. In Boston, the dapper Lynn Patrick, in his second season as the Bruins' coach, was about to push the Canadiens to the limit in the playoffs, forcing Montreal to come back from a 3–2 game deficit to win their semifinal series with a 3–1 game-seven win at the Forum. Fourteen years later, Patrick would be introducing Bowman to the NHL as his assistant with the newly awarded St. Louis franchise.

The Junior Canadiens comfortably ruled the league in 1951/52, finishing atop the standings at the end of February with a thirteen-point lead over the Citadels and Reds. In thirty-six games, Bowman had contributed four goals and nine assists while attracting seven penalty minutes. On March 1, the Junior Canadiens' drive for a Memorial Cup title began with a league semifinal series against the Three Rivers Reds. The Reds were looking forward to avenging a bitter loss to Montreal in the 1949/50 semifinals, when the Canadiens had required the entire best-of-nine series to eliminate them. The Reds, however, were given little chance in this rematch. Montreal had defeated them in seven of ten regular-season meetings, and the Reds did not have the talent depth of Montreal's most important Junior farm club.

The Reds' pride and ambition soon turned to resentment and chippy play as the Junior Canadiens built a comfortable series lead, winning the opening games 3–1 and 5–1. In the second game, the outclassed Reds earned nine of thirteen penalties, including a ten-minute misconduct to one player for mouthing off at officials. In game three, Jean-Guy Talbot contributed one of the goals that gave the Reds a 2–1 lead at the end of the first period, but a pair of Canadiens goals in the third period put Montreal up 3–0 in the series.

Game four, on March 6 at the Forum, saw another surly Reds performance as a playoff sweep threatened. Ten of fourteen penalties went to the Reds, who could not handle Montreal's confident offence or the goaltending of Charlie Hodge.

With one minute to play, the game was comfortably in hand—Montreal was up 5–1—and the series was all but lost for the Reds, as the Canadiens were about to move into a 4–0 lead in the best-of-nine. As the clock wound down through the final seconds, the play took an unexpected turn. Scotty Bowman got a breakaway.

As a checking winger, Bowman's scoring chances were few and far between. He rarely recorded even an assist, although in this game the Canadiens were in such control that he had assisted on Montreal's fourth goal. As the game drew to a close, Sam Pollock had sent out the line of Bowman, Herb English and Sandy Morrison to keep an eye on the Reds. By now the teams were going through the motions. Montreal had more scoring than it needed to win, and there was no danger of the Reds exploding with four goals in the final minute to force overtime. Reds coach Jacques Toupin as much as surrendered by making no attempt to pull his goaltender, Gilles Boisvert.

As Bowman drove for Boisvert, the last man back for the Reds was the team's defensive star, Jean-Guy Talbot, whose temper had been boiling over as the game wore on. He'd drawn a minor penalty late in the second period, and then had been assessed two more minors in the third. Talbot had been on the ice for the fourth goal, on which Bowman had assisted, and now, in the final seconds of play, with the game a foregone conclusion, Bowman was gunning for personal glory, chasing the goal that had thus far eluded him in the 1951/52 playoffs.

Bowman could hardly have been expected to put on the brakes when opportunity presented itself in the last shift of the game, but he was also indulging in a bit of nose-thumbing known as running up the score. The Reds were down and out. All Montreal needed to do was keep the Reds away from Hodge, throw the puck around, run down the clock and take their four-goal victory margin into the dressing room. But Bowman was face-to-face with a rare personal opportunity, and he was not going to turn away from it. If this had been a football game, Bowman would have been a defensive back encountering a fumble on the last play of the game, with his team winning 42–7. Nothing was going to stop him from scooping up the ball and running at the opposite end zone.

Jean-Guy Talbot swung his stick at the dashing Bowman, cracking it against his skull.

In the Scotty Bowman mythology, this terrible moment on the Forum ice is the end of hope for Bowman as a Montreal Canadiens prospect. A young and promising career is snuffed out in one spasm of violence. Horribly injured, Bowman must have his fractured skull repaired with a steel plate and find his way back into the game through coaching.

There is no disputing that the Talbot assault was a brutal one. Even Bowman's thumb-nosing sprint at Boisvert could not have justified the attack. Bowman would recall that "It was like being scalped." Accounts of the game reported a gash four to five inches long on Bowman's head and a trip to the hospital to receive fourteen stitches. Talbot received a ten-minute and match misconduct penalty for deliberate injury and was not dressed for the next game. The seriousness of the incident was further underlined by the Quebec Amateur Hockey Association's decision to issue a one-year suspension to Talbot, an extremely rare disciplinary measure in a sport in which athletes regularly take their sticks and knuckles to each other.

However, the Bowman injury and its consequences do not match the script later written when Bowman became a successful NHL coach. While there is no question Bowman's injury was serious, Talbot refutes the notion that he had attempted to decapitate him. Talbot had taken a whack at Bowman's arm and when he swung at it a second time, says Talbot, Bowman ducked and caught the stick in the head. "There is no way I would hit him on the head on purpose," he insists, and notes that he visited Bowman in hospital after the incident. And Talbot says his suspension had more to do with a contract dispute with the Canadiens, who held his rights, than with the Bowman slash. The 1951/52 season was supposed to be Talbot's last one in Junior hockey, he notes, and Montreal wanted him to play minor pro hockey in Buffalo or Cincinnati. But Talbot refused to report, as he wanted to play for the Quebec Citadels Senior club with Jean Beliveau. For refusing to answer the call-up—not for slashing Bowman—Talbot says he was suspended by the QAHA, and this suspension was lifted in January 1953.

As for the longstanding and erroneous assertion that Bowman suffered a fractured skull, this part of the script had echoes of a true encounter: in a 1969/70 pre-season game in Ottawa, the hockey world was horrified by a vicious stick-swinging duel between Chicago's Wayne Maki and Boston's Ted Green. While Green was the instigator, Maki made himself infamous by smashing in Green's skull. A steel plate was required to repair Green's head. The star defenceman missed an entire NHL season as he recovered from the attack.

Scotty Bowman, in contrast, missed only one game as a Montreal Junior Canadien.

It is impossible to reconcile the standard tale of Bowman's downfall as a player with the printed record. The press was remarkably mute on such a catastrophic incident. Bowman's injury was noted without fanfare as part of the game report. Two days after the incident, the *Gazette* said that, because of the gash, Bowman "will likely be out several games."

Bowman missed the final game of the series with the Reds on March 8. Though they were without Talbot, the Reds played well at home and were leading 3–2 when Pollock pulled Hodge and the Junior Canadiens tied the game with three seconds to play. An overtime goal gave Montreal a five-game sweep. Meanwhile, the Quebec Citadels and Montreal Nationales were grappling in a hard-fought series that would go to all nine games before the Citadels prevailed. The league finals between the Junior Canadiens and the Citadels did not start until March 20, two weeks after Bowman had been cut down by Talbot. When the Junior Canadiens skated onto the Forum ice for the first game they had played there since Bowman's injury, Bowman was with them, sporting a helmet. He did not play like someone whose career had just been derailed by a crippling head injury. Bowman was, in fact, singled out for rare praise; the *Gazette* reported that he played "a great two-way game for the Habs," who nonetheless lost 3–1. Two nights later, Bowman was in the lineup again for a hard-hitting game that Montreal won 3–1. The record indicates that Bowman was as capable a player after the injury as before it, that he was relied upon by Sam Pollock in the Memorial Cup playdowns, and that his downfall as a player in the Canadiens system lay not with Jean-Guy Talbot, but with someone else.

Bowman played every game in the Quebec Junior League finals, a series that initially did not unfold according to plan. The Junior Canadiens were again heavily favoured, having dominated the Quebec Citadels in the regular season. The Citadels were the farm team of the New

York Rangers, and its best players in 1951/52 were Camille Henry and goaltender Marcelle Paille, who would play for the Rangers from 1957/58 to 1964/65. Coached by former Ranger star Philippe (Phil) Watson, a native Montrealer, the Citadels defied the 3:1 betting line by taking a 2–1 series lead in game three, their first home match of the series. But after Pollock urged from his players three straight wins, the Junior Canadiens were off to meet Ottawa's Eastview St. Charles team in the next round, a best-of-three that would decide who met the Ontario Junior League champion in the eastern Memorial Cup playoffs. The winner of that series would meet the western champion in the Cup finals.

With the Eastview St. Charles series, the Junior Canadiens were now subject to the Memorial Cup tournament regulations. In the Quebec playoffs, teams had been allowed to dress seventeen players, plus a reserve goaltender. Memorial Cup regulations allowed only fourteen players. Pollock's response was to create a platoon of four players who could be rotated through one available starting position. The selected players were Marc Boileau, Ross Murray, Ken Naylor and Scotty Bowman. As a result of the platoon system, Bowman didn't see any action against Eastview St. Charles.

He didn't miss much. In the 1949/50 playdowns, Pollock's Junior Canadiens had overwhelmed the victor in the Ottawa-Halifax series, Halifax St. Mary's, 11–3 and 10–1. Eastview St. Charles wasn't quite so outclassed, but the Junior Canadiens moved them aside easily with 4–2 and 6–2 wins, to advance to the eastern finals.

Pollock's Montreal prospects were back playing the next generation of New York Rangers as they greeted the Guelph Biltmore Mad Hatters at the Montreal Forum in the opening game of the eastern Memorial Cup finals. Sponsored by the Guelph Biltmore Hat Company, the team's disconcertingly whimsical name was shortened simply to the Biltmores by sporting purists.

The Junior Canadiens had eliminated Guelph in the 1949/50 playdowns, but this was a much tougher bunch of Mad Hatters. Andy

Bathgate was back, on a team that was a veritable snapshot of the future Rangers. Harry Howell, a Norris winner in the 1960s who would log twenty-four seasons in the NHL and the WHA, starred on defence. Another blueliner was Aldo "Bep" Guidolin, who would move up to the Rangers with Howell and spend more than three seasons as a Ranger and later coach. Also on defence was the pugnacious "Leapin' Lou" Fontinato, who would play seven seasons with the Rangers and two with the Canadiens, and who would become famous for losing a heavyweight bout to Gordie Howe in 1957. On left wing were Ron Murphy and Dean Prentice, both of whom would graduate with Howell and Guidolin to the Rangers the next season. Prentice would last twenty-two seasons in the NHL, Murphy eighteen. A third left-winger, Bill McCreary, made occasional NHL appearances from 1953/54 to 1962/63 before finding a starting job for four seasons in St. Louis, playing for Scotty Bowman. Their coach was Alf Pike, who had starred at centre with the Rangers from 1939/40 to 1946/47, excluding a two-season interruption during the war.

The Junior Canadiens were facing an offensive marvel, a team that had broken the league scoring record with 34 goals to spare by pumping out 341 in fifty-four games—an average of 6.3 per game. Although he never made the NHL, they were paced in offence by Ken Laufman, who set a new Ontario Hockey League scoring record that season, with 139 points.

But their biggest threat was a player whose participation did not sit well with Pollock. Ron Stewart had been added to the Guelph roster as a professional call-up substitution. Ray Ross had been summoned for a three-game tryout by the Seattle Totems, a Western Hockey League (WHL) farm team of the Cleveland Barons of the American Hockey League, with whom Ross had signed a C-form, a promise of services that permitted the club to require him to turn professional within one year. (It was Jean-Guy Talbot's refusal to answer his C-form call-up and play in Buffalo or Cincinnati that got him suspended by the QAHA.) But after the tryout, Ross had refused to sign a contract.

The Ontario Hockey League directed professional hockey—the network of leagues whose player-status regulations were administered by the NHL—to suspend Ross, which meant he could play neither as a professional nor as an amateur. Under Memorial Cup rules, the Biltmores were allowed to replace Ross with a player from another team, and they had chosen Stewart, a prolific scorer on right wing who had already been borrowed by the Barrie Flyers from the Toronto Marlboros. As a Toronto property, Stewart would join the Maple Leafs that fall and play twenty-one NHL seasons.

Sam Pollock thought there was something rather convenient about the timing of Ross's call-up. The suspension, he learned, had been issued before Ross had even completed his tryout. Ross, for his part, said he had refused to sign because "they wouldn't pay me enough," but also because he claimed to have a letter from Cleveland's scout, written at the time he signed the C-form, assuring him he would not be called up until he had completed his Junior career.

Pollock did nothing about his distaste for the Stewart substitution right away, choosing simply to play the opening game. The performance of Hodge would be critical to Pollock's chances, but so would his team's checking game. Pollock abandoned his rotation system for the fourteenth spot on the bench and assigned it exclusively to Scotty Bowman.

The Junior Canadiens were a smaller, faster team than the Biltmores, but Pollock decided they should open the series by hitting hard and often. It backfired, as the Biltmores led 2–0 on power-play goals after the first period. At intermission, Baldy George, the Canadian Amateur Hockey Association (CAHA) representative in charge of the series, went to Frank Dillon, registrar of the Quebec Amateur Hockey Association, and George Horward, president of the Quebec Junior League, and told them to inform Mr. Pollock he was to "cool out his players." Pollock claimed after the game that Alf Pike was delivered the same message, but Pike denied it. Whoever did or did not get the message, the game settled down after the first period and Guelph cruised to an easy 6–1 win.

After the game, Pollock decided to file a protest with the CAHA over Stewart's use by Guelph, even though the CAHA had already ruled him eligible. He received support from Rudy Pilous, coach of the St. Catharines Teepees, whom the Biltmores had earlier eliminated. "It smells a bit," was Pilous's description of the Ross-Stewart switch. "I think the Guelph management knew more than they said." The Teepees' protest, however, was declared ineligible. Even though Pilous said he was acting on new information—Ross's claim of a letter from Cleveland's scout and the fact that the suspension was issued before he had even completed the call-up—the protest was disallowed. Technically, Pilous was required to file one within forty-eight hours of his last game against Guelph, and that had taken place ten days earlier.

Game two in Montreal was back to brutal play. Guelph star Bep Guidolin fractured his leg when he slid into the boards. Andy Bathgate and Bucky Hollingworth had a fight, which ended when Bathgate threw Hollingworth right over the boards; Bathgate was also struck in the face by a slash the officials did not call. Twenty-one penalties were dispensed as Pollock's team won 7–5. Neither side was happy with the refereeing. Pollock wanted Hap Shouldice and Stan Pratt of Ottawa dismissed by the CAHA for the rest of the series. Alf Pike was in complete agreement, having blamed them for a mishandled face-off that he believed led to Guidolin's leg fracture, and an offside call missed on the Junior Canadiens' winning goal. "You can quote me on this," he told *The Globe and Mail*. "In fact, please do. Hap Shouldice is the stupidest referee I've ever seen and Pratt isn't much better. This is big business and we're being saddled with incompetent homers."

The series moved to Guelph for game three, a controversial decision for the Biltmores' backers as it was played on Good Friday, and their refusal to host a game on Easter Sunday meant game four would be played at Maple Leaf Gardens. New referees—Jerry Orlinski of Kitchener and Andy Bellemer of Bala—were supplied.

Guelph was enjoying a 4–1 lead in the second period when Bowman, in one of his rare offensive opportunities, hit the goalpost. The

Biltmores had stretched their lead to 5–1 by the end of the period; fifty-seven seconds into the third period, they were up 6–1. Then came a parade of penalties to Guelph players, which ignited a Junior Canadiens comeback. Harry Howell went off for elbowing at 3:17, and Connie Broden scored on the power play. Don Marshall scored an even-strength goal thirty seconds later, and after Lou Fontinato went off for highsticking at 6:30, Broden again connected on the power play to make it 6–4. Fifty-nine seconds later, an unassisted effort by Yvon Chasles drew the Junior Canadiens to within a goal.

Less than a minute later, Montreal's Les Lilley drew a hooking penalty. Scotty Bowman was sent out to help kill the penalty, but he was unable to contain his anger over the penalty call, which had broken the momentum of the Junior Canadiens' comeback. He sprayed a stream of abusive language at Jerry Orlinski, who slapped him with a misconduct. Bowman would not quit. Teammate Butch MacKay had to physically restrain Bowman from going after Orlinski, and a further game misconduct was awarded. With Bowman gone from the ice, the Biltmores' Bill McCreary scored on the power play to make it 7–5. Hollingworth responded with a goal a minute and a half later to return the gap to one goal, but the Junior Canadiens' rally was over. The Biltmores were up two games to one, with the series headed for Toronto.

The Junior Canadiens were dreadful on the Maple Leaf Gardens ice, losing 7–2 to drop behind 3–1 in the series. "We smelled out the joint," Pollock volunteered. "That was the worst game we ever played, and it was our ninety-first of the year." He publicly criticized the play of goaltender Charlie Hodge, who had also disappointed him in the opening-game loss. But the only player change he made was on left wing. Pollock benched Bowman and replaced him with Ken Naylor for the rest of the series. Bowman's only noteworthy contribution to game four had been a hooking penalty halfway through the second period, when Montreal was trailing 3–1.

Back home on Forum ice, Hodge played superbly. Outshot 36–17, Montreal won 1–0 to put the series at 3–2. The teams returned to

Maple Leaf Gardens for game six. Shortly before the game, Pollock learned that his protest over Guelph's use of Stewart, who had scored six times in the first four games, had been dismissed. Guelph scored four times before Montreal responded with one of their own late in the second period as the Mad Hatters won 5–2 to advance to the Memorial Cup finals.

Pollock was so bitter about the loss that he refused to offer the customary congratulations to his coaching adversary, Alf Pike, who called him a "crybaby" over the Stewart fracas. "Don't misunderstand me," Pollock explained to reporters. "I give full credit to the Guelph kids, but I still think the Guelph management pulled a fast one in the Stewart deal and I'd be a liar if I went out and congratulated them when I didn't mean it." Even with his team eliminated, Pollock would not let the Stewart issue die. He promised to launch another appeal in concert with the western Memorial Cup finalists, the Regina Pats, which was another Montreal farm club. "We're going to spend a lot of money to prove that Guelph put over an illegal deal." Nothing came of Pollock's threat. The Junior Canadiens proved to have given Guelph its toughest competition, as the Pats went down 8–2, 4–2, 8–2, 10–2.

Game four of the eastern finals was Scotty Bowman's last as a Junior Canadien. He wasn't with the team the next season, when Pollock added future Montreal stars Henri Richard, Phil Goyette and Claude Provost. The Montreal Royals Junior club was revived, and after appearing in three games with the Kitchener Greenshirts (a Canadiens affiliate), Bowman joined the Royals. Far from having seen his career ended by Talbot, Bowman appeared in thirty-six Royals games in 1952/53, producing five goals and eight assists. In the Royals' short-lived playoffs, Bowman contributed two assists and eighteen penalty minutes in four games. In 1953/54, he played virtually a full season for the Royals, with twenty goals, thirty-four assists, and seventy-five penalty minutes in fifty-six games. In another brief playoff run, Bowman produced four assists and two penalty minutes. About to turn twenty-one, his Junior years were officially over.

In the standard version of his life, Bowman's prospects for a professional career ended when he crossed paths catastrophically with Jean-Guy Talbot in the spring of 1952 and was unable to recover from a severe head injury. The seriousness of the injury seems to have ballooned once Bowman was coaching in the NHL, its severity inflated with details inspired by the Ted Green incident. (However, Jimmy Roberts, who first encountered Bowman in 1958, feels the stories of a career-ending skull fracture were in circulation before the Green incident.) While Bowman was coaching St. Louis some eighteen years after the slash, Brian Macfarlane would write that the slash had produced forty-five stitches and a fractured skull—a far more serious outcome than reported by the *Gazette* at the time of the injury. The fractured-skull story gained fresh life in a profile of Bowman published by *Sports Illustrated* in 1993, in which Bowman's mother is quoted as having said, "Scott put his hand up and a piece of his skull came off of his head."

The steel plate widely presumed to have resulted from the attack has provided Bowman's enemies with their favourite insult. "Platehead!" has been shouted at him more than a few times by opponents, most spectacularly by opposing coach Marc Crawford of the Colorado Avalance during the 1996/97 playoffs. After the Crawford incident, Bowman both clarified and obscured the record on the Talbot incident. "I don't have a plate in my head," he said. "I never fractured my skull. I just got a bad cut that ended my career."* But the cut obviously did no such thing, even though this had become Bowman's standard explanation. A decade before the Crawford outburst, Bowman had firmly blamed the Talbot incident for ending his career. In *Lions in Winter*, the Montreal Canadiens history by Chrys Goyens and Allan Turowetz, published in 1986, Bowman summed up the consequence

---

* Bowman further muddied the record in a June 24, 1998 column by Jerry Sullivan in *The Buffalo News*. "I fractured my skull playing in Junior hockey," Bowman said.

of the Talbot slash this way: "That was it for me. I was never the same player afterward. I just didn't have the confidence. I had a lot of headaches and blurred vision and things like that in the off-season and the club recommended that I quit as an active player." He may have finished his career as a Junior Canadien, but having played sixty three regular-season games with the Junior Canadiens before the Talbot incident, Bowman played eighty-nine regular-season games with the Royals after it.

Talbot has long been an unfortunate scapegoat for Bowman's failure to become a professional player. Talbot himself has been under the impression that Bowman underwent some sort of surgery and that his slash ended Bowman's playing days. When interviewed by this writer, he was surprised to learn that Bowman went on to play two more seasons of Junior hockey.

By all accounts, Bowman did not hold the incident against Talbot. "I don't think Scotty Bowman is capable of holding a grudge," says Glenn Hall, who played with Talbot for Bowman in St. Louis. And the fact that Talbot would even have such a terrible incident in his past surprises Hall. "Jean-Guy was the easiest going guy. If you couldn't get along with him, you couldn't get along with anybody." Hall's opinion reinforces Talbot's insistence that the injury was not deliberately inflicted.

The most compelling fact to emerge from Bowman's playing career is that the wrong man has long been fingered for snuffing his professional prospects. It seems that Jean-Guy Talbot didn't do the deed. One can argue instead that Sam Pollock did, by benching him after Bowman's performances in games three and four of the eastern Memorial Cup finals. It has been said that Bowman got his competitive ardour from his mother, who when losing at cards would throw her hand in the fire. Bowman may have thrown away his hand when he lost his composure in game three and was tossed out for spraying invective. When his checking game failed to avert a 7–2 rout in game four, Pollock singled him out for replacement and ended his Junior Canadiens career, leaving him to play on with the second-class Royals for two more seasons. Bowman simply wasn't good enough to play professionally. He was a one-way player, a determined checker with occasional offensive spark and a growing penchant for accumulating penalties.

The ending of Scotty Bowman's playing career is important in that it affected the way in which he was received as a coach by professional players, almost two decades later. Players who are given the same message by two different coaches are more likely to respond to the coach who has actually played the game at a high level. Such a coach can speak from experience, which is particularly important when that coach, like Bowman, is an old-school taskmaster. Toe Blake had enormous authority in Montreal because he had done it all himself. There was nothing he demanded of his players that hadn't been demanded of him. Scotty Bowman could never claim to have played in the NHL, but he carried the aura of someone who might well have, if not for the stickwork of Jean-Guy Talbot. Other players whose careers immediately preceded his had segued into coaching and managing after catastrophic injuries. Tommy Ivan had turned to coaching in the Detroit system in the 1940s after suffering a career-ending whack on the head. Aldege "Baz" Bastien began a long coaching and managing career after his role as heir-apparent to Maple Leaf goaltender Turk Broda was denied him by a training camp puck that blinded him in one eye in 1949. Bowman has tended to be lumped in with these figures, rather than being associated with someone like Punch Imlach, who played the game at the Junior and Senior levels but whose real abilities lay in coaching and managing.

In many sports, great coaches have been found among players whose genius for the game outshone their ability to actually play it. While some players might have given Bowman his due because they considered him someone who was denied his opportunity to play, his real authority would derive from the fact that he got results. Ultimately, this was far more important to Bowman's staying power as a coach than the cachet of a might-have-been. All around him, players who did achieve greatness fell by the wayside as coaches when their charges were unable to execute winning game plans. Just because the man at the chalkboard had been through a Stanley Cup double-overtime victory didn't automatically make him capable of urging a similar feat out of a new generation of players.

There is some poignancy in Pollock's apparent inability to recall the troubled details of the beginning of their long relationship. (Initially, Pollock ventures that Bowman was playing for the Royals when Talbot struck him, and he cannot recall the details of the 1951/52 playoff run.) One suspects that Bowman must well remember those details. It would help explain why he could seek out Jean-Guy Talbot to play for him in St. Louis without a hint of remorse or resentment. There was no reason to resent Talbot for ending his playing career if Bowman knew deep down that Talbot didn't do it. Scotty Bowman had not performed to Sam Pollock's stern expectations in a critical playoff series. Whether or not Talbot's slash had anything to do with Bowman's ability to play against top Junior talent, it is irrefutable that Pollock struck him out of the lineup in the midst of the Memorial Cup eastern finals after showing the confidence to dress him for every game of the series. At the very least, even if the slash did preface the end of Bowman's playing days with a top Junior club like the Junior Canadiens, associates like Roberts feel that Bowman had the sense to recognize that his prospects for an NHL playing career were not promising. Whatever the true circumstances of the 1951/52 season, they represented the beginning of Sam Pollock's sometimes cryptic relationship with a player of limited promise who turned into a coach of enormous talent.

3

✧ ON OCTOBER 10, 1956, the principal characters in Scotty Bowman's professional future were gathered in Ottawa for an exhibition game between the Ottawa-Hull Junior Canadiens and the Rochester Americans. Running the Junior Canadiens was Sam Pollock, in concert with Bowman, his new assistant. Playing defence for them was Claude Ruel, part of whose assignment for the night was stopping Al MacNeil of the Americans, who the previous spring had won his second Memorial Cup as captain of the Toronto Marlboros.

Nearly fifteen years later, Pollock, Bowman, Ruel and MacNeil would gather again for one of the most convoluted and controversial episodes in Montreal Canadiens history, but their convergence had begun with a 2–1 victory by MacNeil's Americans. The man known as "Sad Sam," for his dour expression and grim determination, was the weaver of fortunes, drawing the threads of their lives together and then unravelling them again.

Change was in the air that October. The previous year, the Montreal Canadiens had made an important management change when Frank Selke had ended the coaching run of Dick Irvin. Irvin had lasted fifteen years in Montreal, but had been undone by the same inability to secure Stanley Cup success that had cost him his coaching job in Toronto. With the Leafs, after winning the Cup in 1931/32 in his first season with the team, he had taken the club to six more finals in eight seasons, and lost every one. After his third consecutive loss in 1939/40, Conn Smythe had elected to replace Irvin with the team's former captain, Hap Day, and recommended to the struggling Canadiens that they hire him. Working with new general manager Tommy Gorman, Irvin rapidly created a powerful lineup in Montreal, but once their rivals were back to their prewar strength, the Canadiens found Stanley Cups hard to come by. The 1944/45 season had already provided a foreshadowing of frustrations to come, as the Canadiens ruled the regular season, only to be upset in six games by Hap Day's inspired rag-tag Leafs in the semifinals. After winning in 1945/46, the Canadiens went through a six-season dry spell, in which they lost three final series. The most disconcerting run was from 1950/51 to 1954/55, in which Montreal appeared in all five finals but could win only one, the 1952/53 series against the underdog Boston Bruins. The 1950/51 finals were lost to Toronto, but the most galling losses were yet to come, when Montreal lost three finals to the resurgent Detroit Red Wings. The 1953/54 and 1954/55 finals against the Wings went all seven games, and on both occasions the Wings prevailed. The exciting club Frank Selke had built could not defeat the equally exciting Red Wings club built by Jack Adams and coached so well by Tommy Ivan.

The suspension of Maurice Richard in March 1955 after his attack on players and an on-ice official in Boston, which cost the Canadiens the use of their most celebrated scorer in the playoffs, was Irvin's ultimate undoing. Selke felt that his coach was incapable of productively harnessing the Rocket's ferocious temper. There was a coaching job for Irvin in Chicago, helping to resurrect the moribund Blackhawks, and Selke went about selecting Irvin's replacement.

The Leafs had found success under Day, winning two Cups during the war and then four more in five seasons. Selke looked for a similar veteran who could inspire, motivate and strategize. Stories vary on how Toe Blake was chosen. Though he was fluently bilingual, born to a francophone mother, Blake was from northern Ontario and didn't fit the mould of the pure Quebecois coach some of the Canadiens felt that the team deserved to have. According to the authors of *Lions in Winter*, Selke had been considering hiring Billy Reay, the former Canadien who had helped Pollock coach the Junior Canadiens to the 1949/50 Memorial Cup title. As an anglophone Winnipegger, Reay hardly fit the francophone bill, and Blake's old linemate, Maurice Richard, argued for Blake's hiring. Since it was Selke's mission to find a coach who could productively channel Richard's temper, he could do worse than choose someone who had once played alongside Richard and had his confidence and respect.

Blake had been steered into coaching after the double ankle fracture ended his playing career in January 1948. His playing record was exemplary: he had won the Cup twice, as well as the Lady Byng (for gentlemanly play), the Art Ross (for scoring) and the Hart (as league MVP). He had made the first All Star team three times, the second team twice. Blake had been given six years of coaching experience, with Valleyfield in the Quebec Senior League and Houston in the United States Hockey League. Initially, the word on Blake as a coach was that he suffered from the same disease of congeniality that had hampered the efforts of former Leafs great King Clancy. Clancy loved the game and above all the players; when coaching Pittsburgh of the AHL, Clancy wanted to be with the players at the arena and after hours, basking in the camaraderie of the game at the dinner table. Blake would learn the delicate art of distancing himself from the players without being remote, remaining close enough to inspire and motivate, yet not so close that he couldn't discipline or demote.

"Toe Blake was probably the greatest motivator of talent I've ever seen," Sam Pollock reflects. And Pollock and Ken Reardon, in running the development system under Selke, had supplied him with a cornucopia of talent from which to shape a winning lineup.

The crowning achievement of Selke's Montreal years was the string of five straight Cup victories from 1955/56 to 1959/60, made possible by Blake's coaching and his own wisdom in securing and nurturing promising amateur talent. Selke had inherited a few major stars who would win Cups under him—Elmer Lach, Butch Bouchard, Maurice Richard, Ken Mosdell and Billy Reay—but the rest of the team was his, its members brought along from the time they were teenagers. Selke was not a blockbuster trader like Conn Smythe or Jack Adams. For the most part, the players who won Stanley Cups for him in the 1950s had never played for any NHL team but the Canadiens. Among the rare exceptions was left-winger Bert Olmstead, acquired from Chicago via Detroit in December 1950. That deal in itself confirmed Selke's savvy. Olmstead proceeded to play in ten straight Cup finals (the last two with Toronto), helping Montreal win four. The player Selke gave up for him, right-winger Leo Gravelle, promptly played his last NHL season.

When Montreal avenged its two preceding Cup losses to Detroit by defeating the Red Wings in five games in 1955/56, Blake was able to ice an impressive slate of new talent. Don Marshall had become a Canadiens regular in 1954/55, and in 1955/56 the development system gave Blake centre Henri Richard, right-winger Claude Provost and defencemen Bob Turner and Jean-Guy Talbot, his purgatory attributed to the Bowman slash firmly behind him. Over the next few seasons, Blake would collect from the farm system centres Phil Goyette and Ralph Backstrom, left-wingers Marcel Bonin and Ab McDonald, and right-winger Bill Hicke.

Not every new talent was coming out of Sam Pollock's domain. Ken Reardon's efforts out west had produced strong Junior affiliates in Manitoba's St. Boniface Canadiens and Saskatchewan's Regina St. Pats. After defeating Pollock's Junior Canadiens in the 1951/52 eastern finals, the Guelph Biltmores had met the St. Pats in the Memorial Cup finals. While Regina was no match for the Biltmores, its lineup did include Bob Turner and Ed Litzenberger, who Selke sent to Chicago in 1954/55 (along with Johnny McCormack, Dick Gamble and former Junior Canadien Bucky Hollingworth) in a league-wide effort to rescue the lowly Blackhawks. In the 1952/53 Memorial Cup, Reardon's efforts saw the St. Boniface Canadiens reach the finals with Ab McDonald in the lineup, but lose to the Barrie Flyers (whose own lineup included Bowman's future Stanley Cup coaching opponent, Don Cherry). In 1954/55 the Regina Pats were back in the finals, still with Bob Turner, losing to the Toronto Marlboros. The Pats and Marlies staged a rematch in the 1955/56, a series the Marlies again won with a roster stocked with future Maple Leafs Bob Baun, Bob Pulford and Bob Nevin; the 1954/55 Marlies had already produced Billy Harris for the Leafs.

A horse race was developing between Reardon and Pollock, two very capable hockey minds, in what would prove to be a neck-and-neck drive to succeed Selke as Montreal's general manager. In the fall of 1956, Sad Sam Pollock was running a new enterprise, the Ottawa-Hull Junior Canadiens. More than a geographic relocation of the Montreal Junior Canadiens, the Ottawa-Hull team was a new phenomenon, a super-team that belonged to no particular league. While playing Junior hockey games in both the Quebec and Ontario leagues, it would also participate in the Ontario Eastern Senior League and the Quebec Hockey League, a professional loop created by the Canadiens when Frank Selke turned the entire Quebec Senior League into a minor pro league to get Jean Beliveau into a Canadiens uniform in 1953/54.*

The Ottawa-Hull Junior Canadiens were just one of Sam Pollock's many responsibilities in the fall of 1956. The Rochester Americans club

---

*Béliveau was an enormous star with the Quebec Aces of the Senior league, earning $25,000 a year as a drawing card who could put 10,000 fans in Colisée seats. He had set a Junior league scoring record in 1950/51. Selke, after failing to get his signature on a C-form (which would have allowed Montreal to call him up to play within one year), had to be satisfied affixing his name to a B-form at the beginning of the 1951/52 season. This promise of services from Béliveau whenever he decided to turn "professional" had a three-year term, after which Béliveau could remain in Quebec or pursue a number of other options, which didn't necessarily involve the Canadiens. With two years having passed on the B-form, the Canadiens essentially forced Béliveau to join the Canadiens by acquiring the entire Quebec Senior League and making it an above-board professional operation. This made Béliveau a de facto professional, and as such he was obliged to join the Canadiens.

that paid the exhibition-game visit on October 10 were also in his managerial bailiwick. The Toronto Maple Leafs' AHL farm team in Pittsburgh, the Hornets, had ceased operations after the 1955/56 season when its arena was condemned; the Americans were then formed as a joint venture between the Leafs and Canadiens, and Pollock installed former Montreal star Billy Reay as coach. Pollock needed an assistant to work alongside him in Ottawa-Hull and watch the fort when he was away. Pollock found him in the player he had benched in the 1951/52 Memorial Cup eastern finals, Scotty Bowman.

When his playing career ended after the 1953/54 season, Scotty Bowman had turned to coaching at the minor level in Montreal while pursuing a "proper" career. It has been said that the Canadiens paid for business courses at George Williams University for Bowman after his injury; while that's certainly possible, Pollock doesn't remember it. Given that Bowman had been injured by a Canadiens property, the club might well have felt some responsibility for him.

Bowman would recall making $250 a year coaching Junior B hockey, which was hardly a living wage, and in 1955 a sales job was arranged for him with the paint company Sherwin-Williams in Montreal— Pollock feels Ken Brown, a Montreal scout who was running minor teams in Verdun, might have had a hand in securing Bowman's employment. Bowman had a memory some would describe as photographic; at Sherwin-Williams he put it to use memorizing the product codes for his arsenal of paint chips as he made his salesman's rounds. He took early lunches so he could watch Dick Irvin run the Canadiens through their practices at the Forum. When his working day was done, the young and single Bowman devoted his evening energies to coaching hockey. In 1955/56, at twenty-two, Bowman took the Park Extension Flyers, a Verdun Junior B team, to the league finals.

Pollock was impressed with Bowman's dedication and acumen, and he offered him the assistant's job with Ottawa-Hull. He had sought out someone who was not just hockey smart, but also reliable as a manager, who could run the whole show while he was on the road.

He had other clubs to tend to, amateur and professional alike, and scouting efforts to oversee, all of which meant regular travelling that would take him away from the Ottawa-Hull team. (In 1958/59, Pollock had to parachute himself into Rochester and coach the Americans for twenty games.) Running the Junior Canadiens in his absence involved far more than devising forward lines and running skating drills. The Ottawa-Hull team was a complex operation, moving through several leagues simultaneously. Pollock needed a disciplinarian, chaperone, account manager and travel agent all rolled into one, and that person also happened to require first-class coaching skills. The abilities Bowman honed with Ottawa-Hull would serve him well for years. Right into the 1970s, as coach of the Canadiens, he was the master of ceremonies of a major touring show, booking flights and hotels and changing travel itineraries with seasoned dexterity. If coaching hadn't panned out for Scotty Bowman, he could easily have found work moving a three-ring circus around the world.

Bowman was afraid to burn his bridges, but he couldn't resist Pollock's offer. He asked for, and received, a leave of absence from Sherwin-Williams. In December 1956, Bowman told his paint boss he wasn't coming back.

As a super-team, the Junior Canadiens were a mix of Juniors and older professionals, with six overage players including four professionals. They played ten games in the Quebec Hockey League schedule, using Verdun for home ice in five of them. Pre-season action included a series of exhibition games against NHL and AHL clubs such as Al MacNeil's Rochester Americans, and the Junior Canadiens acquitted themselves well. Though they didn't win any of these games, they showed tremendous skill, tying the Cleveland Barons of the AHL 4–4, losing to the Chicago Blackhawks 2–1. Most impressive was their 5–4 loss to the Detroit Red Wings, who iced essentially the same lineup that had skated against the Canadiens in the Cup finals the previous spring.

The goaltender was Gilles Boisvert, a Detroit property who had confronted Scotty Bowman's breakaway as a Three Rivers Red when

Jean-Guy Talbot cut him down in March 1952. On defence was Claude Ruel, a five-foot, five-inch dynamo from Montreal. The forward lines included Claude Richard, brother of Maurice and Henri; Ralph Backstrom, who would be called up for three games by Montreal that season and join the parent team full-time at centre in 1958/59; and Gilles Tremblay, who would make the Canadiens on left wing in 1960/61. The team had also acquired from the Regina St. Pats right-winger Murray Balfour, who had played in the last two Memorial Cup finals. Balfour would see action in five games over the next two seasons with Montreal before being dealt to Chicago.

One of the team's final exhibition games was against the Boston Bruins, who would play the Canadiens in the next two Stanley Cup finals. The game was one of the Junior Canadiens' few emphatic defeats of the pre-season, as they bowed 6–2. For Bowman, the Bruins tilt was another noteworthy brush with his future, in the person of Lynn Patrick. The key players in the first years of Bowman's NHL career had all passed before his eyes in the first weeks of his new job with Sam Pollock.

Bowman's campaigns with Pollock gave him a thorough introduction to sporting success, failure, connivery and controversy. The Junior Canadiens defeated the Guelph Biltmores in the 1956/57 eastern Memorial Cup finals, avenging for Bowman and Pollock their 1951/52 loss. Next they were on their way to Flin Flon in northern Manitoba, to play one of the most exasperating series of their careers.

The Flin Flon Bombers had earned the right to represent the west in the Memorial Cup finals by defeating the Edmonton Oil Kings and then the Fort William Canadiens, the latter four straight. Flin Flon, straddling the border of Manitoba and Saskatchewan about 350 miles northwest of Winnipeg, rests deep in the Canadian Shield. The mining town was delirious with the thrill of their Bombers making their well-deserved first trip to the Memorial Cup finals: the Bombers had dominated the Saskatchewan Junior league, winning forty-eight of fifty-five games. Their coach was Bob Kirk, who had starred with Winnipeg's

Elmwood Millionaires when they lost the 1929 Memorial Cup to Frank
Selke's Toronto Marlboros, and who had gone on to play thirty-nine
games for the 1937/38 New York Rangers.

There were not two more intense characters in Canadian Junior
hockey than Sam Pollock and Scotty Bowman. Shortly before Bowman had joined the Junior Canadiens in late 1952, Pollock had smashed
a chair on the ice in two different games against the Montreal
Nationales to express his displeasure with the officiating. While Bowman would regularly cite Toe Blake as his greatest coaching inspiration, in his basic ferocity he was an obvious protege of Pollock's.

"Sam was a fiery coach," says Al MacNeil, who came to play for
Pollock in Rochester, and in Ottawa-Hull, when the Canadiens turned
their team there into a minor pro operation in the Eastern Professional
Hockey League. "He did a lot of stuff for effect. He could have written an acting school manual on how to get the most out of a situation. His greatest strength was that, even when he won nine Cups in
fifteen years as Montreal's general manager, he never believed he was
going to win another game. He approached every game at that level.
He never assumed that because he beat Boston or the Soo yesterday,
he was going to beat them today. He always took the worst-case scenario as far as being prepared. He made you a winner by making you
understand you could never assume anything in the game. It was only
over when the final buzzer went. Sam was a driven guy who never
looked like he took any satisfaction in a win, because there was still
a win to come. That's probably why he got out of it a little earlier than
he planned, because it took such an emotional toll on him."

MacNeil attributes much of Bowman's coaching style to the tutoring he received from Pollock. "Sam and Scotty fed off each other,"
MacNeil explains. "They didn't suffer fools gladly. Scotty has that great
sense of outrage about mediocrity when he knows there's better there.
That came directly from Sam."

The Junior Canadiens had completed their series against Guelph on
April 21, and the first game of the Memorial Cup finals was set for

April 24 in Flin Flon. The Junior Canadiens made it as far as Winnipeg before bad weather grounded their plane, and the opening game had to be postponed.

Sad Sam lived up to his name by finding little in the finals to be happy about. He began his visit to Manitoba by making it clear that he didn't like the series format—three consecutive games in Flin Flon, followed by three consecutive games in Regina. He didn't think the third game should be in Flin Flon. As a matter of fact, he didn't think any of the games should be in Flin Flon. The town's rink, Whitney Forum, had seating for only 1,400, with space for another 800 in standing room. Pollock brandished the Memorial Cup rulebook, pointing out that a rink in the finals was supposed to have seating for at least three thousand. Using Whitney Forum, Pollock said, was "absurd." Why couldn't the Flin Flon games be played in Winnipeg, which had an arena with seating for ten thousand?

This didn't go over well with the fourteen thousand locals who were relishing their remote town's rare moment in the national limelight. "Flin Flon citizens are up in arms over criticism levelled at the town and its facilities by Ottawa officials who do not recognise, apparently, any part of Canada west of Ottawa," complained Jimmy Wardle, executive president of the Bombers. "We feel that the nationally known, warm-hearted hospitality and a fine hockey club make up for the lack of a Chateau Laurier and what they amusingly call an 'ice palace' in Ottawa."

Pollock heaped further scorn on the west in general by complaining about the choice of referees, both of whom were from Edmonton (the series was employing a two-referee system). Normally the Memorial Cup chose one ref from the east and one from the west. Asked if he was going to file a protest with the CAHA over the arena and the officiating, Sad Sam waved it off. Perhaps he had learned from his fruitless protest in the Stewart case. "It's like talking to a statue in the park," he explained. The series hadn't even started, and already Pollock was unhappy with the officiating and at odds with his opponent's entire community.

The Bombers were not stacked with future NHLers, but they were a quick-skating, disciplined club whose lineup for the series had been bolstered, as competition regulations permitted, by three key additions: centre Orland Kurtenbach of the Prince Albert Mintos, defenceman Jean Gauthier, a Montreal property from the Fort William Canadiens, and goaltender Lynn Davis from the Port Arthur Bruins.

In the rescheduled first game, the Bombers showed their mettle, leading 2–1 in the dying moments. Pollock's decision to pull Claude Dufour for an extra attacker resulted in an empty-net goal for the Bombers. The Bombers appeared on the verge of taking firm control of the series with a 3–2 lead in game two when Pollock made another last-minute pull of Dufour. Bill Carter scored for the Canadiens with thirty-three seconds left; nine seconds later, captain Ralph Backstrom broke the hearts of the Bombers fans by notching the winner.

Like it or not, Pollock had to play game three in Flin Flon, and the Bombers mounted a 2–0 lead in the first period. Trailing 2–1 in the third, the Junior Canadiens rifled four unanswered goals to win 5–2 and take a 2–1 series lead into Regina.

In game four, the officiating began to get under Pollock's already aggravated skin. A 1–0 lead turned into a 3–1 loss as the Bombers scored three times in the final period. Six of nine minor penalties in the game had gone to the Canadiens.

By now, the series had become a roving carnival of hockey's heavy hitters. Coaches and general managers from around the NHL were dropping in on the games in Flin Flon and Regina to see how Pollock and Bowman were handling Kirk's crew. The Stanley Cup finals had ended April 16, with Montreal defeating Boston four games to one, and Toe Blake had decided to take in the sights in the company of Montreal vice-president, western talent czar and former teammate Ken Reardon. The old Canadiens teammates were big, confident old pros, and their size and demeanour contrasted with the high-octane energy of the Pollock-Bowman duo, both smaller men, harried, and sensing a western conspiracy against them. Knowing how exercised Pollock was about the officiating, Blake, fresh from his second Stanley Cup win in as many tries, delighted in tormenting him and could not resist making observations about what a good job the referees were doing whenever he was in earshot. Reardon, for his part, seemed privately pleased with the solid effort the Bombers were turning in. A team from the western Memorial Cup playdowns hadn't won the event since 1946/47. The lengthy reign of the eastern teams was attributed to their superior skating, but it was felt that the west was catching up as more artificial-ice arenas were built, creating more playing time.

Game five was when Pollock at last erupted. The betting line on the game favoured Montreal by a goal and a half. Flin Flon had had its breaks; now the Junior Canadiens were going to take control of the series. Flin Flon, however, didn't follow the betting line: it was a 1–1 game after two periods. Most of the penalties had gone Ottawa's way in the first and second periods, and for Pollock the shockwave that triggered his eruption came shortly before the second intermission. Jean Gauthier had applied an elbow to the face of Ottawa-Hull's John Annable, which attracted a minor penalty for Flin Flon. Annable wasn't satisfied, pursuing the referee to argue for a major, as Gauthier had drawn blood. For his persistence, Annable was awarded a misconduct.

When the period was through, Pollock verbally lacerated the officials for their treatment of Annable. They responded by suspending Pollock from the rest of the game. Toe Blake, watching Pollock's performance, turned to Reardon and asked, "Tell me, do I look like that when I coach?"

Oh, what fun. With Pollock out of the game, the Junior Canadiens were left to Scotty Bowman to coach. His debut as a Memorial Cup coach was a disaster. Handed a 1–1 game, he was down 3–1 after less than four minutes of play in the third period. Trailing 5–2 at the end of the game, Bowman tried to organize a six-man attack, but Flin Flon's Patty Ginnell grabbed the puck and threw it into the Junior Canadiens' end. The easterners never got the puck across their own blueline again before the buzzer sounded. Bowman was so enraged by the referees' failure to penalize Ginnell that he made his own sharp-tongued pursuit of the officials when the game was over.

Down three games to two, Pollock was labouring under an increasing load of slights and improprieties. He wouldn't stop talking about the fact that games were played in Flin Flon—they would be going back to Whitney Forum for game seven if Pollock could win game six and tie the series. The officiating had inspired a four-alarm tirade, and now he was mad about the series scheduling. He thought game six was going to be on Saturday, May 4, but because the series was not allowed to play a second set of back-to-back games (a pair had been played in Flin Flon), and because Sunday was the Sabbath, game six would not take place until Monday . . . when two of Pollock's most valuable players were due back home to write exams—Mike Lagace at Laval, Gilles Tremblay at Hull College.

"I hate to sound as if I'm complaining," Pollock complained, "but we've been getting the dirty end of the stick ever since we arrived in the west."

His team rose above its miseries. Down 2–1 in game six, the Junior Canadiens scored three third-period goals to win 4–2 and force the seventh game, back in Flin Flon. The deciding tilt lived up to Pollock's pessimistic expectations. Of ten penalties called, seven went to the Junior Canadiens, including all four penalties in the third period, when his team was trailing 3–1. Mike Lagace, who had been flown back with Tremblay to participate in the deciding game, scored with two seconds left, to make it 3–2, but the clock had nothing left for them. The Bombers were Canada's Junior champions.

When a reporter suggested Pollock had had a tough time with officiating, he muttered, "Yeah. I guess it had to be that way." Reardon admired the effort the Bombers players turned in, but could not abide the lopsided penalty calls. "This was a historic series with some historic calls by the referees," he cracked.

✧   ✧   ✧

Pollock and Bowman went home to plot their comeback, and returned to the Memorial Cup in 1957/58 with an even stronger team. Joining holdovers Gilles Tremblay and Ralph Backstrom were J.C. Tremblay and Bobby Rousseau, all impending stars of the Montreal Canadiens. Travelling east to contest the title were the Regina Pats, making for an all-Montreal final, a showcase of the reigning Stanley Cup champions' brightest prospects for the 1960s. In this in-house series, the Pats brought to bear Terry Harper, Dave Balon, Bill Hicke and Red Berenson.

Bowman and Pollock got to the finals with a clever bit of lineup manipulation. For the eastern finals against the Toronto Marlboros, they brought in Bruce Gamble from the Guelph Biltmores as a substitute goaltender, claiming their regular starter was too sick to play. Gamble had been a standout for Guelph in the eastern finals against the Junior Canadiens the previous year. A Rangers property, Gamble would be an NHL starter with Boston, Toronto and Philadelphia. The Marlies protested Gamble's use, to no avail, and they went down in five.

The Ottawa-Hull Junior Canadiens were a fine facsimile of their parent NHL club: solid defensively, with an ability to pump goals past opponents in machine-gun bursts. If Pollock and Bowman could catch you out on line matches, could confuse your defensive coverage, you were in very serious trouble. After losing game one, they took a 4–0 lead in the first twelve minutes of game two to win 4–2. They did it again in game three, mounting a 3–0 lead in the opening thirteen minutes before winning 6–2. An overtime win for the Pats evened the series, but in a second-period span of less than a minute and a half the Junior Canadiens rifled three unanswered goals and won game six 6–3. An easy 6–1 win gave the Junior Canadiens the series. It was a far cry from the politically and emotionally charged series against the Flin Flon Bombers. After eight seasons of trying, Sam Pollock had another Memorial Cup win. Scotty Bowman, for his part, had begun his coaching career at a breakneck pace. Two seasons in Canadian Junior A hockey had brought him two trips to the Memorial Cup. As an assistant to Pollock, he had learned and accomplished a lot. Sad Sam was ready to give Bowman a team of his own.

4

❖ "I'VE GOT A NEW NAME for Scotty Bowman," Wayne Cooper, public relations director of the St. Louis Blues, declared in the spring of 1968. "I'm calling him Cecil B. DeMille."

The National Hockey League Western Conference final series between the Blues and the Minnesota North Stars, which Cooper had just witnessed, would not be enshrined in the game's lore the way some of the great Stanley Cup finals have been—like the seven-game tilts between the Montreal Canadiens and the Detroit Red Wings of the mid-1950s, or the down-three-nil reversal of fortune by the Toronto Maple Leafs against Detroit in 1942. These were truly epic struggles, in fact as well as in the public perception. But what the Blues were up to that spring was, nevertheless, remarkable.

The St. Louis Blues was an expansion team that had just gained a Stanley Cup finals berth, a berth that most people did not believe any one of the league's new franchises deserved to have reserved for it, as had been ordained under the controversial playoff structure of 1967/68. The expansion clubs, sequestered in the West division, were built out of hockey's spare parts, and, not surprisingly, over in the East every Original Six club but one, Detroit, had finished ahead of them on points in the regular season. Nonetheless, the league had decided (over the initial objections of president Clarence Campbell) that one of the newcomers, however inferior, would be guaranteed a spot in the finals, after advancing through their own playoff rounds. But how St. Louis reached the finals would matter little in the game's lore if the consensus was that they didn't deserve to get there.

How they got there was nonetheless a marvellous story. In brief: two playoff series, each requiring all seven games; they tied Philadelphia on goals 17–17 and were outscored by Minnesota 22–18, yet defeated both teams. Six of the fourteen games required overtime; four of those overtime games, including the clincher, came in the division final against Minnesota, a league record for any series; and St. Louis won all but one of the six games that went into sudden death.

While the Blues' playoff drive might not have had the epic scope of a DeMille four-reeler, it did have a tour de force director whose attention to fine detail and micromanaging instincts made possible the breadth and depth of this narrative. This was Scotty Bowman's show. In the course of a few months, after assuming control of the Blues as coach and general manager in November 1967, he had taken a newly minted and struggling team from last place to Stanley Cup contention. People like Cooper could only watch, amazed, as Bowman's Blues put on a show that had the dramatic guts of a Hollywood screenplay. It was a script written for underdogs that the audience would love to cheer for. It had all the right subplots. The rivalries and old scores were in absurd abundance, and Bowman, in addition to directing the script, was perhaps the leading character.

Bowman was thirty-two, the youngest coach or general manager in the league. *The Hockey News* had named him coach of the year after his Blues overcame the North Stars 2–1 in overtime on May 3 to advance to the finals. Bowman had brought heart-attack playoff hockey to the banks of the Mississippi, and just two days after outlasting Minnesota, his Blues would be playing in game one of the finals. Waiting for him there was his own past, and his future as well: five days earlier, the Montreal Canadiens had defeated the Chicago Blackhawks 4–3 in overtime to reach the finals for the fourth consecutive season.

No one gave the Blues any kind of chance. The team had won twenty-seven of seventy-four regular-season games, finishing third in its division and eighth overall. The Canadiens had won forty-two games and finished first in their division and overall. And confronting Bowman behind the Canadiens bench was the winningest coach in NHL history, who was also one of its most celebrated players. In 1967/68, Toe Blake was reaching for his eighth Stanley Cup as a coach, and the ground was laid for a sporting massacre.

But for Bowman, this scenario of adversity was an old bit of script. Nine years earlier, in his first job coaching in the Juniors, he had risen to the occasion of the underdog role, mounting a playoff drive that rivalled anything Wayne Cooper would marvel over in St. Louis. Though he was a rookie NHL coach in the spring of 1968, his performance with the Blues was, in fact, vintage Bowman. That spring, his goaltender was Glenn Hall, who would remark that Bowman was thinking when everyone else was sleeping. Nine years earlier, his goaltender had been a teenage Denis DeJordy, who would remark that Bowman was always twenty-four hours ahead of the game, that he never stopped thinking about the game. In the end, both playoff drives were not about who won or lost. They were about how much Scotty Bowman could accomplish with so little, and they invited the question of how much he could accomplish if given more.

It was hailed as the most stirring playoff performance in the history of Junior hockey in Ontario. Scotty Bowman had guided the Peterborough Petes to the 1958/59 provincial title, against expectations and the tide of playoff momentum, overcoming an array of setbacks. He did not have the most talented team, but Bowman had enough talent and cunning of his own to fashion a winner—Peterborough's first since 1901.

The Petes were a second-string amateur development club of the

Montreal Canadiens. The main Junior talent continued to be assigned to the Ottawa-Hull Junior Canadiens; the Petes got what was left over. After a long period of dormancy, Junior hockey had returned in 1956 to Peterborough, an industrial town in the heart of Kawartha Lakes cottage country about an hour's drive northeast of Toronto. The Petes had been coached in 1957/58 by former Leafs captain Ted Kennedy, after a comeback bid with the Leafs had failed. One year in Peterborough convinced Kennedy that coaching Junior hockey was not his calling, and as the 1958/59 season approached, the Petes had no one behind the bench.

The Petes' sponsors approached Sam Pollock for help with their Canadiens affiliate. He had two candidates: Scotty Bowman and Claude Ruel, the compact Junior Canadiens defenceman, who had just suffered a career-ending eye injury in an exhibition game in Belleville. "I wanted Ruel to start in the system the way Bowman had, and felt that Bowman would be a great help to Claude," says Pollock. "But Peterborough didn't have a coach and were pleading with Montreal to supply one." Rather than having Bowman and Ruel work together, the way he had hoped, Pollock was forced to assign one of them to the Petes. He gave the Petes the choice of either man, and they understandably opted for Bowman, who had the experience of two Memorial Cup campaigns and the Junior Canadiens' victory the previous spring. Pollock gave Ruel the Junior Canadiens to coach, under his own tutelage.

Bowman's first game as a coach with his own team in the Montreal organization was on October 18, 1958, at Maple Leaf Gardens, against the Toronto Marlboros, whose bench was being run by former Leaf goaltending great Turk Broda. Bowman's coaching debut was a 1–0 loss, but the game was more noteworthy for the fact that Bowman was slapped with a two-game suspension for a bench-clearing brawl. Broda, who was also iced for two games by the league, blamed Bowman's Petes for the fracas, in which eight players earned seventy-two minutes in penalties and seven players who left their benches received twenty-five-dollar fines. Broda claimed the Petes had taken to the ice first and that his players had had no choice but to follow. Bowman refused to take the blame, charging instead that the referee had simply lost control of the game.

While poorer cousins to their counterparts in Ottawa-Hull, the Petes were not without talent. They had Jacques Caron, the top goaltender in the OHA that season, and a bruising defenceman from Kirkland Lake named Barclay Plager. Up front was Wayne Connelly, who scored thirty-six goals in 1958/59 and was named to the league All Star team. Bowman also had Jimmy Roberts, a defenceman and defensive forward who personified the underdog nature of the 1958/59 team. As a teenager in Port Hope, he had travelled to Toronto to try out with the Marlies, but ended up playing Junior B hockey in Peterborough. In 1958, the Canadiens got his signature on a C-form and he was assigned to the Petes, just in time for Scotty Bowman to arrive. It was the beginning of a professional relationship that would stretch almost thirty years. Roberts, the second-string Montreal prospect, would end up winning five Stanley Cups with the Canadiens in the 1960s and 1970s and playing in four more finals.

From the beginning, Bowman displayed a wicked talent for toying with people's motivational equilibrium. He benched players or gave them irregular shifts to make them hungry, leaving them to stew and want more ice time, and to give more when they got it. "There were days of turmoil in Scotty's career even back then," says Roberts. "George Montague was in and out of the lineup. He'd play two shifts, then not dress. Play five shifts, then not dress. One game he got up on the bench, threw his gloves into the middle of the rink, turned around to Scotty and told him, 'I'm quitting!' In the next couple of days he was back, and he ended up doing well in the Memorial Cup. Even in those days, the Bowman manipulation of the mind was going on. It worked. It was painful for the people it was working on, but it worked for the whole team."

Having finished far out of the running in their first two seasons, the

Petes enjoyed a finish of second overall on the 1958/59 season. They moved aside the Barrie Flyers in their opening playoff pairing, bringing on a semifinal series against the Guelph Biltmores, the New York Rangers affiliate whose lineup included Jean Ratelle. While the Petes had finished four points ahead of Guelph in the standings, in their games together Guelph had enjoyed a significant edge, coming away with twelve of eighteen points. The Petes won the opener 6–3, but in the pre-game warmup for game two, calamity struck. A shot by Wayne Connelly hit Caron in the face, causing a hairline fracture to his jaw. As in the rest of his coaching career, goaltending was going to be a major factor in Bowman's playoff fortunes. The Petes' backup, Chuck Adamson, responded superbly to the task of replacing Caron. Bowman ordered his team to check unfailingly, and they came away with a 6–2 win.

A 1–1 tie was followed by a comeback effort that seemed to crush any hope Guelph had of getting back in the series. Trailing 3–1, Bowman's Petes scored twice in twelve seconds to salvage a tie and move one win away from advancing to the provincial finals. The playoffs used a points format: two for a win, one for a tie (there was no overtime), with the first team to reach eight points the winner. The Petes got their win in a 2–0 shutout by Adamson, on goals by Plager and Connelly.

In the provincial finals, the Petes faced the St. Michael's College Majors, a venerated component of the Toronto Maple Leafs' amateur talent system. The Majors' last great season had been 1946/47, but the Toronto Catholic school continued to produce major-league talent for the Leafs. Tim Horton had played there in the late 1940s, and he had been followed by such alumni as Dick Duff and Frank Mahovlich. In 1958/59, St. Mike's had an impressive assembly of talent playing on both its Junior B Buzzers and Junior A Majors. The Majors' goaltender was Cesare Maniago, and Dave Keon was on right wing; other gifted players at the school then included goaltender Gerry Cheevers, defenceman Arnie Brown, and left-winger Larry Keenan.

The Leafs had provided the team with a new coach, former defensive great Bob Goldham, who had won two Stanley Cups with Toronto and three with Detroit before retiring in 1956. After finishing fourth overall in 1958/59, Goldham's Majors had reached the provincial finals by upsetting the favoured St. Catharines Teepees, a Chicago Blackhawks affiliate that featured Denis DeJordy in goal and Stan Mikita at centre. Mikita had enjoyed the maximum three-game call-up permitted to amateurs with Chicago that season, and at age twenty, he would make the parent club that autumn. DeJordy, twenty, would become a tag-team netminding partner with Glenn Hall in Chicago in 1964/65 and share a Vezina with him in 1966/67. Though a loser in the playoff series against St. Mike's, DeJordy was soon to become a wild-card factor in Scotty Bowman's first playoff drive as a coach.

With a Stanley Cup–winning defenceman coaching, with Maniago in goal, with a defensive-minded forward like Dave Keon on hand, the Majors were tremendously difficult to score against. St. Mike's led the first game 2–0, but the Petes came back to tie the game and salvage a point. In game two the Petes were weak defensively and couldn't generate much offence, going down 4–1. Bowman had stuck with his netminding fill-in from the first series, Chuck Adamson, for the opening games, but after the 4–1 loss he decided to revert to Caron, whose jaw was healed enough to allow him to play. A tie and another 4–1 loss followed. The Petes were down six points to two in a first-to-eight series; they hadn't been able to produce a single win in the first four games, and they were one loss away from elimination.

"We can't skate with those guys on this big ice surface," Bowman admitted after the 4–1 loss at Maple Leaf Gardens. "The only player we had who was hitting at all was Plager. I wish we had fifteen Plagers. We got only one penalty in the game [a Plager trip in the second period]. You can't win on that kind of hockey, especially in the playoffs."

Bowman's players got the message and got chippy. In the fifth game, at home in Peterborough, Barclay Plager accounted for five of the Petes' eight penalties, as St. Mike's attracted six. As important as the hitting was the performance of centre Gary Darling. Their scoring star, Wayne Connelly, had been struggling, but the 127-pound Darling was filling in admirably. His hat trick, scored in a span of seventy-nine seconds, helped secure a 4–2 win and avoid elimination.

It was back to the Gardens for game six. A tightly played game saw Peterborough take a 1–0 lead. During the second intermission, Bowman traded punches with a fan. ("He was swearing at me, using filthy language.") With just over two minutes to go, St. Mike's scored to get the tie and move one point away from advancing to the provincial finals. The Petes needed three consecutive wins to avoid elimination.

Which is exactly what Bowman's Petes produced, concluding the streak with a convincing 4–1 win at Maple Leaf Gardens. Goldham strove to hide his disappointment at having downed the mighty Teepees only to be levelled by the Petes, a team that it had had seemingly at its mercy. Three times in the series against St. Mike's, the Petes had been one goal away from elimination. "They beat us at our own game," Goldham said. "They were skating and checking, and we weren't."

The miracle over St. Mike's propelled the Petes into the eastern Memorial Cup playoffs against the Ottawa-Hull Canadiens; whoever won would advance to the Memorial Cup finals against the western playoffs winner. It was the A squad versus the B squad, another Montreal house league Junior series. Claude Ruel had the juggernaut, Scotty Bowman the tramp steamer.

Ruel had an able crew: Bobby Rousseau and Gilles Tremblay from the 1957/58 champions had been bolstered by Jacques Laperriere and Keith McCreary. Laperriere would join Terry Harper and J.C. Tremblay from the 1957/58 Memorial Cup finalists in creating a new defensive corps for the champion Canadiens teams of the 1960s. Right-winger Keith McCreary's career would come in expansion, with the Pittsburgh Penguins and Atlanta Flames.

The Junior Canadiens were the favourites, but there were concerns about their somewhat listless performance in casually dealing with the Quebec Baronets 6–3 and 8–3 in their lead-up playoff series. Ruel's team had played only a few exhibition games in addition to the two matches against the Baronets, while Bowman's Petes had been through eighteen playoff games. The Junior Canadiens might be well rested, but they might also be susceptible to upset by a playoff-hardened opponent.

It didn't look that way, as the Junior Canadiens won the first two games, 4–1 and 5–2. Jacques Caron, whom Bowman had given much of the credit for the turnaround against St. Mike's, disappointed him with his play in the opening game. And Bowman's chances were further dimmed by an ankle fracture suffered by Bill Mahoney in the first period of the first game, which broke up his top line of Mahoney, Larry Babcock and Wayne Connelly.

"We've got them on the run," Ruel crowed. "If these boys play the hockey they're capable of, we should take them in four straight."

"Saturday, it was my goalie who let me down," Bowman countered. "Yesterday, it was the forwards. They weren't checking the way they should. However, we've been behind the eight ball before and we came out of it."

Then something happened, something awfully familiar to members of the Canadiens organization. A goaltender on a Junior team being coached by Scotty Bowman had to bow out of the playoffs for health reasons, to be replaced by a star netminder from an eliminated team.

Bowman (with Pollock) had pulled this manoeuvre in 1957/58, when they'd parachuted in Bruce Gamble from Guelph for the eastern finals against the Marlboros. Now Bowman was trying the same thing, in mid-series. Jacques Caron had been packed off to hospital to have a cyst removed from his leg. In his stead, Bowman was going to use Denis DeJordy.

DeJordy very nearly wasn't available. After his Teepees had been eliminated, DeJordy had gone home to Ste. Hyacinthe, Quebec. Some local lads were putting together a team to play in a weekend tournament in Maine and had invited him to come along. DeJordy had considered the trip, but his mother had talked him out of it, telling him it would be a waste of time. Unbeknownst to him, Scotty Bowman had slipped his name onto the Petes' injury reserve list. Bowman called him and got him on a train to Toronto.

Bowman met him at Union Station and drove him to Peterborough for game three, talking hockey the whole way, running through game strategies. DeJordy had never met anyone like him: "He was hockey hockey hockey." Bowman was completely obsessed by the task at hand: defeating Claude Ruel's Junior Canadiens. DeJordy found himself in the company of someone who absolutely hated to lose. In the 1960s, DeJordy would coach at a summer hockey camp in St. Andrew's, New Brunswick, where Bowman was also an instructor. It amused him then to see Bowman, even in the camp games held between kids, totally focused on victory.

Some believed Scotty Bowman had pulled a fast one in replacing Caron with DeJordy. Jimmy Roberts, however, defends the substitution as perfectly legitimate. Caron had received a bad bruise on his hip, which had developed an enormous cyst that required constant attention for Caron to play. "It came to the point where he could hardly make it onto the ice." He had finally been sent to the hospital to have it removed, long after he should have.

Claude Ruel moved to protest the substitution, but the effort went nowhere. "With the selection of players they had, they had no business protesting," says Roberts. "That was just sour grapes from Pollock's prized pupils, getting beaten by a bunch of kids they had no use for."

With DeJordy in goal, the Petes took a 2–0 lead in game three, but the Junior Canadiens came back to get a 2–2 tie. "We've got our first point from them now and these kids are fired up," Bowman said the next day. "Canadiens will have to dig if they want to win tonight in Hull." Bowman's confidence was remarkable. The Petes were down five points to one. Ruel needed only a win and a tie, or three ties, to get the necessary eight points. Instead, Ruel got four straight losses as Bowman's Petes cruised to the Ontario Junior title. DeJordy was brilliant, and so was Connelly. Held scoreless for the first three games of the playoffs, the team's top goal-producer in the regular season scored four times in the 5–2 win in game four, three times in the 4–1 win in game five, and did all the scoring in Peterborough's 2–1 win in game six. Ruel was regularly seen moaning in the dressing room after a loss, wondering what had gone wrong.

The western finalists, the Winnipeg Braves, had their own future NHLer in net, Ernie Wakely, as well as two highly skilled defencemen: Gary Bergman, who would begin playing for Detroit in 1964/65, and Ted Green, a permitted addition from the St. Boniface Canadiens, who would join Boston in 1961/62. But when Bill Allum, their coach, heard that the Petes had knocked off the Junior Canadiens in the eastern final, he felt trepidation, wondering what kind of team was coming his way.

The Petes managed to win the opening game 5–4, but then lost the next three. Despite having fallen behind three games to one in the best-of-seven series, Bowman tried to sound optimistic. "Don't forget, we've been down worse than this. St. Mike's had us down three to one with one tie, and we bounced back. We'll do it again, just watch."

Sam Pollock was watching. He had gone west in the middle of the Petes–Junior Canadiens series, to await its outcome and welcome the winner to the finals. What he saw was not another Scotty Bowman comeback. What he saw was Scotty Bowman losing his temper in the third period of game five, being assessed a bench minor for slapping a stick on the boards, and then being ejected from the game for opening his wallet and pantomiming a payoff to the referee. After a 2–0 Petes lead melted into a 6–2 loss, Bowman was gracious enough to return at the end of the game and extend his congratulations to Bill Allum. Scotty Bowman would not be coming home with a Memorial Cup of his own.

Pollock did not blame him for the third-period outburst. After all, Pollock had gotten himself heaved out of a game in the 1956/57 finals when he could no longer control his temper over the refereeing. The Pollock School of Acting had graduated a distinguished performer. But Bowman's performance was as much genuine outrage as act. Four decades after Bowman's loss, Pollock has not lost his own mistrust of Memorial Cup officiating on the road. He still feels that if the 1958/59 series had been held in the east, the Petes could well have won. At the time of the loss, Pollock made sure people understood that Bowman had been in the last three finals, an unprecedented record for a coach.

It was the closest Bowman would ever come to winning a Memorial Cup on his own, although he would coach the Petes for two more seasons and take charge of two other Junior teams in the 1960s. Until he reached the NHL, the 1958/59 Petes campaign stood as his greatest accomplishment. He would become famous in the NHL for winning championships with great teams, but it was in Peterborough in 1958/59 that he first demonstrated his innate coaching ability. The Petes' playoff drive showed that Bowman possessed a cleverness and dedication that could make a legitimate contender out of an underdog. He demonstrated a refusal to fold when he was at a deep disadvantage, a resourcefulness in the DeJordy affair that suggested, if not a slippery cunning, then at least an attention to detail, and, in his final-game outburst a ferocious temper, a disdain for officiating, and a theatrical flair that would resurface regularly in his NHL years.

The 1958/59 Petes season was his dress rehearsal for his performance with St. Louis in the 1967/68 NHL playoffs. Some of the players from that series were even sitting on the Blues' bench. The parallels, for those who were around for the first campaign, were impossible to miss in the second. Bowman was dangerous, especially when coaching a second-class outfit against a world-class team like Toe Blake's Montreal Canadiens. After the Petes' loss, Bowman spent nine years waiting for another chance to show the hockey world what he could do, and that lag time honed his skills. When Bowman got another chance at success, he was not going to treat it lightly. He was going to fight harder than anyone to achieve his goal, and his effort would make a figure as great as Toe Blake reconsider whether he still had the stomach to risk defeat.

5

✧ AFTER SCOTTY BOWMAN'S playoff performance with the
1958/59 Peterborough Petes, his career moved into a period of relative stasis, with some movement but no real progress. There was little
chance of a rapid rise through the Canadiens organization, for Toe
Blake wasn't going anywhere and, like his fellow NHL coaches, he
didn't employ an assistant. After winning his fourth Stanley Cup in
as many years that spring, Blake was ebullient and boastful. "It'll
take anybody five years to beat me," he told a television interviewer
as he savoured his record Cup performance. No NHL coach had ever
won more than three Cups in a row. And since becoming an NHL coach
in 1955/56, Blake had never *not* won a Stanley Cup. He did not know
what defeat was.

Bowman's success in Peterborough attracted an offer to run the
Toronto Marlboros, but he turned it down, banking for his long-
term future on the Canadiens. He stayed in Peterborough for two
more seasons but never again came as close to a Memorial Cup win
as he did in 1958/59; his team was twice eliminated before he could
reach the provincial finals. The years of domination of Junior hockey
by the Canadiens organization were over. Claude Ruel spent five seasons coaching the Junior Canadiens, from 1958/59 to 1962/63, but
he came no closer to Memorial Cup success than Bowman—in fact,

the Junior Canadiens never advanced into the Memorial Cup play-downs in those years.

After Bowman's near-miss in the 1958/59 Memorial Cup, Sam Pollock moved to add to his stable of young proteges. Bowman remained in Peterborough while Claude Ruel moved back to Montreal with the Junior Canadiens. A new operation, the Ottawa-Hull Canadiens, was established, managed by Pollock. This club was part of the new Eastern Professional Hockey League, an outgrowth of the professional Quebec league which absorbed a few Senior teams in Ontario and added franchises in St. Louis and Syracuse. Pollock collected from Bowman's Petes Jimmy Roberts, and secured Al MacNeil. After winning the Memorial Cup as captain of the Toronto Marlboros, MacNeil had been called up to the Leafs in 1956/57 to join former teammates Bob Baun, Bob Pulford, Billy Harris and Bob Nevin. MacNeil managed fifty-three games on defence, but was back in Rochester in 1957/58. There seemed to be no hope of a starting position after Punch Imlach arrived in 1958 and put together the superlative defence corps of veterans Tim Horton and Allan Stanley, and ex-Marlies Bob Baun and Carl Brewer, with Marc Reaume providing relief.

Pollock had known MacNeil since his Junior days as a Toronto Marlie, and playing in Rochester in the late 1950s placed MacNeil directly under Pollock's management. To make him a Montreal property, Pollock traded Stan Smrke to Toronto. With MacNeil as Ottawa-Hull's captain and former Red Wing and Blackhawk Glen Skov as player-coach, Pollock won the Eastern Professional Hockey League title in 1960/61.

Pollock admired MacNeil's character ("just a great guy") and hockey sense, and offered him the chance to move to an off-ice career, like Ruel and Bowman. "We had a good relationship and were always on the same wavelength," says MacNeil. "He wanted me to coach Ottawa-Hull." MacNeil, however, could not bring himself to abandon the possibility of an NHL career, and turned Pollock down. Pollock, MacNeil and Frank Selke discussed his future, and agreed he should keep playing. MacNeil made the Montreal Canadiens' lineup in 1961/62, but it was a momentary success. Toe Blake had the veteran Jean-Guy Talbot anchoring the defence corps, J.C. Tremblay had just arrived, and Jean Gauthier, Terry Harper and Jacques Laperriere were on the way. A trade was arranged, with MacNeil sent to Chicago for Wayne Hicks. MacNeil's instincts were correct: he could play in the NHL if given a chance, and he spent the next four seasons as a Blackhawks starter. Though he had left the Canadiens, MacNeil understood he would be back. "As soon as I was finished playing, I knew that I was going to end up as a coach somewhere with Sam."

While Pollock was attempting to recruit MacNeil, he was also giving Scotty Bowman new duties. In September 1961, Bowman was made chief scout of amateur talent in the east. He held the post for two years, but the job was less glamorous and less critical than it appeared. Local bird dogs did the main work, and with no universal draft, Bowman wasn't called upon to assess mature young talent for possible acquisition in an annual cattle-call. These were the still the days of C-forms, in which the best prospects were tied up by sponsor clubs, thereby removing from Bowman's view any players who were already owned by the Canadiens or any other professional club. And with the Canadiens so omnipresent in the Quebec game, there wasn't much unknown talent to search out. This was particularly true after 1962, when the Canadiens secured a seven-year right of refusal on all amateurs whose fathers were francophones born in Quebec, a measure intended to preserve the unique nature of the club. Although he did make some important signings, Bowman spent much of his time thinking about the long-term prospects of fourteen-year-olds.

A fresh job was found for Bowman, a promising one with a new NHL venture. In August 1963 the NHL established its own professional development league for young talent by acquiring the Central Hockey League. While sponsorships were maintained with clubs in the AHL and elsewhere, the new Central Professional Hockey League (CPHL) was meant to provide a springboard out of the Junior ranks for prospects, without those players having to compete for starting positions with minor pro veterans. Each CPHL team was allowed only one player age twenty-five or older and three between twenty-three and twenty-five; the rest had to be younger. The Eastern Professional Hockey League was folded as the new venture was established. In the inaugural 1963/64 season, Chicago sponsored the St. Louis Braves, Detroit the Indianapolis Capitals, Boston the Minneapolis Bruins, New York the St. Paul Rangers, Toronto the Tulsa Oilers (who did not begin playing until the league's second season, when a new arena had been completed) and Montreal the Omaha Knights. Pollock was made general manager of Omaha, and Bowman became his coach.

The CPHL proved to be a finishing school not just for new players, but for new coaches as well. In addition to Bowman in Omaha, Harry Sinden was the player-coach in Minneapolis, Fred Shero the coach in St. Paul.

Bowman had just turned twenty-seven when he arrived in Omaha. Among the players under his charge were his former Petes Jimmy Roberts and Barclay Plager. The goaltender was Ernie Wakely, a twenty-three-year-old Montreal property from Flin Flon who had opposed Bowman's Petes in the 1958/59 Memorial Cup final and had played one game for the Canadiens in 1962/63. Roberts, Plager and Wakely would all figure in Bowman's coaching future.

The Knights' season began with a road trip that gave Bowman a guided tour of the new league. His Knights won every one of six road games, as well as their home opener. But after racing to the top of the standings with a 7–0 record, Bowman wanted out. Pollock released him from his duties, and one of his players, Bill McCreary, was given the coaching job. The lone permitted over-twenty-five veteran on the team, McCreary, who was twenty-eight had played fourteen games for Montreal the previous season; he had also opposed Bowman and Pollock when the Junior Canadiens had tangled with the Guelph Biltmores in the 1951/52 Memorial Cup eastern finals. As with Roberts, Plager and Wakely, McCreary would not be permanently removed from Bowman's career with his departure from Omaha.

Pollock announced Bowman's departure from the Knights on November 1, with no explanation offered. A puzzled *Hockey News* reported, "It was learned that Bowman is suffering from ill health." But it seems that the only ill health Bowman might have been suffering from was homesickness.

"I remember him saying, 'I would prefer to come back and work in the system,'" Pollock recalls. "For some reason, it didn't appeal to him."

Bowman would later blame the parsimony of the local team owners for his decision to leave. Being forced to tour the American midwest by bus was a cost-saving measure that rankled him, and he was upset by their penny-pinching in player meals. Montreal scout Ron Caron met Bowman at Dorval Airport when he returned home. "He wasn't depressed, but he was very upset. His nerves were bad. It wasn't the fear of failing. He felt the owners were interfering and not treating his team like professionals. He couldn't cope and needed a break to get away from that atmosphere."

And perhaps chaperoning a roster of young pros around the American Midwest was not what Bowman wanted from life, even for one season. He was a relentless disciplinarian, and he would have had his hands full with a gang of young men so many miles from home. In his first seven games, Bowman had proved overwhelmingly that he could coach in the CPHL, but one road trip had apparently convinced him that he didn't want the baggage.

For Jimmy Roberts, Bowman's decision to leave Omaha was understandable. Stuck out in the American Midwest, he was too far from the heart of the Canadiens organization. Pollock was busy back in Montreal, and though he was the team's general manager, he didn't have time to get anywhere near Nebraska. Bowman was the lone sentry at a distant Canadiens outpost. In Roberts's mind, Bowman left partly because he was homesick, and partly because he felt professionally isolated. Bowman lived and breathed the game, and with the Knights there was no one else to talk hockey with except his own players.

It must have looked as though Bowman had just stepped off the fast track to an NHL coaching career. He had walked away from the CPHL challenge, returning to an unclear future at home in Montreal. Harry Sinden would be called up from the CPHL to coach Boston in 1966/67 at age thirty-three—at the time he would be the youngest coach in the NHL. Certainly the track record of coaching suggested that most candidates for an NHL coaching job required experience at the minor professional level. However, Sinden's experience aside, toiling in the minor pro ranks was no guarantee that the big job would follow. Fred Shero persisted in coaching in the minor pro system of the Rangers, in the CPHL and AHL, without attracting an invitation to handle the parent club. When New York's general manager, Emile Francis, decided George Sullivan had to go as the Rangers' coach in 1965/66, he initially took over the job himself; he later tried Bernie Geoffrion (who had been claimed on waivers from Montreal's protected list in June 1966) for part of 1968/69, but ultimately reclaimed the bench. The breakthrough in the NHL for Shero, the faithful company man, didn't come until 1971, when the Philadelphia Flyers hired him, at age forty-six.

There was, in fact, no clear career path to an NHL coaching assignment. Generally, the job fell to former NHL players. In this respect, Scotty Bowman was still cutting against the grain of coaching tradition.

In the history of the postwar modern game, the great teams were usually coached to Stanley Cup success by old warriors, who had often won the Cup themselves as players. Hap Day and Joe Primeau, both former Toronto greats who had played on the 1931/32 champion Leafs team, guided Toronto to Cup victories—Day in 1941/42, 1946/47, 1947/48 and 1948/49; Primeau in 1950/51. Dick Irvin, who had starred in the professional western game and joined the new Chicago Blackhawks lineup in 1926/27 after his old league folded, never won a Cup as a player but coached the Canadiens to the 1943/44, 1945/46 and 1952/53 championships. And in 1955/56, former Canadiens great Toe Blake had taken over.

The Leafs' and Canadiens' penchant for hiring former playing stars as coach was followed by New York, Chicago and Boston in the immediate postwar years, but not by Detroit. General manager Jack Adams was a former blood-and-guts NHLer who had also coached Detroit until 1947/48, when he hired Tommy Ivan as his replacement. Ivan's playing career had been cut short by a head injury before he could reach the NHL, and after the war (during which he had run the powerful Canadian army hockey team at the Cornwall, Ontario training base) he had entered Detroit's exemplary development system, coaching minor-pro affiliates before taking over from Adams as the Red Wings' coach. And when Ivan moved to the Blackhawks after winning a third Cup, in 1953/54, to accept a promotion to general manager, the Red Wings' Adams continued to defy tradition, hiring another non-veteran as his coach. This time it was Jimmy Skinner, the last player cut at the Red Wings' 1944 training camp, who was coaching the Red Wings' Ontario Junior A affiliate. But when Skinner quit the Wings during the 1957/58 season, traumatized by management's ruthless reaction to the stillborn players' association movement, Ivan steered the Red Wings back onto the more traditional coaching path by hiring former Detroit captain Sid Abel.

By the late 1950s, the NHL coaching ranks were dominated by former league players. Toronto was a notable exception, with Punch Imlach holding down both the general manager's and coach's jobs, beginning in 1958/59. At the start of the 1960s, Montreal had Toe Blake, Detroit had Sid Abel, and New York had Alf Pike, who had coached the Guelph Biltmores against Bowman and Pollock in the 1951/52 Memorial Cup eastern finals. Chicago joined Toronto in casting against type, with non-vet Tommy Ivan employing non-vet Rudy Pilous. But when Pilous was replaced by Billy Reay in 1963/64, every NHL team except Toronto had a veteran for its coach.

Consequently, though there was no written rule that said to coach in the NHL you had to have played in it, by the early 1960s it was a fairly powerful trend. At the very least, a coaching candidate had to have been groomed with experience in the minor pros. Jumping directly from the Junior coaching ranks to the NHL was a rare feat, though it had been achieved by Joe Primeau in Toronto in 1950 and Jimmy Skinner in Detroit in 1954. Perhaps coincidentally, both achieved immediate Stanley Cup success, and both made quick exits from the league. Primeau had decided as soon as he won the Cup that he wasn't interested in the NHL grind under Conn Smythe, but he stuck it out for two more seasons. Skinner similarly decided that the pressure of coaching in the fractious house of Jack Adams was more than he could stomach. Bowman's brief tenure in the CPHL suggested that he might prove to be another Primeau or Skinner, a gifted Junior coach who had no enthusiasm for the professional ranks.

Bowman returned home to Montreal from the CPHL stint to spend the 1963/64 season scouting prospects for the Junior Canadiens. As the playoffs in Canadian Junior hockey began, he drew a new assignment. He was parachuted by Sam Pollock into the Notre Dame de Grace (NDG) Monarchs, a Junior club in Montreal's Canadiens-sponsored Metropolitan League. (Notre Dame de Grace was also the neighbourhood in which Pollock grew up.) At the time, there was no province-wide Quebec Major Junior League; the Junior Canadiens were playing in the Ontario Hockey League, and the Metropolitan League was the best Junior competition Quebec could manage, with ten teams playing in two divisions. The Monarchs were a good team in a strictly second-tier league, finishing second in the West division under coach Alex Rennie. The Monarchs were hardly the calibre of the Montreal Junior Canadiens, who boasted centres Jacques Lemaire and Andre Lacroix, right-winger Yvan Cournoyer (the OHL's most valuable Junior player that season), defenceman Serge Savard and goaltender Rocky Farr. Lemaire, Cournoyer and Savard would become mainstays of the Montreal Canadiens, while Lacroix would go on to play thirteen seasons in the NHL and WHA, and Farr would draw three seasons of backup duty with the NHL's Buffalo Sabres. Coach Yves Nadon was taking the express route to the Memorial Cup playdowns, meeting the

Toronto Marlboros in the OHL finals, while Bowman and his Monarchs were touring unplowed backroads.

Though it lacked the glitter of the Junior Canadiens, the Monarchs' lineup had bright spots. Carol Vadnais was on defence, Lucien Grenier was on right wing, and in goal was Rogie Vachon. By some quirk of fate, all would end up Los Angeles Kings. Bowman also had centre Larry Pleau, a sixteen-year-old from Lynn, Massachusetts. In August 1963, Pleau had attended a hockey school in Worcester, where the instructors included Ralph Backstrom and Charlie Hodge from the Canadiens. Hodge and Backstrom sent the word back to Montreal that there was a kid worth looking at, and Bowman ventured to Massachusetts to see Pleau play in a summer high-school league. Back at the Pleau home, Bowman asked him if he wanted to come up to Canada and play Junior hockey. Pleau didn't even know what Junior hockey was, but he signed a C-form and headed north to join the NDG Monarchs. Pleau would play three years of Junior hockey for Bowman and one season under him as a Montreal Canadien before jumping to the WHA.

Vachon was a seventeen-year-old sleeper talent whom Bowman had personally secured for the Canadiens organization the previous year. As chief scout, Bowman had made the trip to the Vachon family dairy farm near Palmarolles in northern Quebec with scout Ron Caron (a future general manager of the St. Louis Blues). They got the sixteen-year-old's signature on a C-form; although the form was supposed to pay a minimum $50 signing fee ($100 was the typical bonus), Vachon doesn't recall getting any money at all. The next year, in the fall of 1963, Vachon was brought down to try out with the Junior Canadiens. He made the team and began alternating in goal with Farr, but he was judged too green for top-flight Junior hockey. As he recalls, he was only seventeen, still in school, and had never really had a coach before. On November 26, Sam Pollock reassigned Vachon to the NDG Monarchs (along with Grenier and two other players), replacing him with Andre Gagnon.

At five-foot seven, Vachon was only about an inch taller than the diminutive Charlie Hodge, and he would be the smallest goaltender in the NHL when starring with Los Angeles in the 1970s. But he was also a ferocious competitor, and under Bowman at NDG he showed promise of major talent. It nonetheless would have seemed extraordinary at the time to imagine that the NDG's goaltender, a castoff from the Junior Canadiens, would be playing for the Montreal Canadiens in the Stanley Cup finals a mere three years later.

The Monarchs' quarterfinal opponents were the third-place Verdun Maple Leafs, and the Monarchs were favoured to win. After an uncomfortably close 3–2 victory in the opening game, however, NDG was upset 6–5 in game two, and Sam Pollock moved in to dismiss Rennie and install Bowman. Juggling the roster to produce an effective three-line system, Bowman ran up wins of 7–3, 6–0 and 10–7 to take the Monarchs into the West division semifinals, against the first-place Lachine Maroons. Knocking off Lachine in six games, the NDG Monarchs were in the league finals against Rosemount, the best team in the weak East division.

After defeating Rosemount 2–1 in the opening game, Bowman noted he had four players who had been demoted from the Junior Canadiens. "During the year they had to play in the shadow of the Junior Canadiens," he explained. "Now they've knocked out Verdun and Lachine and are eager to get back into the Junior OHA next season." As with the Peterborough Petes of 1958/59, Bowman had found the right motivational button and was pushing it as hard as he could. The NDG Monarchs were out to prove that they didn't deserve their second-class status in the Canadiens organization. And having quit Omaha and the CPHL, Bowman was out to prove that he had the coaching skills to rescue him from his uninspiring scouting duties.

The temper that caused Bowman to be ejected from a game in the 1951/52 Memorial Cup eastern finals had not subsided over the ensuing decade. Junior players excelled for Bowman in part because they were terrified of being subjected to one of his temper tantrums. "He was a screamer. When he lost it, you didn't want to be around," Vachon recalls. "He went absolutely crazy." Pleau remembers him as "very demanding, very intimidating. We would come off the ice in warmups, and he'd be checking us for sweat. We'd go into the bathroom and put water on us to make it look like we were sweating."

Bowman was a disciplinarian who expected the young men under his charge to behave with the pride of the Canadiens organization in mind. "He was very well organized, on and off the ice," says Vachon "He got the message across of what he wanted, fast. Off the ice, he forced every kid to wear a hat. We were always well dressed. We looked like a real professional team."

It took six games for the Monarchs to down Lachine and claim the Metropolitan League title. Next came a pasting of the Victoriaville Bruins with 4–0, 5–0 and 8–3 scores in their best-of-five series. The Monarchs were then required to play the Port Alfred Nationals of Lac St-Jean in a best-of-five Quebec Junior final. In a practice for the series, Vachon had his nose broken, and he had to be replaced temporarily by Jacques Rivard of the Quebec Citadels. Even without Vachon, the Monarchs had little trouble. Flu reduced Bowman's lineup to only three defencemen for the opening game, but the Monarchs won regardless, 13–3. Repeat 5–1 wins moved aside the Nationals and sent the Monarchs into a double-round-robin series at the Montreal Forum against the Ottawa Montagnards and the Legionnaires of Summerside, Prince Edward Island.

With Vachon's return, the Monarchs beat Ottawa 4–0 and the Legionnaires 15–0. The Summerside team, which had lost 9–1 to Ottawa, was sent home early by the Canadian Amateur Hockey Association as the round-robin was abandoned in favour of a showdown game between the Monarchs and the Montagnards. The Monarchs won 11–3 to advance to a best-of-five eastern final series against the OHL champions. The Monarchs had won ten straight games; since taking over the team, Bowman had compiled a record of twenty wins and five losses.

Bowman girded his Monarchs for the next round by gathering additional talent. Among the five players he added were Billy Plager, younger brother of Barclay and Bob, and Craig Patrick, son of Bruins general manager Lynn Patrick, both from the Lachine Maroons. Meanwhile, the Junior Canadiens had managed to tie the Toronto Marlboros 5–5 in the opening game of the OHL championship, but had then gone down in straight defeats. The Marlboros had not lost a game since February 19, two months earlier. Their lineup was one of the most powerful that Canadian Junior hockey had ever seen, or ever would see. Gary Smith was the goaltender; the defence featured Jim McKenny and Rod Seiling. The forward lines were an array of yet more future NHL and WHA regulars: Pete Stemkowski, Ron Ellis, Mike Walton, Wayne Carleton and Brit Selby (who would win the Calder in 1965/66). Few other Junior teams have ever graduated so many players into NHL starting positions.

The Marlboros were obliged to meet and annihilate the North Bay Trappers of the Northern Ontario Hockey Association before contending with the NDG Monarchs, the last opponents they would have to entertain before reaching what they believed to be their rightful spot in the Memorial Cup finals. Marlboros coach Jim Gregory was impatient to get on with the "real" hockey. These games just put unnecessary wear and tear on his wonderful team, and he said as much in the press as he awaited the arrival of Bowman and the Monarchs at Maple Leaf Gardens.

Bowman's hackles were raised. "It appears that the Marlies feel they are in for a cakewalk against us. Well, I feel that we can surprise them in a short series, and we'll prove without a doubt that we are no pushovers."

Unfortunately, when the Marlies pushed in game one, the Monarchs fell hard, humbled 7–2. The Marlies weren't just a more skilful team overall. They were physically bigger, full of older players who were on the verge of NHL careers. Many of the Monarchs were only fifteen or sixteen, and while overall they were a heftier team than most in the Metropolitan League, compared to the Marlies they looked and played like kids. "Those guys were so big," Vachon remembers. "Some of them were 185 pounds. They were just a huge team."

The combatants headed to the Montreal Forum for game two, where fewer than two thousand fans were on hand. Only the most devoted Monarch supporters turned out to lend moral support for what was expected to be a thorough drubbing. Among the dutiful fans was Lynn Patrick, who had come to cheer on his seventeen-year-old son, regardless of the grim prognosis.

Before the game, Pete Stemkowski taunted Bowman with the promise that the rematch was going to be a high-scoring one. Trash talk has a long and even honourable tradition in sport. Rival players and coaches routinely sling disparaging remarks in each other's direction before a big game or series, either because mockery is part of their game plan or because they just can't help themselves. Sometimes it backfires, offering a motivational tool to an opponent who might otherwise have been an easy mark. Gregory's disdainful words about the Monarchs before the series had not left Bowman's mind. He heaped Stemkowski's words atop Gregory's, worked them into the wound the Marlies had inflicted on his players' egos in the opening blitz at the Gardens, and sent a surreally motivated group of Monarchs onto the Forum ice.

Rarely has a coach accomplished so much with so little. At the end of the first period, the Monarchs were winning 4–0. The stunned Marlies refocused and began chipping away at the deficit. Bowman later admitted that when the Marlies made it 4–2, he began to worry. Early in the third period, the game was tied 4–4. But instead of collapsing, the Monarchs dug deeper and came up with two unanswered goals as they outshot the Marlies 28–23 in the 6–4 win.

Far greater victories had been witnessed in the fabled Forum, but there had never been one so joyous. Playing to a near-empty building, an underdog had achieved a genuine sporting upset. Bowman was in heaven. "This has got to be my biggest thrill in hockey," he proclaimed, happily setting aside his Memorial Cup win of 1957/58 with Pollock and the Junior Canadiens. His pride was rivalled by that of Lynn Patrick, who knew only too well what it was like to be browbeaten and disrespected—his Bruins had not made the playoffs in the last five seasons. Here, before him, was evidence that the right coach, virtually singlehanded, could turn a loser into a shocking winner. The spectacle of the Monarchs' performance was made even more uplifting for Patrick by the transformation of his own son into a playoff hero under Bowman's guidance. Craig Patrick had scored twelve goals all season in Lachine and one in the team's playoff appearances. In just one game with Bowman, Patrick had scored twice, opening the scoring with an unassisted effort and contributing the fourth goal in the last minute of the first period.

The revenge of the Monarchs did not end in the Forum that night. Back in Toronto for game three, Bowman promised a seismic playoff upset as his team took a 3–2 lead, with another Craig Patrick goal, into the first intermission. It was a rough game, and Vachon was brilliant as the Monarchs clung to a 3–3 tie in the third period. But the Monarchs could not find the second wind that had rescued them in game two. The Marlies rammed three goals past Vachon to win 6–3 and put the Monarchs one game away from elimination.

Despite exhaustion and a parade of injured players, the Monarchs refused to lie down in game four. Patrick assisted on the Monarchs' first goal, and the opening period ended with the Marlies ahead 4–2. Patrick scored in the second to make it a one-goal game; the Marlies replied with one of their own, and the third period dawned with a 5–3 score. Bowman was not without hope, but his team was finished. It had absorbed more punishment than could be expected, and its thin defence had little strength against the ceaseless Marlboro attack. Six unanswered goals in the final period made it an 11–3 Marlie victory. Despite the score, Vachon had been extraordinary, turning away forty-seven Toronto shots.

The Marlies had their Memorial Cup berth, but one could not imagine

Jim Gregory or his players ever underestimating an opponent again. As it turned out, the lowly NDG Monarchs had given the Marlboros their toughest hockey of the 1963/64 playoff season: tougher than what was offered by the Junior Canadiens in the Ontario finals, tougher than what was soon after offered by the defending-champion Edmonton Oil Kings, who lost in four straight games in the Memorial Cup finals. There had been terrifying moments for the Marlies in three of the four games against the Monarchs, when it had appeared that Bowman might actually figure out how to derail their Memorial Cup drive. It was a performance that was not lost on the fascinated hockey world. A season that had begun for Bowman with a professional setback, as he had bolted from the American Midwest for an unclear future at home, had ended with a showcase of his ability. The next season, Sam Pollock made him the new coach of the Montreal Junior Canadiens.

Scotty Bowman was the greatest coach in the game without an NHL job. Unfortunately, in Montreal, the job of coaching the Canadiens was the territory of Toe Blake—for now, and, it appeared, for as long as he wanted it.

As Bowman had guessed, the NDG Monarchs players he inherited in the spring of 1964 were out to prove they belonged in the OHA Junior A. When Bowman was rewarded by Pollock with the Junior Canadiens coaching job after NDG's extraordinary playoff run, he in turn rewarded many of those players by taking them with him. The entire forward line of Larry Pleau, Craig Patrick and Norm Ferguson came along, as well as Serge Grenier and Carol Vadnais. Included in the 1964/65 Junior Canadiens lineup were future Canadiens stars Serge Savard and Jacques Lemaire, and Christian Bordeleau, who would play for Bowman in St. Louis.

The Junior Canadiens squeaked into the fifth and final OHA playoff spot in the final weeks of the 1964/65 season, which meant playing the league-leading Toronto Marlboros in the opening round. The Marlies still had a number of talents from their 1963/64 Memorial Cup–winning team, including Jim McKenny, Wayne Carleton and Brit Selby, as well as Brian Glennie on defence and Jerry Desjardins in goal. Bowman felt his team, with so many Monarchs on board, was still in awe of the team that had defeated NDG in the 1963/64 playoffs. A 5–1 Montreal lead in game one collapsed into a 5–5 tie, and despite playing well in game two, the Junior Canadiens lost 4–3.

Ironically, the one significant Monarch Bowman hadn't taken with him to the Junior Canadiens was Rogie Vachon, who was assigned by Montreal to a Junior B team in Thetford Mines as the Junior Canadiens starting job was given to former Quebec Citadels goaltender Jacques Rivard. After the loss in game two, Bowman publicly promised to switch to Rivard's backup, Ted Ouimet, but ended up sticking with Rivard for the rest of the series. Rivard rewarded Bowman's confidence in a 5–3 win, but then the Marlies humbled Bowman with 5–1 and 4–1 defeats. A 2–1 win in game six staved off elimination and gave the Junior Canadiens fresh hope. The 8–1 loss that followed, however, which eliminated the Junior Canadiens, left Bowman mercilessly critical of Rivard. Saying he was talked out of replacing Rivard after game two, he promised that Ouimet would be his starter in 1965/66. "I figured Rivard let me down in that series."

Ouimet did get the starter's job, as Rogie Vachon was making the amazing leap from Junior B in Thetford Mines straight into the professional ranks with the Quebec Aces in the AHL and the Houston Apollos in the CPHL. Ouimet played well, and in another late-season drive the Junior Canadiens moved from fifth to second. Eliminating the sixth-place Hamilton Red Wings with four wins and a tie, the Junior Canadiens ran their unbeaten streak up to fourteen games. It ended with a 5–3 loss to the first-place Oshawa Generals in the opening game of the OHA semifinals. While the Junior Canadiens won game two, 2–1, the Generals won the next three to continue on their path to a Memorial Cup appearance. After defeating the Junior Canadiens, Oshawa coach

Rudy Pilous confessed that Bowman's team was the one that had given him the most concern, and that the only way they could fail to win the Memorial Cup now was to drop dead. The Boston-sponsored team had a tremendous lineup, which included future Bruins Bobby Orr and Wayne Cashman, but they still lost the Memorial Cup finals to the Edmonton Oil Kings.

Despite the loss to Oshawa, Bowman was proud of his team, and said so. He could not know then that a 3–2 loss to Oshawa would stand as his last game behind the bench in Junior hockey.

For Larry Pleau, who had played about ten high-school hockey games back home in Massachusetts in 1962/63, his introduction to Junior hockey in 1963/64 was an almost inconceivable leap forward in intensity and personal growth. When the season was over, he had played more than seventy games, more than thirty of them in playoff action under Bowman as an NDG Monarch. "I'll never forget that stretch in the playoffs, because Scotty played me all the time. It was unbelievable."

Pleau was with Bowman for both his seasons as the coach of the Junior Canadiens. Pleau would graduate to the Montreal Canadiens' lineup in 1969/70 after playing for the 1968 U.S. Olympic team. He was a Canadiens utility forward—"a benchwarmer" as he puts it—for three seasons, the last of them under Bowman. Jumping to the Hartford Whalers as a hometown hero in 1972, he played seven full seasons until the Whalers joined the NHL in 1979/80. Pleau then moved into coaching and managing in Hartford, with the Whalers and their minor-pro affiliates. In 1989, he was hired by the Rangers as assistant general manager of player development, and he later rose to vice-president of player personnel. In June 1997, Pleau was named senior vice-president and general manager of the St. Louis Blues.

"You were terrified of him," Pleau says of his Junior days under Bowman. "I can remember him getting guys almost crying. You *feared* him. My memories of him, there are negatives, but I wouldn't be where I am today if it wasn't for Scotty, because of the way he handled me as a person when I was young—because of what I learned from him and the direction he gave me in my hockey career."

Pleau was shown the ropes by a peerless tutor. "Looking back, you can understand why he's done so well. He had a great mind, he really knew the game, and he taught you things." With the NDG Monarchs, "We had systems—face-off plays, forechecking, penalty killing. You were enthused. You wanted to learn." Against the Marlies in the Memorial Cup playoffs, Bowman used a defensive system in which the centre stayed back with the defencemen to thwart the rushes of an offensively superior team. Pleau would recognize the same system in Bowman's first NHL playoff coaching run with the St. Louis Blues in 1967/68, against the Philadelphia Flyers and the Montreal Canadiens.

Part of the learning process for Pleau was learning about Scotty Bowman, a tremendous disciplinarian off the ice as well as on it. Playing in the Ontario Junior league, the Junior Canadiens spent many days on the road, travelling by bus to games as far away as Windsor in southwestern Ontario, always returning for a regular Sunday home game at the Forum. Bowman would get the hotel master key and check on players' rooms, if only to make sure they weren't watching television in the middle of the afternoon, an indulgence he loathed. One night in Hamilton, Pleau and a teammate missed curfew and tried to sneak into their hotel room by the back stairs. "And there he was, sitting, waiting for us. I'll never forget that."

On another occasion, the Junior Canadiens played poorly in a Saturday road game against the Niagara Falls Flyers. They faced a 400-mile bus ride back to Montreal for their usual home game at the Forum the next day. Suddenly, the bus was pulling off the highway in Kingston, heading for a local rink. Bowman had called ahead and arranged some ice time for a road-weary team that hadn't played to his satisfaction. "He got us out of the bus, we put on wet equipment, and we skated hard for an hour without any pucks. Then we got back on the bus and went to Montreal."

For all the terror Bowman inspired, he could be disarmingly sociable, joining players in the back of the bus or walking with them, chatting away (mainly about hockey) as if he were a friend and not a demanding coach. But then, he could also be utterly bewildering, changing tacks in his behaviour without warning. "I was walking down the street with him in Peterborough after a morning practice," Pleau remembers. "We were going by a store that had wedding gowns in the window. He looked at me and said, 'Ah, you're never going to be a hockey player. You're going to be married with five kids before you're a hockey player.' He said it sarcastically, out of nowhere. You could never figure out why he said these things. It was like he was trying to find a way to keep you off balance. Never predictable. Practices were always different. One practice, he tied my lower hand to the stick so I wouldn't let go of it."

Ron Caron, who had scouted talent with Bowman in the 1960s and was in charge of amateur scouting during Bowman's NHL coaching run in Montreal, would remember him as "very focused. He loved to take charge of human beings called hockey players. I think Scotty dreamt of becoming a detective. He liked to use his authority."

In 1971/72, Pleau was a member of the Montreal Canadiens playing under Bowman, the team's new coach. Bowman's methodology was nothing new to him, but his behaviour nonetheless continued to confound. In a game against Chicago, Pleau and Pierre Bouchard were riding the bench as the Canadiens struggled. "Scotty came into the dressing room between periods and started hollering at Pierre and me. We're looking at each other. We haven't even played! Scotty says, 'You guys aren't *cheering* hard enough.'"

✧　✧　✧

During its Cup streak of the late 1950s under Toe Blake, Montreal won forty of forty-nine playoff games. After losing back-to-back series to Detroit that went the full seven games in 1953/54 and 1954/55, the closest contest Montreal had in the Cup finals was its 4–2 series victory over Boston in 1957/58. The Canadiens won eight of nine games against a resurgent Maple Leafs club in 1958/59 and 1959/60, sweeping Imlach's team in the second encounter.

After Montreal's fifth straight win in 1959/60, success was no longer so readily attained. It was not a case of the Montreal club getting worse—far from it, as the Canadiens extended their regular-season title streak to five, from 1957/58 to 1961/62. Rather, Montreal was brought up short by a league recovering some semblance of parity. While the New York Rangers continued to flounder and Boston faded badly after 1957/58, Toronto and Chicago had assembled strong lineups. After appearing in ten consecutive finals from 1950/51 to 1959/60, the Canadiens were shut out of the finals in four consecutive seasons—eliminated in the semifinals twice by the Leafs and twice by the Blackhawks.

Many hockey clubs in the game's history would have welcomed Montreal's burdens in the early 1960s. The lineup was tremendous, a mix of veterans and youth, with yet more talent in the amateur pipeline. Montreal had problems, but they were hardly insurmountable. Maurice Richard had retired after the 1959/60 Cup win, closing out a career that had been played exclusively as a Canadien. The need became apparent to move veteran players out of the way, to make room for fresh talent, to strengthen the Montreal checking game in the face of tenacious Detroit and Toronto squads. General manager Frank Selke acted with little apparent sentiment, dumping All Star defenceman Doug Harvey in New York after the six-game semifinal loss to Chicago in 1960/61, sending perennial Vezina winner Jacques Plante to the Rangers after the five-game semifinal loss to Toronto in 1962/63. Only six members of the 1959/60 championship lineup were still on hand when the Canadiens regained their championship form with a seven-game defeat of Chicago in 1964/65.

The club had changed hands in September 1957, as the aging Senator M. Donat Raymond sold his 60 percent interest in the publicly traded Canadian Arena Company (owner of both the Canadiens and the Forum) to Senator Hartland Molson and his brother Tom. One year later, the brothers sold their majority interest to cousins David, Peter and Bill Molson. The new ownership had little effect on the day-to-day operation of the club. For the most part, the Molsons let management do its job, although Senator Molson intervened with a steadying hand soon after buying the club, dissuading Frank Selke from punishing Doug Harvey, the team's ringleader in the 1957 players' association effort. Toronto's Conn Smythe and Detroit's Jack Adams had succumbed to self-destructive wrath, shipping union advocates Jimmy Thomson and Tod Sloan of the Leafs and Glenn Hall and Ted Lindsay of the Red Wings to the NHL's gulag, the Chicago Blackhawks. As brewers, the Molsons knew that unions were part of doing business, and they couldn't see the point of letting the argument damage their team. The players' association, as it happened, did not come to pass that year, and the Canadiens continued to rule the league while Detroit and Toronto suffered for their venom (and Chicago began its return to respectability).

The organization continued to demonstrate its unparalleled knack for rolling over a winning lineup, measuring its occasional slumps not in poor regular seasons but in playoff shortfalls. The challenge before the Canadiens under the Molsons in the early 1960s was within the organization itself, making seamless management changes that would not upset the team's ongoing quest to return to Stanley Cup glory. Frank Selke was approaching seventy, and the Molsons made repeated suggestions to him that perhaps it was time to consider retirement and make way for one of the younger talents who had been toiling under him for so many years. Selke was finally persuaded to move aside, reluctantly, at the end of the 1963/64 season. The Molsons had informed him that the company had a mandatory retirement age of seventy, and Selke was now seventy-two.

The shortlist for the position of general manager consisted of two names: Ken Reardon and Sam Pollock. Both men had contributed greatly to the flow of young talent filling Toe Blake's bench. The task of choosing Selke's successor fell to team president David Molson, who went with the front-line manager, promoting Pollock on May 15, 1964; Reardon continued in his vice-presidency.

One of Pollock's first moves was to launch Scotty Bowman on yet another quest. As a reward for his brilliant performance with the NDG Monarchs, Pollock had given him the Montreal Junior Canadiens coaching job. Bowman had replaced Yves Nadon, who in turn had replaced Claude Ruel the previous season when Pollock made Ruel Montreal's chief scout.

Pollock had immediate success as the Canadiens' new general manager. The roster changes continued, and when Montreal won its first Cup in five seasons the following spring, there were fifteen faces new to the lineup since the 1959/60 victory. The defence had been completely transformed, with the addition of J.C. Tremblay, Terry Harper, Jacques Laperriere and Ted Harris playing in front of goaltenders Charlie Hodge and Gump Worsley (acquired from New York in a multi-player trade that surrendered Jacques Plante, Don Marshall and Phil Goyette). Three veteran centres—Jean Beliveau, Henri Richard and Ralph Backstrom—provided pivot points for a raft of new wingers—foremost among them Jimmy Roberts, Yvan Cournoyer, Gilles Tremblay, Bobby Rousseau, John Ferguson and Dick Duff. All except Duff, a former Leaf acquired from the Rangers in December 1964, were products of the Canadiens' development system. The team possessed an enormous amount of skill, perhaps even more than the lineup that had dominated the playoffs in the previous decade.

As the Canadiens embarked on another string of Cup successes, appearing in five consecutive finals from 1964/65 to 1968/69 and winning four of them, it remained to be determined who, eventually, inevitably, would take over from Toe Blake as coach. Blake was hardly over the hill when the club returned to its winning ways in the spring of 1965. He was not yet fifty-three when Gump Worsley shut out the Blackhawks in the decisive seventh game on Forum ice to bring Cup honours to the city for the thirteenth time, the sixth for Blake as coach. But it was also Blake's thirty-third season in professional hockey, since he'd debuted as a player in 1932/33 with a one-game appearance as a Montreal Maroon. He had been with the Canadiens organization since 1935/36, thirteen years as a player, six as a minor-league coach, ten as head coach. His playing career had ended against his will with the double ankle fracture in January 1948; he was going to end his coaching career on his own terms.

There was obviously nothing wrong with Blake's coaching acumen. But as the team lineup changed, as general managers came and went, Blake was the unresolved question for the organization. How long would he stay? Another season? Another decade?

No one was addressing the question directly. Pollock avers that life after Blake simply wasn't on the organization's formal agenda. "In retrospect, it was something we should have thought about, but succession planning wasn't a big thing in those days. Even today in sports, people hire a coach, and nobody thinks of who the next coach is going to be." Blake had been going from one single-season contract to another. "We never considered his retirement. We felt he was just going to go on and on."

Then in March 1965, the league announced that it would expand from six to twelve teams in 1967/68. In a league that had supplied limited opportunities to junior management, doubling in size would open new doors to immediate advancement. The Original Six organizations would inevitably face losing future executives along with players. The players would have no choice when it came to answering the call of the expansion draft. The members of junior management, on the other hand, were in a seller's market. New clubs needed managers, coaches, scouts and more. It would be a rare opportunity for job candidates to make a great leap forward professionally, jumping out of the queue in which they had been expected to wait patiently for a promotion that might take years to come, if it ever came at all. Succession planning, ignored in Montreal to this point, suddenly became a pressing issue.

In the summer of 1966, Lynn Patrick telephoned Sam Pollock. He wanted Pollock's permission to speak to Scotty Bowman, the fellow who had made his son Craig a playoff hero with the NDG Monarchs in the spring of 1964 and had coached him on the Junior Canadiens. There was a new NHL franchise in St. Louis, called the Blues. Patrick had just been hired as its general manager and coach, and he needed an assistant.

6

✧ THE NHL'S ANNOUNCEMENT in March 1965 of its plan to double in size in 1967/68 was the first expansion initiative by the league in almost forty years. The NHL had not grown since 1926, when the Chicago Blackhawks, New York Rangers and Detroit Cougars (later named the Falcons and then, in 1932/33, the Red Wings) joined the Montreal Canadiens, Montreal Maroons, Ottawa Senators, Toronto Maple Leafs, Boston Bruins, New York Americans and Pittsburgh Pirates to create a ten-team league. The Depression and wartime had whittled the league down to its "Original Six" configuration by 1942/43, and there the league was content to remain for more than twenty years.

It was a cosy railway league and it controlled the overwhelming source of its talent, the Canadian amateur system. The American Hockey League, which had been founded in 1936, had increasingly shown signs of aspiring to major-league status, but it had been hobbled by the Second World War, and by the 1950s it was firmly in the NHL's back pocket as a quasi-independent development league. Territorial agreements with subservient leagues like the AHL, the Western Hockey League and midwestern American loops like the United States Hockey League meant that the NHL could not expand into certain viable major-league cities, particularly ones in the east, like Philadelphia and

Pittsburgh. For the small circle of NHL owners, thinking small really meant thinking big. So long as they reined in their membership, the owners could continue to control the professional game. No one was going to challenge their supremacy and, as owners of arenas as well as teams, they were making pots of money.

Television and air travel changed their world. The passenger jet made it feasible to consider west-coast teams and a regular-season schedule of seventy-plus games. The higher travel costs could be off-set (hopefully even exceeded) by the new bottom-line contribution from television revenue. Pete Rozelle had shown how an also-ran sport like professional football could be turned into a national obsession through television. NHL owners wanted an American television con-tract, which they hadn't had since 1959, and they couldn't get one without turning their northeastern league into a truly national one. To satisfy the market demographics of broadcast executives, the league was going to have to grow dramatically. Expansion would mean not simply adding more teams, but adding more geography to its foot-print as well.

Expansion was also fast-tracked because, for the first time in decades, league owners were actually worried about competition. The minor-pro Western Hockey League had far more operational independence than the AHL; unlike the AHL, its teams tended to have the bulk of their rosters under contract, so that they were less reliant on loaner players from NHL teams. In the 1964/65 season, for example, the Portland Buckaroos had all but two of their players under their own contracts. The two loaners were Pat Stapleton and Andy Hebenton, who were Boston Bruins properties, and when Boston traded them to Toronto in June 1965, the Buckaroos were so angered by the move that they broke off their farm-team agreement with the Bruins. The WHL, whose game was closer to the quality of the NHL than that of any other professional league, was toying with the idea of expanding eastward. Quality would quickly take care of itself if the league could get the necessary geogra-phy under its belt, a handsome television deal and the star players the new money would bring in. An alarmed NHL had to move quickly to cut them off at the pass.

The NHL expansion fee was $2 million, and the league was besieged with more than a dozen applications. The expansion process, however, was not going to be conducted on the grounds of something as elemental as merit. The league was going to grow on terms micro-managed by its existing owners. Los Angeles was reasonably viewed by them as a must-have site—but so, curiously enough, was St. Louis.

St. Louis was actually a far from obscure choice. The gateway to the American west was a major-league town, home to the Cardinals of baseball and the old Browns of football. Located south of Chicago on the Mississippi, it would give the Blackhawks a companion franchise in the Central time zone. The city was also no stranger to hockey, having briefly enjoyed an NHL franchise in 1934/35, when the ailing Ottawa Senators were moved there and called the Eagles. While the Eagles didn't fly in their one-season, Depression-era experiment, hockey did become part of the St. Louis sporting scene through the Flyers, who played in the AHL from 1944/45 to 1952/53.

In 1962, Chicago moved its minor-pro affiliate in Syracuse, New York, to St. Louis in the Central Hockey League, and the following season, 1963/64, the Central Professional Hockey League made its debut as a NHL development loop, featuring the St. Louis Braves. Jimmy Norris and Arthur Wirtz, owners of the Blackhawks, had made sure that St. Louis was at the foundation of the CPHL initiative. So when the NHL's announcement of its planned expansion came, late in the 1964/65 season, they made sure that St. Louis was at the foundation of the NHL expansion, even though there wasn't yet an actual applicant for a St. Louis franchise.

The reason for their insistence wasn't complicated or visionary. Norris and Wirtz owned the decrepit St. Louis Arena, and they wanted to dump it. They told their fellow NHL owners that St. Louis had to be reserved as one of the expansion sites. With each of six new franchises paying $2 million to a league consisting of six established franchises, it was easy for Wirtz and Norris to reason that this pool of franchise fees wasn't really a pool. The basic math of redistribution meant that, essentially, every new franchise would pay $2 million to one of the existing franchises. Wirtz and Norris could argue that they wanted "their" franchise fee to come from St. Louis. Exactly who was going to come forward with that $2 million wasn't the most important point, and their deal-making made a mockery of the well-organized bids from hopeful franchisees in viable locations like Vancouver and Buffalo (who would not make it into the league until the second phase of expansion, in 1970). Wirtz and Norris would enjoy the bonus of offloading $4-million worth of unwanted arena, for a net profit of $6 million on the league expansion.

So it happened that, while St. Louis was one of the first franchise sites determined by the NHL, it was the last to actually fall into place. By February 1966, when the league drafted the final lineup of expansion sites—San Francisco, Los Angeles, Philadelphia, Minneapolis/St. Paul, Pittsburgh and St. Louis—the only location still without an owner was St. Louis.

Of the six new sites, all but one, Philadelphia, were established hockey towns. Like St. Louis, Minneapolis/St. Paul was a CPHL whistle-stop, home to the New York Rangers' farm club. San Francisco and Los Angeles were WHL markets. San Francisco's WHL Seals were to become the Oakland Seals when the franchise moved across the bay before making its NHL debut. Los Angeles had the Blades, which gave way to the Kings of the NHL. And Pittsburgh was a long-time hockey town whose roots in the professional game reached right back to the beginning of the century; the steel town had enjoyed pro hockey before Toronto did. Except for a pause from 1956/57 through 1960/61, after its rink had to be torn down, the Pittsburgh Hornets had been a leading member of the AHL since 1936/37, and Pittsburgh had enjoyed NHL hockey via the Pirates from 1925/26 to 1929/30.

NHL hockey finally found firm footing in St. Louis through a rich man's son. Sid Salomon III was the hockey-mad offspring of one of the city's leading citizens. Sid II (aka Sid Jr.) was an insurance titan and a mover and shaker in the political arena who had dabbled in professional sports, owning a piece of the NFL's Browns. As Sid III would tell it, he was at the country club when he heard that St. Louis was going to get an NHL franchise, no owner mentioned. Sid III became so excited that he almost fell in the pool. He shared the news with his father, who made the phone calls that quickly put together the investment circle necessary to secure the franchise, take the arena off Norris's and Wirtz's hands, and make the old barn look respectable. Final tab: about $8 million.

Sid Salomon II was the lead investor, and he handed the team over to his son, not yet thirty, as something to keep him busy and happy. Sid III had a year to get an NHL franchise up and running. He had no team, no farm system and no management. Whatever he came up with was going to have to share the ice with operations as mighty as the Montreal Canadiens and not embarrass the league, the city or the Salomon family. He needed a point man to get this Everest assault rolling, and he ended up turning to Lynn Patrick, a man with the finest hockey pedigree.

The Patricks were hockey's first family, a clan of remarkable on-ice skill and off-ice savvy. The dynasty began with brothers Frank and Lester, turn-of-the-century stars who went west to convince their father that his money would be better invested in professional hockey than in his sawmill. They formed the Pacific Coast Hockey Association (PCHA) in 1911 with teams in Vancouver, Victoria and New Westminster, B.C. They built the country's first artificial-ice arenas, and raided the NHL's precursor, the National Hockey Association (NHA) back east for its better players, setting off a salary war. By the spring of 1915 they had been able to convince the trustees of the Stanley Cup that their league champion deserved to challenge the NHA champion for the trophy, and in a home-ice tilt Lester Patrick played, coached and managed as his Vancouver Millionaires demolished the vaunted Ottawa Senators in a three-game sweep.

Frank Patrick ran the PCHA, while Lester continued to play, as well as coach and manage. The league played sterling hockey, but as the 1920s dawned it began to lose ground economically to the NHL. A merger in 1925/26 with the Western Canada Hockey League, which had teams in Alberta and Saskatchewan, failed to stave off failure. The NHL was then expanding into the United States, and it was winning the player salary war. For the 1926/27 season, the Patricks arranged to sell player contracts en masse to NHL teams, and the folding of the brothers' league helped to fill the rosters of new NHL teams in Chicago, New York and Detroit.

Frank and Lester followed the suitcases filled with their former players' contracts east to find work themselves. New York City was getting its second NHL franchise in two seasons—the Americans team had begun playing in the new Madison Square Garden facility in 1925/26, and now the Rangers were going to share home ice with them. Colonel John Hammond had hired an impresario of Toronto amateur hockey, Conn Smythe, to assemble the Rangers, and Smythe had done a superb job. But rather than make him general manager, Hammond cashiered Smythe, paid him a $10,000 severance and hired Lester Patrick instead; Frank joined him on the Rangers' management team. Smythe rebounded by levering a purchase of the Toronto St. Patricks in 1927 and turning them into the Maple Leafs. The Patricks settled in at Madison Square Garden to establish another family empire.

Lester Patrick coached the Rangers until 1938/39, when he chose to concentrate on managing the team and turned the bench over to a western league alumnus, Frank Boucher, who had ended a twelve-season playing career with New York in 1937/38. A first-class coach and innovator, he brought New York the Stanley Cup in 1939/40. And he did it with two sons of Lester Patrick in the lineup: Murray ("Muzz") and Lynn.

Lynn was the elder of the Patrick brothers by three years, and the more talented player. Both brothers had their NHL careers interrupted by the war, and played their last games in 1945/46. Father Lester then moved upstairs and out of the way to allow Frank Boucher to become general manager as well as coach, and both Patrick sons entered the coaching profession in the Rangers' minor system.

In 1948/49, the thirty-six-year-old Lynn took over from Boucher as the Rangers' coach. Although he was back in the NHL, Lynn had not drawn a plum assignment. The Rangers had been turned into the whipping boys of the league during the war, their lineup decimated by military service obligations, and the club could not find its way back to greatness in the fast-paced game introduced by the two-line offside in 1943/44. There was a glint of hope under Lynn in 1949/50, when a Cinderella squad reached the Cup finals against the Detroit Red Wings. The glass slipper shattered in overtime in game seven, however, when a Pete Babando shot eluded goaltender Chuck Rayner and gave the Red Wings the title.

With that loss, Lynn left the Rangers and accepted the coaching job in Boston, taking over from Frank Boucher's brother George. The Bruins did not have the development system of Detroit, Montreal or Toronto, but the team was scrappily competitive. From 1951/52 to 1957/58, Boston was the only club other than Detroit and Montreal to reach the Cup finals. It never won, losing in 1952/53, 1956/57 and 1957/58, all three to Montreal. But Boston fought gamely, and the team was proud to have taken Montreal to seven games in the 51/52 semifinal. After the 1954/55 season, Lynn took over as general manager from Art Ross, who had been in the job since the team's creation in 1924, and turned coaching over to former Bruins captain Milt Schmidt. The next season, brother Muzz took the position of general manager in New York after a brief warm-up as coach.

For ten seasons, two of the six NHL franchises were in the hands of the brothers Patrick. Unfortunately, they turned out to be two of the poorest performing franchises. After appearing in the 1957/58 Cup final, the Bruins faded badly. The Rangers never got untracked, despite showing promise in Muzz's first three seasons on the job, in which he tortured himself trying to teach the blueshirts how to play two-way hockey. Beginning in 1959/60, the Bruins missed the playoffs for five straight seasons; beginning in 1958/59, the Rangers missed the play-offs in seven of eight seasons.

The end for Muzz came after the 1963/64 season; for Lynn, after 1964/65. Lynn landed in Los Angeles, where he would serve as coach and general manager of the WHL's Blades. It was a caretaker manage-rial job, for Los Angeles would be entering the NHL in 1967 as the Kings, and Lynn did not figure in the plans of the new franchise, owned by expatriate Canadian Jack Kent Cooke. No one else had Lynn Patrick at the top of their hiring lists. For tier-one hockey, Lynn Patrick was yesterday's man.

The long string of losing seasons in Boston was not what any team owner would have been looking for on the resume of a prospective hiree. The new franchises were filling their coaching and management posi-tions with fresh prospects—men recently retired from playing the game, managers who had shown winning ability in the development leagues. The Kings hired former Leaf Larry Regan as general manager, and he in turn hired as his coach Red Kelly, who won his eighth Stanley Cup in the spring of 1967 as a Maple Leaf. The Minnesota North Stars brought aboard as their general manager Wren Blair, who had been in charge of the Bruins' Junior affiliate, the Oshawa Generals, when they defeated Bowman's Junior Canadiens in the 1965/66 playoffs. After a long search, Blair decided his best coaching candidate for the North Stars was himself. The Philadelphia Flyers hired as GM former NHLer Bud Poile, who was general manager for the WHL's San Francisco–based California Seals. Poile hired as his coach Keith Allen, a marginal Red Wings defencemen of the 1950s who had made a sporting and finan-cial success out of the Seattle Totems of the WHL. The Seals franchise, meanwhile, in entering the NHL, was going through a messy front office shuffle. Rudy Pilous, the former Chicago Blackhawk coach who had coached the Oshawa Generals in 1965/66, was hired to replace Poile, then fired by team president Frank Selke, Jr.; the son of the former Canadiens general manager hired former Canadiens workhorse Bert

Olmstead as his coach and general manager. And the Pittsburgh Penguins hired as general manager Jack Riley, who had overseen the U.S. Olympic gold-medal effort in hockey in 1960; George ("Red") Sullivan, the former Rangers player and coach, got the coaching job.

That left St. Louis, the last franchise out of the blocks in the personnel race. The fact that Patrick ended up being hired by the Salomon group as their general manager had nothing to do with their own head-hunting acumen. Patrick was running the L.A. Blades when Red Auerbach, general manager of the Boston Celtics basketball team, learned that none of the NHL expansion teams had approached Patrick about a job. Auerbach and Patrick had gotten to know each other while Patrick was running the Bruins, and so Auerbach contacted the Salomon group and made his considerably weighty recommendation. Lynn Patrick was back in the big leagues, his NHL career having come full circle: in 1934 he had played his first professional game as a New York Ranger in St. Louis, tangling with the short-lived Eagles.

Patrick went to NHL president Clarence Campbell to hear from the horse's mouth the league's position on tampering with employees of other franchises. With Campbell's blessing, Patrick approached Sam Pollock and received his permission to speak with Scotty Bowman.

As Bowman would later assert, at the time Patrick approached he was at an impasse with Pollock over his salary. He had been making $7,000 as coach of the Montreal Junior Canadiens, and he wanted $10,000, a hefty sum for a Junior coach. Patrick was offering him $15,000 to meet him in St. Louis.

Money would seem to have made the decision obvious, but so did career planning. Bowman was always shrewd in the choices he made. By the summer of 1966, his career path in Montreal was far from clear. He was plainly one of the bright young stars of the Canadiens organization, but he was far from the only one. Claude Ruel was one rung ahead of him on the management ladder, having passed the Junior Canadiens job to him via Yves Nadon in 1964/65 to become Montreal's chief scout and then, in 1966, director of player development. Unless Bowman wanted to try his hand in the minor-pro game again, he was going to be coaching Junior hockey for an unforeseen period. While his coaching record was indisputably better than Ruel's, there was no guarantee he would be Sam Pollock's leading candidate for the Canadiens' bench whenever Toe Blake tired of winning Stanley Cups. In the summer of 1966, Blake had just won his second in a row, the seventh in eleven seasons, as the Canadiens defeated the Red Wings in six.

Bowman's list of accomplishments would have been well known to anyone in the professional game, but Lynn Patrick's personal experience of Bowman's valiant but doomed tilt at the Marlboros in the 1963/64 Memorial Cup eastern finals, employing his own son, Craig, gave him a special insight into Bowman's skills. Patrick could not have had any delusions about the chances he had for pillaging an edifice like the Montreal Canadiens with the new team in St. Louis, but he could certainly use someone who was more than willing to try, and who held out a hope, however, faint, of actually succeeding. And even in defeat, Bowman's effort had been exciting. Excitement sold tickets and garnered media interest, which in turn sold more tickets. With Bowman in St. Louis, Patrick would have several years of ticket-selling, headline-grabbing excitement.

For his part, Bowman would be going to work for someone who had gained the respect of the Canadiens organization as the mastermind of the sometimes dangerous Bruins playoff efforts of the 1950s. Patrick's gentlemanly air, underscored by impeccable tailoring, seemed incongruous with his fondness for war on the ice. In the late 1950s, as Bowman was making runs at the Memorial Cup title with Pollock, Patrick was not at all shy about outlining his overarching Bruins strategy. He wanted a physical team that intimidated the opposition, that made them afraid to share the ice. His words would anticipate almost verbatim, the playing philosophy of the Philadelphia Flyers as articulated by Fred Shero in the mid-1970s.

Bowman, too, knew how this game worked. He had seen the aggressive physical game played under Sam Pollock in the 1950s and had encouraged it himself while running the Petes, measuring the team's dedication to winning playoff hockey by the number of penalties it took. Bowman was a master strategist, but it would be a mistake, when admiring his stylish Canadiens teams of the 1970s, to think that he didn't appreciate how much hitting and hurting—and, when necessary, fighting—was part of a winning strategy. Together, Patrick and Bowman set out to create a bruising late-1950s Bruins team for the people of St. Louis. The Blues of Patrick and Bowman would be the "Black and Blues."

Bowman was initially announced as the Blues' coach when hired in the summer of 1966, but his role soon proved so elastic—part coaching, part managing—that he would be referred to simply as Patrick's "aide," while Patrick formally held both the coach and general manager positions. Working out of his home in Montreal, Bowman spent a year scouting every possible player he could who was either available as an unsigned amateur or might come up for grabs at the expansion draft in June 1967.

Expansion was a near-disaster for the league. The principle was sound enough, and the six new markets had been reasonably well chosen, but the mechanics of creating these new teams created a shambles. The ice surface of the expanded league was far from level. The established Original Six teams still had their farm systems and the hordes of amateur and minor-professional talents they had under contract. Two full NHL seasons would pass before the amateur talent pool would be opened to everyone via a universal draft in June 1969 and sponsorship of amateur teams would be eliminated. In the meantime, the Original Sixers were draining the pool by signing teenagers to professional contracts and sending them to the minor-pro ranks, safe from the reach of both the league's dispersal draft (as they weren't NHL starters) and the forthcoming universal draft (as these teenagers were no longer amateurs). To ensure long-term success, the expansion clubs needed first crack at exciting young talents, but this was not going to happen. In the future, NHL expansion clubs would benefit from high initial draft picks, but for the six teams that entered the league in 1967/68, their main options for players were found among those that the Original Six clubs had left unprotected. They were players who were retired, deemed over the hill, marginally skilled, or, in a precious few cases, talents for whom there was no room on the protected lists.

Sam Pollock had been given the job of drawing up the league's expansion-draft strategy. Presiding over one of the NHL's great development systems as general manager of the Canadiens, he was not in a mood to be generous to the new operations. He had spent his entire professional life building up Montreal's stock of players. Why should these new owners come along, lay down two million dollars, help themselves to his prospects and starters and be competitive overnight? There was so much talent in the Canadiens system that Montreal could have iced a seventh expansion club all by itself and given itself a scare in the Stanley Cup finals. Pollock's initial proposal was that, for the 1967 expansion draft that would stock the rosters of the new teams, the existing clubs should be allowed to protect fourteen players, as they customarily did for the annual intra-league draft. But the board of governors saw this as too harsh. Pollock and his fellow general managers would be allowed to protect eleven, plus two goaltenders.

In drafting the schedule and playoff format for the 1967/68 season, the NHL had the sense to recognize that these new, talent-poor clubs would be competing at a disadvantage, and so it gave them a few breaks. The new teams were grouped together in the awkwardly named West division, and they would play the majority of their games—fifty of seventy-four—among themselves, so as not to be obliterated by the established teams. They would then hold their own playoff series, from which a Stanley Cup finalist would emerge (a concept league president Clarence Campbell initially opposed, but accepted on the urging of the Original Six owners). In other words, no matter how bad these teams turned out to be—and hopes for them were far from high—at least one of them would get a shot at the league championship. The downside of this scheme was that fans in these new markets would spend most of their time watching games against other lowly expansion teams, with only twelve home games a year featuring Original Six clubs. That meant seeing just two games a year featuring the Stanley Cup champions, the Toronto Maple Leafs, or the Montreal Canadiens, the league's acknowledged powerhouse, while the Oakland Seals would come knocking five times that season.

Hiring Bowman had been Patrick's first step in building his team. The next step was working with Bowman to scout and sign two dozen of the best available amateurs. "Finally," Patrick would recall, "we scouted every pro player in the business at least five times so that when we went to the [expansion] draft we would not make any silly mistakes. We knew who and what we were after."

They based their team-building strategy on the possible outcome of those twenty-four critical games against the Original Six clubs. They needed to put together a team that could hold its own in those encounters. Scanning the lists of unprotected players, there was no possible way to assemble a lineup that could go toe-to-toe with any Original Six lineup in an offensive shootout. Wide-open hockey would kill them. They needed to build a defensive fortress from which to launch the occasional raiding party across the opposition's blueline. If they could take care of their own end and not embarrass themselves against the Original Sixers, winning against their fellow expansion clubs would be much easier. They also knew they had to ice a team that could please the fans over the short term while a team with more long-term potential took shape. As Bowman explained after the draft, "We wanted to buy ourselves some time so that we would have a team that could keep us in contention while we were building our younger players to the point where they could move into the big time."

In their quest to forge an impregnable defence, Patrick and Bowman identified as their cornerstone Blackhawks goaltender Glenn Hall. A backup was found in Don Caley, a Detroit property playing with Pittsburgh in the AHL. To anchor the defence corps in front of Hall, they chose from the Toronto list Al Arbour, who was playing with the AHL Rochester Americans. An old teammate of Hall's, Arbour had broken into the NHL with Detroit in 1953/54 and played on the Red Wings' Cup-winning team that season. He hadn't been able to secure a starting job, however, and in the 1958 intra-league draft he was taken by the Blackhawks. There he won a Stanley Cup with Hall in 1960/61, but at the June intra-league draft that followed the win an unprotected Arbour was taken by Toronto.

As a Maple Leaf, Arbour was a spare wheel on a gleaming vehicle, a replacement for utility defenceman Marc Reaume, whom the Leafs had dealt to Detroit for Red Kelly. With Bob Baun, Carl Brewer, Tim Horton and Allan Stanley the regular starters, and fellow former Red Wing Larry Hillman available when healthy, Arbour's ice time in Toronto depended on injuries to the star players. The arrival of Kent Douglas only further distanced him from a starting job with the Leafs. He shuttled between Toronto and Rochester, playing enough in 1961/62 and 1963/64 to put his name on the Stanley Cup for the third and fourth times, but most of his time was spent with the Americans, where he served as captain.

Arbour was a solid, stay-at-home defenceman, an unflappable, level-headed old pro who was renowned for his shot-blocking skills—in spite of the fact he wore glasses while on the ice. He was one of the best examples of a capable talent that had become trapped in the minors during the Original Six years.

In all, Patrick and Bowman plucked three defencemen from the Leafs' list. In addition to Arbour, they took Darryl Edestrand, a youngster who had played only nine games in Rochester in 1966/67, and Fred Hucul, who was playing with Toronto's WHL affiliate in Victoria. The Blues' wise drafting of Edestrand showed the strengths that Bowman, after a decade of coaching and scouting amateur talent, brought to the team-building process. While Edestrand was scarcely known to the professional game, Bowman knew him from his Junior days.

Also chosen from Toronto's list were left-wingers Gary Veneruzzo, John Brenneman and Larry Keenan. Veneruzzo would spend the majority of his St. Louis career in the minors before finding a starting job in the WHA. Brenneman, who in the past three seasons had played for Chicago, New York and Toronto, would be dealt away shortly by Bowman. As a St. Mike's Major, Keenan had played against Bowman's Petes in the 1958/59 Ontario Junior A finals. Apart from two games with the Leafs in 1961/62, Keenan had spent his years as a Toronto property playing with Al Arbour for the Rochester Americans. He became a St. Louis regular for more than three seasons.

The Blues chose from the Rangers Max Martinsek and Rod Seiling. Martinsek never made the majors, a rare disappointment for Patrick and Bowman in their carefully considered selections. Seiling was a former Toronto property who had been an add-on to the major 1964 trade that sent Dick Duff and Bob Nevin to New York in exchange for Don McKenney and Andy Bathgate. When picked by St. Louis, Seiling was seeing duty with the Rangers' AHL affiliate, the Baltimore Clippers.

As it happened, Don McKenney also figured in the Blues' drafting. McKenney's spell with Toronto after the 1964 trade was brief and complicated by injuries. He had broken into the NHL under Patrick with the Bruins in 1954/55, and had spent most of his playing career there before landing in New York the year prior to being dealt to Toronto. Demoted to Rochester, McKenney (along with Bathgate) was sent to Detroit in May 1965. The Red Wings made little use of the veteran; he was playing with Pittsburgh in the AHL when Patrick brought him back into his employ.

With so few NHL regulars available in the draft, Patrick and Bowman were compelled to select from the Blackhawks centre Bill Hay, the Calder winner in 1959/60, who had called it quits after playing thirty-six games in 1966/67. Though inactive, as a retiree he remained a Blackhawks property, and he was available for selection by any team who wanted to gamble their pick against the odds of convincing him to return to the ice. Pollock and Bowman could not coax his signature onto a playing contract. It was a rare miscalculation in a draft in which they were better prepared and made better choices than any other expansion team.

From the Montreal list came one of their most important acquisitions: right-winger Jimmy Roberts, a Canadiens starter since 1963/64 who had played in the last three Cup finals. With Hall having being chosen in a separate goaltending draft, Roberts was the first player Bowman and Patrick selected in the draft of all other players. No available player was better known to Bowman. Roberts had been to the Memorial Cup finals with him as a Peterborough Pete, and had been part of Bowman's short-lived coaching stint in Omaha in the CPHL. A stalwart defensive forward, a great checker and a penalty-killer who could also play defence, Roberts was made expendable in Montreal by the awesome depth of talent the Canadiens enjoyed at his position. The Canadiens already had Claude Provost, Bobby Rousseau, Claude Larose and Yvan Cournoyer, and in the new season they would introduce Mickey Redmond. Roberts was an experienced role-player, a veteran of two Montreal Stanley Cup wins who had played in the big games and, having played for Bowman, knew how to respond for him and could serve as an example for others. Also from the Montreal list they chose Noel Picard, a tough defenceman who had played fourteen games for the Canadiens in 1964/65 before being parked in Seattle in the WHL.

As a former Bruins general manager, Lynn Patrick helped himself to four players from Boston's unprotected list: Nineteen-year-old left-winger Dan Schock, who had not yet reached the NHL; centre Terry Crisp, who was with the Oklahoma City Blazers of the CPHL in 1966/67; right-winger Wayne Rivers, who had played off and on for Boston and was with the AHL's Hershey Bears in 1966/67; and Ron Stewart, Bowman's old foe from the 1951/52 Memorial Cup eastern finals.

After all the grief Stewart had caused Sam Pollock in that series,

Stewart's career had finally fallen under the control of the teenage left-winger who Pollock had hoped would help neutralize him. Stewart had gone on to play thirteen seasons in Toronto, winning three Stanley Cups. Hap Emms had just replaced Lynn Patrick as Boston's general manager when he made a four-player deal with Punch Imlach in June 1965 that turned Stewart into a Bruin. Stewart played two full seasons in Boston before being left unprotected in the expansion draft.

Stewart was the only NHL regular other than Roberts whom St. Louis had come up with in the draft who was still interested in being an NHL regular, as Hay would not answer the call and Glenn Hall, who was a friend of Hay's, had also announced his retirement. It was essential for Patrick to convince Hall, who was capable of becoming the very foundation of the franchise, that his career was not over.

Twelve years had passed since Lynn Patrick had first thought he was about to bag Glenn Hall. In the summer of 1955, the Detroit Red Wings were Stanley Cup champions for the second consecutive season, the fourth time in six seasons. Patrick was the new general manager of the Boston Bruins, and he needed a netminder. For the past four seasons, the Red Wings had had a marvel named Hall parked in Edmonton, playing for their WHL minor-pro affiliate, and the only thing keeping him out of the NHL was a shortage of starting jobs in a league whose teams were only required to employ one full-time goaltender. Like Johnny Bower, who was sequestered in the American League with the Cleveland Barons, Hall was toiling just out of the limelight, with no firm date for when he might emerge into the bigtime. The Red Wings, after all, had Terry Sawchuk, who had come to the NHL full-time in 1950/51 and in five seasons had won three Stanley Cups, three Vezinas and made three first and two second All Star teams. In 1952/53 Hall had been called up from Edmonton for six games to relieve Sawchuk, who had broken a bone in his foot. His goals-against of 1.67 for those appearances—which included a 4–0 shutout of the Bruins—made it known that Hall, then twenty-one, was a comer.

When Patrick spoke to his Red Wings counterpart, Jack Adams, about making a deal for a goaltender in the summer of 1955, Adams indicated that he was willing. Patrick prepared for a deal that would land him Hall. Instead, to his amazement, Adams allowed that it was Sawchuk who was up for grabs. The two men hammered out a nine-player blockbuster deal that sent Sawchuk and three other Red Wings to Patrick's Bruins as Adams executed a brazen house-cleaning of his championship lineup.

In the process, Hall got his NHL starting job, promoted to the Red Wings that autumn. He played brilliantly, finished second in goals-against, won the Calder as rookie of the year and was voted to the second All Star team. An outstanding NHL career was born from that monster deal, but little else. Patrick did not get the goaltender he needed. Sawchuk played well for one season, but in 1956/57 a bout of mononucleosis was followed by a nervous collapse in January. When he refused to play for Boston any more, Adams and Patrick were back to deal-making, sending Sawchuk home to Detroit in exchange for defenceman Larry Hillman and left-winger Johnny Bucyk.

It had worked out, in a strange way, for Patrick. Bucyk became an exemplary team leader who played twenty-one seasons as a Bruin. But the Bruins tried one netminder after another for a decade, and while each achieved moments of greatness, no one could claim the job unequivocally, and get it done the way Glenn Hall would have.

Hall, for his part, was made expendable by the return of Detroit's favourite son, Terry Sawchuk, and emphatically expendable by his sympathies for the players' association movement that so vexed Adams. Along with Ted Lindsay, he was sent to the lowly Blackhawks as punishment.

The banishment did not faze him. With other teams also dumping union sympathizers in Chicago, the Blackhawks emerged from years of ineptitude to become Stanley Cup contenders. They had Hall's goal-tending to thank for much of it. Outstanding in the regular season, Hall was terrific in playoff competition, when performance matters most in the NHL. In the spring of 1961, the third-place Blackhawks were a playoff dark horse, paired with the first-place Canadiens, finalists in the previous ten Stanley Cups and winners of the last five in a row. Hall won the adoration of the fans as the Hawks upset the Canadiens in six, then downed his old team, the Red Wings, in six, to win the club's first Cup since 1937/38.

The Blackhawks then became an enigma of the 1960s, a powerful club that could not quite convert its regular-season performances into another Cup win. The 1960/61 performance, as it turned out, would be the last Blackhawk Cup victory to date. Stacked with high-scoring All Stars like Stan Mikita and Bobby Hull, the Hawks fell victim to close-checking opponents who were able to shut down their big guns. It was a team that couldn't seem to summon the combination of meanness, desperation and determination that made other clubs champions.

After losing the 1965/66 finals to Montreal in a game-seven showdown, Hall decided to retire to his farm in Stony Plain, about thirty miles west of Edmonton. He was surprised when training camp time rolled around and the Blackhawks demanded to know where he was. So he went back, and played another season, one of his and the Blackhawks' greatest and, ultimately, most disappointing.

The league had made it mandatory in 1965/66 for teams to carry two dressed-to-play goaltenders, and Hall had carried most of the weight for Chicago, subbed off by understudy Dave Dryden, older brother of future netminding star Ken. For 1966/67, the Blackhawks had in mind more of a tag-team arrangement, and they paired Hall with Denis DeJordy, Scotty Bowman's netminding ringer from the 1958/59 Peterborough Petes Memorial Cup drive. Together, Hall and DeJordy won the Vezina as the Blackhawks dominated the regular season. Chicago outscored all other teams and finished seventeen points ahead of second-place Montreal. Five of the six positions on the first All Star team were claimed by Blackhawks, while Hall was named to the second team. But in the playoffs, an aging Maple Leafs roster was waiting for them. Checked relentlessly, the Blackhawks' shooters could not find the Leafs' net, and Chicago was upset in six.

Hall decided that it was again time to retire, and the Blackhawks were certainly making it easier for him. It occurred to Hall that when they brought him back from his brief retirement for 1966/67, the team had no long-term enthusiasm for him. The expansion draft was coming in June 1967; they would be allowed to protect only two goaltenders, and they were going to be the younger member of the Vezina-winning pair, DeJordy, and Dave Dryden.

Hall was not past his prime. Some goaltenders are brilliant for brief periods before burning out, or are erratic over a long period, like Sawchuk after his return to Detroit in 1957 and his subsequent move to Toronto in 1964. Hall was a wonder in that he began his career with brilliant performances and kept on turning them in. He was nearly a fixture on the All Star team—in twelve seasons he had made the first team six times and the second team four times, and he was not yet thirty-six. He had revolutionized goaltending with his butterfly style, and his impact on the game was just over the horizon, with Tony Esposito, a devotee of his playing technique, a few seasons away from making his spectacular debut with Chicago. An entire generation of new goaltenders was about to enter the game, indebted to his innovation. Hall was capable of continuing to play and to inspire. But he could no longer justify the hazards of the job for the pay he was getting. He saw goaltending as one of the worst positions in professional sport in terms of stress and danger to life and limb. Even when he was a kid, Hall's mother couldn't bear to watch him play. He had collected his share of facial stitches during his career, and in practices with his own team he simply refused to stand in for more than a few shots, as players like Stan Mikita, wielding scythe-like curved sticks, loosed slapshots that danced like knuckleballs and whizzed past his ears.

He didn't dislike the game, even though he became famous for routinely throwing up before taking to the ice. Hall considered himself fortunate that he had been able to have a job he liked, in hockey, and then had been able to find another job he liked, in farming. But he'd never really had a raise as a hockey player. He would be presented with a contract, told its terms and shown where to sign. The NHL was a cosy cartel, and if players didn't like the terms of employment, they could always be replaced, or punished with banishment to the minor leagues. In the summer of 1967, Glenn Hall decided they could replace him.

Patrick and Sid Salomon III made the pilgrimage to Stony Plain to convince Hall that it wasn't yet time for the defending Vezina holder to become a full-time farmer. Hall made it clear that money was the one and, possibly, only issue.

"How much do you want," he was asked.

"Fifty thousand dollars," he flatly declared.

Patrick leaned his head back, eyed the vaulted ceiling of the living room in the Hall ranch house and proclaimed, "Holy Mackerel!"

"Well, how much did you think you were going to have to pay me?"

"Forty-five thousand dollars," Patrick conceded.

It was Hall's turn for astonishment. "Holy Mackerel!" he shouted back at his visitors. "Why don't we just split the difference?"

They did. Hall bought another 320 acres for his farm and with Patrick's permission skipped most of training camp before reporting to the Blues.

The expansion draft was just the beginning of the construction job on the Blues' lineup. Patrick and Bowman immediately traded their fourth draft choice, Rod Seiling, to New York for the Rangers' defenceman Bob Plager and right-winger Gary Sabourin, plus two amateurs, defenceman Gord Kannegiesser and right-winger Tim Ecclestone. The deal left them with three solid defencemen: Arbour, Picard and Plager. A pleased Bowman declared, "Nobody will be pushing us around."

During the June meetings, Patrick and Bowman went to Sam Pollock and executed a complex player purchase and trade that netted them two starters, Ron Attwell and Bill McCreary, and two amateur properties. A hulking centre, the twenty-two-year-old Attwell was new to the NHL, while McCreary had a long and varied career on left wing. After playing in the 1951/52 Memorial Cup eastern finals against Bowman as a Guelph Biltmore, McCreary had embarked on a minor-league career, joining the Rangers for ten games and the Red Wings for three in the 1950s. Acquired by Montreal, he saw fourteen games of NHL action in 1962/63 before heading back to the second tier. McCreary was thirty-two when the Blues acquired him and at last gave him his big-league break.

At the beginning of the 1967/68 season, Bowman and Patrick sent John Brenneman to the Red Wings for right-winger Craig Cameron, defenceman Larry Hornung and centre Don Giesbrect (who had played for the Hamilton Red Wings against Bowman's Junior Canadiens in the 1965/66 playoffs). Cameron started right away, Hornung would wait until 1971/72 to break into the Blues' lineup, and Giesbrect never played at all. With three deals—the Seiling trade, the player purchase from Montreal and the Brenneman trade—Bowman and Patrick had gained eleven players and given up only two.

The season began with promise. The Blues defeated Boston 5–1 and Detroit 3–2, and gave up only eight goals in the first four games. But the team was soon struggling, and sinking. The Blues were dead last in the league, with four wins, ten losses and two ties, when Lynn Patrick decided he could no longer serve as both general manager and coach. Wren Blair in Minnesota was the only other expansion team executive still attempting to hold down both jobs. On November 22, Patrick turned the coaching job over to Scotty Bowman, so that he could concentrate, as general manager, on developing talent at the Blues' CPHL farm team in Kansas City.

Bowman acted swiftly to turn the Blues around. The next day, he called up from Kansas City Frank St. Marseille, one of the team's more enigmatic discoveries. Two years earlier, Lynn Patrick had been managing the L.A. Blades in the WHL when he received a letter from St.

Marseille's brother, a singer in town. The letter extolled the skills of Frank, who was playing for Port Huron in the International League. Frank's brother urged Patrick to give him a tryout; Frank would pay his own expenses to Los Angeles and stay with his brother. Patrick never bothered replying, but then found himself noticing Frank's name in the lists of top IHL scorers. When Patrick was hired to put the Blues together, he decided they should have a look at this play-making right-winger. Bowman scouted him and pronounced him the Gordie Howe of the IHL. When Patrick and Bowman saw him play at the IHL All Star game, they were disappointed in his performance but decided he still merited attention. Patrick and Bowman took Sid Salomon III on his first scouting trip, to see St. Marseille play in Toledo. No NHL team had his rights; he was twenty-eight years old. After the game, they got St. Marseille's signature on an A-form, which committed both parties to nothing more than St. Marseille coming to the Blues' training camp.

"I thought he was the best player in our training camp," Patrick would recall. "Scotty and I talked it over and decided that he can't be as good as he seems to be and we decided to send him to our training camp at Kansas City and see what happens." St. Marseille began playing for Kansas City, but with the Blues struggling, Bowman and Patrick decided it was time to give him his big-league break. He would play in the NHL for the next ten seasons.

Soon after promoting St. Marseille, Bowman brought up Tim Ecclestone, Ray Fortin (acquired as an amateur) and Darryl Edestrand. On November 29, at the end of his first week as coach, Bowman engineered a major deal with the Rangers. Ron Stewart, the Blues' leading scorer, and Ron Attwell were sent east in exchange for two names from Bowman's past: Barclay Plager and Red Berenson. With Jim Roberts and Barclay Plager, Bowman now had two members of his 1958/59 Memorial Cup finalist team—and two Plager brothers on the blueline.

He also had a scoring star. Berenson was a castoff of the Canadiens' talent system. An American who had played Junior hockey in Canada,

Berenson had skated for the Regina Pats against the Ottawa-Hull Junior Canadiens when Bowman won the Memorial Cup with Sam Pollock in 1957/58. Berenson had played for the U.S. Olympic gold-medal team in 1960, but in the new decade was unable to find a long-term starting position at centre with the Canadiens. While he participated in the 1964/65 Stanley Cup win, Berenson played only three games that season, and after logging twenty-three games in 1965/66 he was sent to the Rangers. While Barclay Plager became an intimidating anchor on the Blues' defence, Berenson took over from the departed Stewart as the team's top scorer.

With a few quick and key changes, Bowman took the Blues from last to third place in the West, three points behind first-place Philadelphia. Bowman had many years and more than half a dozen Stanley Cup victories ahead of him, but Jimmy Roberts would come to feel that Bowman's finest moments as a coach were in those first seasons in St. Louis. The team, Roberts reflects, "was a bunch of castoffs. We had all types, and we weren't a bunch of choirboys. We would have been a tough group to handle, and every member had to be handled a little differently. There weren't many buttons he pushed with players that didn't get the best performance out of them. For the young man he was at the time, it took pretty decent coaching to do that. It wasn't a team that was there and had all this talent and was used to winning, and could win. It was a team that he had to make win. He moulded it, motivated it, and the record speaks for itself. He deserves the lion's share of the credit for what happened, and I still look at it as his best coaching years."

For four seasons, Bowman enjoyed the goaltending services of Glenn Hall, who in turn enjoyed Bowman's coaching. They became lasting friends and mutual admirers. "I'd always gotten along with my coaches," says Hall. "Bowman was the best coach I ever had, and that I've ever seen."

Hall had been around the professional game since the early 1950s, but he had never had a coach so systematic in his approach to winning.

That should not, however, be confused with a coach who is known for a particular playing system. Bowman did not preach a complex game plan with neutral-zone transitions or crisscross play-making by forwards. It was a basic game that set out to minimize the scoring chances of the opposition. With their own end taken care of, the Blues could try to score goals. If they got a lead, their tight checking style made them difficult to come back against. And any coach that made reducing goals-against a priority was going to find deep respect in the goaltending ranks.

"I don't think there was anything more in his system than players moving up the ice together and then getting everybody back into your own zone," says Roberts. "It was a good forechecking system that he probably hasn't changed much since then. It was basic 'up and down the ice' hockey, with everybody playing their positions and over-extending themselves to get the job done."

Hall had heard about Bowman's screaming fits with his Junior players. He had even watched him (as he would put it) erupt in the dressing room like Vesuvius, burying players in sarcasm rather than hot ash. But he never personally suffered his legendary wrath. "I never had any problem with him. He expected you to give your very best, and if you did, there was no complaint." Bowman, for his part, practically worshipped Hall, and would list him as one of his top five favourite players of all time. The keys to winning, Bowman would say, were a good general manager and good goaltending. Hall was "a coach's dream. Hall would come to me and say, 'Are you sure you want me to play tonight?' That meant he wanted to play. With him, you knew every time he was in the net, he was going to give you his best."

Early in Bowman's coaching tenure in St. Louis, Hall had watched Bowman set the psychological tone of his relationship with the team. It was, as Roberts notes, a team that had many players who were older than him, who had been around the block. Bowman looked to the ceiling with his hands in his pockets and said: "There are twenty guys in here who probably have twenty different ways to make out the lineup. I suppose you all have a better way to shuffle this deck and come up with a winning hand." After a theatrical pause, he jabbed, "But let me tell you this, gentlemen: You can't shuffle deuces and threes." He then made his exit. In that one dressing-room encounter, he'd made clear to many of them what they were, and what his job was. He then went about coercing them into overachieving. He made young players earn their starting jobs, letting them know that just because they had been drafted or had their name on a contract didn't mean they were actually NHLers. Bowman also infused them with a sense of purpose beyond winning games for St. Louis. He felt that their achievements would carry the division, would make expansion a success.

The team felt just like Bowman's underdog Peterborough Petes: being together in St. Louis gave them something to prove. They knew this without Bowman having to remind them. Noel Picard would make the rounds of the dressing room before a game against an Original Six team, stop before a player who'd been left unprotected or dealt away by that night's opponent, and tell him: This is the team that didn't want you.

Larry Keenan was typical of the veteran players who got their first real shot at the NHL through expansion. "When I was in the minors, because there were already a lot of guys there ahead of you in the National Hockey League, and because there were only six teams, it was very difficult to come up. And in those days, they could bury you in the minors. In expansion, the attitude of a lot of guys was, 'I'm here to prove I could have been here a long time.' Guys were playing with pride in themselves, with self-motivation."

A sense of vengeance would be well honed for many players by the time Bowman's Blues had battled through their two seven-game playoff series against Minnesota and Philadelphia in 1967/68, winning five of six overtime games, to come face to face with the Montreal Canadiens in the Stanley Cup finals. Bowman's Blues had Red Berenson,

Jimmy Roberts and Noel Picard, plucked from the Montreal discard bin early in Bowman's first season as coach. Before the season was out, he added old pro Dickie Moore, whose career was supposed to have ended several seasons earlier. His knees a wreck, Moore had retired from Montreal after the 1962/63 season, but Toronto's Punch Imlach coaxed him back in 1964/65, in an effort to fill the hole he had created on left wing by trading Dick Duff to New York. Moore tried, but in thirty-eight games the winger who had produced ninety-six points for the Canadiens in 1958/59 was held to two goals and four assists. Bowman was looking for poise and experience more than scoring power, and he put Moore, at thirty-seven, back in the NHL for twenty-seven regular-season games in 1967/68.

Halfway through the season, Bowman brought his own career full circle by signing the Three Rivers Reds defenceman who had cut him down with his stick in the spring of 1952. After twelve seasons and seven Stanley Cups with Montreal, Jean-Guy Talbot had been left unprotected in the expansion draft. Selected by Minnesota, he had been dealt to Detroit and then let go on waivers. Without a hint of ill-will or resentment clouding his judgment, Bowman moved in quickly to sign Talbot and put him to work with the rest of his former Canadiens.

One addition was still to come, one perhaps even more difficult to imagine than Talbot. Down in Kansas City, forty-four-year-old Doug Harvey was working as the farm team's player-coach. Bowman and Patrick had debated calling him up, but regulations prohibited it until Kansas City's playoffs were completed. Bowman wanted Harvey for his steadying influence. The multiple Norris winner had spent much of the 1960s trying to play hockey when the general consensus was that he was past his prime. At one point he had offered to play for the Quebec Aces, the Rangers' farm team, for free, just to be able to prove himself.

Harvey's playing purgatory had resulted from the Canadiens' 1960/61 semifinal loss to Glenn Hall and the Blackhawks. Furious with the performance of the defence, general manager Frank Selke had made an example of Harvey by trading him to New York. Harvey was sure it was Selke's way of finally getting back at him for his participation in the players' association drive of the late 1950s. Harvey had just won his sixth Norris Trophy in seven seasons when Selke banished him to the Rangers, and he won his seventh, as player-coach, with New York in 1961/62. Harvey gave up the coaching position, claiming it interfered with his ability to have a beer with the boys, and his playing career sputtered out. After starting in fourteen games for the Rangers in 1963/64, he sank into the minors. He was a tragic figure, a gifted athlete who could not make the transition to life away from the rink, who drank more than he should have and could not embrace the authoritarian role of coach that could have provided the logical continuation of his career.

On April 18, 1968, Scotty Bowman gave Harvey another chance to play in the NHL. St. Louis had enjoyed a 3–1 series lead over Philadelphia in their opening quarterfinal playoff encounter, but the Flyers struck back with two wins. Their 2–1 overtime win in St. Louis on April 16 forced the seventh game, back in Philadelphia. Harvey joined the Blues' lineup for the decisive game, and the castoffs and spare parts came through. Dickie Moore assisted on Frank St. Marseille's goal to open the scoring for St. Louis, Glenn Hall held the Flyers to one goal, and in the second period Doug Harvey set up what proved to be the game- and series-winner.

Bowman was named coach of the year by *The Hockey News* before the semifinal series against the Minnesota North Stars. The best, however, was yet to come from Bowman and his team. A record four of seven games in the semifinals were decided in overtime, with St. Louis prevailing in three of them. After winning the opener 5–3 at home, the Blues had lost game two 3–2 in overtime, and were then humbled 5–1 in game three. Passing the halfway mark of the third period in game four, the Blues were down 3–0. Dickie Moore took the puck up ice and fed Roberts, who scored St. Louis's first goal. One minute later,

Moore scored to make it 3–2. Facing a 3–1 series deficit, Bowman pulled Hall; Roberts scored on a Barclay Plager rebound to tie the game with eleven seconds left. One minute and thirty-two seconds into over-time, Terry Crisp moved down the left side, drew the Flyers' defence out of position and slipped the puck to Gary Sabourin, who scored the game-winner and evened the series at 2–2. It was vintage Bowman player manipulation: he had been holding Sabourin back on the bench, making him hungry, and only let him loose when the game moved into sudden death.

After the tremendous rally of game four, St. Louis moved ahead in the series with a 3–2 overtime win, then suffered a game six collapse, losing 5–1. Overtime was again required in game seven, and after the 2–1 win, Bowman's Blues had only two days to prepare themselves to meet Toe Blake's Canadiens in the finals.

Montreal was eminently overqualified to win the series. There was nothing, on paper, that St. Louis could point to as evidence of their competitiveness. Montreal had all the stars and the first-place record (forty-two wins to the Blues' twenty-seven). Montreal had scored more goals, 236, than any other team, and showed their awesome depth by doing it without a single top-ten scorer. St. Louis produced 177 goals, the third-worst offensive output in the league. Montreal had allowed 167 goals, earning its netminders Gump Worsley and Rogie Vachon the Vezina. St. Louis had allowed 191 goals, a middling performance. Montreal's captain, Jean Beliveau, was runner-up for the Hart Trophy as the league's most valuable player; Jacques Lemaire was runner-up for the Calder Trophy as the league's top rookie; J.C. Tremblay was runner-up for the Norris as the league's top defenceman. Claude Provost won the Masterton as the league's most sportsmanlike player. Worsley made the first All Star team, Tremblay the second team. No Western division player, let alone a St. Louis Blue, won any individual award or made either All Star team. And the Canadiens had Toe Blake, who had seven Stanley Cup wins as a coach.

The raw numbers could not assuage Montreal's concerns that they might be in for a fight. Bowman's skills were greatly respected, and he had his "Over the Hill Gang" (seven players thirty-five or older) playing with giant-killing finesse. Moore and Harvey were doing more than their own jobs, in exemplary fashion. They were leading by example. "They played with such joy," says Hall. "They were an inspiration to the younger players." At times, Montreal seemed to be playing its own past. At the start of game four at the Forum, four of six Blues on the ice were former Montrealers: Harvey, Berenson, Talbot and Roberts.

Moore would finish the playoffs—his last NHL appearances—in a four-way tie for second in scoring, with seven goals and seven assists. Harvey would credit Bowman with making him a star again. "Scotty Bowman taught me more in three practice sessions," he would say, "than Toe Blake showed me in ten years."

And then there was Hall, who had been a central character in some of Montreal's earlier playoff nightmares. His goaltending as a Blackhawk had killed the Canadiens in two semifinals, and had forced Montreal to produce a game seven win to capture the Cup in 1964/65. Bowman was going to confront the fleet-footed Canadiens with a suffocating checking game, and his last line of defence would be Hall. The series' outcome would turn on his performance.

The Blues were not expected to win, and they didn't. Superficially, the series was a rout, as Montreal won in four straight. Two games, however, ended in overtime, and every game carried a one-goal margin, with the Blues never trailing by more than a goal. After winning the opener 3–2 in overtime, the Canadiens had eked out a 1–0 win in game two on a short-handed goal by Serge Savard early in the third period. They were losing the game four 2–1 when Henri Richard and J.C. Tremblay scored in the third period to win the Cup.

When the series was over, Sam Pollock pronounced the Blues' defence to be better than Toronto's. Toe Blake gave credit where it was due. "St. Louis got great goaltending and, because of it, were rarely behind in the score for any length of time in the games. That meant they didn't have to open up. They could play their tight, checking style and wait for the breaks. They stayed on top of us with their checking. We didn't get a chance to really break out against them."

For all the praise Bowman received, Hall had been the overwhelming star of the St. Louis effort. The Blues may have tried to play a tight checking game, but they had still been outshot 151–91 in the series. In games two and three, Hall kept the Blues in the contest while they were outshot 36–19 and 46–15. With a save percentage of .927, he became the second goaltender (after Roger Crozier of the Red Wings in 1965/66) to lose to the Canadiens in the Cup finals and still win the Conn Smythe Trophy as the most valuable player of the series.

Bowman passed the credit on to the players who had responded to his demands. "My guys gave as much as I asked and no one could have given more. We lost to the Canadiens in fourteen periods of hockey by only four goals."

The series that launched Scotty Bowman's Stanley Cup career ended that of Toe Blake. Though he had been employed in a series of one-year contracts, Blake's job security had never been in doubt. It was understood that he had work for life with the Canadiens. When he decided coaching was behind him, he could become a kind of in-house elder statesman, an adviser without portfolio, dispensing his wisdom and experience wherever, in hockey operations, it was required.

He announced his retirement right after winning his eighth Cup. "This is my last year," he said. "The tension is getting too much. It gets tougher every year. I'm quitting for good. . . . I told Senator Molson before the playoffs began that I was calling it quits after this series."

Perhaps superstition, and not tension, had overcome Blake. He had played thirteen seasons in the NHL, and coached thirteen more. Montreal had just won its thirteenth Cup of the modern era, which had begun in 1926/27 with the collapse of the Patricks' Western Hockey League. And his Canadiens had taken thirteen playoff games to win it.

If Blake was anything like Bowman, those coincidences would have been enough to drive him from the job. Bowman was terribly superstitious, refusing to stay in rooms on the thirteenth floor of a hotel, which meant refusing accommodations on the fourteenth floor if there wasn't one numbered thirteen. He went the full nine yards: avoiding black cats; never walking under ladders; bristling with good-luck charms; not replacing skate laces, even if they were on the verge of snapping, in case doing so snapped a winning streak.

Bowman didn't meddle with the Fates. As it happened, he was not fated to succeed Blake. The Blues promoted Bowman to general manager and coach after the playoff run, moving Lynn Patrick into the newly created managing director's role to concentrate on improving the team's development system. Bowman now had the kind of power and influence in the NHL he could only have dreamed of two seasons earlier, when he was a Junior coach working for Sad Sam Pollock.

The new season, 1968/69, would be the last played before the old recruitment system was abolished and the universal amateur draft introduced. The system Pollock and Bowman knew so well was dying. A new order was in the making, and in St. Louis, Bowman was poised to rule it. In Montreal, Pollock had to figure out how to keep the Canadiens franchise among the elite NHL ranks, a position it had occupied since he had come aboard in 1947, when Bowman was a teenage prospect in Verdun.

The Canadiens had come out ahead in the first encounter between the new and old leagues, but it remained to be seen how long that domination could extend. Detroit had faltered in the first season of expansion, the only Original Six club to finish behind an expansion team in the overall standings. Montreal had tremendous player resources, but it could not harbour all its talent indefinitely. Further league expansion was coming, its right of first refusal on francophone Quebec talent would soon end, and the universal draft would give the worst teams in the league the best chances at securing the new stars.

Sam Pollock had a Stanley Cup, but he didn't have a coach, and he soon wouldn't have the league he knew so well. Scotty Bowman had the affections of the Blues' ardent fans, the support of the owners, and the respect of the players and the league. He was on top, in command, and he was doomed.

7

✧ SCOTTY BOWMAN'S St. Louis Blues appeared in three consecutive Stanley Cup finals and never won a game; they were defeated in four straight in every series, by Montreal in 1967/68 and 1968/69, and by Boston in 1969/70. In 1970/71, the Blues made their first quick exit from the playoffs, losing to the Minnesota North Stars in six in the quarterfinals. Shortly thereafter, Scotty Bowman was out of a job. It was an astonishing reversal of fortune, and it should never have happened. At the first signs of setback, the Blues' ownership began demolishing an organization of great potential. Bowman was just one of several talented employees who would find success elsewhere in the league, leaving behind a team that would sink into bankruptcy.

How had the Blues and Bowman come to this? Certainly for the first three seasons there was nothing but progress. No more could have been asked of the coach and general manager of an expansion team.

After the first exciting season, the universal draft was still a year away, and Bowman had to rely on the June intra-league draft and trades to find new talent. He raised eyebrows far and wide by selecting former Canadiens goaltending great Jacques Plante from the Rangers' list. Plante hadn't even played in three years. After being traded to New York by Montreal following the 1962/63 season, the six-time Vezina winner struggled to keep the Rangers in the game. He finally quit in 1964/65 rather than accept a demotion to the AHL, and he took a sales job with Molson's. Asthma had also affected his ability to play. By the summer of 1968, however, Plante was making it known that he was willing to try a comeback. Bowman came after him with a $35,000 contract and he readily accepted.

Since the introduction of the mandatory two-goaltender rule for regular-season play in 1965/66, teams had come to employ two regular starting goaltenders, and not just a main goaltender and a backup. The increasing length of the regular season and the playoffs, combined with the exhausting time-zone changes of air travel, made it more difficult for one goaltender to carry a team from October to May. Signing Plante gave Bowman another veteran performer who could spell off Hall. The pair won the Vezina (and Hall was named to the first All Star team) in 1968/69 as St. Louis's goals-against fell half a goal per game; the Blues allowed about a hundred fewer goals than their West division rivals. The Blues also outscored all West division teams but Oakland, with Red Berenson becoming their first top-ten scorer.

Bowman built on the inaugural Blues effort with a marvellous season in 1968/69, and St. Louis took a great leap toward legitimacy. But there was still a considerable gap between the Original Six clubs in the East and the expansion teams in the West. All clubs in the East outscored their West counterparts, and all had winning records. While the Blues' thirty-seven wins were fourth-best in the league and they led the league in goals-against, like the other West division clubs the Blues could not generate the kind of offence seen in the star-packed East. Overall, the West clubs trailed the East clubs in offence by almost a full goal per game. St. Louis was also the only West division club with a winning record.

Philadelphia and St. Louis were emerging as the expansion clubs with the greatest potential. Both sets of owners, the Salomons in St. Louis and Ed Snyder in Philadelphia, represented a new breed of hockey entrepreneur, more oriented toward marketing than the Original Six owners, who either had no real need or saw no reason to sell their product to consumers.

The Salomons also brought a fresh attitude to player relations. For the league veterans, coming to St. Louis was like a trip to some fabulous sporting Oz. In renovating the St. Louis Arena, the Salomons had taken care to spruce up the Blues' dressing room, making it spacious and rolling out carpeting. It was a far cry from the cramped, concrete dungeons most players knew. The dressing room was emblematic of the Salomons' wont to treat the players with respect, as professionals rather than chattels. The Salomons actually socialized with the players; there were beer parties, and trips to Florida. "They were probably the first club that introduced the Wives' Room," recalls Larry Keenan, a married player whose first child was born during his three seasons in St. Louis. "The Salomons' philosophy was that if you have a happy wife, you've got a happy player." Such a philosophy was heresy back into Toronto, where wives were loathed by Punch Imlach and families were expected to take a distant back seat to the Leafs.

The Salomons' player-friendly attitude did not gibe with Bowman's experience or methodology. He was a young man who subscribed to the old school of player management. Intimidation and fear were tools he readily employed. A column by sportswriter Dirk Carroll in the Montreal *Gazette* of November 19, 1963, effectively summarized the attitude toward player motivation popular in Bowman's formative coaching years. "Youngsters resent discipline, whether or not they're athletes. They're also deluded into thinking that adults can escape discipline. What they don't know is that adults must discipline themselves, which is much harder than having somebody else do it for you. . . . The best coaches in hockey and football, and the best managers in baseball, are those who can get the best out of the players under their command, providing the players have the latent ability. The players aren't all alike. Some of them have to be babied and some of them have to be bullied, and the smart coach or manager realises it and acts accordingly."

But how did you decide who to baby and who to bully, when, by the standards of the old NHL, everybody was being babied by the owners?

Bowman felt his way through this marked shift in the owner-player relationship, and managed to instil the discipline and, where he felt appropriate, the degree of fear required. The game was changing, and he would have to change with it. "In those days," says Keenan, "they coached through fear sometimes. You played out of fear for your job. Those days are gone. You could see it changing, even in the late sixties and the seventies: more and more, coaches had to have an answer for your questions. It wasn't, 'Do this because I'm your boss,' or 'You're doing this because I told you to do it.' The big difference today is that when a coach asks a player to do something, he has to have an answer, because if he doesn't, why should you have to do it that way?"

Three decades after arriving in the NHL, regardless of how much he had changed, Bowman would be considered the last of a dying breed of disciplinarian. Bowman was capable of inspiring his players to excel, sometimes by making them hate him. But he was never an inspirational coach in the sense of chalking up positive aphorisms in the dressing room. Nor was he a hand-holder or a group-hugger. Bowman's model of coaching excellence was Toe Blake, who erected an emotional barrier between himself and the players. "Toe was a very aloof person," says Jimmy Roberts, who won two Stanley Cups under him. "He never said much to the team, but when he did, you listened. Toe had great teams. To coach great teams, people think it's easy, but it's very hard handling the kind of great players he had—the Jacques Plantes, the Doug Harveys, the Boom-Boom Geoffrions. He was a coach who didn't get close to his team at all, but the team had the utmost respect for him."

"Toe Blake treated everybody equal—tough," says Al MacNeil. "He was a good coach, fair to the guys. He controlled the dressing room and ran the practices. He rode people a lot, but whether he won or lost, he was still a pretty good guy." MacNeil believes that Blake's aloofness was calculated, insulating him from the highs and lows experienced by individual players. "He did keep a distance that he thought was necessary between the boss and the guys, but there was always respect and it was never done with the idea of making you feel uncomfortable. It was designed to get the maximum out of everybody."

In St. Louis, Bowman had his way, and it was the right way, and if you did things that way, you were fine. You were valued, and you would succeed. "You did your job, and that was it," is how Keenan sums up the employment requirements for Bowman's Blues. If you had some other idea about the nature of the right way, you were gone. It was basic, and it worked. Different players experienced a different Bowman, because he approached each of them differently. And everyone experienced a different Bowman from one day to the next, for reasons known only to him.

"The true Scotty Bowman is seen when he goes to the NHL draft," says Roberts, now an assistant coach in St. Louis. "The people he goes to talk with are the soldiers, the people who were loyal to him when he had them. He comes to you—you don't go to him. He's happy to see these people, to be in their company. When there are three or four of us who played for him together on a casual evening at the draft and he spots us, he comes over, and he's the last one to leave. They are people he's never individually thanked and probably never will, but the appreciation is there. He's had an awful time in his career thanking people who have done a lot for him as players, given him years of service. He doesn't know how to say thanks."

"He always liked the role players," Ron Caron has said. "The stars, he wanted to crush. I would say very few players liked Scotty, but everyone respected him. He never pretended that he had to be liked, but he made those guys better. That's sacrificing yourself for winning."

"He likes character players," Roberts elaborates, "whether the player was any good or not. We had players in St. Louis—the Craig Camerons, the Timmy Ecclestones—he used to be on them mercilessly. He meets them today and they're like sons to him. He's outwardly happy to see them again, even though they meant nothing to him as far as all the great players he's had."

Bowman made a few changes to his lineup after the first Cup appearance. Moore retired, again, after the 1967/68 finals, as did McKenney, and Harvey came aboard full-time as a player-coach. On June 11, Darryl Edestrand and Gerry Melnyk were sent to Philadelphia for Lou Angotti and Ian Campbell. Angotti was promptly flipped to Pittsburgh to get Ab McDonald. The addition of McDonald on left wing gave Bowman a veteran of Montreal's 1957/58 and 1958/59 Cup wins to go along with Harvey, Plante and Jean-Guy Talbot. The Blues also sent Wayne Rivers, who had played twenty-two regular-season games in 1967/68, and backup goaltender Don Caley to New York to get Camille Henry, Bill Plager and Robbie Irons.

The trade worked out well for the Blues. Bowman now had all three Plager brothers (although Bill wouldn't see regular duty until 1969/70), another backup goaltender in Irons, and the experience of Camille "The Eel," whom Bowman had played against in the Quebec Junior league championships of 1951/52, when Henry starred with the Quebec Citadels. The small, slippery centre had begun his NHL career with the Rangers in 1953/54, and at the top of his game he had been good for fifty to sixty points a season. Now thirty-five, Henry could no longer be called in his prime, but he provided the Blues with thirty-nine points in 1968/69.

In August, Bowman was formally named the Blues' general manager as well as coach. The team began the season with far more cohesion than it had in its first one and enjoyed a relatively straightforward run to another appearance in the Cup finals, sweeping both Philadelphia and Los Angeles in four in the quarter- and semifinals. The league had resolved to stay with the configuration of Original Sixers in the East and expansion teams in the West, with the winners of each division advancing to the finals. The East finals were regarded as the "real" Cup series, and certainly the encounter between Boston and Montreal supported that sentiment. The resurgent Bruins took the Canadiens to six games, and Montreal, with Claude Ruel as coach, required three overtime wins (including a double-overtime series clincher in Boston) to advance to a rematch with the Blues.

Bowman started Jacques Plante in the opening game in Montreal, which the Canadiens won 3–1. From then on he went with Hall, but it made no difference. Three consecutive Canadiens wins of 3–1, 4–0 and 2–1 earned Ruel his first Stanley Cup and the Canadiens their fourth Cup in five seasons.

Following the series, Doug Harvey left St. Louis to try his hand at coaching Junior hockey in Quebec. Camille Henry was also effectively finished; he would play only four games in the new season. June 1969 brought the first universal amateur draft to the NHL, but Bowman had discounted its role in his ongoing team-building. While there was desirable talent available, Bowman wouldn't get a shot at it. He had traded away his first-round pick, ninth overall, to the New York Rangers, who used it to select Andre "Moose" Dupont, a future Stanley Cup winner with the Philadelphia Flyers. And after Dupont was selected, a number of quality players were chosen to close out the first round: Jim Rutherford, Ivan Boldirev, Pierre Jarry and J.P. Bordeleau. Bowman didn't get a selection until nineteenth overall, in the second round, when he chose Mike Lowe, who would never play in the NHL or the WHA.

Patrick and Bowman had done a superb job in creating the Blues' lineup in 1967, but the challenge after the first season was icing a team that could win enough games to satisfy fans while developing the talents that would support the club in the future. The new universal draft of 1969 was supposed to supply the exciting new talents, but Bowman began to trade away the marginal young talents he had, who weren't ready to play in the NHL and might not ever be, in order to get experienced NHLers who might be at the ends of their careers but could at least get the job done over the short term.

He was not the only general manager caught in this trade-for-draft-pick trap. In the first universal draft in 1969, three of the expansion clubs—St. Louis, Los Angeles and Pittsburgh—were without a pick in the first round. Boston, which needed no help improving its strong lineup, had gathered three first-round picks through trading and the Rangers picked up two, while Detroit, Chicago and Toronto held one each. Montreal enjoyed special status in the inaugural draft, which marked the last year in which it had right of first refusal on francophone Quebec talent. Granted the first two picks of the opening round to exercise this option, Sam Pollock snared Rejean Houle and Marc Tardif of the Montreal Junior Canadiens.

Before the draft, Bowman sent Ron Schock and Craig Cameron to Pittsburgh for Lou Angotti and the Penguins' first pick in the 1971 draft. Angotti had momentarily been his property in the course of the Ab McDonald three-way deal the previous summer. Angotti again proved to be a quick-flip commodity.

Inspired by his success with veteran players in his first two seasons, Bowman went shopping for more. At the intra-league draft on June 10, he collected ex-Canadien Andre Boudrias from the Blackhawks, sending them Angotti as compensation. After appearing in seven games with the Canadiens, from 1963/64 to 1966/67, Boudrias had been taken by Minnesota in the expansion draft; the left-winger had then been dealt to Chicago in 1968/69. From the Rangers, Bowman acquired another veteran of the 1950s Canadiens, centre Phil Goyette, and from Los Angeles right-winger Ron Anderson.

Bowman also adjusted his goaltending ranks, acquiring Ernie Wakely, the Canadiens property who had played for him during his brief tenure in Omaha and had minded net for the Winnipeg Braves when they defeated Bowman's Petes in the 1958/59 Memorial Cup. Wakely and Plante played the bulk of the season, while Hall, Bowman's playoff ace, was rested, appearing in only eighteen regular-season games.

The Blues had another strong regular season in 1969/70, winning the West division with thirty-seven wins and missing out on the Vezina (won by Tony Esposito in Chicago) by only nine goals. Again, the Blues were the only club in their division with a winning record. Team scoring improved by twenty goals, and while the West clubs overall continued to trail the East in offence, in this season St. Louis and Minnesota at least outscored Toronto. The Blues moved past Minnesota and Pittsburgh in six to reach the finals for the third consecutive season.

This time their opponents were the Boston Bruins, who had finished tied on points with Chicago atop the East. The Bruins had been improving rapidly, with Bobby Orr, Phil Esposito, Gerry Cheevers and others having come along since Lynn Patrick left the operation. They had swept the Blackhawks in the semifinals, and in the finals Bowman had no effective response either to their offence or defence. After being outscored 16–4 in the first three games, the Blues attempted to stave off their third consecutive sweep in the Cup finals by forcing overtime in game four. A dramatic Orr goal brought Boston its first Cup since 1940/41, and the fact that St. Louis hadn't won a single game in the last three finals caused the league to review its division alignments.

The league was also expanding again. Buffalo and Vancouver, whose well-organized bids had been turned aside in the first phase of expansion, were being admitted to the league for the 1970/71 season. The Sabres and the Canucks were placed in the East division, and the Blackhawks were moved to the West, thereby setting a strong Original Six club among the 1967/68 expansion teams. The league was hoping to avoid another Stanley Cup washout. For the Blues, it meant they had serious competition in their division for the first time since 1967/68.

After the 1969/70 finals, Bowman declined to re-sign Jacques Plante. Though Plante was playing well, Bowman still had Hall as his clutch netminder, and he concluded that one veteran goaltender (Hall was about to turn thirty-nine, Plante forty-one) was enough. Plante was allowed to sign with Toronto, with whom he played well enough to make the second All Star team, while tutoring Bernie Parent. Wakely (who at thirty was no youngster) became Bowman's starting regular-season goaltender, with fifty-one appearances to Hall's thirty-two in the expanded seventy-eight-game season.

For the second consecutive year, Bowman was caught in the veterans-for-draft-picks trap. He had no first-round pick in the amateur draft and wasn't able to choose until twenty-third overall, when he took Murray Keogan from the University of Minnesota. Like Lowe, Bowman's first pick in 1969, Keogan never made it to the major leagues.

In the second universal draft, in 1970, the newest expansion clubs were given a considerable advantage over their predecessors: they were awarded the first two draft positions. Buffalo, choosing first, took Gilbert Perreault, one of the most exciting Junior prospects that would ever become available at a draft. Vancouver, choosing second, secured Dale Tallon. Boston held four picks in that first round, Montreal two. Pittsburgh and Oakland were the only 1967/68 expansion teams able to exercise a first-round pick.

At the 1971 draft, the plight of the original expansion clubs became more pronounced. The strong Original Six teams, deep in talent, were steadily dealing away unwanted but highly capable players to struggling expansion teams in order to collect their draft picks and round up the next wave of talent. Sam Pollock had shifted gears effortlessly, moving out of the old system of C-forms and Junior farm teams and into the new draft system. Although the draft was supposed to give the weakest teams the best new players, in fact, through trading, it was giving the strongest teams many of the hottest young talents. The Canadiens held three first-round and three second-round picks in 1971, Boston and New York two each in the first round.

In hindsight, general managers like Bowman would be criticized for dealing away their futures to crafty men like Pollock in order to make short-sighted gains, but it is difficult to see the practicality of the alternative: playing badly and eroding the fan base in hopes that a few draft picks would bail you out several years down the road when they matured into star players. Teams like the Blues were in new markets for major-league hockey, and owners could not tolerate losing efforts. The New York Islanders, who arrived in 1972, would be a rare example of an expansion team's ownership being willing to put up with catastrophic seasons, holding on to draft picks rather than trading them away to stem the bleeding.

The original expansion clubs of 1967 were further harmed by being subjected to the 1970 expansion draft that stocked the Buffalo Sabres and Vancouver Canucks. Bowman lost Andre Boudrias to Vancouver and Phil Goyette to Buffalo. Goyette was bitter to have been left unprotected by Bowman. He had just had a wonderful year, leading the team with seventy-eight points and finishing fourth in the league scoring race. While Bowman publicly expressed regret, he emphasized that he had to start concentrating on youth, and could not hold on to the popular centre, who was about to turn thirty-eight.

Before the draft, Bowman swapped defencemen with Los Angeles, sending them Ray Fortin for Bob Wall. That fall, Bowman began doing business with Punch Imlach, who had become coach and general manager of the new Sabres franchise after being fired by Toronto when the Leafs were swept by Boston in the 1968/69 playoffs. In October, Bowman was exchanging right-wingers, sending Imlach Ron Anderson in order to retrieve Craig Cameron, whom he had dealt to Pittsburgh in June 1969. In early November, Larry Keenan and Jean-Guy Talbot were on their way to Buffalo for Bob Baun.

One of the Leafs' stalwart defencemen of the 1960s Stanley Cup teams, Baun's relationship with Punch Imlach had steadily eroded, to the point where he was benched for most of the 1966/67 Stanley Cup final against Montreal. Left unprotected by Imlach in the 1967 expansion draft, Baun had gone to the Oakland Seals. After a season in California, he joined the Red Wings. In assembling his new team in Buffalo, Imlach got hold of Baun's rights. Baun, however, was not going to be playing for Imlach, and his rights were available. Bowman gave Imlach what he wanted, two old pros in Keenan and Talbot who could provide the stability he desired in a team chock-full of young players.

Bowman, however, didn't have a spot for Baun, who was thirty-five, but the man Maple Leaf Gardens fans called "Boomer" was welcome back in Toronto, now that Imlach was out of town. On November 13, nine days after Bowman acquired his rights, Baun was sent to the Leafs in exchange for Brit Selby.

Selby was another name from the encyclopedic cast of characters that filled Bowman's hockey past. He had starred with the Toronto Marlboros when Bowman's NDG Monarchs attempted to block their march to a Memorial Cup title in 1963/64. While Selby had won the Calder Trophy after his NHL debut in 1965/66, his career had not fulfilled the promise of his freshman season. By the time Bowman got the left-winger, Selby had already bounced from Toronto to Philadelphia and back again. He did not turn out to be an effective substitute for the older Keenan. While Keenan had produced thirty-three points in fifty-six games in 1969/70, Selby would come up with only eight in all of 1970/71, and he spent most of 1971/72 in the minors.

With this series of personnel moves, Bowman's fourth season in St. Louis was off to a rough start. He had given up Goyette, who proceeded to contribute sixty-one points to Buffalo's first season. Keenan and Talbot had been lost, and Selby was a flop. Plante, allowed to go to Toronto, was having a brilliant year. The team was without a scoring star, as Red Berenson was in a slump, and with Chicago now in the neighbourhood, the Blues no longer ruled the West division.

But the biggest change was the absence of Bowman from the bench. He had resolved, after the 1969/70 season, that he could no longer both coach and manage the team, and had elected to stick with the more senior post. Bowman elevated his captain, Al Arbour, to the coaching position and withdrew into the executive ranks.

Late in the 1969/70 season, Arbour had run the Blues' bench for two games while Bowman was off on a scouting trip (even though the record book would credit Bowman with all seventy-six games that season). That was the extent of Arbour's coaching experience. In January, the Blues went into a slump, winning five, tying three and losing seven over fifteen games. Although they remained in second place in the division, the Blackhawks were pulling away in first.

While Bowman was off the bench of his own club, he drew the assignment of coaching the West for the third consecutive season in the All Star game. Previously, the game saw the defending Stanley Cup champion playing a team of league All Stars. But in 1969, when Bowman made his first appearance, the format had been changed to an East-West contest. In that first showdown between divisions, held at the Montreal Forum, Bowman brought respectability to the expansion teams by wresting a 3–3 tie against the star-packed East, which was coached by the retired Toe Blake. Bowman had taken a generous supply of Blues into the Forum for that game—Glenn Hall, Jacques Plante, Al Arbour, Doug Harvey, Noel Picard, Red Berenson, Jimmy Roberts and Ab McDonald. Bowman coached the West again in 1970, with the game in St. Louis. Again he brought a raft of Blues—Hall, Plante, Arbour, Berenson, McDonald and Roberts were back, along with Gary Sabourin, Bob Plager, Frank St. Marseille and Phil Goyette. But in this encounter, the East, coached by Claude Ruel, outshot the West 44–17 and won 4–1.

This time, Bowman's All Star assignment came on January 19, 1971, at Boston Garden. Chicago's move into the division gave him more talent to play with, and nine Blackhawks were in Bowman's lineup. For the first time, his Blues were in the minority, but he still had six of them—Wakely, Roberts, Bob Plager, Berenson and Sabourin. Less than five minutes into the game, the West was up on goals by Chico Maki and Bobby Hull of the Blackhawks. At 6:19 of the period Montreal's Yvan Cournoyer scored for the East, and that was the last goal of the game as nearly fifteen thousand fans watched Bowman protect his lead for more than two and a half periods.

Bowman had gone up against Harry Sinden, whose Bruins had defeated his Blues in the previous spring's Stanley Cup final, and he had won. And yet back in St. Louis, he wasn't even a coach any longer.

He returned to St. Louis from the All Star game to watch Arbour struggle with the club. Bowman had apparently learned what his career would demonstrate time and again—that it was impossible for him to give up the visceral thrill of running a bench, particularly when he was so good at it. On February 7, Bowman took back the coaching job from Arbour. In his first game running the bench again, the Blues beat the Flyers 6–2 in Philadelphia, ending an eight-game winless streak on the road. In the final twenty-eight games of the season, Bowman won thirteen, tied five and lost ten.

Both Arbour and Bowman insisted that Bowman's decision to return to coaching and Arbour's decision to return to playing defence were mutual. Bowman also asserted that Arbour would have the coaching job back next season. Bowman, in essence, had come in as a relief pitcher, and didn't want to start the next season in the job. Arbour was his man. It may have been the only time in NHL history in which a general manager removed a coach from a struggling team and promised to rehire him as soon as the playoffs were behind them.

Hours after Arbour was replaced, Bowman was trading away two of the team's most valuable players. The Red Wings were in the throes of a major re-engineering, with a five-player deal having been arranged with New York after the All Star break. When Bowman learned that Gary Unger was available, he started negotiating with Detroit's new general manager, Ned Harkness, who had replaced Sid Abel. Unger was a Toronto property who had been sent to Detroit in March 1968, along with Frank Mahovlich, Pete Stemkowski and the rights to Carl Brewer, in exchange for Paul Henderson, Norm Ullman and Floyd Smith. Detroit was now unloading all its acquisitions from that deal. Stemkowski had already gone to New York earlier in the season, and Mahovlich, a second-team All Star in 1969/70, had just been sent to Montreal in a one-for-three exchange. Brewer was also available, and Bowman was more than a little interested.

Unger had produced sixty-six points at centre for Detroit, and the twenty-three-year-old had greater things ahead of him. Detroit was willing to package him with Wayne Connelly, who had excelled for

Bowman as a Peterborough Pete. In return, Bowman agreed to give up his team captain, Red Berenson, and Tim Ecclestone. Though Berenson was in a scoring slump, he and Ecclestone still represented the Blues' two top scorers, and Berenson was popular with the fans.

Unfortunately for Bowman, the trade played less like a team-building exercise than a labour-busting action. Berenson was the team representative in the NHL Players' Association (NHLPA), and at the All Star break he had been reelected as the association's president. Bowman was no fan of the NHLPA, and Berenson publicly cited his union activities, and not his scoring problems, as the reason for the trade. "Scotty's very much against the association," Berenson told the press. "I don't think I would have been traded if I were not involved in the association." He revealed that the Blues had asked him several times before the trade to give up his work with the association "without putting any pressure on to force me to do it."

Bowman dismissed Berenson's allegation. "I felt that Red's activities with the association were quite extensive," he told *The Toronto Star*. "But we talked about it earlier in the week, and he assured me that it was only a figurehead job and that it was not the reason he was not having as good a season as last year. A lot of times a player in this situation is devalued to another team, but I assured Ned Harkness that this was not the case, and that the association did not take much of Red's time."

"We're looking for help on defence and I don't think I got it [in the Unger deal]," Bowman explained on February 19. "However I think we got one-eighteenth of a Stanley Cup team in Unger. I hope it doesn't take us fifteen years to win the Stanley Cup but Unger should be around at least that much longer."

Unger did prove to be an NHL ironman with St. Louis and a franchise player in the 1970s. And Berenson would come back to St. Louis in 1974/75 to play with him. Neither would be around in St. Louis fifteen years later, when Bowman was a few months away from being fired in Buffalo, hamstrung by many of the same issues that surfaced for the first time in his career in St. Louis: troubled roster decisions; a team that wasn't winning the way the owners thought it should; and the struggle to find a coach who could meet Bowman's high expectations and help him resist the temptation to return to a job he did so well.

The Arbour coaching debacle is the traditional explanation for what went wrong in Bowman's St. Louis career, and it certainly played a major role. But Bowman had been feuding all season with Sid Salomon III over his handling of the team, and his roster manoeuvres increasingly became a sore point. One of the last straws was, supposedly, Carl Brewer.

Brewer was a brilliant defenceman, an All Star who in the fall of 1965, at twenty-seven, had quit the Maple Leafs after a contract dispute with Imlach. Rather than play NHL hockey, he'd completed a Bachelor of Arts degree at the University of Toronto, and tried to reclaim his amateur status. His ambition to play for the Canadian Olympic team was thwarted when the International Olympic Committee overruled the International Ice Hockey Federation and refused to allow Brewer, as an ex-professional, to compete for Canada at the 1968 Games. His dream of amateur glory denied, he served as player-coach of Muskegon in the IHL for 1967/68, adamant about not returning to the Leafs. Fed up, Imlach threw his rights into the deal that sent Mahovlich, Stemkowski and Unger to Detroit. Rather than follow his rights to Detroit, Brewer followed his curiosity to Helsinki, to take a coaching job.

Brewer says he crossed paths in Helsinki with Cliff Fletcher, the general manager of the Blues' Kansas City farm club and Bowman's assistant GM, who was in Finland on a scouting trip. "I squired him around Helsinki," says Brewer. "He eventually signed one of the kids who was playing on my team, who ended up in Kansas City." Brewer says Fletcher made no proposal for him to return to the NHL with St. Louis. That came later, in a letter from Sid Salomon III, and Brewer declined the offer. But the Red Wings made him listen, with a huge raise and the help of his former Leafs defensive partner Bob Baun, who was playing in Detroit along with fellow Imlach refugees Mahovlich, Stemkowski and Unger. A condition of his signing was that the Red Wings find a playing position for his brother Jack in their system. Brewer had a terrific season in 1969/70, making the second All Star team. "When I saw how well he played for the Red Wings last season, I kicked myself," said Bowman.

In February 1971, Brewer was available. He was regarded as a prickly customer, unpredictable and difficult. Some would try to paint him as a flake, but without his personal resolve, the NHL's misappropriation of player pension funds and Alan Eagleson's financial indiscretions as head of the players' association would not have seen legal resolution in the 1990s. Brewer says he enjoyed his playing time in Detroit but left over their failure to pay his brother Jack in full on his minor-league playing contract. A cheque for Jack came up $500 short of the agreed-upon fee, which was supposed to be a little over $4,000. Brewer thought it foolish that, when they were paying him about $100,000, the Red Wings risked losing an All Star over such a pittance. "They should have known that I'd walk," he says.

Rather than report to Detroit for 1970/71, he took a job repping Finland's hockey stick manufacturer, Koho, in North America. His rights were dealt to Bowman, and with Unger persuading him to come to St. Louis, Brewer returned to the NHL.

Bowman had been warned that Brewer could be difficult, but he didn't appear concerned. "This guy has a tremendous knowledge of hockey. It amazed me to hear him analyse our team. He knew the strengths and the weaknesses of almost every player."

Brewer played only about six weeks of hockey for St. Louis. "It was the strangest team I'd ever played for," he says. Compared to the united spirit of the Cup-winning Leafs and even the Red Wings of 1969/70, he found the Blues riven by player cliques. The ownership was also meddling in the operation of the team to a degree Brewer calls "insidious."

Brewer would find himself cast in the villain's role of the man who got Scotty Bowman fired in St. Louis, a billing that baffles him. It would be said that Brewer had been a hit with the Salomons, but not with Bowman, who was adamantly opposed to having him back in 1971/72. The split between the Salomons and Bowman over Brewer, coming atop all the other controversial player deals of the year and the Arbour demotion and promised rehiring, was too much to take.

Or so the story goes. "I have no idea what Scotty Bowman thought of me," says Brewer. On the other hand, Brewer has no doubt about what the Salomons thought of Bowman. On April 15, 1971, the night before the sixth game of the Blues' quarterfinal series against the Minnesota North Stars, Brewer had dinner with Sid III. Nursing a sore back, Brewer was a doubtful starter for the Blues, who had finished fifteen points ahead of their fourth-place playoff opponents that season. Coached by former minor pro Jackie Gordon, Minnesota had a strong goaltending tag team in Cesare Maniago, who had played for St. Mike's against Bowman's Peterborough Petes in the 1958/59 playoffs, and Gump Worsley, the Montreal netminding star of the 1960s who had been acquired by Minnesota in the 1969 intra-league draft. The Blues had been leading the series two games to one, but had lost the next two, and were now a game away from elimination.

Sid III appalled Brewer by saying, "I hope we lose tomorrow so I can fire Bowman."

"I'd never encountered anything like that before," says Brewer. "It was embarrassing. Why the hell was he saying that to me?" It was bad enough that an owner wanted to lose a playoff series so he could have an excuse to fire the coach and general manager. Worse was him confiding in a player who, if he sympathized with the owner, could help throw the game.*

Brewer was judged fit enough to play, and the Blues lost, 5–2. Bowman, as Brewer knew, was out of a job. Sid III had already usurped Bowman's authority, firing Cliff Fletcher. A settlement (undisclosed) had

---

*Neither Sid Salomon II nor Sid Salomon III is alive today to confirm or deny his intentions toward Bowman.

to be reached, as Bowman had three years left on a five-year contract.

Lynn Patrick returned to the general manager's job, while Frank Mario continued as director of player personnel. Al Arbour, judged ineligible to coach, nonetheless retired from play to become assistant general manager, with Jimmy Roberts announced as the new team captain, taking over from Barclay Plager, who had replaced Red Berenson when he was traded. Roberts, however, did not take the position, and the captaincy remained with Plager. Glenn Hall chose to retire and return to farming, no longer satisfied that he could play at the peak of his game. Carl Brewer played forty-two games in 1971/72 before hurting his knee. He never returned to the Blues, choosing instead a comeback effort with the Toronto Toros of the WHA in 1973/74. Bill McCreary retired to become manager-coach of the newly acquired Denver Spurs farm club in the WHL. The Salomons hired as their new coach Sid Abel, who had been replaced as Detroit's general manager the previous season.

"I think it was a mutual parting," Bowman told *The Hockey News*, gamely trying to find some way to make his strange fall from grace sound like anything but a firing. "If that's possible, it happened." He plainly regretted the parting, calling the St. Louis job "one of the best two or three in the league."

As he made clear to *The Hockey News*, at the heart of the split was a disagreement over how much autonomy he should enjoy in running the team. His contract gave him "full control" of the Blues "with advice and consent" of the Salomons.

"Advice and consent—how strong is that?" he wondered aloud. "I tried to get their consent on matters in my best way. I always had the impression I would stay, if I could live with the situation. We had our differences and problems. A contract can say a lot of things but it can't say everything, and it would have been difficult for me to remain. I don't know whether they wanted me or didn't want me. I resigned in the best interests of the hockey team and myself. I always tried to do my very best."

"They'd wanted to fire Cliff Fletcher, and have the younger Salomon go in and for Scotty to be a mentor to him," says Al MacNeil, who later worked with both Fletcher and Bowman. "Scotty probably saw the writing on the wall and thought, 'If they don't want him, they don't want me.'"

Bowman's sudden departure in St. Louis became widely viewed as a ridiculous consequence of meddling owners, in particular Sid III, who had apparently concluded that a few years of associating with Bowman had made him the wiser of the two in the intricacies of building and managing a professional hockey club. While there were problems in Bowman's last year, the Salomons did not solve them by removing Bowman. In the first year without Bowman, the Blues went through three coaches—first Abel, then McCreary, then (ironically) Arbour.

The Salomons might have been tremendously wrong about Bowman's management capability, or perhaps they were pinpoint accurate, for the issues that troubled the Salomons would resurface with the Knoxes in Buffalo. But as the 1970s unfolded, the fortunes of the Salomons and Bowman dramatically diverged. By 1975, the Salomons were fending off rumours that the franchise was in financial trouble. In 1977, with both father and son seriously ill, the franchise was in trouble irrefutably. It was sinking into bankruptcy that summer before being resuscitated by new owners, Ralston-Purina. The animal-feed people would soon be attempting to woo Bowman back to St. Louis. But by then, Bowman would be the most celebrated coach in the game, a multiple Stanley Cup winner, the strategic mastermind of one of the greatest dynasties in league history.

However backhanded the compliment, perhaps the Salomons deserved some credit for Bowman's subsequent success. Without their meddling and impatience, Bowman would not have been knocked out of the general manager's job with the Blues, thereby freeing him to become the most successful coach in the expansion era. The Salomons' sporting epitaph would not hail them as the visionaries who brought Scotty Bowman to St. Louis—for that was Lynn Patrick's work—but as the overbearing owners who drove him back into the arms of Sad Sam.

8

✧ ABOUT AN HOUR AND half before game time on May 13, 1971, Sam Pollock was rinkside in Chicago Stadium, awaiting the fifth meeting between his Canadiens and the Blackhawks in the Stanley Cup finals. In two days, he would mark his seventh anniversary as Montreal's general manager. His first five seasons had been something of a dream, with five consecutive trips to the finals and four victories. The last two had been something of a nightmare, by Montreal standards. But then, those initial victories had not always been easy. Dynastic performances are not necessarily turned in by teams that completely dominate the competition. During Frank Selke's last four seasons as general manager, a wonderful Canadiens club had not been able to get past the semifinals. Pollock might have won the Cup on his first try, in 1964/65, but it was no cakewalk. The league was enjoying exceptionally close play among the Canadiens, the Maple Leafs, the Blackhawks and the Red Wings. In 1963/64, Selke's last season, all three playoff series went the full seven games, and in 1964/65, it took Montreal six games to defeat the defending-champion Leafs in the semifinals and all seven in the finals to master the Blackhawks.

Awaiting the start of game five in 1970/71, Pollock was back in familiar territory. As in the 1964/65 series, the Canadiens and Blackhawks were tied at two games apiece, and although he could not know it (but may well have suspected it), these teams were destined for another seven-game tilt. He still had eight players from the 1964/65 championship lineup: Jean Beliveau and Henri Richard at centre; J.C. Tremblay, Terry Harper and Jacques Laperriere on defence; Claude Larose and Yvan Cournoyer on right wing; John Ferguson on left wing. (He also had Leon Rochefort, who had played for the Canadiens in the early 1960s and had been sent to New York in the Jacques Plante trade of 1963. After 1969/70, Pollock got him back, in a six-player deal with Los Angeles.) Almost half the 1964/65 lineup was still with him, a testament to the Canadiens organization's knack for continuity. But Pollock did not have the same coach. Toe Blake, having retired after the 1967/68 victory, had left a gaping hole that might never truly be filled. Three seasons after Blake's departure, in the middle of the Stanley Cup finals, Pollock was still trying to fill it to his satisfaction.

Back in December, Pollock had made the first midseason coaching change by the Canadiens since manager Cecil Hart gave up the coaching job to Jules Dugal in 1938/39. The next season, Dugal was managing the team and Pit Lepine was coach. A year after that, Tommy Gorman was in charge and Dick Irvin was the coach, and the Canadiens' lengthy history of management stability began. Pollock embodied that very stability as he approached his twenty-fourth anniversary with the organization. The uncertain shuffling of the coaching position, however, was an unsettling throwback to the years in which the Canadiens were struggling, not winning. While his Canadiens were winning at a pace any professional sports organization could envy, Pollock nonetheless was striving to guide the organization through not one but three transitions: the protracted succession of Blake; the arrival of the universal draft in the expansion era, which had entirely transformed the development process; and the need to turn the Canadiens roster of the 1960s (and even the 1950s) into the dominant franchise of the 1970s.

Sam Pollock's management style could be described as pragmatic optimism. He believed—or at least he exhibited the belief—that things would work out, whatever the situation or issue; then he proceeded to help them work out in the way only he seemed to be able to manage. The universal draft, which was supposed to be a disaster for the Canadiens as they lost their vast amateur development system, had turned into a bonanza under Pollock. He had amassed so much talent in the 1960s while the getting was good that he was able to trade away some of his quality players to poorly performing expansion teams, still ice a winning club, and collect top draft picks in return. In one month, the next entry draft would be held, and Pollock was holding the first pick overall, despite having finished fourth overall that season. He had pocketed this nugget by sending the California Seals (whose president was Frank Selke's son, Frank Jr.) a left-wing prospect, Ernie Hicke, and a draft choice. With the Seals having finished last in 1970/71, Pollock was set to land Guy Lafleur of the Quebec Remparts.

If he could get through the Stanley Cup finals and win his sixth Cup in eight seasons *and* draft Lafleur, Pollock would be able to close the books on one of the strangest campaigns in the Canadiens' history with a true flourish. But he still wouldn't have Toe Blake's successor in hand. Pollock had started the season with Claude Ruel behind the bench and finished it with Al MacNeil. Only in Montreal could a coach guide a team to a Stanley Cup title and not be considered the leading candidate for the task he had just accomplished.

By the time Pollock, MacNeil and the Canadiens arrived in Chicago for game five, they had already been through seventeen post-season games. Back in Toe Blake's glory years as coach, eight or nine games would usually have been enough to get the team to the Stanley Cup. In 1970/71, one of the league's greatest playoff series was already behind the Canadiens: the opening round against Boston. As defending Stanley Cup champions, the Bruins had utterly dominated the regular season, with fifty-seven wins and 399 goals—well clear of the second-highest number of wins, forty-nine, posted by Chicago and New York, and the second-highest number of goals, 291, produced by Montreal. When the Bruins met the Canadiens in the quarterfinals, though,

Montreal was not entirely the same team that had contested the regular season. In goal was a late-season call-up, Ken Dryden, and on his performance the hopes of the Bruins for a repeat Cup win were dashed in a six-game upset.

In the goaltending trade, Dryden was an eccentric among eccentrics, a talent of multiple personae—an exceptional athlete, a lawyer-in-training, and a social activist, working in consumer advocacy with "Nader's Raiders." He had taken seven years to progress from long-shot prospect to playoff giant-killer. As a Junior B goaltender in Toronto, Dryden had been selected by Boston in the 1964 amateur draft. At the time, NHL clubs were still operating sponsored Junior clubs and securing the professional rights of amateurs through C-forms and the like, which made the 1964 amateur draft a clearing house of over-looked and unappreciated talent. Lynn Patrick was Boston's general manager, and he didn't even choose Dryden until his third pick. He then included him in a four-player swap of draftees conducted with Montreal. Sam Pollock had been in his new job as Montreal's general manager about a month when he made the trade for Dryden's rights. It was one of his first deals as Montreal's boss, and while it attracted little or no attention at the time, the Dryden trade proved to be one of the most important he would ever make.

Dryden had gone his own way, pursuing a law degree while continuing to tend net. His skills gained him a scholarship to an Ivy League university, Cornell, where he became an All American and an NCAA Division 1 champion. He joined the Canadian national team program in 1969 as a salaried player on a three-year contract, rather than joining Montreal's AHL farm team, the Montreal Voyageurs. The intent was for talents like Dryden to form the core of the 1972 Canadian Olympic team, but the Soviet Union pressured the International Olympic Committee to overrule the International Ice Hockey Federation, and the IIHF withdrew its permission for Canada to use paid players at the 1972 Games. With Dryden's national team venture over, in the fall of 1970 the Canadiens dressed him for an exhibition game against the mighty Bruins, and he was impressive in stopping forty-two shots in a 5–4 win. But Dryden began law studies at McGill University in Montreal as planned, leaving the starting goaltender's job to Rogie Vachon.

On December 12, 1970, Dryden made his professional debut with the Voyageurs. The law student shut out the Quebec Aces 4–0. His debut came nine days after Sam Pollock oversaw Montreal's mid-season coaching change. Al MacNeil had just left the Voyageurs to take over the Canadiens from Claude Ruel.

The transition from the Toe Blake era to whatever should or could follow certainly had not been seamless, not in the way Selke had given way to Pollock at the management level. When Blake resigned after winning the 1967/68 Stanley Cup against Scotty Bowman's St. Louis Blues, the Canadiens were suddenly confronted by the succession issue for which they had not prepared. The greatest coaching job in the NHL, occupied by only two men over twenty-eight seasons (Dick Irvin for the first fifteen, Blake for the last thirteen), was up for grabs, and this would be no small hiring. The coach of the Canadiens was a public figure, a symbol as much as an executive. He had to be selected with extreme care; there was more at stake here than simply making a hockey team win. In Montreal, winning had almost become a given under Blake, who made it look dangerously easy. Sam Pollock was said to be sifting through a short list of ten candidates, and Busher Curry, a Canadiens star of the 1940s and 1950s, was thought to be a front runner. Pollock cannot recall ever having a short list. He says the only person he had in mind was the man he actually hired: Claude Ruel.

It was a choice that surprised even Ruel, whose coaching resume was short and not distinguished by any championships. Five seasons running the Junior Canadiens had led to his job as Montreal's chief scout and then, in 1966, the position of director of player development.

Ruel was happy and effective in his role, and Pollock had to talk him into taking the coaching job.

Ruel had two strengths as the new coach. His background in the organization gave him great familiarity with many of the players in the Canadiens' lineup, and he was French Canadian. The dream of a francophone coach had not died during Toe Blake's long tenure. Blake had not fit the cultural bill, but at least (unlike Dick Irvin) he had been bilingual and had a francophone mother. By the time Blake retired, he had become a beloved figure to French and English alike in Quebec. But in the meantime, the Quiet Revolution had taken hold in the province, a resurgent nationalism that would soon turn ugly. Montreal—and many Montreal players, including captain Jean Beliveau—felt that, all other qualifications being met, it was time "one of us" had the chance to coach Les Canadiens. Ruel was all but drafted into a job he had no real desire to take on.

The team rallied to his support, and in their first season together, 1968/69, they won the Stanley Cup, defeating Bowman's Blues in four straight. Ruel became only the third coach in NHL history, after Detroit's Jimmy Skinner and Montreal's Blake, to win both the regular season and the Stanley Cup on his first try. The players bought Ruel a harness-racer in a show of appreciation, and the wisdom of Pollock's hiring decision was celebrated.

The Canadiens, however, were a highly touted blue-chip stock vulnerable to a traumatic market correction. In 1969/70, Ruel's second season, the club underwent a grim devaluation. The team was plagued by injuries, and Ruel fell into disputes with some of his players. Standing only five-foot five and weighing about 230 pounds, Ruel wasn't an intimidating figure, but his penchant for hollering in fractured English lost its comical tone as the team struggled through a difficult season. He tried to quit halfway through, but Beliveau convinced him to stay on, and worked to support him. The season delivered an unthinkable conclusion: the Canadiens missed the playoffs for the first time since 1947/48, when Toe Blake's midseason ankle fracture ended his playing career.

The Canadiens had produced a 38–22–16 record, which left them tied for fourth in the East with the Rangers. Just seven points separated the division's top five teams, and Boston, in second, had won only two more games than the Canadiens. To break the tie between New York and Montreal, total goals were counted. Having scored nine times in the last game of the season, the Rangers edged out the Canadiens, 244 to 242. Scotty Bowman's Blues might have finished six points behind Claude Ruel's Canadiens in the regular season, but it was Bowman who was coaching in the finals while Ruel missed the playoffs altogether.

Ruel did not lose his job, but Sam Pollock made an important staff adjustment, promoting Al MacNeil, coach of the Montreal Voyageurs, to be Ruel's assistant.

MacNeil had moved in and out of Sam Pollock's orbit in the 1960s. After turning down the opportunity to become a coach immediately in the Canadiens system and playing defence for Chicago for four seasons, MacNeil was left unprotected by the Blackhawks at the 1966 intra-league draft. MacNeil's destiny was to work someday for Sad Sam, and his rights were acquired by Pollock in that draft, but they were immediately lifted by the Rangers. After a season in New York, MacNeil was made available in the expansion draft, and the Penguins claimed him. MacNeil was thirty-one when the 1967/68 season ended, and Pollock landed him for the third time, sending centre Wally Boyer (whom he'd just picked up from the Seals) to Pittsburgh to get him.

On paper, it didn't look like such a good deal. Boyer played another 272 games in the NHL and WHA, while MacNeil didn't play one. Pollock, however, had secured the management prospect he wanted.

MacNeil was given two player-coach assignments to choose from: with the Cleveland Barons in the AHL or the Houston Apollos in the CPHL (the Canadiens' league affiliation had been moved from Omaha). Having already played in the American league, MacNeil thought he should take the opportunity to check out the Central league, and so he headed to Houston. Working both sides of a dressing room as player and coach is not for the faint of heart. "I don't think there's anything harder than being a playing coach at the professional level," he says. But he did it successfully in 1968/69, and when the Canadiens decided to move the Houston operation into the AHL, as the Montreal Voyageurs, he took the player-coach job with them as well. MacNeil's Voyageurs recorded a league-leading forty-three wins (with a roster that included Guy Lapointe on defence and Jude Drouin at centre) before losing in a three-team round-robin playoff series.

By arranging for MacNeil to assist the beleaguered Ruel, Pollock had installed a safety valve. If Ruel blew, MacNeil would be there to stop the system from crashing in midseason. And that is what happened on December 12, when Ruel tendered his resignation, saying the team would no longer play for him. As MacNeil recalls, Ruel made the decision to quit after a road game in Pittsburgh. When the team returned to Montreal, Ruel discussed his position with Pollock, who returned him to player development duties. Pollock then asked MacNeil if he wanted to run the Canadiens. "I was young, ambitious and had lots of life," says MacNeil. "I said sure, I'd love to do it."

In hindsight, MacNeil's prospects appeared anything but long-term. He was in his first season as a full-time professional coach, and while he had a long association with Pollock, he did not have the deep roots in the organization that aided Ruel in commanding (initially) the support as well as the respect of players. And MacNeil, having been born and raised in Nova Scotia, didn't speak French. This shortcoming, more than anything else, clouded his future, for he had the misfortune to come into the job at one of the darkest periods in Montreal's history. The Front de Liberation du Quebec (FLQ) terrorist group had pressed its secessionist cause with a bombing and kidnapping campaign in the fall of 1970 and murdered Quebec provincial cabinet minister Pierre LaPorte. The War Measures Act was invoked in October by the federal government, and the suspension of civil rights outraged many Quebecois who had no sympathy with the FLQ.

French-English relations in Canada were so poor that the antagonisms spilled over into hockey. The Memorial Cup finals that spring featured the Quebec Remparts, led by Guy Lafleur, and the St. Catharines Black Hawks, led by Marcel Dionne; Lafleur and Dionne would be chosen first and second in the summer's NHL entry draft. (A rift in Canadian Junior hockey had kept western teams out of the tournament.) Following a brawl-filled game four in Quebec, violence broke out in the stands and a crowd of Remparts supporters attacked the Black Hawks' bus. After winning game five at home to trail the Remparts 3–2 in the best-of-seven series, the Black Hawks refused to return to Quebec for game six. The series was awarded to the Remparts, who then met and defeated the Edmonton Oil Kings in a hastily arranged alternate finals.

It was through this sea of emotion, resentment and violence that MacNeil steered the Canadiens into the Cup finals against Chicago. He had survived the seven-game opener against the Bruins, the runaway favourites. He had survived the semifinals against the surprising North Stars, who had eliminated Bowman and the Blues in six and had the series tied at two apiece before the Canadiens won in six. Win or lose, he was not going to survive the final series against the Blackhawks.

In fathoming Sam Pollock's state of mind in the last few hours before game five, it seems safe to say that he did not want to lose Al Mac-Neil, but he also did not want him back as Montreal's coach. Unlike Sid Salomon III, who had expressed the hope one month earlier to Carl Brewer that his Blues would lose to Minnesota in game six so he could fire Scotty Bowman, Sam Pollock was not interested in losing to the Blackhawks so he could get rid of Al MacNeil. He would not get rid of Al MacNeil any more than he had gotten rid of Claude Ruel. Pollock had good people; he just had to find the right jobs for them. Ruel had gone back to player development, and MacNeil could go back

to the Voyageurs. As for who should replace MacNeil, Pollock understood by then that Scotty Bowman was no longer gainfully employed
by the Salomon family.

"I was sitting in a corner of the arena, by myself, when Bowman
came along," explains Pollock. "I started talking to him. He had just
been let go by St. Louis one or two weeks before. I said, 'What are
you doing?' Bowman said, 'Well, I'm not doing anything right now.
I've had a couple offers from the west coast, but my wife and I don't
want to go.'" Bowman had indeed made a job-search swing through
California and had been offered the coach and general manager's jobs
with both the Kings and the Seals.

"I said, 'Look, if you'd like, you can come to Montreal and work
for me,'" Pollock continues. "'I have no idea in what position at this
time. Think about it and give me a call.' A week later, he called and
said, 'Sam, I'd really like to consider coming to work for you in Montreal.' So he flew up."

Much had transpired between their meetings. In six days, the Blackhawks and Canadiens had played three games. Chicago had blanked
the Canadiens 2–0 in game five to lead the series 3–2. Three nights
later, Montreal had eked out a 4–3 win at home to force game seven.
In the process, Henri Richard had torpedoed any chance Al MacNeil
had of continuing as coach. The "Pocket Rocket" had moved the language war into the dressing room. It was not something MacNeil was
prepared for.

MacNeil had been juggling lines, looking for combinations that
would put an end to the Blackhawks. In the process, he had benched
Richard, who was the most senior team member next to Beliveau. The
Pocket Rocket had the fiery familial pride better known from the outbursts of his older brother Maurice. Having started with the Canadiens in 1955/56, Henri had participated in all five consecutive Cup
wins marshalled by Toe Blake in the late 1950s, then won four more
under Blake and Ruel in the 1960s. Benching Richard had caused
trouble before. Blake had left him idling for a few games in 1967/68

after he'd been injured, in favour of newcomer Jacques Lemaire. Richard was so enraged he failed to show up for a game. "I'd rather pick garbage than sit on the bench," Richard told the press. After spending a week AWOL, he decided to return. But this episode in no way prepared Richard for the personal humiliation of being left off the ice by MacNeil in a game that could have lost the Canadiens the Cup. Richard had won nine of them before MacNeil arrived, and he didn't appreciate being forced to watch as his chance to win a tenth nearly slipped away.

After game six, a seething Richard informed a rapt press in the Canadiens' dressing room that MacNeil was the worst coach he'd ever had and that he was favouring anglophone over francophone players. When Beliveau heard Richard's eruption, he quickly hauled him off to the showers, but the outburst was on its way into the headlines.

Having been around the Montreal organization as a player, Mac-Neil had heard the scuttlebutt that "if you're an English player with the Canadiens, you have to have a little extra or they'll keep a French Canadian instead of you." But as an anglophone who hadn't been able to hold down a long-term starting job with the team, he didn't believe it. "I never thought they let guys go who weren't French who could help the team. They weren't in the business of losing. They put out a club that could win, and it didn't matter if you were French, Jewish, black, green or pink."

The team was one thing—the city was another. MacNeil considered himself politically astute, and he viewed the cultural turmoil gripping Montreal and the province as the work of "just the usual bigots. The relations between the French and English within the Canadiens had always been good." After game six of the finals, however, MacNeil's family received death threats and required police protection.

The Canadiens travelled to Chicago for game seven, and Richard was back on the ice. Trailing 2–0 in the third period, Jacques Lemaire beat Tony Esposito with a sixty-footer. Then Richard scored both the tying and winning goals. Sam Pollock had his sixth Stanley Cup in

eight seasons. Jean Beliveau retired, and Henri Richard, who regretted his outburst after game six and apologized to MacNeil, became
the new captain.

And Scotty Bowman arrived from St. Louis to discuss employment
opportunities. "I said there's three possibilities," Pollock recalls. "Run
the farm system, be my assistant, or you could even end up coaching.
I knew Scotty well, and thought he had done a fantastic job in St. Louis,
and was surprised when they let him go." Pollock felt that Bowman
was the best coach for the Canadiens "going forward," but he didn't
want to lose MacNeil. The Voyageurs were moving to Nova Scotia,
and Pollock wanted MacNeil to go with them, to be coach and general manager. Pollock says he told MacNeil, "'In a few years you can
be my assistant.' He wanted to think about it. A few days later, he
accepted it."

MacNeil had enrolled in a French immersion course that summer
in anticipation of returning as the Canadiens' coach, but the ugly experience of the Montreal playoff drive told him that his cultural baggage
would be an endless source of friction, if not in the dressing room then
in the press and among fans. "Sam said I should go to Halifax and be
coach and general manager, do everything I want. I wasn't sure at first,
but I went along. Sam always made good decisions."

And so Scotty Bowman came aboard as the Canadiens' new coach,
a bilingual Montrealer who came closer to fitting the cultural bill the
job demanded than MacNeil. Outwardly it was a demotion from the
general manager's job in St. Louis, and Bowman would later describe
it as a "stopgap" move. But given his options, the decision is easy to
understand. Bigger jobs were offered Bowman in Oakland and Los
Angeles, but both the Seals and the Kings had missed the playoffs and
had little promise of even medium-term success. The Seals continued
to dwell in the cellar of the standings before moving to Cleveland in
1976/77, where ineptitude persisted and a merger was finally arranged
with Minnesota in 1978/79. The Kings would turn into a middling
team with one great season, 1974/75, on the horizon.

Montreal was the right career decision. Bowman could coach—for the first time—an NHL team packed with talent. The 1970/71 team had nine future members of the Hockey Hall of Fame: Jean Beliveau, Henri Richard, Jacques Laperriere, Guy Lapointe, Jacques Lemaire, Yvan Cournoyer, Ken Dryden, Serge Savard and Frank Mahovlich. While Beliveau was retiring to accept a front-office vice-presidency, an even more powerful club was being assembled for the 1970s. Pollock was holding three first-round and three second-round picks in the 1971 draft, and he would use them to select, among others, Guy Lafleur first, Murray Wilson eleventh, and Larry Robinson twentieth. Ken Dryden, who won the Conn Smythe Trophy, had played so few games in 1970/71 that 1971/72 would qualify as his rookie season and he would outpoll them in Calder voting. By the time Montreal won another Cup in 1972/73, the number of future Hall of Famers in the active lineup would have grown to eleven, with the additions of Larry Robinson, Guy Lafleur and Steve Shutt.

It's difficult to imagine Bowman even mulling over the decision to return to Montreal. It had been almost twenty years since he had played left wing for Sam Pollock's Junior Canadiens. Working for Pollock again, coaching a team that was entirely capable of winning many more Cups, in a city in which he had been born and raised, in a city in which hockey was a life force and the Canadiens a cultural institution—Bowman must have been ready to jump at the chance. And he did jump, after MacNeil had agreed to step aside.

When Frank Mahovlich heard that MacNeil was on his way out, he was sufficiently concerned to approach Pollock. Mahovlich had been acquired from Detroit by Pollock on January 13, when Montreal handed over Mickey Redmond, Guy Charron and Bill Collins in exchange for a once-troubled Maple Leafs star whose career had been revived with his trade to Detroit in March 1968. Mahovlich made the second All Star team in 1968/69, and the big left-winger had long been admired by Jean Beliveau and Frank Selke. Whenever Mahovlich was in Punch Imlach's doghouse in the early 1960s, Selke would offer to make a trade for him, but Imlach always turned him down. In Montreal, Mahovlich found a first-class organization on and off the ice. "I was really impressed with the players. I got my first goal with them in my first game, against Minnesota." Mahovlich finished the season with 73 points, and in the playoffs he scored a record fourteen goals and matched Phil Esposito's record-setting 27-point effort of 1969/70. The point total still stands as the best playoff effort by a Canadien.

Mahovlich, in short, had enjoyed much success under MacNeil, and he was alarmed that his coach was suddenly leaving. "I didn't talk too much to Al," he says. "I just went along with what he said. I think he and Sammy Pollock had a good rapport." Mahovlich, though, wanted to know why this rapport had led to MacNeil's departure, and Pollock told him. "He explained that he'd just wanted Al MacNeil to finish the season, that he'd already set it up that Bowman would be the coach the next year."

The management change required explanation and clarification, even in a business accustomed to ruthless hirings and firings. MacNeil insisted to the press that he hadn't been fired or demoted; Pollock was asked to clarify when he had decided MacNeil was out and Bowman was in. But the controversy, such as there was, remained external to the organization. "I had two major-league coaches," Pollock says, "and I treated them that way."

Pollock had done what seemed impossible. Between December 1970 and June 1971, he had gone through three different coaches—one more than Frank Selke had employed in eighteen seasons. Yet he had managed to keep everyone in the organization—Ruel was back overseeing player development, MacNeil was back in the American league, in a bigger job than he'd had at the start of the season, and Bowman, the prodigal son, was back from banks of the Mississippi and running the bench of the defending Cup champions. "We were lucky to retain all our people," Pollock offers.

He wasn't just lucky. He was Sad Sam.

9

✧ NO CANADIENS TEAM ON A winning streak in the dynastic run from the mid 1940s to the late 1970s was self-contained. They each had players who linked one successful run to another, while a few players managed to have careers that reached across several phases of the dynasty. Henri Richard, for example, who started in 1955/56, lasted until 1974/75, the dawn of the team's last great Cup streak. The Montreal Canadiens team he captained in the early 1970s, however, featured one of the most transitional lineups in Canadiens history, bridging the teams of two great eras, the 1960s and the late 1970s.

It was a time of rebuilding, and of accommodating a flurry of changes in both the sport and the Canadiens organization. The universal draft was in full swing, and the World Hockey Association was about to arrive; both changed the economics and mechanics of team-building, in some respects forever. The Canadiens, however, would take it all in stride, coping with these challenges better than any other NHL franchise. The sale of the team by the Molsons to the Bronfmans in late 1971 had no real effect on the operation, and a stability of sorts resulted from the return to the Canadiens fold of Scotty Bowman. Reunited with Sam Pollock, Bowman turned his stopgap job into the greatest coaching performance of the post-1967 era.

Bowman and Pollock were a complex team, in that each made

implicit demands on the other's performance. Pollock gave the coach a first-class lineup, stood by him when players and press took issue with him (and stood by players Bowman sometimes took issue with), and in return expected results. Bowman delivered those results, and would continue to do so for as long as Pollock could find and retain players that could win championships. They admired each other for their successes in holding up their respective ends of the bargain, and Bowman would come to argue that he had no ambition to become a general manager, so long as Sam was working with him. Indeed, for seven seasons Sam Pollock had the league's best coach, and Scotty Bowman had the league's best general manager.

The first season, 1971/72, was not easy. Two key members of the lineup, Jean Beliveau and John Ferguson, retired, and Rogie Vachon demanded to be traded. The former NDG Monarch goaltender had broken in with the Canadiens in 1966/67 and vied with Gump Worsley for the starter's job, until Worsley suffered a nervous breakdown from a fear of flying in November 1968 and was eventually drafted by Minnesota in 1969. When Ken Dryden arrived in the spring of 1971 and performed so brilliantly in the playoffs, Vachon could see that he would be getting little ice time. He went to Pollock in early November 1971 and asked to be traded, and an understanding general manager had him in Los Angeles in a matter of days. Into the Canadiens' roster in exchange came former Montreal defenceman Noel Price, left-winger Doug Robinson, and Bowman's goaltender from the 1958/59 Memorial Cup, Denis DeJordy.

Offsetting the losses, however, were many new faces. Already the 1970/71 season had seen a host of new players arrive: Dryden in goal; Guy Lapointe, Pierre Bouchard and Bob Murdoch on defence; Claude Larose, Leon Rochefort and Phil Roberto on right wing; Mark Tardif and Frank Mahovlich on left wing; Rejean Houle, who could play either wing; and Bob Sheehan at centre. In 1971/72, Guy Lafleur started on right wing, and on December 13, Pollock retrieved for Bowman from St. Louis his valued checking and penalty-killing right-winger,

Jimmy Roberts, in a deal for Phil Roberto. A few other minor adjustments were made to the lineup that had won the 1970/71 Cup under
Al MacNeil: Bob Sheehan was sold to the Seals, and Leon Rochefort
went to the Red Wings for defensive prospect Kerry Ketter and cash.

Richard's captaincy notwithstanding, this could be called the Frank
Mahovlich era—a span of a few seasons in which the left-winger,
acquired from the Red Wings, played his final NHL seasons as a Canadien. A member of neither the championship lineup of the 1960s
dynasty led by Jean Beliveau nor the late-1970s team associated with
Guy Lafleur in his prime, Mahovlich was the scoring star of the transitional team, leading with points in 1971/72 and 1973/74, and finishing second in goals in 1971/72 and 1972/73.

Mahovlich had suffered famously in Toronto from 1957/58 to
1967/68, badgered and bullied by Punch Imlach, and on two occasions he was hospitalized with nervous exhaustion. "Imlach was lucky
he had us," Mahovlich says. "He was lucky that I couldn't do what
guys do today: if you don't want me to play for this team, get rid of
me. I couldn't go anywhere. It was crazy. We suffered quite a bit and
won in spite of him."

Having endured Imlach, there wasn't much Scotty Bowman could
throw at Mahovlich that he hadn't seen before and survived. Imlach
was an authoritarian taskmaster who brutalized players with exercise.
"Bowman was much better than a lot of coaches I've had. He ran a
fairly good practice. There were a lot of games that I left in the practice in Toronto. People would boo me, but I just didn't have any energy.
When I got to Montreal, I felt like a tiger out there, that I still had
something left."

Many of the players were young and new to the league; others were
aging veterans who would be challenged to hold on to a starting job.
Bowman greeted this complex mixture of talents with an equally complex arsenal of motivational and disciplinary tools.

Larry Pleau, who had played for Bowman on the NDG Monarchs
and the Junior Canadiens, was a spare wheel at centre when Bowman

arrived in Montreal. Playing mainly as a Voyageur for Al MacNeil, Pleau had appeared in twenty Canadiens games in 1969/70 and nineteen in 1970/71—not enough to get his name on the Stanley Cup. Under Bowman, he was still a fill-in, but at least he was dressed for fifty-five games in 1971/72.

"At times," says Pleau, "it was like he was your friend." At other times, it was like Bowman was the KGB. His tough behaviour on the road became legendary. That first season running the Canadiens, he got a master key and searched the players' hotel rooms for liquor while they were taking a pre-game skate in Boston. In successive seasons, he camped out in lobbies, waiting for the curfew-breakers to straggle in. When the team didn't play to his satisfaction on one road trip, he told Canada Customs to check everyone's luggage.

His discipline picked up at the start of the 1972/73 season. After the Canadiens lost to the Rangers in six games in the 1971/72 quarterfinals, he fined nine players for breaking curfew. "I fined only two players last season, and both were for being late for practice," he told *The Globe and Mail* in November 1972. "Now we have curfews and there's no use having them unless you intend to enforce them, which I do. We had an exhibition game in Boston on a Friday night with a Sunday game coming up in New York. I felt it was important because we had played so badly against the Rangers last season. So I put in a midnight curfew after the Boston game. Then I had a bed check. There were veterans wandering in around 1:20 in the morning. I gave them the word at practice the next morning it was going to cost them. They told me the midnight curfew was foolish and said I should have spoken up the night before to let them know about it.

"What's worse, a guy sits around with some teammates and misses curfew and another guy gets in on time and orders a case of beer from room service. Let's face it, in the final analysis, you have to count on a certain degree of self-discipline. When every club sponsored the whole farm system, you could implant good habits in Juniors. Now it's different. You have to make a point of getting the kind of attitude which you used to ingrain in kids."

In other words, Bowman was compelled to treat some of his professionals the way he treated the kids he chaperoned around Ontario while coaching Junior hockey. "He was the same as he was in Juniors," says Pleau. "Intimidating. Everyone was scared of him."

"He was a disciplinarian who kept everybody off balance," says Mahovlich. "You didn't know what to think. One day he'd do something, and the next day he wouldn't."

Bowman could be subtle in the way he wielded authority. According to Jimmy Roberts, Bowman might note that a player had broken curfew, but do nothing about it. A few days later at practice, he would say, "Now, I know some of you missed curfew on Friday," without naming names, but those not named knew Bowman had them. He could use the curfew violation to intimidate a player without openly citing the transgression.

As his career progressed, observers would note that Bowman's methods were mellowing. Even when Bowman was starting his first season as Montreal's coach, his behaviour was seen to have softened. "He did change with the times," says Denis DeJordy. "He changed with the players, too." He recalls how rookie defenceman Pierre Bouchard wanted Bowman's permission to attend midnight mass, which would mean breaking curfew. Bowman permitted it, whereas other coaches would have been inflexible.

Even with four years in St. Louis behind him, Bowman was still learning the NHL coaching game, shaping his tactics off the ice as much as on it. This was the era of the hands-on Bowman, who still ran his own practices (with some help from Claude Ruel), who made travel arrangements for the team, and who listened to people he felt he could learn from.

Bowman's formative years as a coach in the Canadiens organization had been spent in the shadow of Toe Blake, whom he admired, studied and listened to with the intensity the old warrior deserved.

When Bowman became coach of the Junior Canadiens in 1964, he was given an office on the same floor as Blake. As Bowman recalled in 1995 after Blake's death, "I was able to spend a lot of time asking him questions. He spent the afternoons in his office going over stuff. It was interesting for me because he had been an NHL coach for about ten years.

"He was quite an innovator. He really wanted to match up players in a lot of situations. He had some real good offensive players. He liked the role players. He had a pretty good format. He believed the role players were important on the team. He made them feel as important as he could. He was good with the stars because he was demanding, he never let them get too, not complacent, but too happy with themselves.

"He got a lot out of his teams. He really believed in making it tough on other teams to score. He liked skilled players, but demanded balance from his players. I remember when he got Yvan Cournoyer out of Juniors [in 1964/65]. He played him on the power play. That's how he broke him in. He never handed things to players. He believed the young guys had to come in and prove themselves, especially defensively. I think all the players who played for him, they knew how they stood, that they had to play two ways."

The comparisons between Bowman and Blake, who both coached Canadien dynasties, were inevitable, and entirely appropriate. But Bowman has deflected any notion that he might surpass Blake's record of coaching success. When people noted that he might match or break Blake's record eight Cup wins, Bowman pointed out that Blake was unassailable, at least by him, for Blake had amassed his eight in just thirteen seasons.

When Bowman took on the job of coaching the Canadiens, Blake was on hand to dispense advice. "He told me, 'Just keep stressing keep the puck out of your own end, you'll score enough goals.' We had a lot of skill players. He said, 'Don't get carried away with the offence. Get enough to win and then make sure you play the other guys.' He was with them for fifty years. The players that played for him, they liked it because they were winners."

"Scotty Bowman and Toe Blake are the two greatest coaches ever in hockey," says Pollock. "No coach has had the longevity that Scotty has, and that speaks for itself. When Scotty was coaching, you never had to worry that he wasn't getting the very best out of that team. Good coaches can win you maybe six or eight games a year on their own, and I'd certainly put Scotty in that category."

"Toe Blake was the greatest coach I ever had for knowing exactly what was going on with every player on the ice," says Jimmy Roberts. "He was like a video camera. He could see and remember everything. He could almost tell you where you were on the ice for any play he wanted to bring up. Scotty had that vision of the game from the bench also, but it stands out more with Toe in that there wasn't video equipment around, where Scotty had a lot more television and video later on and access to replays."

As with Blake, Bowman's powers of recall often attract comment and awe. (During his tenure as coach of the Pittsburgh Penguins, players gave him the nickname "Rain Man" for his encyclopedic command of, and fascination with, statistics.) Some insist his memory is photographic, but he may simply be overwhelmingly dedicated to the job. His ability to remember players who played for and against him in his long apprenticeship in Junior hockey paid off when he reached the NHL and helped Lynn Patrick assemble the Blues. Once in the NHL, he showed himself to be a devoted student. He constantly gathered intelligence on other teams, watching televised games into the early-morning hours, studying footage of opponents to prepare for them, working the phones to keep in touch with contacts near and far.

In his first seasons with the Canadiens, Bowman also proved himself open to new ideas. Left out of the management of the Team Canada squad that faced the Soviet Union in the 1972 Summit series, but keen to know more about the Russian style of play, he solicited the opinions of Canadiens players like Frank Mahovlich, who had participated.

"Scotty was always learning," says Mahovlich. "He was always asking questions of the players, picking up a few things. He had a good mind. He might not have tried something right then, but if a guy was saying something, he'd put it back in his head somewhere like a filing cabinet, and bring it up years later."

Bowman has never been known as a "system" coach; if he has a system, it is simply a long-standing aversion to predictability. He learned early, under Blake's tutelage, that flexibility in individual game strategies, forechecking styles and the players he dressed for a particular contest was vital to success. Bowman knew that unpredictability was an important part of his coaching style. If his own players didn't know what to expect from him, neither would his opponents. Coaches who can get their team to play only a particular style of game have always been in over their heads when up against Bowman. Any opponent who has a distinctive style knows that Bowman will have dissected it completely before they meet, and they should also know that if they draw up a game plan to counter the way Bowman's team played the last time they met, he is very likely to come at them with another style of play altogether—more (or less) forechecking, different line combinations, double shifts of scoring stars, four regular forward lines instead of three.

Coaching hockey is a unique calling. Baseball managers oversee a game that unfolds at an almost languorous pace. They can call time-outs and walk right onto the field to talk shop with players. Football is a series of highly co-ordinated set pieces, executed in bursts of a few seconds of violence. Basketball has some of the pace and team play of hockey, but it differs critically in that players do not change on the fly. No other sport approaches hockey in the difficulty of strategizing a game in motion; a special skill is required to put the right players on the ice at the right time. Not only must those players work well together, they must be matched against opposing players to their team's advantage. This aspect of coaching hockey is what is known as "running the bench." It is one of the most important skills in a hockey coach's repertoire, and no one has proved to be better at it than Bowman.

Before Bowman's arrival in the NHL, coaching was often seen as a motivational job rather than a strategic one, a job tailor-made for an old pro who could rouse the dressing room with go-get-'em war stories, slap backs on the bench and open the gate to let players on and off the ice. The game was almost deceptively simple, frozen (in North America at least) in its configuration by the introduction of the two-line offside for the 1943/44 season. This rule allowed players for the first time to pass the puck across their own blueline, provided the receiving player was not across the new centre-ice line, and it created overnight the modern, fast-breaking game—the "firewagon" game Montreal played so well. Defencemen were almost always expected to "stay at home," behind their own blueline, helping launch attacks by delivering the breakout passes the new offside rule allowed, but certainly not (except in a few spectacularly skilled cases) leading the rush themselves. Wingers took passes and checked, rigidly patrolling their respective wings. There was, almost always, only one goaltender dressed to play on each team. The league would not make two goaltenders mandatory for the playoffs until 1964/65, for the regular season until 1965/66.

The playing roots of managers and coaches in the NHL tended to make the league hidebound, wary of innovation. Goaltenders had a tough time leaving the crease to play the puck; Glenn Hall's revolutionary butterfly style, the foundation of modern goaltending, earned him management grief when he made the NHL with the Red Wings in 1955/56, despite his superb play. Jacques Plante was able to introduce the face-mask to the NHL only after being badly cut in a game against the Rangers in November 1959. Toe Blake had no choice but to allow him to wear it because Montreal had no goaltender on hand to replace him.

In Toronto, Punch Imlach became legendary for not bothering to hold penalty-killing drills during practice. The prevailing logic was that players were supposed to know how these things worked if they were good enough to play in the NHL. It fell to veteran players to indoctrinate the rookies in game skills. Coaching was more about putting players together in the right mix of lines, not drawing elaborate puck-handling strategies on chalkboards. There was none of the puck-cycling and other novelties that would later come to the NHL, mainly due to the influence of the international game.

And certainly there wasn't much of a bench to manage. Having one full-time goaltender took care of deciding who to start in net on a particular night, or whether someone should be replaced in mid-game. The bench was also short. In 1949/50, teams were allowed to dress seventeen "skaters," exclusive of goaltenders, but this was cut in 1952/53 to fifteen on the road and sixteen at home. In 1954/55 the number of skaters edged up to sixteen and stayed there until 1971/72, when the bench stretched to seventeen. In 1982/83, it stretched again, to eighteen, where it now remains.

Sixteen skaters generally meant icing a defensive corps of five (two pairs plus a utility), and devoting the rest to three forward lines and two utilities. One more player would make a world of difference—it could mean three defensive pairs, or four complete forward lines. The coaches of Toe Blake's day didn't have that luxury, but at least they had more player options than coaches like Dick Irvin did in the early years of his bench career. When Irvin joined the Chicago Blackhawks as a player in 1926/27, NHL teams were allowed to dress a maximum of twelve players. Goaltenders were counted separately beginning in 1928/29, and in 1929/30, with the arrival of the modern blueline off-side rule, the maximum number of players was allowed to balloon from twelve to fifteen. In 1930/31, Irvin used this increase to his advantage in his rookie coaching season. Dressing more players and employing shorter shifts, Irvin's Blackhawks were only narrowly defeated by the more powerful Canadiens in the Cup finals.

Irvin was a pioneer in the art of line matching—getting a checking line against a team's scoring line, keeping a scoring line away from the opponent's checkers. He brought this skill to Montreal in 1940 and made it a foundation of the Canadiens' success. "Montreal was the first organization to really match lines, with the patience that's involved in making changes on the fly," says Al MacNeil. "Scotty perfected it. His great strength is as a bench coach. He's a line or two ahead of whoever he's coaching against. He reads the situation so quickly and counters so well. You never have the wrong guys on the ice when Scotty's on the bench."

Critical to matching lines is having the necessary player resources. The scoring stars get most of the ink and the largest salaries, but teams cannot win championships without role players. Bowman was true to the Canadiens tradition in holding these players in high regard. "When we had the Tremblays, the Risebroughs, the Gaineys, the Jarvises," says MacNeil, "it all went back to the Donnie Marshalls and the Phil Goyettes, the backup guys who supported the star staff like the Beliveaus, the Geoffrions, the Moores. They did all the heavy work. They filled out the club and made for champions."

It has been noted that Bowman can outmanoeuvre rival coaches within the first three minutes of a game, shuffling through line changes until his opponent finds his top scoring line suddenly matched by Bowman's checkers. Game, set and match, with fifty-seven minutes left on the clock.

"Scotty is fantastic at matching lines," says Pollock. "There's a huge difference in what players you have on the ice against certain other players. That's one of the things Scotty learned early and has used to his advantage all through his coaching career."

"He is still the best today in running the bench," affirms Jim Devellano, executive vice-president of the Red Wings.

"He's the toughest guy to coach against because he's so unpredictable about what he's going to do," Chicago coach Craig Hartsburg told *The Detroit News* as Bowman's Red Wings bore down on the Stanley Cup in 1996/97. "He's got great players, but he gets them to play every night. That's not easy."

"It's always something to coach against Scotty, because he is the master of masters," Boston Bruins coach Pat Burns told the newspaper at the start of the 1997/98 season. "I remember the first time I coached against him. I think he was in Pittsburgh, and I spent half the game staring at him on the other bench."

"There has never been anyone who could run a bench better than Scotty," his former St. Louis assistant, Cliff Fletcher, has said. "He was always three or four moves ahead of the opposition. So his players knew they only had to be as good as the other team. Scotty would make the difference."

Taking over the Canadiens, Bowman was completely devoted to and engrossed in the task of winning hockey games. His wife told Bill Libbey of *The Hockey News* in 1973 that Bowman was so intense, he wanted to be reincarnated as a goal post. He frightened, baffled and inspired. And sometimes he drove people right out of town. After the 1971/72 season, veteran defenceman Terry Harper called it quits. As a Regina Pat, he had played against Bowman and Pollock's Junior Canadiens in the 1957/58 Memorial Cup finals, and he became a Montreal regular in 1962/63. Jacques Laperriere and Harper were the team's steady defensive veterans, and Pollock felt he needed Harper enough to offer him a three-year contract. Harper refused to sign it, calling it three years of "high-priced hell," and was traded to Los Angeles. "Bowman was the whole reason" he left, Harper told *The Globe and Mail* columnist Leo Monahan. "I'd made up my mind I just couldn't play under him anymore. I've never spent a year with a more disorganized club since I started to play hockey. But something has happened to this organization. Even the year we won the Stanley Cup, you could sense something going sour. I'm thirty-two now and life is too short to put up with this kind of nonsense. If the league keeps expanding I figure I might play another ten years." As it turned out, he played nine.

In the world inhabited by Sam Pollock, every cloud had a silver lining. He might have lost Harper, but to get him the Kings had paid
dearly, with their second pick in 1974, first and third pick in 1975,
and first pick in 1976 (which netted Pierre Mondou).

Bowman was rarely the direct cause of the loss of a player, though.
When not respected, his methods were at least tolerated, for by 1972
players no longer had to resign themselves to playing in an organization
they despised. The arrival of the WHA in 1972 opened a fresh employment option and a lever for salary increases. The new league, conceived
by a pair of Californians (one of whom, real estate lawyer Gary Davidson, had never even seen a hockey game) was meant to horn in on the
NHL's monopoly in the same way that they challenged the National Basketball Association with their American Basketball Association.

Chicago's Bobby Hull and Boston's Gerry Cheevers were among
the new league's biggest signings, but the first player publicly signed
to a contract with a WHA team was Montreal's Larry Pleau. As a native
of Massachusetts, Pleau was a logical choice for the New England
Whalers. The night before the press conference at which he was to
sign his contract, he telephoned Sam Pollock. "I was a bench-warmer
with Montreal. I just wanted to *play*. I said, 'Mr. Pollock, if you'd
just tell me you'd trade me, I'd stay in the league. I know that Vancouver and the Islanders would probably take me. That's what I want
to do.' He said, 'Larry, I'm not going to trade you, and there's not
going to be a WHA tomorrow, and there's not going to be one ever.'
He hung up." Pleau had his press conference and his signing, and
played seven seasons for the Whalers before becoming their coach
and general manager. Ironically, soon after he signed, Pollock did trade
him, to Toronto for Brad Selwood, but by then Selwood too had signed
with New England.

Despite Pollock's prediction to Pleau, there was indeed a WHA, and
it pestered the NHL for the rest of the decade, driving up wages, changing the management-player relationship and removing the NHL's
certainty that the best prospects would always respond to their selection

at the draft by signing a contract. NHL expansion had already helped start the changes. As Pollock notes, until then, contracts of more than a year were almost unheard of. Then, top players late in their careers began demanding security, and two- and three-year contracts appeared. With the WHA on the scene, multi-year contracts with big salaries and bonus schedules reared their heads as the players found bargaining power: sign me on my terms, or I'll go to the Cincinnati Stingers. "It was the first time any team was faced with losing a player to another team," says Pollock. "The only other time they had lost a player was when a guy retired."

NHL teams reacted by either signing big cheques or battening down the hatches and refusing to bargain. After initially trying to pretend the WHA didn't exist, the Rangers, Stanley Cup finalists in 1971/72, opted for the former strategy.

Sam Pollock resolutely refused to be swayed by the appearance of a rival league. The Canadiens had a long-standing policy of incremental increases in player salaries, of enhanced worth being proven over several seasons. In particular, a player new to the team could not expect a huge salary increase based on one season's performance. The Canadiens organization was vulnerable to losing players in several categories. With so much talent, there were marginal players who could make much more money playing a regular shift in the WHA. Veterans, who might be seen to have a limited future, could secure longer-term contracts in the rival league with clubs who were willing to gamble on their staying power—reaping their box-office appeal in the process. And then there were the young players who had acquitted themselves well in their initial seasons with Montreal, but who couldn't wrest a substantial salary increase from the organization.

Pollock's refusal to get into a bidding war with WHA teams immediately cost him a talented and experienced defenceman, J.C. Tremblay, who signed with the Quebec Nordiques for their first season. "It was a big shock," Pollock concedes. "After we lost a couple of players, we accepted it as a fact of life."

Initially, the WHA had no real effect on the Canadiens. J.C. Tremblay might have left, and Harper might have headed to Los Angeles, but Bowman was able to start three important new players: Larry Robinson on defence, and Steve Shutt and Murray Wilson on left wing. The New York Islanders entered the league that year and won just twelve of seventy-eight games. Bowman's Canadiens lost just ten. Finishing first overall, the Canadiens allowed the fewest goals against and were outscored only by Boston (by one goal). Ken Dryden won the Vezina, Guy Lapointe was runner-up for the Norris, and he and Dryden were joined on the first All Star team by Frank Mahovlich, with Yvan Cournoyer making the second team. Montreal hadn't had this many first-team All Stars since 1960/61.

After dominating the regular season, Bowman's Canadiens quickly found competition in the playoffs. The Buffalo Sabres, who had just completed their third season by finishing fifteen wins behind Montreal, in fourth place in the East division, took them to six games before allowing them to advance. The semifinals brought on the Philadelphia Flyers, playing their second season under coach Fred Shero. Having missed the playoffs in 1971/72, the Flyers had quickly emerged as Cup contenders. The combative Flyers traded overtime wins with Montreal in the first two games before losing three games straight.

The finals brought a reunion of sorts with the Blackhawks, who had lost the 1970/71 Cup to the Canadiens. These Hawks were without Bobby Hull, the WHA's most celebrated signing, but they had still scored more goals in 1972/73 than they did in 1970/71 or 1971/72. The two coaches—Bowman in Montreal and Billy Reay in Chicago—had teams renowned for both scoring goals and preventing them. While the Blackhawks had not turned in one of their greatest defensive seasons, they did have Tony Esposito in goal; Esposito and Dryden were the most celebrated goaltenders of their day, and had shared netminding duties for Team Canada in the eight-game series against the Soviets the previous September.

The teams quickly came to an agreement that, defensive prowess notwithstanding, this series was going to be a shootout. While Bowman oversaw disciplined 4–1 and 4–0 wins in games two and four, in the rest of the series he engaged in a battle of raw firepower, giving up twenty-two goals in four games and scoring twenty-five in response. Montreal won the opener 8–3; Chicago won game three 7–4 and game five 8–7. The Canadiens never scored fewer than four goals in a game, and they took the Cup with a 6–4 win in Chicago in game six. From the perspective of the Toe Blake playbook, it was an ugly win. The classic Blake style entailed minimizing the opposition's scoring opportunities and relying on the team's essential offensive talent to deliver victory. Over the series, Montreal allowed 3.83 goals a game, after a season in which Dryden had held opponents to 2.26. Unlike 1970/71, this Stanley Cup was not going to deliver the Conn Smythe to Dryden or any member of the Canadiens' defence. Yvan Cournoyer won it, after he and Jacques Lemaire tied Gordie Howe's record of twelve points in a series finals and Cournoyer scored fifteen goals in seventeen playoff games.

Following the Cup win, the Canadiens stumbled, as the team fragmented into a collection of individuals. The WHA had survived its first season. Former Canadien Larry Pleau had won the league's inaugural championship, the Avco Cup, with the New England Whalers. John F. Bassett, one of the Canadiens' minority shareholders (who had also been a Leaf shareholder), cashed in and bought the Ottawa Nationals, moving them to Toronto and relaunching them as the Toros. While J.C. Tremblay and the Quebec Nordiques had not logged a winning season, the team had strong fan support, as the provincial capital enjoyed a return to the glory days of the exciting hockey provided in the early 1950s by Jean Beliveau and the Quebec Aces. (The Nordiques even tried to get Beliveau to come out of retirement.) Rejean Houle and Marc Tardif, Sam Pollock's prized picks in the 1969 draft, joined Tremblay as Nordiques for 1973/74. Guy Lafleur, a native son who had starred for the Quebec Remparts in Junior hockey, was struggling in his first few seasons as a Canadien to live up to the expectation that he don the mantle of Beliveau, and he was tempted to follow.

While Houle and Tardif were Montreal's most obvious losses to the WHA, the league's effect on salaries was also an important factor in Ken Dryden's decision to sit out the 1973/74 season. Dryden chose to article as a law student, at $134 a week, rather than continue to be, in his mind, underpaid. Dryden was earning about $80,000 a year, about half of what Bernie Parent had been offered in 1972 to jump to the WHA, before he was a star. In less than three seasons, Dryden had won two Stanley Cups, as well as the Calder, the Conn Smythe and the Vezina, and he had been named to the second and first All Star teams. At the press conference announcing his decision to sit out the season, Dryden said, "I can name six goaltenders who were higher paid than me. That bothers me and I can't see any reason why this should be the case."

Dryden's loss was considerable to Bowman. He admired the rangy netminder more than any other player. "He reminds me of Glenn Hall," Bowman had said in his first season as Montreal's coach. "He can make the big save when you need it. He can give you the big period when you need it. His style is similar to Hall and so is his courage and ability to rise to the occasion." Bowman would tell columnist Al Strachan that Dryden was said to be complex, "but he was a pretty decent guy if you sat down and levelled with him. You always knew he was never going to have two bad games in a row."

Dryden was always Montreal's main starter in the regular season and the playoffs, and his loss, even for a season, was difficult for the organization to bear. (Former Canadiens goaltender Gump Worsley found Dryden's refusal to play unforgivable.) Since Dryden's arrival late in 1970/71, Sam Pollock had steadily cleaned house of starters and strong prospects. He had already let Esposito go in 1969, having Worsley and Vachon at the time. Then he had let Worsley go to bank on Vachon, with Dryden in reserve. When Dryden emerged as a starter, Pollock agreed to Vachon's request to be traded away, and Vachon, with the L.A. Kings in 1974/75, would miss winning the Vezina by only four goals and finish second in Hart Trophy voting. Pollock had also sold Denis DeJordy and Chico Resch to the Islanders; paired with Billy Smith, Resch would be a Vezina runner-up three times and a second-team All Star twice. The issue wasn't whether or not any of the goaltenders were actually better than Dryden; rather, it was the fact that Pollock had surrendered so much goaltending talent, banking on the fact that he could depend on Dryden's services, short of injury. Dryden, however, had foreshadowed the holdouts of Soviet stars Alexei Yashin and Sergei Fedorov by more than twenty years. If Pollock wasn't going to pay him what he thought he was worth, he simply wasn't going to play. The only bargaining chip Dryden had was to withhold his services, and when he did, the team suffered noticeably.

Having to live without Dryden, either for one season or forever, was part of what Bowman had to accept in working for Sad Sam. Pollock was not going to spend the Bronfmans' money freely, and Bowman would just have to coach what he was given.

The 1973/74 season was an extended ordeal for Bowman and the Canadiens. In 1972/73, the team had led the league in wins, points and goals against; in 1973/74, the Canadiens won seven fewer games, to finish second in the East and fourth in the league, scoring thirty-six fewer goals and, in Dryden's absence, allowing fifty-four more of them. In the playoffs, the Rangers—the team with the payroll bloated by the war against the WHA—downed them in six in the quarterfinals.

Sifting through the ashes of the failed season, critics made Bowman a popular target. He had been feuding, in and out of the public eye, with players. His relationship with Wayne Thomas, the former Canadian national team goaltender brought in to replace Dryden, went on the rocks after he pulled him from a pre-game warm-up in Boston. Jacques Laperriere wasn't interested in returning if Bowman was, and retired at the end of the season.

John Robertson, a sports columnist for *The Montreal Star* and *The Toronto Sunday Sun*, laid the blame for the disappointing season at

Bowman's feet—and asked for his head. On April 23, five days after Montreal lost game six to the Rangers 5–2 in New York, Robertson wrote: "I find it difficult to believe as astute a hockey man as Sam Pollock can publicly absolve Bowman of all blame for the Canadiens' problems. Although Scotty was by no means the club's only problem, he was the root of major failing which dragged so many of his players down to mediocrity this season. Loss of pride. Loss of desire. Loss of togetherness. Lack of leadership. Inability to deal with the shirkers and malcontents in his midst. This is what he is paid so handsomely to do."

Pollock refused to consider dumping Bowman. "He was the same man this season as he was in 1972/73 when he won everything," he said at the time. Today, Pollock reiterates that there was no possibility of letting Bowman go. "I never even considered it."

It is a marvellous thing when an entire team—the ownership, senior management, the coach and the players—all work agreeably toward the same ends. Often, though, even when winning, the individual components of the organization have their own agendas to pursue. Players might have bonuses based on scoring that place them at odds with a coach whose total-team approach reduces individual ice time or emphasizes two-way play, either of which can cut back individual offensive output. Ultimately, coaches must bend individual wills and interests to the cause of winning, which is a coach's only measure of success. A player, by comparison, can make a handsome and secure living on a mediocre team by racking up accomplishments that earn him more money and a higher market value. Naked greed is not the only motivator for a player to resist a coach's instructions. Coaches come and go, and players have their own careers to think about. A misguided approach to an individual player's role can derail or damage a career.

Bowman's NHL career has been spent bending individual wills toward his vision of what is required for a team to win. It has won him converts and enemies in equal measure, and has provided him with difficult seasons with different teams. The 1973/74 season was one of his most trying.

"We couldn't get it together," Mahovlich says of the season, when his own production fell but he still was able to lead the team in points and finish second to Jacques Lemaire in scoring. "I think we had the team, but things just weren't clicking. It seemed our minds were somewhere else. Maybe there was too much worry about the WHA."

After the 1973/74 playoffs, the WHA was definitely on Mahovlich's mind as he looked to a new contract. Negotiating with the Canadiens was nothing like negotiating with Punch Imlach in his Leafs days. "Imlach never signed me until after training camp. He'd keep the pressure on me all the time, playing his stupid games. Who the hell needed it? But what could you do? It was a monopoly." He got along well with Pollock, but the monopoly was over and, having just completed his seventeenth NHL season, he sensed the opportunities for making serious money slipping away. "I was thirty-six years old. I thought, 'I haven't got much left. If I'm going to make money, it's now or never.'" He contacted Toronto Toros owner John F. Bassett, whose four-year contract offer beat, hands down, the two-year one with which Pollock responded. Pollock made no effort to match Bassett's proposal.

Having lost Mahovlich, who had contributed 189 points in the past two seasons, Pollock also had to recover from losing his first-round pick in the June entry draft to the WHA. Chosen fifth overall, right-winger Cam Connor of the Flin Flon Bombers signed instead with the Phoenix Roadrunners.

The losses of Mahovlich and Connor were Pollock's last significant ones to the WHA. Pollock held firm, not only in refusing to bid against WHA payrolls, but also against public and private challenges to get rid of Bowman. The coach might not have been popular with players, but Pollock had made it clear that Bowman had his backing. Bowman, for his part, retreated from some of his disciplinary zeal. He relaxed his enforcement of curfews; beer was openly consumed on buses and charter flights. Glen Sather, who played for Bowman in 1974/75, would recall crossing paths with Bowman on a ski hill at Lake Tahoe during a road trip. Sather was in gross violation of club rules on in-season recreational sports, but Bowman feigned not seeing him and never mentioned it.

Bowman and Pollock respected and supported each other, and were the subject of equally contrary perceptions. Some found their manner direct and uncomplicated. Others encountered ambiguity. "Sammy would say things, but they were questionable," says Frank Mahovlich. "It was the same thing with Bowman. He'd say things, but if he had to change his mind, he would. Nothing is in stone—that's what I found with what they'd have to say."

Both Bowman and Pollock provided each other with challenges. Bowman was going to annoy people; Pollock was going to refuse to consider pay raises, to the point of having valuable players like Mahovlich leave for the WHA and Dryden sit out a season. Other coaches might have railed against Pollock's bottom-line intransigence. Bowman accepted it, and worked with the players left to him.

In the end, both were proven right in their faith in one another. Though he had lost Connor, Pollock scored with his second pick in 1974, Doug Risebrough. The Risebrough selection was the most recent in a string of outstanding draft picks Pollock had engineered since Bowman's hiring as coach, beginning with the selection of Lafleur and Robinson in 1971. In 1972, the fourth pick overall, garnered from L.A., had brought in Steve Shutt; the sixth pick, which had belonged to California, had netted Dryden's backup, Michel "Bunny" Larocque; the fourteenth pick produced John Van Boxmeer.

In 1973, Pollock had executed a draft-day masterpiece as he landed what proved to be one of Bowman's most admired and valued players, Bob Gainey. Pollock had identified Gainey, of the Peterborough Petes, as his top pick, but knew that, as a defensive forward, Gainey wasn't likely to be chosen right away. Having secured the second pick overall from the California Seals, Pollock could afford to trade downwards in the draft. His former scout, Cliff Fletcher, now general manager in Atlanta, was eager to land Tom Lysiak, but with the fifth pick couldn't be guaranteed to get him. In agreeing to swap his second pick for Fletcher's fifth, Pollock also received Atlanta's first-round pick for 1974 in the process. The next team to come knocking was Bowman's old Blues, who wanted goaltender John Davidson, but with the eighth pick were in danger of losing him to the Bruins, who were choosing sixth. Pollock accepted the Blues' eighth pick for his fifth and also received another future first-round pick.

Pollock got Gainey as planned, eighth overall, and in 1974 used the picks acquired from St. Louis and Atlanta to select Doug Risebrough seventh overall and Rick Chartraw tenth overall. Another deal paid dividends that summer, as Pollock cashed in the first-round pick he'd received (after the 1972/73 Stanley Cup win) from L.A. in exchange for Randy Rota and Bob Murdoch. Choosing twelfth, Pollock secured Mario Tremblay.

Pollock was unable to sign Cam Connor, his first pick in 1974, but only a month after the turbulent 1973/74 season, a new Canadiens dynasty was taking shape. (And eventually Pollock would win the war against the WHA. Connor joined the Canadiens in 1978/79; Rejean Houle returned in 1976/77. And Dryden, who had spoken with the Toronto Toros during his articling year, chose not to follow his brother Dave, goaltender with the Buffalo Sabres, to the WHA. He returned to the Montreal net for 1974/75.) Risebrough, Tremblay and Chartraw all started in 1974/75. New scoring stars emerged in the roster. Guy Lafleur went from producing 56 points in 1973/74 to 119 points in 1974/75. His centre, Pete Mahovlich, younger brother of Frank, boosted his points production from 73 to 117 and became the power centre the team had lacked.

The Canadiens of the 1970s were operating like the Canadiens of the 1950s and 1960s. The club was built almost entirely from within, now with draft picks rather than with teenagers whose signatures were scribbled on C-forms. Of the twenty players who would win the

1975/76 Stanley Cup for Montreal, only one, Pete Mahovlich (acquired in a trade from Detroit in 1969) did not begin his NHL career in Montreal. With Henri Richard's retirement following the 1974/75 season, the final break with the Canadiens of the 1950s was made, and only four players were left—Jimmy Roberts, Yvan Cournoyer, Serge Savard and Jacques Lemaire—who had played under Toe Blake. Pete Mahovlich was the only other player with experience of the Original Six game. The rest, like Bowman himself, were Sam Pollock's hand-picked selections, and they combined to create what may prove to be the greatest dynasty in the history of the league.

10

✧ THE 1975/76 SEASON would mark the apex of Scotty Bowman's coaching career in Montreal. Not only did he guide the Canadiens to another Stanley Cup win, he slew two dragons for many devoted fans of the North American game. Rampaging on one flank were the Philadelphia Flyers and their orchestrated mayhem, while on the other flank, the stylish Europeans threatened. With the Flyers having won the last two Stanley Cups, fans of the sharp-shooting firewagon game yearned for a white knight to ride to the sport's rescue. At the same time, they wanted the firewagon game as played in North America to be proven no less skilled than the one practised overseas.

By downing the Flyers in the 1975/76 Cup finals, Bowman ended the reign of terror of the Broad Street Bullies, who had won the previous two Stanley Cups. Four months later, as coach of Team Canada, Bowman won the inaugural Canada Cup, mastering the best the Europeans could offer. His team lost only one game, a 1–0 shut-out by Czechoslovakia in the round-robin, before defeating the Czechs two straight in the finals. His Canadiens had already participated in the most memorable cross-cultural contest since game eight of the 1972 Canada-Russia series. The match between the Canadiens and the Soviet Union's Central Red Army club, played on December 31, 1975, ended in a 3–3 tie, with a victory for hockey at its most stylish.

That the job of taking on Philadelphia in the spring of 1976 fell to Bowman was somewhat ironic, for Bowman had inadvertently paved the way for the rise of the Flyers menace with his St. Louis team. He had built the Blues with Lynn Patrick according to Patrick's old Bruins blueprint for a physical team that could intimidate the opposition. The Bruins clubs of the 1950s were the direct forebears of the Flyers of the 1970s, with Bowman's Blues the intermediary party.

The Blues developed a reputation for tough play, and one of the teams they pushed around was the Flyers. The Blues had already eliminated the Flyers in two successive playoff campaigns when Vic Stasiuk arrived as Philadelphia's new coach for 1969/70. In his first game coaching the Flyers at the St. Louis Arena in November 1969, Stasiuk was tanned 8–0 by Bowman's bunch. "There's no doubt about it, they intimidate you in this rink," Stasiuk said afterward. "I had heard a lot about this place and now I believe it. The Blues have everyone in the place working for them—the organist, the policemen, the ushers and even the gatekeeper in the penalty box. He's the guy who turned the whole game around." Stasiuk charged that the gatekeeper didn't allow Wayne Hillman back on the ice from a penalty right away, permitting Red Berenson to tee up a thirty-footer that beat Bernie Parent. "It's all part of the scheme to get the visiting team intimidated so it won't play its regular game," Stasiuk charged, and he fingered Bob and Barclay Plager and Noel Picard as the worst offenders when it came to running opponents.

Bowman never promoted goonery, and it would be wrong to think the Flyers were merely emulating the Blues' style. But Flyers general manager Keith Allen would assert that the manhandling of the Flyers by the Blues in 1967/68 and 1968/69 left him fed up and in search of bigger, tougher players. At the inaugural universal amateur draft of 1969, which came after the Blues' commanding sweep of the Flyers in the quarterfinals, Allen loaded up on pugnacious players from the western Canadian Junior game: Bobby Clarke, Dave Schultz and Don Saleski. With further additions like Andre "Moose" Dupont (originally a Canadiens property) and Terry Crisp, who had played three seasons for Bowman in St. Louis, and the hiring of coach Fred Shero in 1971, the Flyers became a team that was as feared at home as St. Louis had been under Bowman.

The fact that the Canadiens, the standardbearers for speed and style, had failed to reach the finals twice since winning in 1972/73 had nothing to do with the Flyers. The team could not blame escalating violence for keeping them out of the running. The team's own fractiousness and lack of focus harmed it in 1973/74, when the Rangers downed them in six games in the quarterfinals, and in 1974/75, a young and talented Sabres team simply outplayed the Canadiens to win the semifinal series in six.

In their drive to win the 1972/73 Cup, Bowman's Canadiens had first been called upon to deal with the retooled Flyers in the quarterfinals, and had won that chippy series. In 1975/76, Bowman laid the groundwork for eventual Stanley Cup success by having his team hit and hurt the Flyers in their first encounter of the new season. Bowman's Canadiens were more than a pretty passing and shooting team. They had a defence with physical presence and speed. The Shero game plan—short passes with small battles along the boards that ensured any opponent wanting the puck would have to deal with two Flyers at a time—wasn't going to work against Montreal. The Canadiens were big and fast, and they hit right back. When the teams convened for the 1975/76 Cup finals, Bowman demonstrated his ability to control the play. This series was nothing like the shootout that had brought Bowman his first Stanley Cup, in 1972/73. The Flyers were too good a team, and Bernie Parent was too good a goaltender, to be overwhelmed, and three games were decided by one-goal margins. But all the margins were in Montreal's favour, and overtime was never required as the Flyers were swept in four games.

A profile in *The Hockey News* in February 1976 captured Bowman as he approached the showdown with the Flyers and the beginning of his greatest Montreal years. "I love coaching and I love the game," he said. "It is a continuing challenge, trying to get the most out of eighteen to twenty men and plotting strategy. I suppose it would be frustrating if you had inferior players and were outclassed by the competition. I felt that at times playing Montreal when my St. Louis team was just starting. But it is fascinating if you have top players and can compete with anyone.

"It is fascinating coaching the Montreal team. Everyone wants to get to the top in his profession and in this sport this is the peak. I don't know if we have the best talent but we have to be close. I know the best talent doesn't always make the best team. The team has to pull together to win. I really don't think there is a lot of difference in talent or in teams among five or six teams in the league the last few years and I don't think of the ones who don't win the Stanley Cup in a given year as losers.

"In some ways it is easier to coach in Montreal than in St. Louis. I expected to coach in St. Louis, not to manage also. I wanted it after a while because you want control of your team, but I found you get no rest and your ability to concentrate on coaching goes out the window. I was always negotiating contracts. I was always on the phone. I couldn't get away from the game. In Montreal I have a manager to do the difficult job of managing for me. I don't think anyone could do it better than Sam Pollock. I know some think he must be a tough boss, but he's really very fair. He consults with you, but he leaves you to run the club. Our rapport is excellent. He is the glue which holds this organization together. He takes the long look at things. He has built stability into the operation.

"The tradition that is supposed to make it tough to win here makes it easier. It inspires and motivates the players. They put out because no one will accept anything less in Montreal. And because there are good players pushing them from behind. I have not had any trouble with them. They do as they are asked to do. They think team. They understand you must sacrifice yourself for the team. They want to win, too."

Formal recognition of his ability did not come readily. In 1974 the

National Hockey League Broadcasters' Association had presented the NHL with the Jack Adams Award to honour the league's top coach, with the recipient chosen in balloting by NHLBA members. The first presentation went to Fred Shero, mastermind of Flyers mayhem. In 1975, the recipient was Bob Pulford, whose Kings rode the outstanding goaltending of Rogie Vachon (as Bowman did in the 1976 Canada Cup) to a franchise-high regular-season finish of second place in the Norris division.

Voting on the award consistently ran against coaches who actually produced Stanley Cup victories. In 1975/76, the award went to Don Cherry, a player's coach with a lunch-bucket squad that lost to the Flyers in the semifinals. Al Arbour won it once, but not when he was winning four successive Cups with the Islanders. Glen Sather had won two Stanley Cups with the Oilers before he received the award in 1985/86, when Edmonton came up short in the playoffs. The award has tended to honour coaches who do a lot with a little, not coaches who do a lot with a lot. In Bowman's case especially, the voters seemed to have a hard time assessing the talent of a coach who had such an overwhelming amount of playing skill at his disposal. In 1975/76, Ken Dryden won the Vezina Trophy, and Guy Lafleur earned the Art Ross Trophy as leading scorer, as well as the Lester B. Pearson Award as the league's most valuable player, based on players' association voting. Dryden and Lafleur also made the first All Star team, with Guy Lapointe making the second team. Bowman's bench contained eight future members of the Hockey Hall of Fame: Dryden, Lafleur, Lapointe, Steve Shutt, Yvan Cournoyer, Serge Savard, Larry Robinson and Bob Gainey—as well as Bowman himself, who would be inducted in the Builders category in 1991. In comparison, the Philadelphia Flyers, winners of the 1973/74 and 1974/75 Stanley Cups, had three future Hall-of-Famers: Bill Barber, Bobby Clarke and Bernie Parent. The Bruins, winners in 1969/70 and 1971/72, had four: John Bucyk, Gerry Cheevers, Bobby Orr and Phil Esposito. Of those, only Bucyk and Orr were with the team when Cherry won the Adams in 1975/76.

In 1976/77, the Canadiens recorded one of the greatest seasons in franchise history. Montreal became the first team to win sixty games, losing only eight. The sixtieth win came in the last minute of the last game of the season, with two quick goals downing the Washington Capitals. Four Canadiens made the first All Star team that season—Dryden, Robinson, Lafleur and Shutt—with Lapointe returning to the second team. The Canadiens cornered the market on individual awards, as Lafleur single-handedly rounded up four: the Hart, Pearson, Art Ross and Conn Smythe. Robinson took the Norris, and the Vezina went to Dryden and his backup, Bunny Larocque. And the Adams at last went to Bowman, as he outpolled the Capitals' Tom McVie.

Bowman's professional recognition was fleeting. The 1976/77 Adams was the only one he would receive while in Montreal. In 1977/78, when he won his third consecutive Cup, Detroit's Bobby Kromm, who got the Red Wings as far as the quarterfinals after they had missed the playoffs in seven straight seasons, won it, with Don Cherry, whose Bruins lost to Bowman's Canadiens in the finals, voted runner-up. In 1978/79, Bowman's St. Louis protege, Al Arbour, topped the voting. Arbour's Islanders lost in the semifinals to Fred Shero's Rangers, and Shero, in being voted the Adams runner-up, became the second coach in a row to lose to Bowman in the finals and outpoll him in Adams voting.

Even within his own team, Bowman's genius was not always recognized or appreciated. He cultivated the aloofness of Blake (a quality Pollock had also cultivated in his coaching days), almost challenging players to dislike him. In March 1972, at the end of his first season with the Canadiens, Bowman nearly died in a St. Louis hotel fire while on a road trip. Several players commandeered a ladder from the volunteer fire department and got Bowman out of his room. "He was in bad shape," Denis DeJordy says, "and when he finally breathed fresh air, the first thing he did was count all the players for curfew."

Yet Bowman interpreted the ordeal by fire as a team-building exercise. "I'll tell you something. It sometimes takes an incident like that fire to really knit a bunch of guys together as a unit. We're shaping up nicely for the playoffs, but that togetherness is the little extra which can get you through the tight spots."

"Togetherness"—at least, between player and coach—would not be a factor in the success of the Canadiens under Bowman. "If this had happened when I was running the club, those guys would have been pouring coal oil on the fire," Toe Blake quipped when he heard about the fire. But Blake, despite his authoritarian distance, had a concern for players he would show in private meetings, and the admiration he commanded was deeply felt. Bowman never seemed to develop a close relationship with his charges. His appreciation and respect for stars and grinders alike was genuine, but he strove not to show it. Many players resented Bowman's methods, but they did not resent collecting the salaries, bonuses and fame that went along with winning Stanley Cups.

"Scotty would always put people on notice, " says Al MacNeil. "He has always been able to handle great players because he understands them and presses the right keys on them. He has always challenged them. They would intensely dislike him at times, and then almost become fond of the guy, when they saw where he was going with them."

In February 1985, Guy Lafleur was honoured with a ceremony at the Forum; his number was retired as he played his last season with the Canadiens. Bowman attended the ceremony, and Lafleur called him the best coach he ever had. "He was so sharp behind the bench that I never saw anyone out-coach him. I had some tough times with him, but I couldn't ever say that I hated him. I love him more than I could hate him."

"He's been extremely successful," says Rogie Vachon, who after getting his trade to Los Angeles in 1971 became a star of the 1976 Canada Cup, starting every game for Bowman's Canadian team. "A lot of players who played for Scotty would say, 'I hate this guy, I would never play for this guy again.' Then you'd say, 'Well, how many Stanley Cup rings do you have?' 'Oh, three...' And they were pretty happy with that."

Perspective on Bowman's methods and manner was clouded by the fact that, for the vast majority of players on the great Canadiens teams of the late 1970s, Bowman was the only NHL coach they'd ever had—and in some cases, ever would have. Bowman may have seemed to some of them a tyrant, and certainly he could be difficult, but there was no measuring stick for most of the players to judge him against, beyond their experience in Junior hockey.

For a few players—those who had played in the Original Six era and came to Bowman in St. Louis late in their careers—there was little to Bowman they hadn't seen before. And some of the Canadiens had personal experience of Toe Blake. Bowman, as a protege of Blake, probably the greatest coach in the history of the game, was bound to suffer by comparison. Few proteges match their mentors in ability, and comparison invariably serves to exaggerate the mentor's strengths and the protege's weaknesses. Just as Bowman suffered in direct measure against Blake, Mike Keenan would be found wanting in comparison to Bowman.

Bowman was, to be sure, a manipulator. He worked a player's anxieties and insecurities to his advantage. He courted the press (when feuding with a player or negotiating a contract) and used it assiduously. Bowman made all sorts of people angry when he wanted them that way. Occasionally he crossed a line, and the players themselves would chastise him. Early in his Canadiens career, he tried to punish the team for a poor performance with an 8:30 a.m. practice, a trick from his Junior days. Cournoyer objected to the exercise, telling Bowman it did needless harm, and he didn't do it again. At one practice, from which Serge Savard was absent, Bowman railed at players about the defenceman's off-ice behaviour. Captain Henri Richard, a veteran of Toe Blake's one-on-one style, told Bowman that if he had an issue with Savard he should speak with him privately.

"The team succeeded partly because it felt it could succeed without him," says Jimmy Roberts. "It made them want to win games he said they had no right winning. The small slights added up."

He was less a master of managing player egos than he is often given credit for, and it would fall to Pollock to deal with the collateral damage of Bowman's experiments in motivational psychology. Pollock had built the great Canadiens club of the 1970s like a Swiss watchmaker, and he was loath to start discarding or replacing pieces just because Bowman had decided he couldn't work with them. A rare disciplinary trade came on November 29, 1977, when Pete Mahovlich was shipped to Pittsburgh with Peter Lee for Pierre Larouche and Peter Marsh. A running battle had broken into the open in February 1977 after Mahovlich was moved from his once-productive line with Lafleur and Shutt to a new assignment centring Cournoyer and Yvon Lambert. Having contributed 105 points in 1975/76, Mahovlich was on his way to only 62 points in 1976/77 as his ice time underwent a corresponding halving. Mahovlich crossed a line with Bowman by complaining about his lot in the press.

"I don't think he will play next year," Bowman responded icily. "That's not how this team operates. We'll either sign him or trade him. You're far better off to trade a guy than wait for compensation. That way, the matter is in somebody else's hands." Bowman said Mahovlich had chosen the wrong time to complain. "This is the kind of thing that you usually get in the off season. Certainly not at this time of the year. . . . My job is to win hockey games. We've lost seven games all year. He says he's not playing enough, but we've got three centres, Jacques Lemaire, Doug Risebrough and Doug Jarvis, all playing well most of the time. His record is the poorest of any forward on the team. Nobody on the team has been on the ice for more goals against than he has. You couldn't say that he has been having a good year."

The following November, the promised trade was made. Mahovlich was a rarity among Canadiens regulars in not participating in all four consecutive Cup wins. Yvan Cournoyer, Serge Savard, Jacques Lemaire, Guy Lapointe, Ken Dryden, Guy Lafleur, Larry Robinson, Steve Shutt, Yvon Lambert, Bob Gainey, Bunny Larocque, Doug Risebrough, Mario Tremblay, Rick Chartraw and Doug Jarvis all saw the streak through, with Rejean Houle participating in the final three after returning from the WHA.

But the stability in the lineup belied a fractiousness within the organization. The dynasty was coming apart even as it seemed to be promising an almost unlimited run of greatness.

The course of events that led to the end of Scotty Bowman's career in Montreal began before he had even won the third in the Cup streak of the late 1970s. Some might say that the end began long before that, before he had won his first Cup as the Canadiens' coach, when Bowman and his wife Suella learned the heartbreaking truth about the health of their third child, David.

To understand Bowman, people tell you, you must understand the tragic circumstances of that child.

On December 22, 1972, *The Toronto Sun* ran a photograph of Scotty Bowman with his three-year-old son Stanley, two-year-old daughter Alicia and six-month-old son David at the Canadiens' Christmas party at the Forum.

Sporting a Canadiens jersey over his winter clothes, David's eyes are closed, and the boy rests peacefully. The caption writer composed the sort of whimsical description that children invite. "Six-month-old David Bowman wasn't very interested in what was happening at the Forum yesterday. His sister, two-year-old Alicia, didn't have any luck trying to wake him up."

But David was no ordinary child, slumbering through a public outing. It was just about this time that the Bowmans were learning that David was hydrocephalic, a condition that left him blind and severely mentally disabled. Not even Suella's professional skills as a trauma unit nurse could avoid their having to institutionalize the boy.

"It is painful, but it is something that has to be borne," he would tell *The Hockey News* in February 1976. "My wife is a nurse and she has a lot of guts. She has helped me to be strong.... There is no hope, but he is comfortable. We visit him the first Sunday of every month. I try to make up any visits I miss in season. The other children are fine. The family means more to me than anything else."

Bowman is indeed a deeply devoted family man. His very humane qualities as a husband and father often made him attractive to those who found his coaching persona unbearable. It was the side of him that fans, opponents and many players never saw—precisely because Bowman strove to erect a firewall between his professional and private lives. The Bowmans would raise five children in all; like Toe Blake, Bowman bought a farm outside Montreal as a family retreat.

With David requiring institutional care for the rest of his life, with his other children bound for university, Bowman's quest for personal security in the unpredictable world of professional coaching was hardly surprising. When he first came into the game, one-year contracts for players and coaches were the standard. Not even the great Toe Blake ever had more than one year guaranteed to him on paper at any time. While Blake understood that he had lifetime employment with the Canadiens, the Canadiens had never suggested to Blake a job in management. Bowman began to worry that if he stayed too long in coaching, the door to the executive suites would be closed to him too. Job security and steady wages went hand-in-hand with the general manager's job. He had held it once, in St. Louis, and he began to covet it in Montreal. Far from wanting Sam Pollock out of the way, he only desired that, if and when Pollock chose to retire, he would be next in line. Later, when his Montreal years were behind him, he would assert that he never actually wanted Pollock's job at all. "A lot of people think I left Montreal because I didn't get Sam's job," he would tell sportswriter Al Strachan, who came closer than anyone to being Bowman's journalistic confidant. "I didn't want his job. If I could have written my own ticket in Montreal, it would have been to keep everything the way it was. Me as coach, him as manager."

At the very least, though, Bowman wanted the security of a multi-year contract. As the 1977/78 playoffs were unfolding, he was surrounded by Canadiens who were beginning to enjoy more secure pacts; Bob Gainey was getting a contract for three years.

Montreal opened its 1977/78 Cup drive with a 4–1 series defeat of the Red Wings in the quarterfinals, which concluded with a 4–2 win at the Forum on April 25. After guiding the Canadiens to their second consecutive Cup win the previous spring, Bowman had become a hot commodity and a hot rumour. Former Canadien John Ferguson was the general manager in New York, and Bowman had been touted as a possible candidate for the Rangers' coach after the 1976/77 season—perhaps he would even replace Ferguson. Ferguson had hired that long-standing figure in Bowman's career, Jean-Guy Talbot, to serve as coach in 1977/78. But when the Rangers lost in the 1977/78 preliminary round to Buffalo, both Ferguson and Talbot were vulnerable. There was talk that Bowman might return to St. Louis, at least as coach. Emile Francis had settled in there as general manager after leaving the Rangers and was working to revive the bankrupt operation Ralston-Purina had acquired from the Salomons in 1977. Vancouver had also been thought to be open to him, but in 1977/78 the Canucks ended up replacing general manager Phil Maloney with Jake Milford. After failing to make the playoffs, however, Orland Kurtenbach's job as coach was up for grabs.

Following the Red Wings series, Bowman told a *Globe and Mail* reporter that the rumours of him moving to another team were "pure fiction," but he did allow that he was willing to "consider alternatives."

He told the newspaper that he had made a contract proposal to Pollock at the end of the season. "I was hoping to get this sorted out prior to the playoffs. But now management says it will be the end of May before anything is decided. In my seven years here, I have been operating on one-year contracts. I have proposed something long-term, five or six years. I have no idea what the reaction will be. I went to Sam some time ago, asking what was in store for the organization over the next five years. He could not tell me then. It seems there's a lot of intrigue going on."

Bowman's hunch was correct. Although he couldn't know it, and no one could tell him, the Canadiens franchise was up for sale.

Bowman told *The Globe and Mail* that he was looking for a deal that would involve coaching, management, or both. Pollock, he said, had suggested to him that he might be completely removed from running the Canadiens within three years. Bowman didn't want to sign a contract with the Canadiens unless he was guaranteed the opportunity to take over as general manager from Pollock.

Bowman was now forty-four, and he didn't want to find himself coaching after he turned fifty. Seeking a long-term contract, he wanted to know what the Canadiens had in mind for him. "If Sam leaves and someone else is brought in as a replacement, I wouldn't stay," he said. "The Canadiens may think I'm not qualified in a management capacity. Maybe Sam is slow on getting to me with the Canadiens' plans for the next five or six years. Maybe he only sees himself involved for, say, three years and can't commit himself to anything beyond that point. A month from now I'll know if I have to move."

At the time, Bowman was drawing a base pay of about $80,000, plus bonuses. He told *The Globe and Mail* he was optimistic that the contract could be settled with Montreal and he wouldn't have to go anywhere else. "I'll know what the Canadiens think of me when I see their final offer."

Toronto was moved aside in four straight games in the Cup semifinals. The finals brought a rematch with Don Cherry's Boston Bruins. After a straightforward 4–1 win at home, Montreal was given a battle over the next three games. The Canadiens went up 2–0 with an overtime win, then lost 4–0 at Boston Garden. With an overtime win at home, the Bruins tied the series at two apiece. The Canadiens then got down to business and finished off the Bruins with back-to-back 4–1 wins.

The third consecutive Cup win had come on May 25, at Boston

Garden. Naturally, the lead issue for many reporters was Bowman's future. Asked if he would be coming back as Montreal's coach, Bowman begged off answering. "Let me savour the victory. There's nothing to talk about really because it's out of my hands. This could be my last game behind the Montreal Canadiens' bench and my last game as a coach."

Where might he be headed? Bowman wasn't saying. *The Toronto Star* reported that Bowman would be meeting with Pollock over the next few days. "Sam said that I should wait until May and the time has come," Bowman told the *Star*. "My contract ended when that game finished and in the next few days we're going to talk over my future. Coaching has become a high-profile, demanding job and I think coaches have the same right as players to ask for long-term contracts and a good salary."

Bowman's window of opportunity for hardball negotiating was closing, and he admitted this. If he wasn't going to remain in Montreal, he had to go somewhere else, and the short list of potential employers was getting shorter. If he was going to make the jump to a general managership, he would have to do it quickly, as teams didn't like to go into the league annual meeting and draft in mid-June without the chief hockey job filled. In the middle of his semifinal series against the Bruins, Philadelphia coach Fred Shero had arrived at a new deal that made him coach and general manager of the Rangers. Vancouver, which had missed the playoffs, had just hired as its new coach Harry Neale, who had been coaching Hartford in the WHA.

The negotiations between Bowman and Pollock stretched into June. "I'd like to get it out of the way," Bowman admitted at the beginning of the month. "I like the ownership and management in Montreal. I'm happy where I'm working. They are good people to work with. It's always easier to work with people you know."

When the deal was done, Bowman did not have the five- or six-year package with a guaranteed promotion to the general managership. Instead, he had a two-year coaching contract, a verbal understanding from Pollock that he was capable of succeeding him, and a rider that would extend the contract to four years if the club changed hands.

Despite the inclusion of the rider, Bowman appeared to be walking blindfolded into the biggest crisis of his professional career. The rider would give Bowman job security in the event of the arrival of new owners, but it failed to address the question of whether Bowman would actually still want the job. If the Canadiens were sold, what would happen to Pollock? If Pollock did not go along with the sale, Bowman would be orphaned, very possibly left working for a new boss rather than becoming that boss.

The contract negotiation that was meant to give Scotty Bowman security and a future with the Canadiens organization ended up serving as a prelude to the end of his career in Montreal. Bowman's departure would not be precipitated by his relationship with players, the media or his superiors, or even a sudden inability to deliver winning performances. Rather, it would come about because of changing priorities in one of Canada's great financial empires, the tangle of cross-ownerships and subsidiaries overseen by the brothers Edward and Peter Bronfman.

The Montreal Canadiens had become part of the Bronfman portfolio on the last day of 1971, in Scotty Bowman's first season as coach of the team. The brothers Peter, David and Bill Molson had decided to cash in the market value of the team before a new capital gains tax went into effect on New Year's Day, 1972. On December 31, their majority interest in Canadian Arena Company, which owned the Canadiens and the Montreal Forum, was sold to Edper Investments, a consortium comprised of Edgar and Peter Bronfman, the Bank of Nova Scotia (later Scotiabank) and Baton Broadcasting (which participated for one year, until owner John F. Bassett decided to buy a WHA franchise). The Canadian Arena Company was subsequently turned into Carena Bancorp as the operation became entwined in the Bronfmans' Trizec real estate venture.

The sale to the Bronfman group resulted in a new president for the club, Jacques Courtois, and for the Forum, Irving Grundman, but the team carried on essentially untouched. The key vice-presidents—Toe Blake, Ken Reardon and the newly retired Jean Beliveau—remained in place, as did Sam Pollock and Scotty Bowman. The group rewarded the Bronfmans' utter lack of meddling by winning a slew of Stanley Cups.

After Montreal won its third Cup in a row in the spring of 1978 and the fourth since the ownership change—and just as Scotty Bowman was deciding he needed more job security and a promotion to go with it—the Bronfmans opted to cash in their investment. By then Carena held 52 percent of Trizec and about 20 percent of a company called IAC, which became the Continental Bank of Canada and was subsequently sold to Hongkong Bank. To offload the investment in the Canadiens (while holding on to the Forum), the Bronfmans appointed Sam Pollock as the point man in the search for the right owner. Pollock had become an investor in Edper—his holdings were worth about $1 million in 1978—and he would be acting in his own best interests in selling the team. But in selling the Canadiens, he would lose his job as general manager, for he was the only executive who would not be going along with the sale. "I really didn't have a choice," he says. Pollock was, and would have to remain, an Edper man. After spending more than thirty years in the Canadiens organization, Sam Pollock was about to cut all direct ties with the game. In 1979, Pollock was named chairman and president of Carena Bancorp and a director of Trizec and Brascan.

The cross-promotional potential of television rights made a brewer the most obvious candidate. At the time, Canada's three main brewers were Molson Breweries of Canada Ltd. (no longer connected in any way with the Molson family), John Labatt Ltd. and Carling-O'Keefe Breweries Ltd. The smallest of the three, Carling-O'Keefe, had already become the majority investor in the Quebec Nordiques of the WHA in 1976 and was not interested in bidding for the Canadiens, according to Pollock. Labatt was definitely interested—the company, based in London, Ontario, had become the majority owner of the

Toronto Blue Jays when the American League baseball franchise was awarded in 1976.

The ownership search proceeded quietly through the summer, with serious negotiations taking place in August and an actual deal concluded at the beginning of September. The new owner of the Canadiens was Molson. One of the reasons Molson got the deal, says Pollock, is that it was, at the time, a Montreal-based company. Ironically, one year later, the Bronfmans would take over Brascan, which was the largest shareholder in Labatt, and would thus wind up controlling the company to whom they had decided not to sell the Canadiens. Pollock would become the chairman of Labatt in 1981, and after Labatt was sold to Interbrew of Belgium in 1995, Sad Sam would begin a new career, at age seventy-one, as the chairman of the Blue Jays and Toronto Argonauts in 1997.

The entire senior management of the Canadiens stayed in place with the 1978 sale—except, of course, for Sam Pollock, who on September 6 officially retired. He was given a seat on the board of directors and an alternate governorship in the NHL. In replacing him, Molson's created a new post, managing director, and hired Irving Grundman, the Forum's president, to fill it. Grundman, while retaining his duties at the Forum, would run the club with input from a management committee comprised of new player personnel director Al MacNeil, player development director Claude Ruel and assistant general manager Floyd "Busher" Curry.

Scotty Bowman's reaction was as close to panic as possible. It wasn't just that Grundman had the management job he thought would be his; Bowman also couldn't help but notice the forest of managers blocking the path of his upward mobility.

According to Jean Beliveau, Bowman was never a candidate to replace Pollock—and he claims that Pollock himself agreed to this. In his memoirs, Beliveau wrote that Bowman's behaviour away from the bench disqualified him: "Whenever Scotty took issue with a player for any reason at all, he'd run upstairs to Sam's office and demand an instant trade. Bringing all his experience and knowledge to bear, Sam would calm him down. . . . Sometimes Scotty would barge in while I was meeting with Sam, whereupon I'd personally witness these unfortunate harangues. I made my mind up that if this guy was ever in the running for general manager, or for any position within the organization in which he'd have the final say on personnel matters, the Canadiens were going to be in trouble. . . . [V]irtually any player who had a bad game would be enough to send him scampering to the Second Floor. He wouldn't be general manager if I had a vote. With Scotty at the helm, it seemed likely that our team would change dramatically from year to year, if not from hour to hour."

Beliveau attributed Bowman's front-runner status as the successor to Pollock as the product of a Bowman media campaign: "Like any good general manager, Sam Pollock had refrained from tipping his hand, but I'm pretty sure he had made up his mind on Scotty's aspirations long before. . . . Sam and I both agreed that [Irving Grundman] should get the job, and Morgan McCammon, as president, made it unanimous."

Pollock continues to maintain, however, that Bowman was a candidate for the general manager's job. "In my mind, I thought that would happen, in the course of time, whether that would be in one year, or two. I thought that was the logical thing that could happen." While the wheels were in motion to find a new owner when Pollock signed Bowman to a new contract, he could say nothing to him about it. "We had no idea we were going to sell the team," Pollock emphasizes, noting that the real negotiating didn't begin until later in the summer. When Bowman was re-signed, there was no guarantee that the club would actually change hands. But Bowman, unfortunately, had committed himself to two more seasons working for a general manager he thought would continue to be Sam Pollock, having no idea that Pollock might not even be around for the start of the very next season.

While Bowman was blindsided by the sale, Al MacNeil had been obliquely primed by Pollock to prepare for a major change, and to position himself accordingly. After the 1976/77 season, when his Voyageurs won their second consecutive Calder Cup, MacNeil had drawn a new assignment from Pollock. The Canadiens held the rights to about forty WHA players, and with the rival league showing signs of decline, Pollock called on MacNeil to spend the season scouting every one of them, to determine their worth. Pollock had wanted MacNeil to relocate to Montreal, but when MacNeil balked, he allowed him to work out of his Halifax base. After the 1977/78 season, however, Pollock was adamant that he get himself to Montreal. "He said, 'You have to come up now,' MacNeil recalls. 'It looks like things are going to come to a head. I can't say exactly what it's going to be, but you're going to have to be in Montreal, because things may change here.'"

Asked if he recalls ever agreeing with Beliveau that Bowman should not be general manager, Pollock says, "I don't recall that. In fact, Irv Grundman was not the next general manager. He was the managing director of the team. The general manager's appointment happened a year after that. You must remember, when I left, the season was just starting, so mainly I think they were going through that year and then going to appoint a general manager." In Pollock's version, Grundman was an interim appointment that did not rule out Bowman eventually becoming general manager.

Bowman and Pollock had been around each other for decades, and their relationship was one of the most complex, intriguing and, ultimately, inscrutable in professional sport. "I don't know what went on between Sammy and Scotty," says Jimmy Roberts, who left the Canadiens after the 1976/77 season on good terms and went to work for Bowman in Buffalo in 1979/80. "I think there was always some turmoil between those two. Sammy being the type of operator that Scotty learned from and turned into, he manipulated Scotty, prodded him to get the team to win, probably through the whole process told Scotty what he wanted to hear when he had to, but really didn't know if he was the right guy to take over his job when all was said and done. In his coaching, Scotty is all over the park. One day he's one type of Scotty Bowman and another day he's another type of Scotty Bowman. I don't know whether that fit in to the brewery's thinking of the kind of general manager they wanted representing the team. Certainly there was a lot of controversy in the team every day, which always managed to bring a winner home, but I don't know if that's what the upper bracket of the Montreal Canadiens was looking for in a general manager."

"I would never have signed on for two years as coach if I knew Sam was leaving," Bowman immediately informed the press when he learned of the sale and Pollock's departure. "I have worked with Sam so many years. We were a real team together. I have my own future to think about, and I don't want to spend the rest of my life standing behind the bench."

Bowman pondered aloud the possibility of tearing up his new contract. "I know I'm bound to the contract I signed at the end of last season," he told *The Globe and Mail*, "but I'm now wondering if I can't review it on a technicality. I'm disappointed and I certainly would not have signed the new contract if I knew of this change beforehand.... I certainly don't have much enthusiasm at this point. When I signed the contract Sam was my boss and now he's not. I signed my contract believing Sam to be my boss during the duration of the contract. I had other irons in the fire at the time I signed it and I could have gone elsewhere. I stayed on because of the present format with Sam as general manager."

Bowman said that he had been aware Pollock was withdrawing from day-to-day hockey work with the Canadiens, but he had no idea he would be actually leaving. "Maybe I wasn't sharp enough when I negotiated the new contract.... I'm just basically disappointed that I've coached in the NHL for eleven years and managed in four of those years and no one has communicated with me on the matter. Maybe, my success as a coach might have hurt me as a general manager."

A week after the stunning news of Pollock's retirement and the club's sale, Bowman was putting on a cheery face. He had met three times with Grundman, and also Courtois, and now pronounced the crisis over. "All the points of contention are solved, and I'm now able to say I will continue as coach next season. We worked hard to find grounds for agreement. I explained to them where I wasn't satisfied before and they told me their point of view. I'm happy to say everything is in order."

But everything wasn't in order. While the Canadiens still had their coach, the sale, Pollock's departure and Bowman's own thwarted career ambitions brought changes to the club. The change in ownership provoked more aggressive contract demands from some players. Bowman appeared to sleepwalk through the season, his ambitions searching out a fresh opportunity. In past seasons, the Canadiens had kept themselves sharp by setting team goals for the regular season, aspiring to the sixty-victory plateau. The team had just missed, with fifty-nine, in 1977/78. In 1978/79, the Canadiens didn't come close, though winning a still-impressive fifty-two.

MacNeil agrees with Pollock that the door had not been slammed on Bowman ever becoming general manager. Grundman was less a successor to Pollock than a spokesman to the ownership for a five-man hockey operations group, whose actual composition, MacNeil says, was Grundman, himself, Bowman, Claude Ruel and Ron Caron. "It was going to be run on consensus," MacNeil says. "The five of us were going to work together. That was fine with me. Looking at it from the French and English point of view, I wasn't going to be picked as the general manager or president of the Montreal Canadiens, because of the language problem a few years earlier. That was just going to open up old wounds. I was content to do what I was going to be doing, but Scotty felt slighted."

Bowman's media campaigns would make him sound like the sole logical successor to Pollock, but there were others within the organization who merited serious consideration. While MacNeil had disqualified himself on language grounds, his relationship with Pollock was almost as historic as Bowman's, and he would go on in his career to become director of hockey operations with the Calgary Flames. And Ron Caron, an easily overlooked cog in the Canadiens machine, showed even greater potential. Caron was officially director of amateur scouting for the Canadiens in the 1970s, but in fact he was far more than that. He was management's idea guy, an effervescent "what-iffer" who bombarded Pollock with visions of potential deals. "He would have about fifty new ideas every day to throw at Sam," says MacNeil, "and Sam would cull the good from the bad and act on them. I think we 'made' 2,200 deals and acted on about five of them. We were always ahead of the opposition, reviewing what was possible. When we did go to make a deal, it was made." In 1983/84, Caron became general manager of the St. Louis Blues, and he was promoted to executive vice-president in 1994/95.

In the 1978/79 playoffs, the Leafs proved pesky under coach Roger Neilson, and Montreal required two overtime wins to move them aside in four. This brought on the third consecutive playoff meeting between the Canadiens and the Bruins, this time in the semifinals. Like Montreal, Boston had experienced a small letdown after the 1977/78 season. Though still the best team in the Adams division, the Bruins had won eight fewer games and scored seventeen fewer goals while allowing fifty-two more than in 1977/78. Montreal jumped to a 2–0 series lead in the opening games at the Forum, then saw Boston recover with two wins of its own at home, including an overtime win in game four. Back in Montreal, the Canadiens collected an easy 5–1 win to put the Bruins one game away from elimination, but Don Cherry's team again rebounded, winning 5–2 in Boston to force a deciding seventh game back in Montreal.

With less than two minutes to play, the game appeared decided. Boston was winning 4–3. The most famous incident of Don Cherry's coaching career then unfolded. Guy Lafleur was on the ice, looking for the tying goal, and Bowman gave him a double shift. Bruins left-winger Don Marcotte had stayed with him in his assigned checking role through the missed line change. When Lafleur went off, so did Marcotte.

"I believe when you get down to the short series of a playoff or the last game for the Stanley Cup, breaks are going to play a big part and you have to be lucky to win," Bowman had told *The Hockey News* in 1976. "If you are the best you should win, but from one season to the next intangibles will enter into it and you will not always win. An injury here, a lucky shot there." In the dying moments of game seven, Scotty Bowman got deliriously lucky.

The Bruins' bench allowed a costly error to unfold. When Lafleur came off, the left-winger on the Bruins' line that normally followed Marcotte's shift jumped over the boards. But so did the left-winger on the subsequent shift. Bowman's penchant for the unpredictable, as much as luck, turned the game in his favour. The double shift he had assigned Lafleur had thrown Boston's shift assignments into disarray. For nearly a full minute, six Boston skaters covered five Canadiens before the referee noticed and assessed a minor bench penalty for too many men on the ice.

Sam Pollock had impressed upon Bowman during their Junior days together the importance of going with his top players when victory hung in the balance, even if it meant punishing amounts of ice time. In this game, he had been relying overwhelmingly on just three defencemen, Robinson, Lapointe and Savard, and having drawn the Bruins' penalty with his double shift, Lafleur was back on the ice for the powerplay. He scored to tie the game at 18:46, forcing overtime. At 9:48 of the extra period, Yvon Lambert scored and the Canadiens were in another Cup final. Almost giddy with the miracle of their last-minute reversal of fortune, the Canadiens greeted the New York Rangers three nights later at the Forum to begin their fourth consecutive Stanley Cup final.

Fred Shero was the new Rangers coach; he had left behind him the Broad Street Bullies of Philadelphia to prove his worth as a strategist and not just an orchestrator of mayhem. Defensively, the Rangers were no match for Bowman's Canadiens, having surrendered 292 goals to Montreal's league-leading 204. Shero brought to the Forum an aggressive forechecking game and caught Bowman off guard, scoring a 4–1 win in the opening contest. Unperturbed, Bowman adjusted his game, catching the Rangers' forecheckers up ice and out of position as the Canadiens broke out. Shero never altered his strategy, and the Canadiens rolled up four straight wins. The decisive match, a 4–1 victory at the Forum, was pronounced by Bowman a perfect game.

The Canadiens' 1978/79 Stanley Cup victory was the first for Montreal on home ice since 1967/68, when Bowman's Blues had lost 3–2 in game four. Bowman left himself with little time to savour the win. Seated in a corner of the Canadiens' dressing room as the celebrations unfolded, Bowman produced a piece of paper and addressed a group of reporters with his first pronouncement on the Future of Scotty Bowman.

"I figured it out," he told them. "I've coached 435 games in the last four years—104, 114, 107 and 110 this year. It's just too much. I'm not complaining because we're winning but it's not good for my family and I'm looking for something else. The management here has been good to me, but I don't know if I'll be back behind the bench again. I don't know if I want to coach again. I don't know what the alternatives are, but maybe I'll get out of this type of hockey."

The post-season Bowman employment derby was off and running. Under his contract, Bowman had three weeks in which to explore offers from other would-be employers. After that, he was obligated to commit to coaching the Canadiens. Bowman floated the idea of leaving the NHL altogether. "Before long, I'll have done just about everything I wanted to do as an NHL coach and at that point, I'll seriously consider a U.S. college job," he told *The Toronto Star* on May 26. "When my kids get a bit older, I won't want to travel as much as I do now. They'll need me and I'll want to be with them. Summers with my family won't be enough.... Coaching college hockey would provide a challenge and at the same time, offer me the kind of lifestyle I'll be looking for."

Bowman had apparently explored the idea of going to Notre Dame or Michigan State, but the college route was soon ruled out. Within about a week of winning the Stanley Cup, Bowman's agent, Jerry Petrie, was dealing with offers from four different NHL clubs. The Buffalo Sabres, Toronto Maple Leafs and Washington Capitals were all prepared to offer him the general manager's job. What the Canadiens were prepared to offer him remained to be thrashed out.

The front-runner, should Bowman choose to leave Montreal, was thought to be Toronto. "I am very interested in the prospects of coming to Toronto, but only as general manager," Bowman told *The Globe and Mail* in remarks published May 31. "If I decide to continue coaching it will be back in Montreal."

During the first week of June, Bowman was holidaying in Florida, and so was Maple Leafs owner Harold Ballard. The two met three times; Bowman told *The Toronto Star* that he came away "feeling very impressed." Back in Toronto on June 8, United Press Canada sports editor David Tucker appeared to have the scoop on Bowman's future when Ballard confided to him that, based on Petrie's assurances, he was "80 percent sure" Bowman was going to accept his offer. Ballard would make him head of hockey operations, Toronto's alternate governor with the NHL, and offer him a salary package of $140,000 to $150,000. It was a big step up in prestige and earning power, as Bowman was making about $100,000 in Montreal. Ballard had already tried, and failed, to hire Don Cherry, who had taken the coaching job in Colorado, and he allowed that if Bowman didn't accept, "It's not the end of the world, but it's pretty close to tipping it over the brink."

While Bowman pondered his options, the Canadiens were hit by two important losses. Jacques Lemaire announced his retirement, and his plans to go to Switzerland to play and coach. Lemaire was a forty-goal man with a knack for scoring playoff winners, and he would be missed. But from a management perspective, the most disturbing news was Al MacNeil's decision to leave the Canadiens. Cliff Fletcher had offered him the chance to return to coaching with the Atlanta Flames, and he'd accepted, weighing the opportunity against the turmoil in which Bowman's job hunting had left the Canadiens. "After the Cup," MacNeil sums up, "there was a lot of stuff in Montreal that didn't feel very good." He took the organization's instability as a sign that it was time to seek out new opportunities.

The loss of MacNeil, however debilitating to the Canadiens, gave the team some additional room in which to manoeuvre in negotiating with Bowman. This Irv Grundman did, proposing a new contract with escalating responsibilities. In year one, 1979/80, Bowman would continue to serve as coach; in year two, 1980/81, he would receive the additional responsibility of director of player personnel; and in year three, 1981/82, he would attain the general manager's job. The Canadiens seemed to think Bowman was amenable to the idea, but a few days later he broke the news: he was going to Buffalo.

The Sabres, who had been considered also-rans along with Washington (and St. Louis, who had also shown some interest), had come through with the clinching offer: a five-year contract worth about $1 million with bonuses and complete control of the Sabres operation as general manager, coach and director of player personnel.

Two important factors in Bowman's decision to sign with Buffalo were the scope of the job and the money. Montreal was offering only a graduated increase in his responsibilities. Toronto was offering the desired package, but appeared to come up short on cash. In April 1985, Petrie, who was no longer working as an agent, told *The Toronto Star's* Jim Proudfoot, "Our first preference was Toronto. I felt there were tremendous opportunities in this city for a guy who could come in and turn the hockey club around. Moreover, at that point the Maple Leafs had a pretty good nucleus. I've often wondered how the history of the Toronto franchise might have developed if we'd been able to work something out. I mean, look at it now and think, if Scotty would have been here for the last six seasons and if the Leafs had come up with 'X' dollars more, who knows what he might have done by now?" Proudfoot, though, wondered how Bowman would have handled Ballard—a legitimate concern, given Bowman's unhappy experience with the meddling Salomons in St. Louis. "To interfere with Scotty," Petrie explained, "you must first understand what he's doing. Nobody has been able to figure him out yet and I don't know why Ballard would be different."

It appears, however, that Bowman turned down the most lucrative offer. According to Jim Devellano, who would engineer Bowman's hiring in Detroit in 1993, Bowman had been offered 10 percent of the Washington Capitals by franchise chairman Abe Pollin, but turned it down. So why did he end up in Buffalo?

"Scotty has a wonderful talent and an ability to pick his spots," says Devellano. "He's partially been able to do that because he's very qualified, and partially because of circumstances. When Scotty went to St. Louis, between Scotty and Lynn Patrick they were able to make St. Louis the premier franchise of the new league. Let's give them some credit for that. After Scotty lost his job in St. Louis, he had an interview with Jack Kent Cooke, who offered him the coach and general manager's job with the Kings. Next he met with Charlie Finlay, who wanted him to be coach and general manager of the Seals. The third offer was just head coach of the Montreal Canadiens. Most people would have picked L.A. or Oakland, because they were expansion clubs and you would have both positions. Scotty had enough foresight to see and believe. He knew the Montreal Canadiens had a lot of talent coming. They had an extremely, extremely capable general manager in Sam Pollock. He could go there and win. He wasn't going to win in L.A. He wasn't going to win Oakland. He could win in Montreal with only one job.

"Five Stanley Cups later, his decision turned out to be right. He went to the right place. He went to a team with talent."

It was no different in 1979, says Devellano. "In Buffalo, Punch Imlach had been building a pretty good young team: Gilbert Perreault,

Richard Martin, Jim Schoenfeld. He liked the talent on the team that Imlach had assembled."

On Saturday, June 11, at the league's annual meeting in Montreal, Claude Mouton, the Canadiens' director of publicity, hosted a curt press conference. He informed the gathered journalists that Bowman had exercised his contract option and had resigned as coach. "Scotty Bowman won five Stanley Cups for the Canadiens in eight years. That's it." No questions were entertained.

"I left the Montreal organization in 1967 [sic] to go with St. Louis with mixed emotions," Bowman told the press. "But I knew it was the best for me. I returned to Montreal in 1971 as a stopgap. That turned into eight years. I only hope I can give to the Sabres what the Canadiens gave me to work with. The players in Montreal made me what I am today and I'm reluctant to leave. It's a new challenge for me and a new lifestyle for my family. They say it's harder to make it in your home town. I think it's harder to leave."

The reactions of Canadiens players to Bowman's departure were diplomatic but mixed. There seemed to be as much or more concern that Al MacNeil had left. "I guess if [Bowman] were ever going to leave, it was going to be this year," said Brian Engblom, one of many Canadiens who had played for MacNeil in Halifax. "People kept on asking us what was going to happen. I'm not surprised he's gone. He's had the experience with St. Louis before. Buffalo is a good team. They're right near the top. I couldn't see him going to a team such as Colorado as some people had been saying. It sounded like they gave Scotty what he wanted. There is going to be a big change of face around here without Scotty and Al around."

Engblom's defensive partner, Rod Langway, noted that some players had thought Bowman would stay and try to match Toe Blake's record of five consecutive Cup wins. "He got what he wanted and good luck to him. It's his decision, just like whoever gets traded is [the club's] decision. The big shock was Al going to Atlanta."

"He can be replaced," declared Mario Tremblay. "Scotty was looking

Bowman (right) celebrates the 1958/59 Ontario Junior A Championship, his first coaching success, with members of the Peterborough Petes.

Bowman coached the Montreal Junior Canadiens in 1964/65 and 1965/66.

Ev Tremblay, Bowman, and Lynn Patrick sign an agreement for the new St. Louis Blues NHL franchise to sponsor an Ottawa Junior league in June 1966.

Sid Salomon III ran the St. Louis Blues and ultimately forced Bowman from his general manager's post in April 1971.

Bowman poses with his mentor Toe Blake at the NHL
All Star dinner in Montreal in January 1969.

*Glenn Hall was
fundamental to
Bowman's playoff
successes with the
St. Louis Blues.*

Claude Ruel, groomed in the Canadiens' system with Bowman, was Toe Blake's initial successor as coach of the Canadiens in 1968/69.

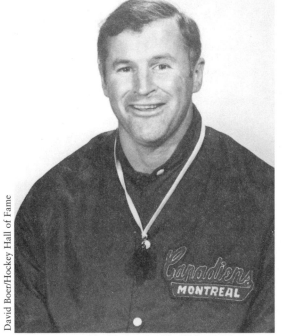

Al MacNeil capped a half-season stint as coach of the Canadiens with a victory in the 1970/71 Stanley Cup, but was immediately replaced by Bowman.

Bowman coaches the Canadiens in January 1972, his first season behind the Montreal bench, as new team president Jacques Courtois looks on.

Sam Pollock's association with Bowman stretched back to the Junior Canadiens of 1950/51. Pollock's departure as general manager of the Montreal Canadiens in September 1978 precipitated Bowman's own departure as coach the following summer.

No player was more admired by Bowman than Ken Dryden, his goaltender for five Stanley Cup wins in Montreal.

Jimmy Roberts, who first skated for Bowman as a Peterborough Pete in 1958/59, played for him in St. Louis and Montreal. He then became an assistant coach of the Buffalo Sabres under Bowman in 1979/80.

Craig Ramsay ended a long playing career in Buffalo to become an assistant coach to Bowman. He was head coach of the Sabres when Bowman was fired as general manager in November 1986.

Jim Devellano was a St. Louis scout under Bowman; as senior vice-president of the Detroit Red Wings, he engineered Bowman's hiring as coach in 1993.

Paul Coffey works out at a Red Wings practice under Bowman's watchful eye on October 7, 1996, after Bowman's initial attempt to trade him to Hartford for Brendan Shanahan fell through.

Carlos Osorio/Associated Press

Colorado coach Marc Crawford and Bowman exchange increasingly heated words in the closing minutes of game four of the Western Conference final series on May 22, 1997.

Carlos Osorio/Associated Press

for the general manager's job and I'm not surprised. I didn't always agree with what he said, but he was a good coach."

"He is going to be hard to replace," offered Pierre Larouche. "But other things have happened to the Canadiens before and they have made adjustments when they have had to. But I guess when you are coaching for eight years, it gets to a point like a player playing for thirteen or fourteen years. You have enough."

"We'll miss him," said Bob Gainey, "but it won't be like there's going to be no one else to step in. He was an integral part of our team."

The Canadiens' losses continued. Before the new season began, Ken Dryden chose to retire at the peak of his profession, a Stanley Cup champion and the Vezina winner in the last four seasons. Grundman dithered over hiring Bowman's replacement and chose poorly in selecting former Canadiens great Boom-Boom Geoffrion. Geoffrion's coaching record was spotty; his biggest problem was nerves, which had forced him to quit in New York in 1968/69 and Atlanta in 1974/75. No city's fans or media were tougher on the coach than Montreal's. Bowman had survived eight seasons in that blinding spotlight. Geoffrion lasted until mid-December. Claude Ruel was dragooned in to finish off the season. The quest for a fifth consecutive Cup ended with an upset loss to Minnesota in the seventh game of the quarterfinals on the Forum ice.

Bowman left Montreal with mixed feelings. In his eight seasons, he had accumulated his fair share of friends and foes on and off the ice. Both Bowman and the Canadiens were determined to prove they could win without each other.

Ultimately, both did, but only after enduring lengthy dry spells. The Canadiens waited seven seasons, Bowman eleven. By the time the Canadiens won again in 1985/86, they were on their fifth coach and second general manager since Bowman left. Success returned under general manager Serge Savard, who replaced Grundman in 1983/84, and coach Jean Perron, who took over from Jacques Lemaire in 1985/86. By the time Bowman won again, he was with his second team since leaving Montreal, and he was neither coaching nor managing. Buffalo had become a drawn-out professional disaster, which justified for some the Canadiens' failure to anoint him Sam Pollock's successor. Bowman had gone to Buffalo to build a dynasty of his own. Instead, he nearly dug his own professional grave.

11

✧ IT WAS OVER, WITNESSES said, in less than a minute. A seven-year relationship that had begun with such fanfare and promise was terminated with a brevity of explanation that still managed to speak volumes about the team ownership's displeasure. Seymour Knox III, acting on behalf of himself and his brother Northrup, entered a room filled with reporters and cameramen on December 2, 1986, consulted a single sheet of paper and read the words that fired Scotty Bowman as general manager, sometimes coach, and director of player personnel of the Buffalo Sabres.

"The Sabres' record under his leadership has not met our patient expectations," Knox explained. "Our fans, especially the solid core of season ticket holders who literally made our franchise possible, deserve better results than they have received."

Twenty-three games into the 1986/87 NHL season, five wins, fifteen losses and three ties had produced thirteen points, good enough for last place in the league. It was the worst season start over twenty games in the franchise's twenty-six-year history. The previous spring, the Sabres had missed the playoffs for the first time since 1973/74. In the latest season, Bowman had at first tried holding down the coaching job in addition to his other duties, then changed his mind and turned over the Sabres to Craig Ramsay, who had played his entire fourteen-season NHL career on left wing with Buffalo before becoming an assistant coach to Bowman in 1985/86. Ramsay had become the fourth coach in seven seasons to try to run the Sabres' bench under Bowman; he also became the last person ever to coach an NHL team managed by Scotty Bowman.

Bowman had considered himself, at one point in his career, near-impervious to dismissal. "Management in Montreal has treated me well," he said in *The Hockey News* in 1976. "It is a mature management which does not make snap judgments in anger or disappointment. . . . If they think they can do better with someone else they will replace me, but that is true in any town in the league, not just in Montreal. I am not one of those coaches who has been fired frequently and may feel nervous. I don't even think about being fired. I don't expect to be. They can't put any more pressure on me than I put on myself. I want very much to win every game. I suppose every coach does. I'm disappointed by every defeat. There's no pressure that could make me try any harder. I try to maintain an even emotional level but I suffer inside."

Bowman still appeared to consider himself untouchable when the Knoxes lowered the boom. "I never saw it coming," he avowed. "It always comes as a surprise."

He had left Montreal a refugee of his own success as a coach, desiring the executive role he had enjoyed in St. Louis. Driven by a trio of irresistible forces—the expectations of the Sabres' owners that he fill the coaching role, his inability to hire a subaltern that could meet his own expectations, and the essential lure of the job he strove to move above and beyond—Bowman kept returning to the bench. Unlike the Canadiens, a team created by the endlessly clever Sam Pollock, the Sabres team Bowman wound up coaching was largely of his own making. He had inherited an outstanding lineup from the outgoing general manager, Punch Imlach, and over seasons of drafting and trading had reduced it to a lineup that couldn't meet the league's generous playoff qualification standard. He had no one to blame but himself for the performance of the team he sent to the ice.

"I have no excuses," he said. "I think I did an acceptable job."

The Knoxes had not hired Bowman away from the Canadiens in pursuit of the acceptable. And Bowman was not a coach who would ever accept a player defending his play as acceptable.

Back on June 11, 1979, an ebullient Seymour Knox III had told the press who attended the announcement of Bowman's hiring, "Scotty is the best hockey man in the world and we have given him a multi-year contract. We're very impressed with his record and we're hopeful he will win us a Stanley Cup. That's our objective and our goal."

Hope had faded entirely as Christmas 1986 approached. The Knoxes were now engaged in damage control to shore up a battered franchise in a tier-two major-league market. The damage control Bowman faced was equally daunting. The reputation for hockey wizardry he had built in the Montreal organization and twice sold to the highest bidder—first to St. Louis, then to Buffalo—was now seriously devalued. He had been forty-six years old when he arrived in Buffalo, married, a father of five (each child the owner of one of the Stanley Cup rings he'd earned with Montreal), concerned about being able to provide for his family. Seven years later, he was fifty-three years old, still married, still a father of five, but now without any security and little marketability. Fairly or not, the Buffalo years had cast him as a coach who was incapable of managing—and worse, as a coach who was no longer capable of winning.

Bowman's glory days, it seemed, had come and gone, just as they had for his former rivals, Don Cherry of the Bruins and Fred Shero of the Flyers. Coaching in the NHL was rarely a long-term employment opportunity. If you were fortunate enough to find yourself running the right team at the right time, success could be yours, but it was almost always fleeting. The fortunate coaches—Emile Francis in New York, Harry Sinden in Boston, among others—scrambled up the corporate ladder into management. In attempting the same scramble, Bowman had broken just about every rung he stepped on. He never really climbed it, because he could never really leave the coaching behind.

Bowman was inclined to blame his misfortune on the burden of being both a coach and general manager, but his critics placed the blame for the Sabres debacle squarely on his own shoulders. As Buffalo sports-writer Jim Kelley summed it up, "An almost uninterrupted decline in points and a corresponding lack of playoff success... was only a part of Bowman's undoing. A history of failed draft choices, poorly exe-cuted trades, uneven player development and excessive spending (in relation to results) also figured in his demise."

In the spring of 1986, as Bowman missed the playoffs for the first time in his NHL coaching career, his old team in Montreal won its first Stanley Cup since his departure in 1979. Montreal could no longer hope to dominate the league the way it had in the 1950s, '60s and '70s, but the Canadiens' five-game defeat of the Calgary Flames brought relief to a hockey-mad city that had come to fear that win-ning had left town with Bowman. He had not taken the magic of the Canadiens with him. Nothing, it seemed, had rubbed off on Buffalo.

There was a time in the history of the Montreal Canadiens when Buffalo was a departure point for future glory, when the Bisons of the American league served as a Montreal farm club. Jacques Plante had plied the goaltending trade there before being called up to anchor the stingy Canadiens defence in the 1950s. But for Bowman, Buffalo gave every indication of being the end of the road, a dead end for a career that had already reached its greatest heights back in Montreal.

Scotty Bowman's move to Buffalo in 1979 filled him with more than a little fear. After his career with the Sabres flamed out, Bowman shared those early concerns with his admirer and confidant, sports-writer Al Strachan. As Bowman related, delays in severing his con-nection with Montreal in June 1979 were making Seymour Knox III concerned that Bowman wouldn't actually come to Buffalo. "I called Seymour Knox and told him I needed another day and a half to wind things up. He wasn't too happy about it, so I said, 'Just to show you how sincere I am, I'll acquiesce to coach the team the first year.' That's what he really wanted. I didn't really want to do it. I was leaving Montreal as a winner and it could only be downhill from there. You're always concerned about the worst part. What if I went to Buffalo and finished tenth?"

Bowman immediately approached Roger Neilson, one of the greatest technical coaches in the game. He proposed that Neilson leave his coaching job with Toronto to become his assistant in Buffalo, with the understanding that he would soon succeed Bowman as head coach. Neilson was interested. "But on the other hand it would be hard to leave the Leafs. I would feel like it was two years down the drain." However, Harold Ballard had made it easier for him to leave, by having tried to hire first Don Cherry and then Bowman to run the Leafs. It was far better for Neilson to go to Buffalo, where he was wanted, than hope to stay in Toronto, where Ballard was actively scouting out his replacement.

Bowman and Neilson were friends, their association stretching back to the Montreal organization of the 1960s. In his rookie season as an NHL coach in 1977/78, Neilson had led the Maple Leafs to their best regular-season finish in expansion-era history, with forty-one wins and ninety-two points. While scoring had dropped by thirty goals, goals against had plunged by forty-eight. Playing a physically intimidating defensive game, the Leafs had upset the New York Islanders in the quarterfinals with a game-seven overtime win, then lost to Bowman's Canadiens in the semifinals. The 1978/79 season, however, had been less successful for Neilson's Leafs, as wins fell to thirty-four. In the quarterfinals, the Canadiens swept them in four, but Bowman's team had required overtime wins in the last two games to do it.

"Technical" coaches are often miscast as strategy wonks who focus on intricate play-making rather than good old-fashioned hockey values, like hitting, fighting and intimidation. Observers incorrectly assume that anyone who systematically dissects the game must be a devotee of stylish Swedish or Russian play-making, ignoring the large physical and psychological components of the game. Scotty Bowman and Fred Shero in the 1970s put the lie to that notion. After winning the 1973/74 Stanley Cup, Shero, the mastermind of the Broad Street Bullies of Philadelphia, travelled all the way to Russia to take a coaching clinic run by Anatoli Tarasov, but Shero understood more than anyone how important a nasty team disposition can be to winning in the NHL. Scotty Bowman similarly never failed to address the importance of the physical game. His Canadiens had to beat the Flyers "in the alley" to take the Cup away from them in 1975/76, with a team of strength and presence. Bowman revealed his sense of completeness when he once complained that Phil Esposito lacked greatness because he wasn't a fighter.

Roger Neilson, who may be the most "technical" coach the NHL has ever seen, was similarly well-rounded in his approach to the game. No one could run a practice as effectively as Neilson, or take apart a game or a player's style on videotape the way he could. (He was such an innovator in his use of video replay that players christened him "Captain Video.") But at the heart of Neilson's game, as he had demonstrated with his Leafs against the Islanders in the 1977/78 playoffs, was a tough defensive style that favoured big players who could hit and a penalty-killing system that could keep the team in the game when the infractions inevitably mounted.

Neilson was a Peterborough high school teacher who came to coaching prominence through the Petes, Bowman's old Junior team. Neilson's first coaching efforts were at age seventeen, followed by a stint scouting Ontario amateur prospects for the Canadiens, before he became the coach of the Petes at twenty-two, in 1966/67, just as Montreal's sponsorship of Junior clubs was coming to an end with the impending arrival of the universal draft. Neilson spent ten years running the Petes' bench, sending on to the NHL players who were exceptional practitioners of the two-way game—in particular, forwards with tremendous defensive skills.

Neilson's Petes reached the Memorial Cup finals in 1971/72, and the 1973 NHL draft saw four players from that team selected in the first two rounds: Bob Gainey by Montreal (eighth), Bob Neely by Toronto (tenth), Colin Campbell by Pittsburgh (twenty-seventh), and Jim Jones by Boston (thirty-first). All had professional careers, and Gainey and Campbell went on to become NHL coaches, a destiny shared by other Neilson-trained players.

By the time the 1973 draft came along, Neilson's reputation for producing well-trained NHL prospects was already established; his Petes had been graduating top picks since the very first NHL universal draft in 1969. In that draft, the Oakland Seals had chosen Tony Featherstone seventh overall and Ron Stackhouse eighteenth. In 1970, Boston took Rick MacLeish fourth overall and Ron Plumb ninth. And in 1971, the Buffalo Sabres chose Craig Ramsay with their first pick, nineteenth overall.

Ramsay was a dedicated checker on left wing who could also contribute offensively. In his long career with the Sabres, he was dependable for twenty-plus goals and sixty-odd points a season, all the while keeping track of opponents' high-scoring stars. It was the two-way play of Sabres like Ramsay, Don Luce and Danny Gare in the 1974/75 semifinals, when Montreal was eliminated by Buffalo, that showed Bowman his team needed two lines that could keep an opposing team at bay.

In Peterborough, Ramsay had been tutored rigorously and effectively by Neilson. Arriving in the NHL was something of a shock to him. Buffalo was the domain of general manager Punch Imlach, who could not have been less systematic. A throwback to the classic persona of the Original Six blood-and-guts motivator, Imlach believed in hard work and little else.

"Basically, Punch's system was 'Go get 'em,'" Ramsay recalls. "It was work, grind his players, push them and drive them and tell them they're no good and make them hate him so they would work harder. The wingers went up and down the boards, picked up their wingers, and had lots of one-on-one battles. You followed your winger back, made sure he didn't score, and then you tried to beat him back down the ice. When I came out of Junior, I didn't ever want to do that. That wasn't the way I'd played."

Ramsay tried to play the way Neilson had taught him to play, and because he produced results, he caught no grief. But his first eight seasons in the NHL were symptomatic of the problems the league faced in its elimination of the sponsored amateur development system. If newcomers weren't trained properly in Junior, the way he had been by Neilson, they weren't likely to get much help in the NHL. It was sink or swim for too many talents. The level of coaching—of moulding a player's skills and developing and executing a playing system— was often better in Junior competition than it was in the NHL. In the Original Six days, in which Imlach had whip-cracked the Maple Leafs to four Stanley Cups, players were expected to have the bulk of the necessary skills once they reached the NHL. If they didn't have them at the end of their Junior days, they were sent to the minor pros for seasoning. Too often in the post-1967 NHL, players were rushed into starting positions, as available talent was greatly diluted by the NHL's ongoing expansion and the arrival of the WHA. And initially, the league saw little reason to have assistant coaches, whose main jobs were to run practices and work one-on-one with individual players. While assistant player-coaches existed (Bowman had used Doug Harvey as such in St. Louis), no NHL coach voluntarily hired his own assistant coach, until Fred Shero brought in Mike Nykoluk in 1972/73.

Imlach had been fired by the Knoxes as Buffalo's general manager (and Marcel Pronovost as coach) after back-to-back weekend losses (8–1 and 4–1) to Bowman's Canadiens in December 1978. John Anderson finished the season as general manager and Billy Inglis as coach on an interim basis. When Scotty Bowman arrived as coach and general manager for 1979/80, he brought with him two assistant coaches: Jimmy Roberts and Roger Neilson. Craig Ramsay, who had been part of the player revolt that ended Imlach's reign, found his career coming full circle with the arrival of Neilson in Buffalo.

Bowman's relationship with Jimmy Roberts was even deeper than the one with Neilson; it went all the way back to the Peterborough Petes of 1958/59, and carried on through St. Louis and Montreal. After the 1976/77 Stanley Cup season, Roberts was thirty-seven and facing retirement. "I was getting pretty old," says Roberts. "They had replacements for me, the next wave of talent. I'd married a girl in St. Louis, and they were good enough to arrange for me to finish my career there."

The Blues, which had gone bankrupt under the Salomons, had just been bailed out by Ralston-Purina. Roberts spent the 1977/78 season with the Blues before retiring. He was away from the game entirely in 1978/79, and then Scotty Bowman called. "He said, 'What've you been doing? I'm going to Buffalo. Would you like to come with me?' That was the start of my coaching career." As a model defensive forward, Roberts complemented the defence-minded strategic style espoused by Neilson.

Bowman's plan—to start out as Buffalo's coach and then turn the job over to Neilson—was sound, but there was a problem with it that not even Bowman seemed able to foresee: he would find it extraordinarily difficult to tear himself away from coaching. "Scotty likes to control all of the issues, which he could do by being general manager," Ramsay explains. "But what he found out is that he didn't have that day-to-day excitement of being on the bench." The consequences for Buffalo, Bowman and the people he hired would be considerable.

In Bowman's first season in Buffalo, with Neilson and Roberts at his side, Buffalo was transformed as a hockey organization. The skate-till-you drop practice sessions Imlach had been running since his Leafs days were gone, and in their place were precision operations in skills development and game preparation. "Our practices were high-tempo, well organized and planned," says Ramsay. "In fifty-five minutes, not two hours, you were exhausted and you had done things. You had legitimately covered things you had to understand or had to be ready to do in a game. They could really run a practice. Roger's a brilliant practice guy, and Scotty's great, too."

In that first season, most of the practices were run by Neilson and Roberts, with Bowman usually showing up only for games. Hands On Bowman was becoming the Imperial Bowman. "He came in for a six o'clock game meeting, stomped around a bit, showed us his intensity, and we went out and played," says Ramsay. "That intensity was okay. We were a good team, and it was different. The level of intensity he brought, which was phenomenal, was sort of refreshing."

Playing under Bowman and his assistants that first season, Ramsay discovered the essential skills that had made Bowman so successful in Montreal. "When he coached me, my job was to cover Guy Lafleur, Wayne Gretzky. I spent all night going against them. It felt like we were always in control of the game. We always had the right match-ups. Being in control is what Scotty brings with him to the job.

"Scotty is a great coach of a great team. I admired him for the way he ran the bench. He always gets his match-ups. He'll make fine adjustments to his lineups to make sure of that. In my case, sometimes I would go out with Gilbert Perreault instead of with Don Luce."

In that first season, Bowman drove the team from an 88-point season, with thirty-six wins, in 1978/79, to a 110-point season, with forty-seven wins, which earned them first place in the Adams division and the Prince of Wales Conference, and second place overall, behind Philadelphia, in the league. His goaltending duo of Don Edwards and Bob Sauve led the league in goals against to win the Vezina. But Bowman's concern with his own expectations for the team flared in the last game of the season, a home tilt against Toronto. The Sabres had won their second-last game, against Pittsburgh, 9–1 the previous night, and as the time ran down on the season finale the Sabres were enjoying a 7–2 lead. Defenceman John Van Boxmeer then broke his stick in his own end; the Leafs pounced on the loose puck and scored. The goal had no effect on the outcome of the game or the Sabres' position in the standings, or Edwards and Sauve's lead in league goaltending, but it did mean that the Sabres had now allowed 201 goals, not 200, that season. "Scotty went berserk over a goal that was absolutely meaningless, except to him," Ramsay recalls.

He had also driven the team hard—motivated, perhaps, by a desire to live up to the regular-season standard he had set with the Canadiens, to show forthrightly that he could achieve with a team other than Montreal. Roberts sensed that making the break with the Canadiens, having been passed over for the general manager's job when Pollock retired, was wrenching for Bowman. His past returned to haunt him in 1981/82, when a division realignment brought the Canadiens into the Adams with Buffalo. In the six full seasons that followed in Buffalo, Bowman's Sabres were able to finish ahead of Montreal only once, in 1983/84.

"Scotty had given a lot to that organization, and he was like a lot of people who had been there for years—they had tattoos of the Canadiens crest all over them," says Roberts. "It took him a long time to break out of that mould. I think it really hurt him along the way, in Buffalo. That scar was still there, and he couldn't understand, with what he had given them, why he wasn't accepted." Al MacNeil agrees that the break from Montreal was difficult for Bowman. "No team anywhere was as well organized in the business of winning," MacNeil says of the 1970s Canadiens. "To leave that would have been quite traumatic for him."

In the 1979/80 playoffs, Bowman paid for the Sabres' regular-season success. The team was hurt; half a dozen starters, including Ramsay, missed games, which meant another half a dozen players were filling in, playing unfamiliar roles. Hobbling forward, this powerful team was still able to down Vancouver in the preliminary round and sweep Chicago in four in the quarterfinals, before meeting Al Arbour's Islanders in the semifinals. The battered Sabres, who could well have gone all the way were it not for the parade of injuries, fell to the Islanders in six games. In the finals, the Islanders won their first of four consecutive Stanley Cups with a six-game defeat of the Flyers.

The 1979/80 lineup had been Punch Imlach's team; Bowman had made few personnel adjustments. But beginning in 1980/81, he set out to put his own imprint on the club, at the same time turning over the coaching job, as he had promised, to Neilson.

It was the beginning of the end for Bowman in Buffalo, and very nearly for Bowman in the NHL. Over the next seven seasons, he went through a flurry of coaches, all of whom were with him as players or assistant coaches at the beginning of his Buffalo term. No one measured up to his standards. No one, not even Bowman himself, could make the team he was aggressively overhauling win a Stanley Cup. His first campaign, with the Imlach team in 1979/80, was as close as he would come.

Neilson's effort with the team in 1980/81 was solid, but not as spectacular as 1979/80. The team won the division again, with eight fewer wins, eleven more points, nine more goals for, forty-nine more goals against, and—most important—several fewer stars. Bowman had already sent Rene Robert, one third of the French Connection (with Richard Martin and Gilbert Perreault), to Colorado at the beginning of the 1979/80 season, for John Van Boxmeer, who had played for Bowman in Montreal. And in March 1980, Bowman beat the trade deadline with a deal that helped Los Angeles address the defensive weakness suffered by all the Norris division teams but Montreal. By surrendering a veteran in his tenth season, Jerry Korab, who was the club's leading offensive defenceman, Bowman collected the Kings' first pick in the 1982 draft.

Bowman saved his most aggressive trading for his second season. With Neilson taking on the responsibility of coaching the team, striving to satisfy the ownership's desire for a Stanley Cup, Bowman continued to deal away the team's most celebrated players as he accelerated his rebuilding program. Bowman turned to the veterans' roll-call for more trade bait that could garner him future draft picks, and he again found a willing buyer in George Maguire, general manager of the L.A. Kings. On March 10, Richard Martin and Don Luce were sent to the coast in a deal that, once again, just beat the league trade deadline. Martin, the second member of the old French Connection to be traded, had a bad knee, but the Kings obviously didn't think it was a career-threatening injury; Maguire gave Bowman a third-round draft choice in 1981 and a first-round pick in 1983 that had originally belonged to Detroit. For Luce, an accomplished checker and penalty-killer who had spent most of the season riding the bench, Maguire sent an undisclosed amount of cash and the Kings' sixth pick in 1982.

Bowman made out handsomely with these deals, as Martin played only three games for the Kings in 1981/82 before his knee forced him to retire, and Luce's career ended after thirty-nine games in Toronto in 1981/82. Maguire had handed over three draft picks to gain the limited services of these veterans. But the Sabres paid as well, in that Bowman's management decisions were creating a rift between him and Roger Neilson, who had to take the heat for the team's failures.

Martin and Luce were both ten-season veterans, with Martin the Sabres' all-time leading scorer. Korab had already been sent west; in January, Bowman had placed another veteran, left-winger Rick Dudley, on waivers, and he had been picked up by Winnipeg. Bowman was following a traditional team-rebuilding philosophy: offload veterans while they still have some market value to garner draft picks. He was doing it, though, at warp speed. Sam Pollock had been able to roll over the Canadiens' lineup with trades for draft picks, but not by gutting the team of veteran stars.

The age and experience of the Sabres plunged dramatically as Bowman promoted a new generation of players. Steve Patrick, Bowman's first choice in the 1980 draft, had been an underage selection and began the 1980/81 season playing Junior hockey for the Brandon Wheat Kings, but at twenty he was called up on right wing as a regular starter for the last thirty games. Gilles Hamel and Alan Haworth, drafted at nineteen by Bowman in 1979, spent 1979/80 playing Junior hockey. After starting 1980/81 with the Rochester Americans, they were elevated to the Sabres by Bowman, with Hamel on left wing and Haworth at centre. Rob McClanahan, drafted forty-eighth by Imlach in 1978, and Mike Ramsey, chosen first by Bowman and eleventh overall in 1979, had played together on the U.S. Olympic gold-medal team in 1980. Ramsey had broken into the Sabres defence right after the Olympic victory, while McClanahan moved between Buffalo and Rochester before settling into a starting job at centre in 1980/81. In addition, Bowman had given left-winger Tony McKegney and defence-men Richie Dunn and Larry Playfair, who had first appeared in the Buffalo lineup in 1978/79, regular starting assignments.

"In Roger's one year as head coach, we had 99 points," says Craig Ramsay. "Roger is the easiest guy to get along with, but he and Scotty ended up fighting all year. Scotty didn't like the way Roger was doing things and he wanted to make the changes that would let him put his imprint on the team, getting all these young players. Look at his deci-sions at that time, trading a bunch of veteran players for a bunch of draft choices, which in the long run is supposed to make your team better but in the short term doesn't do any of us any favours." Bow-man even approached Ramsay and flatly told him that, while he didn't want to, he should trade him. The trade never came, and Ramsay never knew what to make of Bowman's frankness. "You're taking a pretty good hockey team that had a chance to win it, and you start to trade," Ramsay continues. "We have three first picks, but what's left? Now you're trying to break in all these kids who, maybe they're players and maybe they're not. Roger has a great season, we lose in the second round of the playoffs, so Roger's out. It didn't make a lot of sense."

"Off the ice, away from hockey, [Bowman is] as good a guy as you'd ever hope to meet," Roger Neilson told *Sports Illustrated* in 1993. "Around hockey he's very demanding. He motivates by fear. Players are never quite sure where they stand."

It was a difficult time for the Sabres and their fans. The man who was supposed to make their team into a Stanley Cup champion had decided to start making their team into another team altogether. The next season, 1981/82, the changes continued apace. On December 2,

1981, Bob Sauve, one half of the goaltending team that had led the
league in goals against in 1979/80 and was second in 1980/81, was
shipped to Detroit for future considerations after refusing to sign a
new Sabres contract in his option year. That same day, Bowman cut a
much bigger deal with the Red Wings. Danny Gare, Jim Schoenfeld
and Derek Smith were swapped for Mike Foligno, Dale McCourt and
Brent Peterson. Gare had amassed a career-high fifty-six goals and
eighty-nine points under Bowman in 1979/80 and had another strong
year in 1980/81, but in 1981/82 his numbers were headed into decline.
Schoenfeld was playing as strongly as ever in 1980/81, but as he began
his tenth season, retirement was looming; 1980/81 was the last season
in which he played close to a full campaign. Forward Derek Smith had
turned into a sixty-point man under Bowman, but his points production was off in 1980/81, and he would play only forty-two games in
Detroit in 1981/82.

Ted Lindsay, the Red Wings' captain during the Motor City Muscle
era of the 1950s, had become Detroit's general manager in 1976/77,
and was clearing house of top draft picks as he bet the franchise on
veterans and a pugilistic style. Foligno had been chosen third overall
by Detroit in 1979, McCourt first overall in 1977. The trade netted
Bowman one long-term roster addition in Foligno, as the right-winger
played productively with the Sabres until being traded to Toronto in
December 1990.

McCourt appeared to have potential for Buffalo, but his employment history was unhappy. McCourt had been the all-time scoring
leader in Canadian Junior hockey when drafted. After his first season
in Detroit, McCourt found himself being shipped to Los Angeles as
compensation for Lindsay's signing of free agent Rogie Vachon in
August 1978. McCourt had just signed a new contract in good faith,
and could have taken his services to the WHA if he had known he was
going to be awarded to the Kings. The league avoided a nasty antitrust
ruling in the American courts when the Kings arranged to trade
his rights back to Detroit. (It was ironic that Lindsay, who had fought

ferociously for a players' union in 1957, would cause a player-launched court battle two decades later.) The compensation battle came to be the focal point of McCourt's once highly touted career.

After a career-high eighty-six points with the Red Wings in 1980/81, McCourt's play went into decline in Buffalo. McCourt lacked the speed and heft Bowman liked in a forward, not to mention backchecking skills. He also had what was estimated to be the largest contract in the NHL, at $300,000 a season. For his centres, Bowman felt he was better off staying with Gilbert Perreault, draftee Dave Andreychuk and Brent Peterson. In November 1983, Bowman terminated McCourt's contract. Under the terms of the agreement with the NHLPA, this required the Sabres to pay McCourt one-third the value of the contract for double the number of years left on it. Since McCourt was still under contract for two more seasons, getting rid of him cost the Knoxes about $400,000.

"I have to say, the Sabres treated me pretty fair," McCourt commented. "I suppose I really don't know why they let me go, except for the money. It was tough playing in Buffalo but it was good having the discipline and playing on a good team after playing for Detroit. I was very happy to have the chance to play under Scotty Bowman and the whole operation, but at times it was difficult." A nephew of former Leafs captain George Armstrong, McCourt was immediately picked up by Toronto, with whom he played out his last NHL season.

With Korab, Robert, Martin, Gare, Luce, Schoenfeld and Sauve gone, few players were left from the beloved Imlach lineup. The survivors with deep franchise roots were Craig Ramsay, original draftee and French Connection centre Gilbert Perreault, and defenceman Bill Hajt, who had been with the team since 1973/74. Before the start of the 1982/83 season, the Knoxes were forced to do something that had never been asked of them in franchise history: with a recession in full swing, and with the Sabres undergoing an aggressive lineup overhaul and turning in disappointing playoff performances, the first newspaper ads offering "good" season tickets appeared.

The abrupt break with the team's past engineered by Bowman was darkened by Richard Martin's decision to sue Bowman, the Sabres, and the team doctor who initially diagnosed him and operated on his knee. Martin contended in part that the defendants had conspired to have him play, despite knowing he was physically unable to do so.

In a game against Washington on November 9, 1980, Capitals goaltender Mike Palmateer tripped Martin, causing the knee injury. Bowman, Martin charged, pressured him to return to action before the knee had healed. He sat out twenty games before agreeing to return to the lineup. Martin said the knee would swell and would have to be drained whenever he played, but that Bowman wanted him to play anyway. After undergoing arthroscopic surgery by the team doctor on January 2, 1981, Martin returned to play on January 7, appearing in eight games over the next two weeks. He didn't play for the Sabres again. Seeking a second opinion, he was put in touch by Bowman and the team doctor with a Canadian surgeon, who in performing further surgery on February 3 discovered far more damage than the team doctor had. Still, the surgeon predicted Martin could be back playing in another four or five weeks. On the strength of this optimistic report, Bowman was able to trade Martin to the Los Angeles Kings on March 10 for two draft picks. These picks landed the Sabres Colin Chisholm in the third round in 1981 and Tom Barrasso in the first round in 1983.

After appearing in one regular-season game for Los Angeles in 1980/81, Martin lasted three games in 1981/82 before being told by a doctor he would never play again. The doctor was right. In the fall of 1982, Martin appeared on the CTV show "Sports Hot Seat" in Calgary, thoroughly venting his anger at Bowman. "Scotty's an excellent coach but sometimes he's just a little inconsiderate when it comes to people's feelings," Martin said. "He had a good part in ending my career. When Scotty came to Buffalo he needed a whipping boy, and I became that boy. He figured he could abuse me and I'd still be able to play well. He wanted to scare the other players. He likes to do that. I accepted it. But when I did get my injury, and was told I was a faker, that's when I drew the line."

However overbearing Martin found Bowman's behaviour, Bowman could defend himself by pointing to the initial diagnosis of the team doctor, which simply indicated a sprained knee due to hyperextension, with no evidence of swelling or fracture. Arguing that Martin's compensation rights were satisfied exclusively by the Workers' Compensation Board, Bowman and the Sabres were able to extricate themselves from Martin's legal press in 1988, with a summary judgment that also dismissed the allegations against them and ended the conspiracy case; a summary judgment was then secured by the team doctor in 1989 on the issues of fraud and concealment which said he was not liable. By the time Bowman secured his summary judgment, his career in Buffalo was over, his relationship with the team having been compromised by the messy end to a star's playing career. "Scotty," Craig Ramsay says, "did not endear himself to a lot of players."

The player-acquisition system under which Scotty Bowman attempted an aggressive rebuilding of the Buffalo Sabres was in many respects different from the one in which Sam Pollock had proved so skilled. Players were getting younger, and they were coming from places scarcely heard of before the 1980s. Bowman's drafting efforts were at the forefront of emerging talent sources, in the United States and Europe, but as a trailblazer his results were uneven.

American players had long been part of the NHL, but a sudden streak of quality players from 1975 to 1977, with five U.S. college prospects going in the second round of the NHL entry draft, brought the American pool to the forefront. Brian Engblom and Russ Anderson in 1975, Reed Larson in 1976 and Tom Gorence in 1977 were all from the University of Minnesota, where Herb Brooks was in charge of an outstanding program that won NCAA Division I titles in 1974, 1976 and 1979; the fifth, Rod Langway in 1977, was from the University of New Hampshire. All made the NHL, with the greatest impact registered by Engblom and Langway, for they had both been selected by Sam Pollock, the Canadiens' talent genius who could single-handedly set a drafting trend.

Perhaps more impressive than Pollock's success with Engblom and Langway was Montreal's discovery of Chris Nilan. At the 1978 entry draft, Pollock went pick-happy as most everyone else called it a day, taking selections 201, 212, 222, 225 and 227, and 229 through 234. Nilan, a Boston-born right-winger at Northeastern, was pick 231. He spent the 1978/79 season at Northeastern, then joined the Nova Scotia Voyageurs, coming up to the Canadiens for fifteen games. No finesse player, Nilan led the AHL in penalty minutes with 304 in forty-nine games in 1978/79, and became a full-time Canadiens enforcer in 1980/81, leading the league in penalty minutes in 1983/84 and 1984/85. This entry draft afterthought managed a thirteen-season career in the NHL, including a Stanley Cup win with Montreal in 1985/86.

Pollock's selection of Nilan helped American college draftees rise to a record seventy-three in 1978, representing 31 percent of total draft picks. The next milestone for U.S. talent soon followed, in 1979, the year the four surviving members of the World Hockey Association joined the NHL. In the glut of professional talent resulting from the merger, which reduced the number of tier-one professional clubs in North America, the total number of players drafted almost halved, from 234 to 126. Proportionately, the American pool suffered the most, as the number of draftees plunged from seventy-three to fifteen. But league history nonetheless was made when Bowman, newly in charge of the Buffalo Sabres, chose an American college player as his first pick in the opening round. Mike Ramsey of the University of Minnesota was chosen by Bowman eleventh overall, while the North Stars took Ramsey's teammate Neal Broten in the second round, forty-second overall.

The arrival of the United States as a legitimate talent source came just as a lawsuit was reshaping the draft's dynamics. Ken Linseman, a teenage Canadian prospect, filed his suit because had been unable to begin playing in the NHL as he wanted to, due to the league policy of not drafting players younger than twenty. At the time of the June 1977 NHL draft, Linseman was eighteen.

Before the universal draft, when NHL clubs had direct sponsorship agreements with Junior clubs, players regularly began their professional careers at age eighteen. This had been the call-up age specified under the C-form, a promise of professional services many prospects signed when they were as young as sixteen. When a universal draft was introduced in 1963/64 for players whose rights weren't already secured through Junior sponsorship agreements, the age limit was set at seventeen. This was bumped to eighteen in 1964/65, and when the first truly universal draft was held in June 1969, the age increased to twenty. The higher age was the result of an agreement with the Canadian Amateur Hockey Association to ensure Junior teams would not be stripped of top prospects who were still in their teens.

The WHA was also honouring the twenty-year-old rule in its drafts, but individual teams began disregarding the agreement. Wayne Gretzky was signed directly to a personal services contract by Nelson Skalbania, owner of the Indianapolis Racers, at age seventeen. John F. Bassett, owner of the Birmingham Bulls (previously known as the Ottawa Nationals and Toronto Toros), signed so many underage players that the team became known as the Baby Bulls. Linseman was nineteen when he began playing for Birmingham in 1977/78; as soon as he was legally able, he switched to his league of choice, the NHL, joining Philadelphia for 1978/79. His antitrust suit struck down the NHL's exclusionary age limitation, and the draft age dropped to nineteen in 1980 and eighteen in 1981.

This change in draft and employment policy had an immediate effect on the player market. The United States had no equivalent to the

Canadian Junior system, but in the northeast and in Minnesota there were first-rate high school programs (boosted by the U.S. "Miracle on Ice" at the 1980 Olympics) which prepared teenagers for collegiate careers. The Linseman case meant that the NHL was now in the business of drafting American high school students. In 1980, seven players from American high schools were picked in the entry draft. By 1982, the figure had leapt to forty-seven.

In the 1982 draft, Bowman became the first NHL general manager to make an American high school student his first-round choice, taking Phil Housley of St. Paul, Minnesota, sixth overall. In the second round, Bowman went back to St. Paul for his next pick. Housley had played for South St. Paul High School; from North St. Paul, Bowman plucked Mike Anderson, twenty-sixth overall.

In 1983 came another drafting milestone: three Americans in the top ten, including the first American to be selected first overall. Jumping on the homegrown bandwagon, the Minnesota North Stars made as the draft's first pick Brian Lawton of Rhode Island's Mount St. Charles High School (which turned out twelve draft picks from 1981 to 1990). Holding two first-round picks, Scotty Bowman made both his selections from American schools. Tom Barrasso of Acton-Boxboro High School in suburban Boston went to Buffalo fifth overall, and Normand LaCombe, a native of Pierrefonds, Quebec, playing at the University of New Hampshire, was selected tenth overall. Lawton became a nine-season NHL journeyman on left wing. But it was Bowman's picks of Housley in 1982 and Barrasso in 1983 that truly underscored the potential of American players who hadn't even graduated beyond high school play. Housley joined the Sabres at eighteen in 1982/83, produced 66 points, and was runner-up for the Calder as he began a solid and lengthy NHL career.

In 1983/84 it was Barrasso's turn to star. When he came up to the Sabres (like Housley, straight out of school at eighteen), Barrasso dazzled. Playing in forty-two games, he won the Calder Trophy (ahead of

Steve Yzerman), the Vezina Trophy, and was runner-up (with Bob Sauve) for the Jennings Award.* No rookie goaltender had made such a spectacular regular-season debut since Tony Esposito in 1969/70.

Yet while some teenage picks, like Barrasso and Housley, could move immediately into the NHL ranks, most needed seasoning. Drafting players at eighteen was more of a gamble than selecting them at twenty, when a player would be nearing the end of a Junior or American college career. There was a longer track record on which to base a pick, and the older player was also a more mature player, emotionally and physically, making his potential far easier to judge. Some eighteen-year-olds plateaued and never fulfilled their potential, while others when drafted were still a few years away from realizing theirs. Unfortunately, rushing an eighteen-year-old into the professional ranks, the fault of both the team that drafted him and his own eagerness to make large dollars, could ruin a career that should have been allowed to unfold at a more sensible pace. The difficulty of judging eighteen-year-olds was exacerbated by the fact that they were beginning to come from less-mainstream sources: American high schools and, increasingly, European amateur clubs.

Once eighteen-year-olds began to be drafted, large lag times began to set in between the draft date and the season the selected player actually joined the parent club. An American high school student could still have an entire college career ahead of him, followed by an apprenticeship in the AHL, before he came through for the drafting team. In all, five years could easily pass. The delay became longer if the player was the end product of a trade deal. A veteran might be traded in 1978 for a draft pick in 1980. The draft pick might not be ready to play NHL hockey until age twenty-three, in 1985. In all, seven years would have lapsed between the trade being made and the benefit being

---

*From 1925/26 to 1980/81, the Vezina Trophy was awarded to the goaltender(s) on the team with the fewest goals against. Since 1981/82, the Vezina winner has been decided in voting by professional hockey broadcasters and writers. The William Jennings Award replaced the Vezina as a the fewest-goals trophy.

realized. That was an eon in professional hockey. A team could have gone through several coaches by then, and the general manager who made the trade could have been fired for stripping the lineup of popular and productive veterans to get draft picks, causing a plunge in the standings. A sport whose draft process demanded long-term player development was judging its management on short-term success. In the 1970s, Sam Pollock had shown tremendous success in converting draft picks into starting players—and Stanley Cup champions—almost immediately. But in the 1980s, a general manager who aspired to stick around for more than a few seasons had to hope the ownership was patient enough to wait for draft picks to take the years they often required to blossom into NHL starters.

Trades for players, not draft picks, on the other hand, could realize immediate results, as Bowman had demonstrated in St. Louis and would do again in Pittsburgh and Detroit. When his Buffalo career was over, Bowman would say he regretted not working trade deals in the last seasons with the Sabres. The difficulties of the draft system in the 1980s—the teenage selections, the rise of the American and foreign talent pools—accounted in part for Scotty Bowman's downfall in Buffalo. Trades he made early in his tenure for draft picks were still playing out when he was fired, five or six seasons later.

Bowman's biggest headaches came with his forays into the European talent pools. In the 1970s, acquiring Finns and Swedes had not been a priority for Bowman's Canadiens, and Eastern Bloc players were beyond reach, short of defections. Events like the 1972 Canada-Russia series and the inaugural 1976 Canada Cup had garnered respect for the European game, but the use of Europeans by North American professional clubs had mostly been limited to the WHA. The first European to be selected in the first round of the NHL draft was Sweden's Bjorn Johansson, chosen fifth by Atlanta in 1976, and in 1979 a trio of quality Swedes were claimed in the second round: Tomas Jonsson, Pelle Lindbergh and Mats Naslund.

The "defection" of Anders Hedberg and Ulf Nilsson, from the WHA's

Winnipeg Jets to the NHL's New York Rangers, in time to play against Scotty Bowman's Canadiens in the 1978/79 Stanley Cup, coincided with one of the NHL's most discouraging encounters with ambassadors of the international game. The Soviet national team came to New York for the Challenge Cup, a three-game mini-series against a team of NHL All Stars, whom Bowman was chosen to coach. After the NHLers won the opening game 4–2 and took a 4–2 lead in the second game, the Soviets tied the series by rebounding to win 5–4, and then trounced Bowman's NHLers 6–0 in the deciding match. Two years later, in the 1981 Canada Cup, Team Canada was embarrassed 8–1 by the Soviets in the championship game.

There were no Soviets available to play in the NHL, although some general managers used late draft picks to secure the rights to some of the Red stars in the event they chose to defect or the Evil Empire collapsed. In 1978, Sam Pollock waited until the draft had moved into mop-up territory and used the 201st pick to vouch for twenty-year-old Viacheslav Fetisov, a Red Army defenceman who would never play for Montreal but would still figure prominently in Scotty Bowman's future.

But the Soviets could not claim all the Eastern Bloc talent that was capable of playing in the NHL. The excellent Czechoslovakian national team program had earned world championships in 1972, 1976 and 1977. The Czechs had also reached the finals of the debut Canada Cup in 1976, losing to the Bowman-coached Canadiens. In 1974, Vaclav Nedomansky and Richard Farda defected to the West and joined the Toronto Toros of the WHA. Nedomansky became a star, switching to the Red Wings in 1977/78. When Bowman was coaching his first season in Buffalo, 1979/80, the thirty-five-year old right-winger produced a career-high seventy-three points for Detroit. That same season, defector Jiri Crha began playing goal for the Maple Leafs.

Nedomansky had just left the WHA for the NHL when the WHA's Quebec Nordiques decided they could use some of Nedomansky's style and scoring ability. Marcel Aubut, the team's president, and Maurice

Filion, the coach and general manager, had their eye on the brothers
Peter, Marian and Anton Stastny back in 1978. As the Nordiques
moved from the WHA to the NHL in 1979, Anton was the Nordiques'
fourth choice, eighty-third overall, in the entry draft. Aubut and Filion made two trips to Europe in 1979 and attended the 1980 Olympics
at Lake Placid hoping to contact the Stastnys, but failed on every occasion. In August 1980, they went to Austria for the European Cup
tournament, and at last made contact. Marian, the older brother, was
a lawyer, and he negotiated the contracts with the Nordiques for his
brothers, who then defected. Marian, however, could not leave: his
wife and children were back home in Czechoslovakia. Marian was
suspended by the Czechoslovakian national team for his involvement
in the defection of his brothers, and the Communist regime refused to
allow him to emigrate to join them.

Twenty-year-old Anton, the left-winger, and twenty-four-year-old
Peter, the centre, began playing together with the Nordiques in
1980/81. Anton and Peter combined for 78 of Quebec's 314 goals.
The Czechoslovakian league player of the year in 1979/80, Peter won
the Calder in 1980/81 as he set new league records for points (109)
and assists (70) by a rookie: he had personally been involved in 35
percent of Quebec's scoring.

In June 1981, following the startling NHL debut of brothers Anton
and Peter, the top-rated Junior player in the world, according to the
NHL's Central Scouting Bureau, was Czechoslovakia's Jiri Dudacek.
Like other clubs, Buffalo weighed the temptation of dedicating a high
draft pick to him against the likelihood of ever being able to sign him.
No draft pick is a sure thing, not even one in the first round, but with
a Canadian, an American or a European from a democratic state, a
team at least could count on the prospect being able to show up for a
tryout. Not even the Nordiques, who had been so eager to land the
Stastnys, had the nerve to claim Anton higher than eighty-third in 1979.

The night before the draft, Bowman and his staff gathered to review
prospects and discuss strategy. Buffalo's highest pick was seventeenth

overall in the first round, followed by the thirty-eighth pick in the second round and the fifty-ninth and sixtieth picks in the third round. The Sabres' prospect list was heavily weighted with Europeans—Bowman had personally made two scouting trips in the past season, and he was a vocal booster of the quality of the overseas players. "It's like when baseball broke the colour barrier," he proposed at the time. "The baseball clubs that realized how many good black and Latin ball players there were, and went after them, were the teams that did well on the field in those days." Bowman had personally witnessed this fact as a kid, when Jackie Robinson first cracked the colour barrier with the Montreal Royals in the 1940s. "There are a lot of really good hockey players in Europe," he went on. "They have proved it against North American teams that went over there. NHL clubs are just beginning to dip into a deep supply of talent."

Among the Europeans discussed by Bowman and his staff on the night before the draft was Dudacek. "I remember his name being discussed," recalls Jimmy Roberts, "but the first I knew Dudacek was our top pick was when Scotty stood up and said his name at the draft."

Despite his solo surprise, Bowman cast it as a group decision. "We figured, picking seventeenth, at best we're getting a 'maybe.' Why not take a gamble? In most years, there are about six blue-chippers, and then you're looking at an average hockey player.... So we figured, why not take a chance? There's been some defections, there's been some business done between the two countries. I've been over there. I brought a Czech player to St. Louis fifteen years ago. I know everybody over there."

It was true that Bowman had employed a Czech national in the St. Louis system. Jaroslav Jirik was the first player to emerge from behind the Iron Curtain to play in the NHL. Jirik had joined the Czechoslovakian national team and had played in three Olympics over the course of twelve seasons. At thirty, Jirik was permitted to sign a contract with the Blues in 1969, and he spent most of the 1969/70 season with Kansas City in the CPHL. At the end of the season he got a three-game look at the NHL, contributing no goals, no assists, and attracting no penalty minutes.

If Bowman had surprised his own staff, he had stunned his fellow general managers when he intoned, "From Czechoslovakia, Jiri Dudacek, right wing." No Eastern Bloc player had ever been selected so high in the draft. Committing a first-round pick to a nineteen-year-old Czechoslovakian whose government had been outraged by the Stastny caper struck observers as verging on reckless. Having just lost two Stastnys from their national team program and been compelled to suspend the third as punishment, why would the Czechs allow their game's next great talent to leave the country? And the Stastnys had not been the only losses. Toronto had collected another defector, defenceman Vitezslav Duris, for 1980/81; the Nordiques, after springing another quality player, right-winger Miroslav Frycer, for 1981/82, traded him to Toronto.

Bowman did have a good point in that, by the seventeenth pick overall, the sure choices were passing by and the general managers were entering the realm of speculation, or at least journeymen. A player of Dudacek's ability, Bowman felt, justified the gamble. "Dudacek was clear and away the best Junior prospect to come along since Gil Perreault," Bowman argued, implicitly placing him ahead of Guy Lafleur, who was drafted a year after Perreault. However, it was a perquisite of champion-builders to root out overlooked talents and secure them with later picks. Solid scouting and playing hunches were team-building tools used by Bowman's more successful rival NHL general managers. Glen Sather was building a dynasty in Edmonton with inspired late picks, which included Mark Messier (48th) and Glenn Anderson (69th) in 1979, and Jarri Kurri (69th) and Andy Moog (132nd) in 1980. The Islanders were creating and reconfiguring a championship lineup with the help of picks far from the top six. It would be hard to forget that after Bowman gambled a first-round pick on a teenager stuck behind the Iron Curtain in 1981, Montreal used a second-round pick, at 40th overall, to secure defenceman Chris

Chelios of the University of Wisconsin, a future Norris winner who went on to produce sixty-four points in his first NHL season.

The buzz was that if the Czechs ever agreed to allow Dudacek to leave for the West, it wouldn't be until he was thirty and they had drained the best years of his career from him. But Bowman sounded hopeful that Dudacek could become a Sabre sooner rather than later—and that he could become a Sabre without setting off an international incident. "We're hopeful and expect that he will be able to play for us in the future through normal channels.... We now have the negotiating rights to Dudacek, and whenever he comes here, he belongs to us. Nobody else can get him."

The prospects for a negotiated arrival of Dudacek became less likely with the defection that summer of Miroslav Frycer and the third Stastny, Marian, who simply drove out of the Eastern Bloc with his family on an automobile holiday. Marian was twenty-eight when he joined his brothers to form a Stastny forward line. The united Stastny clan scored 107 goals in 1981/82, almost one-third of the Nordiques' total offensive production, Peter leading the way with 46.

The Czechs did show that they weren't completely opposed to players leaving for the West with official approval. However, as expected, the only stars being allowed to try the NHL were ones who had already given their all to the national team. Four players were granted permission to leave in 1981, but only two took up the opportunity. Ivan Hlinka and Jiri Bubla, both thirty-one, began playing for Vancouver that fall.

In September, following the 1981 draft, the world's elite hockey players gathered for another Canada Cup tournament. Among them was Jiri Dudacek, appearing in his first international tournament with the national team. Confronted by the press at Edmonton's Northlands Coliseum after he had helped thrash the Finns, the blond-haired, moon-faced youngster professed perplexity over the attention he was receiving. "I just can't understand it. I'm just an average player. I still am not so great."

Bowman kept up the optimistic patter. "I know everybody over there. I've talked to the kid; the coach introduced me. I'm not saying he'll come right away, but we're prepared to work something out. We've got a lot to offer the kid. Maybe take him for the season, send him back for the world championships, that kind of thing. Strictly business. No cloak-and-dagger stuff."

The Dudacek selection went on haunting Bowman. The Czechs weren't making any deals to let him leave, and it was noted that Dudacek wasn't with the national team in May 1983 at the world championships in Finland. After the Maple Leafs chose Czechoslovakia's Peter Ihnacak twenty-fifth overall, high in the second round of the 1982 draft, the organization had helped him defect in Finland. The Czechs seemed wise to the tricks of the NHL general managers: secure the rights of their players in the annual draft and then spirit them away under the cover of darkness. The Stastny caper had poisoned relations just as Bowman was drafting Dudacek; the Leafs had then further damaged Bowman's chances of landing Dudacek, by means legitimate or otherwise. The Czechs were thought to have left Dudacek off the 1983 world championship team to keep him out of Finland and deny him the opportunity to escape that Ihnacak had exploited.

But the Czechs had another explanation for Dudacek's absence from the national team: they claimed he was suffering from a respiratory infection. The explanation was at first doubted, but with time it gained credibility. A report in *The Toronto Star* on February 25, 1984, noted that Dudacek's health was almost back to normal after almost two ruined seasons. His career then faded away. Stardom eluded him—not only with the Sabres, but at home as well.

Pessimism over the availability of Czech talents in their prime persisted. Chicago drafted eighteen-year-old Pardubice goaltender Dominik Hasek as an afterthought in the 1983 draft, taking him 199th. (He finally came to the Blackhawks in 1990. Chicago decided to stick with Ed Belfour as their main netminder and traded Hasek to Buffalo in 1992; "the Dominator" then won the Hart Trophy in 1996/97, the first goaltender to do so since Jacques Plante in 1961/62, and took Olympic gold and another Hart in 1998.) In 1982/83, two more permitted signings arrived: thirty-two-year-old centre Milan Novy, who lasted one season with Washington, and twenty-nine-year-old left-winger Jaroslav Pouzar, who played a little more than three seasons with Edmonton and so became the first eastern European to win a Stanley Cup. But the success of Toronto in landing Ihnacak persuaded other general managers that Czech talents were worth gambling higher draft picks on—provided you were, unlike Bowman, willing to launch cloak-and-dagger rescue missions.

Montreal's selection of defenceman Petr Svoboda fifth overall in 1984 was a high-water mark for Czech talent. Not only was it the highest a Czech player had ever been drafted, it was the first time an Eastern Bloc player had been drafted while hidden from view of the draft process in the Montreal Forum. The eighteen-year-old defenceman had defected from the Czechoslovakian Junior team and been stashed away in West Germany. Montreal's general manager, Serge Savard, had been terrified that New Jersey, which held the second pick overall, would speak up for Svoboda if they knew he was in the West. The Devils chose Kirk Muller; Svoboda was then paraded into the Forum so Savard could claim him with the fifth pick.

More intrigue followed. Minnesota took eighteen-year-old defenceman Frantisek (Frank) Musil thirty-eighth overall in the second round in 1983. Musil was eager to come to the NHL but feared that if he were caught attempting to defect before his compulsory military service was completed, he might be shot for desertion. He stayed put, attending four world championships (winning in 1985) and the 1984 Olympics. In 1985, teammate Petr Klima, drafted eighty-sixth by Detroit in 1983, defected to join the Red Wings. In the spring of 1986, Musil was dropped from the national team for refusing to sign a five-year contract that guaranteed he would not defect. Once he had completed his military obligations that June, however, he was permitted a vacation at an ocean resort in Umag, Yugoslavia. There he was met by Minnesota's general manager Lou Nanne and Edmonton agent Rich Winter. Musil's plans to defect were so secretive that he didn't tell his parents—or even his girlfriend, who was vacationing with him. Technically, Musil wasn't a defection. Nanne and Winter got him into the United States on a temporary work visa, and he then secured landed immigrant status. Like Klima, he began a long and productive NHL career. (Traded by Detroit to Edmonton, Klima won the Stanley Cup in 1989/90.)

Musil wasn't the only star of the 1985 world championship Czechoslovakian team to escape via Yugoslavia that July. Twenty-year-old Michal Pivonka also defected while on vacation, slipping away to the Italian seaport of Trieste. Pivonka had been drafted by Washington in third round of 1984, fifty-ninth overall. While the Capitals had secured Milan Novy through official channels in 1982, they were not content to wait for Pivonka to become a spent force before being allowed to sign him. Jack Button, Washington's personnel director, met Pivonka at a hunting lodge in northern Sweden later in 1984 to tell him that he'd been drafted. The Capitals maintained contact with him with security precautions out of a John Le Carre novel. A five-dollar bill was torn in two, with one half given to Pivonka. By matching his with the one carried by whoever was sent to maintain contact with him, he would know the person was legitimate. At age twenty, the skilful centre began a long NHL career with the Capitals in 1986/87.

Amidst the capers of his fellow general managers in springing Czechoslovakian stars from the servitude of Communism, Bowman's misadventure with Dudacek was an unfortunate miscue. He was proven wrong to think he could strike any kind of bargain that would get Dudacek (or any other highly touted young player) to Buffalo before the Czechs had wrung from him his best hockey. Certainly no other general manager was able to get a young Czech player without participating in his defection. Dudacek's illness (if legitimate) relieved Bowman of further humiliation, for the only thing that could have made the consequences of the draft gamble worse would have been Dudacek turning into a

Czechoslovakian star and Bowman remaining adamant about bringing him to Buffalo only by above-board means. Had he waited until the collapse of the Communist regime in Czechoslovakia in November 1989, Dudacek would have been a well-worn twenty-seven-year-old.

The Dudacek gamble was the greatest blot on Bowman's drafting efforts in 1981, but not the only one, as the draft turned into a near-futile fishing expedition in the European talent pool. Bowman dangled plenty of bait, but almost no one bit. Reflecting his personal scouting expeditions and conviction that drafting overseas talent was the key to team-building, seven of his twelve picks were transatlantic selections. His second pick, Hannu Virta, an eighteen-year-old Finn chosen 38th overall in the second round, was the only one to make the Sabres, turning into a points-producing defenceman for four seasons. The rest, beginning with Dudacek and including Anders Wikburg (83rd), Mauri Eivola (101st), Ali Butorac (122nd) and Heikki Leime (143rd), were washouts. (Bowman also chose Venci Sebek, an American of Czech parents, 165th, and he didn't pan out, either.)

In 1982 Bowman did stick to North American talent in the opening round, in which he held three precious picks, two garnered by trades of stars. After doing well choosing Housley with the sixth pick overall, he found a starting left-winger at ninth in Paul Cyr of the Victoria Cougars. An even greater success on left wing came with the sixteenth pick, when he chose Dave Andreychuk of the Oshawa Generals, who would produce eighty points in his second season.

Once out of the first round, though, Bowman was back trying his luck with Europeans, and having no more success than he did in 1981. Jens Johansson, taken 30th, never played, nor did late pick Jacob Gustavsson, chosen 121st, while Timo Jutila, selected 68th, managed ten games on defence with the Sabres in 1984/85. Of ten Europeans chosen by Bowman in the 1981 and 1982 drafts, only one, Virtu, ever became an NHL starter, and only one other, Jutila, ever played a league game.

Bowman was less generous in his European picks in 1983, which proved to be the last draft in which he held a handful of high picks.

With Barrasso his top selection, he didn't go near a European until his 9th pick, when he took nineteen-year-old Christian Ruuttu of Finland 134th. At 214th he chose West Germany's Uwe Krupp, and at 235th Kermit Salfi.

In these late picks, Bowman had success, as Ruuttu emerged a capable centre whose NHL career lasted nine seasons. Standing six-and-a-half feet tall, the longshot Krupp was a defensive pillar who joined the Sabres in 1986/87, produced a career-high forty-four points with the Sabres in 1990/91 and enjoyed an appearance in that season's All Star game. After playing only six regular season games for Colorado in 1995/96, Krupp became a star of the 1995/96 Stanley Cup playoffs, helping the Avalanche defeat Bowman's Red Wings in the semifinals and contributing sixteen points in twenty-two games as Colorado won the Cup.

In the next two drafts, Bowman made Europeans a priority, twice selecting a Swede as his opening pick, with mixed results. Mikael Andersson was eighteen years old when chosen eighteenth overall in 1984. "You can't let a guy like this one pass by," Bowman said of the left-winger who had been the top-rated player at the World Junior Championships in Sweden in December 1983, producing eight goals and eight assists in five games. "I was afraid that he would be signed before we would get a chance at him. I thought the Rangers might take him. He's a real talented player. But I don't think he'll be able to play for us next year." The Rangers had used their pick, at fourteenth overall, to secure eighteen-year-old Canadian defenceman Terry Carkner, who began a long NHL career in 1986/87. Andersson, on the other hand, never developed into a Sabres starter. He spent four seasons, from 1985/86 to 1988/89, bouncing between Buffalo and its AHL farm team in Rochester before being let go on waivers to Hartford in October 1989. Although he continued to play in the NHL, he never became the scorer his Junior performance had suggested. Calle Johansson, a teammate of Andersson's in Sweden, was also eighteen when chosen fourteenth overall in 1985 by Bowman. He didn't leave Sweden until 1987, but he immediately proved himself to be a capable defence-man, and he was named to the NHL All Rookie team of 1987/88.

Johansson was one of a number of players Bowman drafted who were just making the Sabres as he was dismissed in 1986/87, or were due to become starters in 1987/88. Jeff Parker, drafted 111th overall in 1982, didn't play his first Sabres games until 1986/87. Normand LaCombe, drafted 10th overall in 1983, did play his first Buffalo games in 1984/85, but ended up being traded to Edmonton in 1986/87, where he won a Stanley Cup. Adam Creighton, drafted 11th overall in 1983, was tournament MVP in the 1984 Memorial Cup, confirming Bowman's wisdom in selecting him. He didn't get a Sabres starting job until 1986/87, but then he became an NHL regular at centre for the next decade, producing a career-high seventy points with Chicago in 1989/90. Darren Puppa, selected 74th overall in 1983, still had two seasons of American amateur hockey ahead of him, and three seasons in the AHL. In 1986/87, he belatedly rewarded the departed Bowman by making the AHL All Star team. He took until 1987/88 to move up the Sabres' goaltending ranks and merit seventeen appearances. He was named to the NHL second All Star team in 1989/90 as Buffalo's main netminder, and he was the first-string goaltender for Tampa Bay from 1993/94 to 1995/96. Christian Ruuttu, drafted 134th in 1983, proved to be an inspired choice. The teenage Finn became a Sabres rookie in 1986/87 and had a nine-season NHL career. And then there was the utterly unlikely Uwe Krupp, whose draft position, 214th in 1983, was normally reserved for Russians who might hijack a plane to New York. Like Ruuttu, Krupp made the Sabres just as Bowman was being fired.

Ray Sheppard, picked 60th overall by Bowman in 1984, didn't make the Sabres until 1987/88, and ended up playing for Bowman in Detroit. Bob Halkidis, drafted 81st that year, also wound up as a Red Wing under Bowman. Darcy Wakaluk, chosen 144th, upheld Bowman's sixth sense about goaltending talent. This late pick broke in with Buffalo in 1988/89 and was a regular with the Minnesota North Stars/Dallas Stars from 1990/91 to 1995/96.

The 1985 draft brought more picks that blossomed after Bowman was let go. In addition to Johannson, there was Benoit Hogue, chosen 35th, who cracked the Sabres in 1988/89. Joe Reekie became another well-chosen longshot at 119th; his lengthy NHL career on defence was just beginning in 1986/87. And deep in that year's draft, Bowman managed to come away with players who would skate for NHL teams. Guy Larose, chosen 224th, played off and on in the league from 1988/89 to 1993/94. Ken Baumgartner echoed Sam Pollock's success with Chris Nilan in 1978. Taken 245th by Bowman, Baumgartner began a long career as an NHL enforcer with Los Angeles in 1987/88.

Finally, Bowman's 1986 picks produced a few NHL regulars. His first pick, Shawn Anderson, who went 5th overall, started with Buffalo immediately in 1986/87. His second pick, Greg Brown, taken 26th overall, made occasional league appearances from 1990/91 to 1994/95. Bob Corkum, Bowman's next pick at 47th, played his first 8 Sabres games in 1989/90 and went on to play regularly at centre with Buffalo, Anaheim and Philadelphia. And down at 131st Bowman had come up with Mike Hartman, a tough nineteen-year-old American left-winger who played his first 17 games with Buffalo in 1986/87 and went on to play 367 NHL games through 1994/95 with Buffalo, Winnipeg, Tampa Bay and the Rangers.

In summary, Bowman had done a better job in the draft than he was given credit for at the time of his firing, when the fruits of his efforts had not yet ripened. Buffalo's ownership had given up waiting for a turnaround. From their point of view, there never was supposed to be a turnaround. They had handed Bowman a first-class NHL club they felt was underachieving under its architect, Punch Imlach. Bowman was supposed to take that team to the Stanley Cup, not falter in the playoffs, trade away the stars and then expect several years of patience from the owners and fans as he waited for a new generation of prospects to become starters. But even if he had stayed, the owners and fans were bound to be disappointed when Bowman's picks inevitably failed to measure up to the heroes Punch Imlach had assembled. Imlach, after all, had launched the team with a bevy of high picks: first in 1970 (Gilbert Perreault), fifth in 1971 (Richard Martin), fifth in 1972 (Jim Schoenfeld). When Bowman got his hands on high picks in 1982 and 1983, he had done well in choosing Phil Housley and Tom Barrasso. But by then, Bowman's opportunity to win with the Sabres was all but over. The decade that the Knoxes had hoped would belong to the Sabres instead belonged to two teams coached by former Bowman players—Al Arbour's New York Islanders, who won four straight Stanley Cups from 1979/80 to 1982/83, and Glen Sather's Edmonton Oilers, who won five Cups between 1984/85 and 1989/90.

12

✧ IN THE DIFFICULT DAYS in Buffalo, Scotty Bowman took sol-
ace and refuge in ice and trains. At home, away from the team he
could not make win, he flooded the backyard in the winter to make a
rink for his children, an exercise that conjured his own childhood
spent on makeshift ice in Verdun. Indoors, he ran his railway, an elaborate model-train tableau. It seemed the perfect diversion from the
complexities and anxieties of running the Sabres. If Scotty Bowman
were to have a hobby (and few people could imagine him with any
sort of amusement beyond winning hockey games), surely this would
be it. A world in microcosm, systematic, within his control, engines
moving cars hither and yon with the precision of line changes. Scotty
Bowman could take refuge from a day-to-day world that eluded
absolute control in a world of his own construction. The world's great
autocrats have always been able to make the trains run on time.

Back among the Sabres, Bowman shunted cars, sent some to the
scrapyard, parked others on sidings. After he fired Roger Neilson as
coach following the 1980/81 playoffs, it was widely expected that at
the June 1981 league meetings, Bowman would name Jimmy Roberts
the new coach. But Bowman was full of surprises. In addition to
making the Czech teenager Jiri Dudacek his first-round draft pick,
Bowman declined to give Roberts the position of head coach. Instead,

Roberts was named associate coach, albeit with the head coach's responsibilities.

Roberts found it difficult to function with the ambiguity of his position, knowing that Bowman was always upstairs, watching him. (The Sabres used a radio system linking the bench with the press box.) As a rookie strategist, he was expected to perform for one of the most accomplished bench managers in history, and he could not succeed. "No one can coach under him," says Roberts. "No one can live up to his standards. You'd have to do everything he did, which is impossible."

After forty-five games, Roberts reverted to assistant coach as Bowman reclaimed the head coach's job. Roberts had produced a record of nineteen wins, sixteen losses and eight ties, but Bowman drove the club harder down the stretch, producing eighteen wins, ten losses and seven ties to finish third in the Adams division.

In the playoffs, however, Buffalo was downed by the Bruins three games to one in the opening round, surrendering 4.25 goals per game. That June, Bowman overhauled his goaltending. Back in December, when he had sent Bob Sauve to Detroit, he made Don Edwards his main starter and Jacques Cloutier, his fifty-fifth pick in the 1979 draft, the backup. After the playoff loss to Boston, Bowman decided he had chosen the wrong member of his former league-leading goaltending duo. Sauve was re-signed as a free agent and Don Edwards was traded to load up on more draft picks. The general manager in Calgary was his former assistant in St. Louis, Cliff Fletcher. Bowman sent him Edwards, defenceman Rich Dunn and Buffalo's second-round choice in the 1982 draft in order to gain Calgary's first- and second-round choices in that summer's draft and the Flames' second-round choice in the 1983 draft.

Bowman was determined to hang on to the head coaching job. He had learned it was something he could not give up easily to concentrate on managing. "Sitting up there, directing traffic with players [through trades and drafting], is not fulfilling enough for him," says Craig Ramsay. "He needs that battle of the game, which he never got by being a player. He *loves* the game," Ramsay emphasizes. "He watches a game after you've played a game. He's up watching on TV at three in the morning."

Roberts's reversion to the assistant's job was a positive development for both Roberts and the Sabres. He had the same high intensity as Bowman, and with both men in senior positions, that intensity could be overwhelming, particularly for new, young players. "Jimmy really learned how to be a good assistant coach," says Ramsay, who in 1997/98 was an assistant coach with the Ottawa Senators. "He stepped back, and became a guy you could talk to. He could make you feel better as a player."

The Sabres rebounded in 1983/84, aided by the phenomenal goal-tending debut of Tom Barrasso. The Sabres won forty-eight games and finished 1 point behind Boston in the Adams division. With 103 points, the Sabres had broken the 100-point barrier for the first time since Bowman's inaugural season, and Bowman was runner-up to Washington's Bryan Murray in voting for the Jack Adams Award as the league's top coach.

In midseason, Jerry Korab became a Sabre again. Persistent problems with his right foot (which caused back problems that knocked him out of twenty-two games in 1982/83) had finished his career in Los Angeles. Major surgery in the summer of 1983, just as he was becoming a free agent, left him out of hockey. The Minnesota North Stars acquired him, but did not play him. Available on waivers, Korab was signed by Bowman.

"It was kind of funny when I first came back to the dressing room," Korab said of his return to the Sabres. "It was like a new team. I hardly knew anyone and those I did know were quick to point out I'm from a different generation than a lot of these guys."

After an impressive regular-season effort, the 1983/84 playoffs delivered another resounding letdown. Bowman, as expected, gave the starting goaltending assignment to Barrasso, and the nineteen-year-old Calder and Vezina winner allowed eight goals in seven periods of play as Quebec swept the Sabres in three in the opening round.

The poor playoff performance and a slow start to the 1984/85 season earned Barrasso a demeaning trip to the minors. "I wanted to beat the—out of somebody," Barrasso said of the cold-shoulder treatment by Bowman. "It was humiliating."

After his five-game exile in Rochester, in which Barrasso allowed only 1.35 goals per game, he was retrieved by Bowman. In 1984/85, Barrasso's regular-season play earned him the Vezina, and he shared the Jennings with Sauve. In the playoffs, the Sabres tangled with Quebec in a high-scoring opening series. Barrasso's goals-against average, a league-leading 2.66 in the regular season, ballooned to 4.40 in the best-of-five as the Sabres lost the deciding game five 6–5 in Quebec. Two successive playoff efforts by Bowman had been met with first-round losses to the Nordiques.

In the meantime, Bowman had lost Roberts. After he dropped back to the assistant coach's job, says Roberts, "Everything was going well. But Scotty was having problems with ownership at that time. Scotty had a way of deflecting criticism of himself in other directions. I felt some of the criticism was getting in places where it didn't belong. I decided to call it quits for that relationship, with no hard feelings. It was time for me to move on." Roberts was hired by Bob Berry as his assistant in Pittsburgh, and his coaching career carried on, taking him to Hartford and, eventually, back to St. Louis.

Bowman had a coaching protege in the Buffalo system in his first years with the Sabres, but he never got him onto the Sabres' bench. "Iron Mike" Keenan came as close as any coach in the modern game to matching Bowman's authoritarian style. Having coached the Peterborough Petes for one season in 1979/80 and taken them to the Memorial Cup finals, Keenan was hired to coach Buffalo's AHL affiliate, the Rochester Americans. In three seasons under Keenan, the Americans improved dramatically, winning the Calder Cup in 1982/83. Keenan then left the Sabres organization to become head coach of the University of Toronto Blues for 1983/84. In 1984/85, Keenan secured his first NHL head coaching job, and he guided the Philadelphia Flyers to the Stanley Cup finals, losing to the Oilers.

Bowman was back trying out a Sabres coaching successor in 1985/86. This time it was former Sabres star Jim Schoenfeld. After being traded away to Detroit in 1981/82, Schoenfeld had moved on to Boston in 1983/84, where, after thirty-nine games, he retired. Bowman saw his coaching potential and hired him to run the Rochester Americans' bench in 1984/85, but after twenty-five games, of which he won an impressive seventeen and tied two, Schoenfeld decided to give the NHL another try as a player and returned with Buffalo for the rest of the season. Rochester was taken over by retired Sabres defenceman John Van Boxmeer. For 1985/86, Bowman named Schoenfeld the Sabres' coach.

Al Arbour in St. Louis and Jimmy Roberts in Buffalo had already learned that getting much past the halfway point of a season as a Bowman coach was near impossible. Only Roger Neilson had been able to last an entire (if fractious) season. Schoenfeld lasted forty-three games before Bowman fired him. The Sabres were in a tight race for a playoff spot: only six wins would separate first from fifth in the Adams division. Bowman's return to the bench made no difference in the performance of the team. Having won nineteen, lost nineteen and tied five under Schoenfeld, the Sabres won eighteen, lost eighteen and tied one under Bowman. Their eighty-point effort was thirteenth-best among the league's twenty-one clubs, and would have put them in third in the Smythe division or fourth in the Norris or Patrick, but in the closely contested Adams it left the Sabres in fifth, four points behind fourth-place Hartford, the last playoff qualifier. For the first time in his NHL coaching career, Bowman did not take a team into the playoffs.

His career as a general manager had been marked by a predilection for placing unproven, inexperienced coaches into the NHL firing line. Indeed, not one of his hirings, with the exception of Roger Neilson, had ever coached in the NHL. In the case of Arbour and Schoenfeld, he had thrust people with considerable potential into the fray with little or no preparation, then yanked them out after about half a season. Both Arbour and Schoenfeld went on to have lengthy NHL coaching careers, but not under Bowman. It was as if Bowman could recognize coaching potential, but could not find the way to let it develop properly. He was a managerial loner who needed ultimate control. In Montreal, he had enjoyed and appreciated the managerial protection and support he had received from Sam Pollock, who had given him most everything he wanted in terms of player deals. As a general manager himself, though, he had feuded with Neilson, rebuilding a team the way he wanted to and leaving the coach to deal with the consequences.

"He decided he was just going to be the GM," Ramsay says of the 1980/81 season. "That was the deal he had with Roger. But now he wants to make his imprint, so that means you've got to change players. Tinkering and making adjustments with a fine hockey team, Scotty is the best. The only scenario where he didn't succeed was in Buffalo, and that was because we ended up not being a strong team. We just got too young, too fast. The match-ups weren't important any more, because we just couldn't make it work. One problem was that we started to change our system a lot. Instead of finding something and sticking with it, we kept changing to fit the group of players."

Bowman was not a popular dressing-room presence, although he had his fans among the players in Buffalo. "I think the thing I like most about Scotty is that he is honest with you from the start," defenceman Mike Ramsey told *The Detroit News* in 1997. Playing with Buffalo through most of Bowman's reign there, Ramsey followed him to Pittsburgh and Detroit, where he retired after more than sixteen seasons, in 1996. "When I was a nineteen-year-old kid, he was very intimidating. But he was fair. And if you gave him an honest effort, you had nothing to worry about."

But Craig Ramsay saw Bowman's relationship with younger players differently. As Bowman re-entered the coaching job, his presence had a debilitating effect on some of the prospects he had recruited.

Because Bowman had never played the game as a young professional, he didn't know what it felt like to have an intense, charismatic coach leaning on him. Ramsay felt this lack of personal experience worked against Bowman, noting that his coaching success has often come from accumulating veterans who have been through the mill. "For many young players, it was an incredible level of fear, dealing with his intensity. They were just waiting for him to pick them as the daily target. He reacted sometimes in a way that really was too strong for many people to deal with. Young players didn't have a reservoir of experience and courage to draw upon to deal with Bowman's anger."

After being traded to the Rangers by Bowman in 1984, Steve Patrick, his first-round draft pick in 1980, reflected on life as a young professional under Bowman's glare. "I can remember him yelling, 'Patrick, you're nothing but an underachiever.' Once, I had a chance to score in Philly. The goalie was down, and I couldn't get the puck up. Afterwards Scotty walked by me, no eye contact. Nothing. He was like that. Then we walked by each other again, and he sort of stopped in his tracks and said, 'Steve, you had the whole net open, and you couldn't even put the puck in it.' Then he just walked away."

Three seasons had taken their toll on Bowman's reputation as a coaching wizard. His highly regarded effort in the 1983/84 season had been deflated by the quick collapse in the playoffs. The repeat loss to Quebec in the 1984/85 playoffs further tarnished his reputation as a playoff genius. The replacement of Schoenfeld in 1985/86 midway through the season probably did more harm to Bowman's coaching reputation than missing the playoffs that spring, for the margin between success and failure was so narrow that year. Buffalo won only three fewer games than Montreal, yet missed the playoffs, while the Canadiens won the Stanley Cup. What hurt Bowman was the fact that he couldn't do any better than Schoenfeld when it came to coaching the team he had built. The logic was inevitable. If Bowman couldn't make the Sabres win more than a rookie like Schoenfeld, then the problem wasn't Schoenfeld. The problem was the team.

And the man who had created the team stubbornly playing .500 hockey was Bowman.

After Schoenfeld's dismissal, Craig Ramsay was next in line to experience life as a Bowman coaching protege. After retiring in 1984/85, he became an assistant coach to Bowman in 1985/86. At the beginning of the 1986/87 season, Bowman was back behind the bench again, but early in the campaign his interest momentarily wavered. Only minutes before the opening faceoff of a game against Montreal, Bowman walked into the dressing room and confronted Ramsay. "He said, 'I'm going to watch the game upstairs. You coach tonight.' I had five minutes to write something up and talk to the players and tell them I was coaching."

It may or may not have been significant that the opponent was Montreal. In 1967/68, when Lynn Patrick had turned the Blues over to Bowman, he too had faced the Canadiens in his first test behind the bench. On both occasions, Montreal was the defending Stanley Cup champion. Bowman was either testing Ramsay with a true ordeal by fire, or he was avoiding placing himself in the path of his old team, sensitive to the scar Roberts says he bore from being rejected by the Canadiens as management material.

Ramsay quickly found that coaching a game was nothing like overseeing practice drills and working with individual players on their skills. "Being an assistant and running the bench—they're not even close. The decisions are yours. It was quite a night for me, the pressure of it. The guys played really well, and it was great excitement, a nothing-nothing tie against a team that was much better than us. After the game, Scotty said, 'It was a bad game, eh.'"

It was a bad game, from the perspective of fan appeal, but Ramsay had survived it, whereas Bowman had lost his first NHL game 3–1 to the Canadiens. Bowman took the Sabres back from Ramsay and carried on coaching. But after guiding the Sabres to three wins, seven losses and two ties, he telephoned Ramsay. "I don't want to coach any more," he said. And Craig Ramsay became head coach number four for Bowman's Sabres.

Both were doomed by Bowman's decision. The team was struggling, Ramsay was inexperienced, and Bowman, by removing himself from the bench, had taken himself out of the job that the Knoxes had really wanted him for. The lesson of 1985/86 was confirmed in the opening weeks of 1986/87. In the past, when a team he was managing was underachieving, Bowman had not hesitated to step in and resume coaching. The 1985/86 season had shown that the Sabres had reached the point where underachievement was not an issue. Scotty Bowman had created a team even *he* couldn't make win. The start of the 1986/87 season marked the first time in Bowman's management career in which he removed himself from coaching when the team was losing. It was optimistic in the extreme to expect that Ramsay would be able to do any better. As it happened, Ramsay's Sabres had won two and lost eight when the Knoxes decided they were through with Bowman. Gerry Meehan was named the new general manager, and Meehan brought in Ted Sator to replace Ramsay. The Sabres won just twenty-eight games that season, finishing last in the league, but over the next three seasons they rapidly improved, reaching forty-five wins in 1989/90.

Nine days before Bowman was fired, Gilbert Perreault, the last surviving member of the French Connection, chose to retire. Perreault had been the first player chosen by Imlach in the entry draft when the team was formed in 1970. Bowman had come to Buffalo an admirer of Perreault's, calling him in 1981 the greatest Junior talent ever to have been drafted, and he named Perreault the new team captain when Gare was traded away. But Perreault was left unimpressed by Bowman. "They probably should have done it three years ago, the way we were going anyway," Perreault said, when informed of Bowman's firing. "I'm not surprised at all. It was a good move by the Sabres. Scotty was the root of some of the team's problems. Look at the start we got this year and we didn't make the playoffs last year. He built the team, so what can I say."

Perreault said he had approached Bowman about some of the team's problems, among them what Perreault saw as a lack of communication and team spirit. He said Bowman made no effort to address his concerns. "We never had a talk about the team. Three or four years ago they said, 'You're the captain,' and I said okay. There was no communication. He was the big boss and that was the way it was. There was no communication with the captain or the players whatsoever."

For the second time in his NHL career, Scotty Bowman was out of work. But this was different from St. Louis in the spring of 1971. When the Salomons sent him packing, Bowman had a shopping list of job offers to ponder. After the Knoxes fired him, Bowman was bereft of opportunity. He had left a dynasty in Montreal for the big job, angered that he had been passed over for promotion in 1978, and his failure in Buffalo was viewed by some as a vindication of Montreal's decision to give the general manager's job to Irving Grundman. In his memoirs, however, Jean Beliveau wouldn't see the issue in such a clear-cut manner. Bowman had not been "an unqualified success" in Buffalo, but on the other hand, "Irving Grundman wasn't entirely successful, either." On balance, though, Beliveau felt the right decision had been made. Beliveau pronounced Bowman "a great coach, but an impatient general manager." Impatience was not a word that described the Knoxes. They had given Punch Imlach eight seasons to create a winner; Bowman was beginning his eighth season when his time ran out.

And in Bowman's absence, the Canadiens had found their way back to glory. After suffering elimination by the Nordiques in the 1984/85 division finals (a 4–3 defeat that included three overtime losses), the Canadiens returned to Stanley Cup success in 1985/86 with a 4–1 defeat of the Calgary Flames. Buffalo under Bowman was missing the playoffs just as the Canadiens were back adding another victory to their fabled string of wins. Montreal would return to the finals, losing to Calgary in 1988/89, and winning against Los Angeles in 1992/93. The organization had proven capable of overcoming the upheavals of 1978 and 1979. Bowman, single-handedly, couldn't close the chapter on Montreal's winning years, and he couldn't, single-handedly, bring winning years to Buffalo.

Bowman ended up sitting out the late 1980s, watching the league battles from a CBC broadcast booth, commenting on the game that had no room for him.

13

✧ THE SUCCESS OF the Pittsburgh Penguins in 1990/91 and 1991/92 was without precedent in the post-1967 expansion era. No other team except the Montreal Canadiens had rebounded from missing the playoffs in one season to winning the Stanley Cup in the very next. But the Canadiens' reversal of fortune in winning the 1970/71 Cup was hardly in the same category as Pittsburgh's one-season rocket-ride from ignominy to back-to-back Cup victories. Montreal, after all, had been in five consecutive finals, and won four of them, before missing out in 1969/70 on the fourth and final playoff spot in the East division to the Rangers. Pittsburgh, on the other hand, was a 1967/68 expansion team that had never come close to Cup success, missing the playoffs in six consecutive seasons from 1982/83 to 1987/88 before toying with respectability by reaching the Patrick Division finals in 1988/89, only to miss the playoffs again in 1989/90. The next season, the Penguins were champions, and they successfully defended their title in 1991/92.

For four seasons, from 1989/90 to 1992/93, Scotty Bowman was part of the Penguins' success story, first as director of player development and recruitment, then as head coach. It is a phase of his career that tends to be downplayed, as if his success there were due to nothing more than good timing and the hard work of others. To be sure, he benefited from some league intrigue, a familiar face in a position to hire and promote him, and a tragedy in the sudden death of Penguins coach Bob Johnson, which abruptly opened the door to his return as an NHL coach. But once Pittsburgh presented him with a return to the game, even when it appeared that his career was over, it was up to Bowman to demonstrate that he entirely deserved the second chance—and he did.

The Penguins' turnaround ranks among the greatest in NHL history. It was breathtakingly rapid in its execution, and was built on solid player management. The Penguins were no "Miracle On Ice," no brief burst of guts and emotion without staying power. Pittsburgh was built to win more than once, and Bowman should receive more credit than he normally does for the organization's success. His value would be underlined by the unprecedented richness of the offer that lured him away to Detroit in 1993.

Pittsburgh had long shared in the general failure of its fellow expansion teams to achieve parity with the established clubs. St. Louis had been able to reach the Cup finals in three successive seasons under Bowman, but that was due to the skewed nature of the playoff format, which reserved a Cup berth for one of the expansion clubs. When that special provision was removed (and Bowman fired), St. Louis failed to make another serious challenge for the finals. Of the six newcomers, only Philadelphia was able to achieve Cup success, with victories in 1973/74 and 1974/75 and further trips to the finals in 1975/76, 1979/80, 1984/85, 1986/87 and 1996/97. The Los Angeles Kings had still not reached the finals when Bowman came to the Penguins in 1989. The California Seals never came close to the finals before becoming the equally unsuccessful Cleveland Barons in 1976/77. In 1978/79, the Barons were absorbed by the Minnesota North Stars, who made a quixotic trip to the finals in 1980/81. There they were obliterated by the New York Islanders, a defeat that said much about the strange failure of those 1967/68 newcomers. Minnesota and its brother expansioneers had enjoyed a five-season head start on the Long Island club, but after a horrible debut it had taken the Islanders only three seasons to develop a club of great promise. Buffalo, which had come into the league in 1970/71, had similarly been quick to establish itself, reaching the finals in 1974/75.

Edmonton's success in the 1980s showed that it was possible for an also-ran club to reach the top quickly if scouting and player development were made an absolute priority. But teams like the Penguins seemed to have made an art of mediocrity: icing mediocre teams, producing mediocre results and using mediocre draft positions to gather more mediocre players.

Pittsburgh had missed the playoffs in its first two seasons of operation, and settled into a lengthy run as a poorer-than-average club. After winning thirty, then thirty, then thirty-one games in eighty-game seasons from 1979/80 to 1981/82, the Penguins nose-dived to eighteen wins in 1982/83, beginning their six-season playoff absence. By finishing dead last in 1982/83, the Penguins should at least have enjoyed first pick in the 1983 draft, but the club had traded away the right to Minnesota, and didn't choose until fifteenth (a position it had, coincidentally, acquired from Minnesota). It was a huge miss by Pittsburgh, although Minnesota wasted a golden opportunity by choosing Brian Lawton, who never lived up to the potential of his pick in eight and a half seasons on left wing in the NHL. Hartford, choosing second, took Sylvain Turgeon; the Islanders, choosing third with a pick obtained from New Jersey, took Pat Lafontaine; Detroit, choosing fourth, took Steve Yzerman; Buffalo, choosing fifth with a pick passed through Los Angeles from St. Louis, took Tom Barrasso. Pittsburgh was fortunate to pick a solid left-winger in Bob Errey down at fifteenth, but the team was not going to make the same mistake again. Pittsburgh became resolute about holding onto its first-round picks, even trading to accumulate more of them. In 1983/84, Pittsburgh held three first-round picks, including first overall, by virtue of having finished last again. The team was perfectly positioned to nab the prospect of the decade: Mario Lemieux.

Lemieux was not yet nineteen years old when the Penguins chose him in the 1984 draft. Playing as team captain for the Laval Voisins of the Quebec Major Junior league, Lemieux had laid waste to offensive records, scoring 133 goals and 149 assists in a seventy-game season. He added another 29 goals and 23 assists in fourteen playoff games, and while his team disappointed in the Memorial Cup round-robin final, Lemieux was far and away the best of the draft-eligible Juniors. While a smattering of players on the Memorial Cup teams would go on to have NHL careers (including Lemieux's Laval teammate, Vincent Damphousse, who won a Stanley Cup with Montreal in 1992/93), no one in the 1984 draft pool came close to radiating the promise of the six-foot, four-inch, 225-pound scorer and play-maker. Kirk Muller, Ed Olczyk, Al Iafrate and Stephane Richer (who remained untouched until the second round) were all up for grabs, but there was no doubt who would be grabbed first.

Beginning with Lemieux in 1984, the Penguins picked high in the first round (never worse than fifth) for five consecutive seasons, a happy by-product of the team's continuing failure to make the playoffs. Presiding over this gloomy period of Penguin history was Eddie Johnston. The former Bruins goaltender, who had won Stanley Cups in 1969/70 and 1971/72, had been hired to coach the Penguins in 1980 after a baffling year in Chicago. In 1979/80, his first season as the Blackhawks' coach, he had guided them to their third consecutive Norris division title, with their most wins since 1974/75. But after the Blackhawks made their third consecutive playoff exit in the quarterfinals (losing to Scotty Bowman's Sabres in four straight), Johnston was fired.

The dismissal was no great slight on his abilities, and he was hired to coach Pittsburgh for the next season. In 1983 Johnston became general manager, and the club's tenacious devotion to first-round picks began. On the ice, the team slowly but steadily improved. Though they were still missing the playoffs, the Penguins were winning more games, up from sixteen in 1983/84 to thirty-six in 1987/88. Along the way, the team ran through a series of coaches: Lou Angotti, Bob Berry,

Pierre Creamer. For several seasons Pittsburgh seemed to begin and end with Mario Lemieux, aka Super Mario, aka The Next One (in deference to Wayne Gretzky, The Great One). The Calder Trophy winner in 1984/85, Lemieux had emerged as a perennial All Star, a league MVP and, for the first time in 1987/88, NHL scoring champion.

After 1987/88, however, the Penguins courted management disaster. Johnston was fired, replaced by former Chicago goaltending star Tony Esposito, who had retired after 1983/84. According to Ross Conway's *Game Misconduct*, Johnston had been a victim of league politics. Esposito had been a favourite of NHL Players' Association president Alan Eagleson, having served as NHLPA vice-president, and Eagleson had persuaded Penguins owner Ed DeBartolo to ditch Johnston and give his job to Esposito.

Esposito had no previous experience to suggest he was ready to manage an NHL team. Gene Ubriaco was hired to replace Pierre Creamer as coach, and the club had some apparent success. Mario Lemieux had what would prove to be the greatest regular season of his career, with 199 points, as Pittsburgh finally returned to the playoffs after finishing second in the Patrick division, with a franchise-record forty wins. In the division semifinals it took them only four games to eliminate the Rangers, who had finished five points behind them. Then they lost a seesaw, seven-game division finals to Philadelphia, who had finished in fourth, seven points behind the Penguins, in the Patrick.

But enjoying the welcome return to playoff hockey was a club with serious problems. It was an offence-minded team, scoring 347 goals, third-highest in the league—but it was a defensive sieve, allowing 349, second-worst in the league. Goaltending was not at issue; at the beginning of 1988/89, Esposito had acquired from Buffalo Tom Barrasso, a major talent. But the rest of the team wasn't paying enough attention to its own end. In the division finals against Philadelphia, the Penguins had taken a 3–2 series lead in a 10–7 shootout, but the Flyers had been able to shut down their offence and outscore them 10–3 in the next two games to eliminate them. The Penguins were terribly one-dimensional. Even though there were seventeen players in the Penguins system who would figure in their Stanley Cup wins, the team lacked key role players and a commitment to a two-way game.

Esposito and Ubriaco managed to start the 1989/90 season in charge of the Penguins, but they wouldn't come close to finishing it. The Penguins had won ten, lost fourteen and tied two when the change came. Esposito (who was never as well liked by the players as Eddie Johnston) and Ubriaco were ousted on December 5.

If DeBartolo had any thought then of returning to Johnston as coach or general manager, he was too late; Johnston had been hired that season to manage the Hartford Whalers. (The Penguins would, however, bring Johnston back as coach in 1993/94.) Instead, Esposito was replaced by Craig Patrick, a favourite son of the famous hockey dynasty that had given the Penguins' division its name.

Craig was the son of Lynn, who had recruited Scotty Bowman to work for him in St. Louis. Like his father, uncle, great-uncle and grandfather, Craig had played the game at an elite level, winning a U.S. collegiate championship as captain of the University of Denver Pioneers in 1969. Trained by Scotty Bowman in the Montreal Junior system, Patrick was one of seven American collegiate players chosen in the inaugural 1969 universal draft. As a journeyman right-winger, Patrick played for the woeful California Seals from 1971/72 until 1974/75, when he was dealt to St. Louis. A season in another poor cousin of the NHL family, the Kansas City Scouts, led him to jump to the Minnesota Fighting Saints of the WHA. The Saints survived for forty-two games of the of 1976/77 season before folding; Patrick played in thirty, and took his services to the Washington Capitals. It was another down-on-its-luck franchise, and after appearing in only three games in 1978/79, Patrick quit playing to turn his attention to coaching and management, joining the U.S. Olympic program as assistant coach and assistant general manager. It was a broad role that mirrored Bowman's own experiences working for Sam Pollock with the Ottawa-Hull Junior Canadiens and for Lynn Patrick with the St. Louis Blues.

The Americans struck gold at Lake Placid, and Patrick converted the triumph into a plum job with the New York Rangers. The Rangers had hired Fred Shero away from Philadelphia in 1978, offering him the coach and general manager's job, and he had taken the Rangers to the Cup finals against Bowman's Canadiens. In 1979/80, though, the Rangers were ousted in the quarterfinals by his old Flyers (who went on to lose in the finals to the Islanders). Shero was drinking, and unaware he was slowly succumbing to cancer. After twenty-one games in 1979/80, Shero was replaced as both coach and general manager by Patrick, who was given the title director of operations. Craig Patrick represented the third generation of Patricks to work for the Rangers.

As had his father Lynn and his grandfather Lester, Craig Patrick attempted to hold down the jobs of both the general manager and coach of an NHL club. His effort lasted one season. The Rangers skidded twelve points in the standings, but he took them farther than Shero had, bowing in four straight to the defending-champion Islanders in the semifinals. For 1981/82, he replaced himself on the bench with Herb Brooks, the coaching hero of the 1980 American Olympic performance.

Patrick and Brooks failed to conjure the magic of Lake Placid in Madison Square Garden. Patrick was loyal to Brooks through three seasons, in which the team produced respectable results but came out on the short end of what had become an annual "subway series" play-off tilt against Al Arbour's Islanders. Shero might have prevailed in the 1978/79 encounter, but from 1980/81 to 1983/84 the Islanders triumphed, moving aside the Rangers to reach the Cup finals in every season and winning three of four.

In 1984/85 the Rangers were struggling in the regular season when Patrick fired Brooks and returned to the bench himself. Wins fell from forty-two to twenty-six, and the Rangers were knocked out of the opening round in three straight by the Flyers. The team rebounded in 1985/86, winning thirty-six games under new coach Ted Sator and reaching the conference finals, the last hurdle to a Stanley Cup series.

The Canadiens downed them in five, and advanced to defeat Calgary in the finals.

The last Patrick reign in New York was ended in November 1986. Phil Esposito was brought in as general manager, and Patrick returned to his alma mater, the University of Denver, to serve as its director of athletics and recreation. Esposito replaced coach Ted Sator with Tom Webster, and Sator quickly found work in Buffalo, replacing Craig Ramsay after Scotty Bowman was ousted there as general manager.

When Patrick was summoned back to the NHL by DeBartolo to replace Phil's brother Tony, he immediately turned to an old family acquaintance, Scotty Bowman, to serve as his director of player development and recruitment, hanging on to the coaching job himself. That he wouldn't name Bowman his coach—after experiencing the resourcefulness of Bowman's coaching first-hand as an NDG Monarch and Montreal Junior Canadien—shows how much Bowman's reputation had suffered through his Buffalo misadventure. As director of player development, though, Bowman could apply the skills he had so ably demonstrated to Craig's father in engineering a hockey club. This situation was not unlike that in St. Louis in the fall of 1967, where with a few player changes, Bowman had a last-place team bound for the Cup finals. Pittsburgh, despite its playoff problems, was rich in player resources, thanks to the pioneering work of Eddie Johnston. The younger Patrick, working with Bowman, would engineer a Cup contender in surprisingly short order.

Bowman had spent the last three seasons as a colour commentator with "Hockey Night in Canada." He was neither good nor bad, merely unmemorable. The best commentators are the ones who have unequivocally put their days working within the game behind them. Those who treat the media job as a place to park themselves between assignments can be too reserved in their observations, afraid to give offence to people they might hope will hire them. Bowman lacked the boisterous persona of NFL commentator John Madden, a Super Bowl–winning coach who had quit the game to preserve his health, or, for that matter, former coaching rival Don Cherry. Nor did he show the incisive wit of HNIC's Harry Neale, a former NHL coach who showed no signs of wanting to give up the broadcast booth. Bowman was ready and available to return to the game, and when he did, hockey broadcasting was not faced with a great loss.

Patrick had hired Bowman essentially as a high-powered roving scout. He would work out of his home in Buffalo, investigating prospects as Patrick overhauled the club. Bowman had resolved not to move from Buffalo, even though he was no longer employed there. He wanted his family to have stability, regardless of his own professional circumstances. This was particularly important with David in institutional care in Buffalo and his two youngest children in high school. Bowman's home in Pittsburgh was a hotel room.

It would take more than one season for Patrick and Bowman to turn the Penguins around. Only fourteen points separated the six clubs in the Patrick division in 1989/90; Pittsburgh finished fifth, its wins having dropped from forty to thirty-two. Back problems had limited Mario Lemieux's season to fifty-nine games (in spite of which he still finished fourth in the scoring race). With the fifth-worst record in the league, Pittsburgh missed the playoffs. The Penguins continued to show their defensive weakness, scoring 318 while allowing 359; for the second consecutive season, the club had the second-worst goals-against tally.

Patrick and Bowman did virtually nothing with their lineup in that first season together, despite the fact that the team was struggling. The two men had both been out of the NHL for several seasons, and did not act with the speed that comes from confidence in having an immediate solution. They seemed content to let the season unfold, finish badly if fate so dictated, and have a shot at more talent in the 1990 draft. Only one trade was made that would have any impact on the lineup that would soon begin reaping Stanley Cups.

On January 8, 1990, Patrick and Bowman made a six-player swap with the Vancouver Canucks. Of the three players the Penguins acquired, one, Barry Pederson, would hang in to play on the first Penguins Stanley Cup team. Boston's first choice (eighteenth overall) in the 1980 draft, the veteran centre had briefly been a forty-goal scorer with the Bruins. In the 1982/83 division finals against Bowman's Sabres, Pederson had produced seven goals and nine assists in seven games, the fourth-best individual performance in a playoff series in league history. Now a Penguin, he was an available extra hand on a club coping with the back pains of star centre Lemieux.

After the club's poor performance in 1989/90, the wheeling and dealing began in earnest. Craig Patrick decided to replace himself as coach. Bowman was being kept neatly compartmentalized in the player development role, unable to acquire too much power within the organization. Patrick passed him over in favour of another old face, Bob Johnson.

Like Patrick, Johnson was a product of the American college game. Herb Brooks's success with the 1980 U.S. Olympic team made him more famous, but Johnson was probably the greatest coach ever produced by the U.S. collegiate system. An army veteran and former University of Minnesota player, Johnson had also pitched C-class ball in the Chicago White Sox system. He was twenty-five when he began his hockey coaching career, running a high school team in Minnesota. In 1963, Johnson was named head coach of Colorado College, where he also coached basketball and was assistant coach of the football team. In 1966 came his hiring as head coach of the University of Wisconsin Badgers. His fifteen seasons there earned him the name Badger Bob, and under his direction the Badgers won four national collegiate titles. In 1977, he was named the NCAA hockey coach of the year. From 1973 to 1975, Johnson was also head coach of the U.S. national team, and in 1976 the U.S. Olympic team finished fourth under him in Innsbruck. He also coached the U.S. team (on which Patrick played) in the Canada Cup tournaments of 1976 and 1981.

Johnson was a fully tenured professor in 1981 when Flames general manager Cliff Fletcher persuaded him to take on a new challenge. The

Atlanta Flames had moved to Calgary for 1979/80, and after the 1980/81 season Al MacNeil decided to give up coaching and become Fletcher's assistant. Johnson was a garrulous, energetic optimist, beloved by players, a coaching yin to Bowman's yang. "It's a great day for hockey" was his signature all-occasions salutation.

Johnson was not, however, a pushover, and his initial NHL coaching assignment in Calgary required considerable adjustment in his approach to players and game preparation. He was accustomed in college hockey to training four days a week and playing on two, and this ratio of practices to games was simply not possible in the NHL. He bemoaned the fact that professionals—even his own son, Mark, who had been part of the 1980 Olympic effort and played in the NHL—would not commit to a Russian-style dry-land training regimen in the off-season. He spoke wistfully of wanting to pack the roster off to Fort Benning in the summer and put them through basic training. Veterans like Lanny McDonald, however, made it clear that players felt they spent enough time around the game during the long regular season and playoff run, and that summers were for families. If players wanted to spend their spare hours on the golf course, there was nothing Johnson could do about it. As Scotty Bowman was struggling in Buffalo, Johnson was labouring in his new hockey milieu. "You try different things," he said of his efforts to get his Flames to win in 1983. "You praise some, you embarrass others. You bench them. I've chewed them out one-on-one in my room. I've tried everything to get the most out of them."

Johnson turned the Flames around, in part by turning himself around. He conceded that the NHL was not the U.S. college game. He backed off prioritizing practices over games, stopped what he himself admitted was over-coaching, and learned that a win is a win, no matter how ugly.

Under Johnson, the Flames developed a bitter enmity with their provincial rivals, the Edmonton Oilers. Johnson oversaw their stunning upset of the two-time Cup champions in a seven-game division finals in 1985/86, and after outlasting St. Louis in another seven-game series, defeated Montreal 5–2 in the opening game of the Stanley Cup. The Canadiens, however, rebounded to win four straight and claim their first Cup win since Scotty Bowman left town.

Fletcher was eager to have Johnson back for 1986/87, but Badger Bob decided to end his NHL career. Taking a pay cut, he accepted the position of executive director of the Amateur Hockey Association of the United States (AHAUS), and moved to Colorado Springs. Johnson was enormously committed to the task of raising the profile and skill level of American hockey, and the new job gave him power over the entire U.S. amateur system.

After three years running AHAUS, Johnson was approached by Craig Patrick, who had crossed paths with Johnson many times during his own years in the U.S. collegiate and amateur game. Patrick offered Johnson Pittsburgh's coaching job. Cliff Fletcher had remained a friend after Johnson decided to leave Calgary (Fletcher consistently made American amateurs the Flames' top draft picks during Johnson's tenure at AHAUS), and he tried to talk Johnson out of giving up AHAUS for the troubled Penguins. But Johnson had always been motivated by fresh challenges, and Patrick certainly had one waiting for him.

Johnson's arrival in Pittsburgh was tempered by the disturbing news that Lemieux would be lost for most, if not all, of the new season, as he underwent surgery for a herniated disk in July. Patrick needed to begin making significant lineup changes. As the Penguins had demonstrated in the 1980s, losing regularly did have its bright side: you collected top draft picks in the process. In 1990, thanks to their failings in the first season under Patrick and Bowman, Pittsburgh was able to pick fifth overall. And in their first year with Bowman in charge of player development, the Penguins went overseas, choosing an eighteen-year-old Czech, Jaromir Jagr.

After Bowman's misadventures in Buffalo gambling on Swedes and Czechs in the first round, professional Bowman-watchers must have been given pause by the Penguins' choice. But the NHL's resistance to gambling top draft picks on Europeans (reinforced by Bowman's uneven success) was ebbing. The crumbling of the Eastern Bloc, which had begun in earnest in 1989, was also opening the market to Russian talent, although uncertainty over actual player availability was causing teams to limit their selections of outstanding talent to late picks.

In November 1989, the Velvet Revolution had unfolded in Czechoslovakia and a bloodless coup had ousted the Communist regime. The following June, Bowman and Patrick gambled their first-round pick on Jagr, who happened to play for the same team, Kladno, as Bowman's star-crossed 1981 pick, Jiri Dudacek. Playing fifty-one games for his hometown club in 1989/90, Jagr had produced thirty goals and twenty-nine assists. Jagr was a big kid, six-foot two and over two hundred pounds. He was a flashy player, a wonderful stickhandler with a scoring touch, whose instincts were to go it alone with the puck. If he could be taught to share it, he would make a dazzling linemate for Lemieux, once the Penguins' captain had recovered from back surgery.

Patrick and Bowman had already surrendered their second-round pick to Fletcher in Calgary to get Joey Mullen. Originally signed as a free agent by St. Louis out of Boston College, Mullen had come to the Flames in a trade in February 1986, when Bob Johnson was the Flames' coach. Mullen had logged a career season with the Flames in 1988/89, becoming a first-team All Star, Lady Byng winner and NHL leader in plus/minus, who had then led the Flames in scoring with sixteen goals in twenty-one playoff games as they won the Stanley Cup. In 1989/90, though, Mullen's points production had fallen from 110 to 69, and the veteran of nine NHL seasons was deemed trade bait as the Flames sought draft picks. Mullen would be a Penguin for six of his next seven seasons.

Heading into 1990/91, the Penguins had a host of talent. There was Lemieux and Barrasso, and Paul Coffey, the Edmonton Oilers' star defenceman acquired in a trade in November 1987. On defence with Coffey was Randy Hillier, acquired from Boston back in October 1984. The club had a trio of veteran left-wingers: Bob Errey, Pittsburgh's first-round pick in 1983; Troy Loney, the club's third-round pick in 1983;

and Phil Bourque, signed as a free agent in October 1982. Jim Paek, chosen 170th overall as Johnston's 9th pick in 1985, was with the Canadian national team program in 1990/91 but would come up for three regular-season games and then join the Penguins in the playoffs. Another longshot draft pick by Johnston was Paul Stanton, a defence-man taken 149th overall as his 8th choice in 1985, who entered the University of Wisconsin that fall. After playing in Muskegon in the International League in 1989/90, the collegian Stanton would get a starting position with the Penguins under Badger Bob. Another colle-gian Eddie Johnston secured was left-winger Kevin Stevens. Selected 108th overall in the June 1983 draft by Los Angeles, Stevens's rights were acquired by Pittsburgh that September. After four years at Boston College and a position on the 1988 U.S. Olympic team, Stevens had become a Penguin and would star in the team's 1990/91 Cup drive, scoring a playoff-leading 17 goals.

Emerging as a star on right wing was Mark Recchi, a pleasant sur-prise from the 1988 draft. Johnston had made him his fourth pick, sixty-seventh overall. This product of the Kamloops Blazers spent most of 1988/89 with Muskegon, but in 1989/90 he became a Penguins reg-ular and scored thirty goals. In 1990/91, Recchi would reach the forty-goal plateau and amass 113 points as the team's leading scorer.

Right-winger Jay Caufield was a hulking enforcer signed as a free agent by Craig Patrick when he was running the Rangers in 1985. Having played thirteen games with New York in 1986/87, after Patrick had been replaced by Phil Esposito Caufield was dealt to Minnesota, where he played one game. After a season in Kalamazoo in the IHL, Caufield was available on waivers, and Johnston claimed him in Octo-ber 1988. Injury would limit him to twenty-three games in 1990/91 and keep him out of the playoffs.

A fill-in on right wing was Jamie Leach, who had been drafted by Johnston as his 3rd pick, 47th overall, in 1987. On left wing, the Pen-guins could call up from Muskegon Jeff Daniels, Johnston's 6th pick, 109th overall, in the 1986 draft.

Clearly Eddie Johnston deserved a lot of the credit for the 1990/91 Penguins as they rose from ignominy to Stanley Cup champions in one season. Even Tony Esposito deserved some credit, for having secured Scotty Bowman's goaltending star from Buffalo, Tom Barrasso. But the Penguins' lineup was far from complete, and Patrick and Bowman would be busy right through the season tinkering with the roster Badger Bob was given to coach.

Having drafted Jagr, a player of the future, in June 1990, the Penguins signed a player of the past in July. After fifteen celebrated seasons with the New York Islanders, Bryan Trottier had been cut loose and was available as a free agent. Trottier was no longer the scoring machine he had been when the Islanders were ruling the league, but he had always been a superb defensive forward, and he offered the experience of a four-time Stanley Cup winner and skills that could be devoted to cutting down Pittsburgh's dreadful goals-against stats.

The season had just begun when Bowman and Patrick brought aboard Gordie Roberts from St. Louis, an old defensive hand. Roberts had turned pro at eighteen, in 1975, with the New England Whalers of the WHA; Sam Pollock had drafted him as an NHL property in 1977, taking him as his seventh choice, but Bowman had never gotten the chance to put him on the ice as a Canadien. Roberts stuck with the Whalers, and when the team entered the NHL in 1979 as the Hartford Whalers, he was claimed by his own club from the Montreal list in the expansion draft. A few days earlier Bowman had decided to leave Montreal for Buffalo, and so they would not work together in the same hockey club until the fall of 1990, thirteen years after Pollock had secured Roberts's rights.

In December 1990, the Penguins executed a flurry of trades. The first, on December 11, was a four-player deal with Minnesota, where Bob Clarke was the new general manager and Bob Gainey was making his NHL coaching debut. In an all-defencemen swap, the Penguins gave up Chris Dahlquist and Jim Johnson in return for Larry Murphy and Peter Taglianetti. Both Dahlquist and Johnson were American collegians signed as free agents by Johnston in 1985. Johnson had been a regular Penguins blueliner since 1985/86, while Dahlquist had gradually earned more time with the Penguins and less time with minor-pro farm clubs. The deal gave the Penguins a more experienced defence-man in Larry Murphy, who had been Los Angeles's first draft pick (fourth overall) in 1980 and was a second-team All Star with Washington in 1987. Like Johnson, Murphy had size, but also scoring ability, often producing more than 60 points a season. Taglianetti had been Winnipeg's fourth pick (forty-third overall) in 1983, and had made the NHL full-time in 1987/88. The American-born Taglianetti could provide blueline muscle, having attracted 203 penalty minutes in 1988/89. He had been a Minnesota North Star less than a month when he was dealt to the Penguins.

Two days after the Minnesota deal, Patrick and Bowman were executing a one-for-one swap with Calgary. Jim Kyte, a defensive strong-man acquired as part of the six-player deal cut by Esposito in June 1989, had seen action in only one game with Pittsburgh in 1990/91 and spent the rest of the season in Muskegon. In return for Kyte, the Penguins received Jiri Hrdina, a draft afterthought for the Flames back in 1984. Selected 158th overall by Calgary using their 8th pick, Hrdina became available after the 1988 Olympics, in which he played for the Czech team. Hrdina was thirty-two when he reached Pittsburgh, a vet-eran of the 1988/89 Stanley Cup win, and he would give the team two seasons of service at centre.

Eight days later, on December 21, came another deal, a one-for-one with Eddie Johnston in Hartford. Rob Brown had been a star of the Canadian Junior game with the Kamloops Blazers, leading the West-ern Hockey League in goals and assists in 1985/86 and 1986/87. Despite his performance, he had been overlooked in the opening rounds of the 1986 draft. Johnston had chosen him fourth, sixty-seventh over-all, and saw his prospect named Canadian Major Junior player of the year in 1987. In his first NHL season, 1987/88, Brown scored twenty-four goals for Johnston. In 1988/89 he erupted with 49, and his 115 points (garnered in only sixty-eight games) placed him fifth in league scoring, one position ahead of teammate Paul Coffey, while Lemieux won the scoring title. In 1989/90, though, his production fell back to 80 points, and in twenty-five games in 1990/91 he scored only six times. Johnston was saddled with an anemic offence in Hartford (the Penguins would score 104 more goals than the Whalers in 1990/91) and wanted to give Brown a try. (Brown's career, however, would prove to have gone into freefall.) In return for Brown, the Penguins secured Scott Young, a two-way right-winger who had come out of Boston University to play on the 1988 U.S. Olympic team; Hartford had made him their first pick (eleventh overall) in the 1986 draft.

Patrick and Bowman left the team alone through the first two months of 1991 as Bob Johnson struggled to squeeze .500 hockey out of them in Mario Lemieux's continued absence. At last, Lemieux returned, and in the first week of March the Penguins unveiled a pair of major trades in preparation for the playoffs. On March 4 they were back doing business again with Eddie Johnston in Hartford, this time in a six-player deal. Off to Hartford went John Cullen, Jeff Parker and Zarley Zalepski, and into Pittsburgh came Ulf Samuelsson, Grant Jennings and Ron Francis.

The Penguin players sent packing to Hartford were known to both Bowman and Johnston. Cullen had been picked by Bowman for Buffalo in a 1986 supplemental draft of American college players. He never did play for Bowman there, as he was still at Boston University when Bowman was fired. In June 1988 Johnston had added him to his stable of U.S. collegiate talents, and he turned into a ninety-point centre for the Penguins. Jeff Parker had also begun his career with Bowman's Sabres; the checking winger would play only four games with Hartford before his NHL career ended. Zarley Zalepski had been Johnston's first choice (fourth overall) in the 1986 draft, and the eighteen-year-old defenceman had embarked on a three-season hitch with the Canadian national team program before joining the Penguins after the 1988 Olympics. He was having his best offensive season, with forty-eight points in sixty-six games, when the Penguins sent him back to Johnston's care.

It was a trade that paid huge dividends for the Penguins, as it gave them a pair of tough defencemen in Samuelsson and Jennings and a demi-superstar in Francis. In the 1984 draft, Hartford general manager Emile Francis had selected Samuelsson sixty-seventh overall as his fourth pick. For some of the brighter NHL minds who had tagged Swedish players as too afraid to go into the corners with Canadian boys, Samuelsson became the Anti-Swede, a tough, borderline-dirty defender who wore a football-style collar to protect his neck when he threw his weight around. He had been good for about two minutes of penalties a game with Leksand, his team back home, and he maintained the same pace in the NHL; he already had 174 minutes in sixty-two games with Hartford in 1990/91 when sent to Pittsburgh. Jennings was a western Junior player who had come to the NHL as a free agent in 1985, another heavy hitter who had notched 171 minutes in sixty-four games in 1989/90 with Hartford. It was hard not to imagine Bowman back in St. Louis at this point, lining up an impervious, nail-tough defence with the elder Patrick. Getting Samuelsson and Jennings was as close as Bowman could come to reinventing Bob and Barclay Plager. It was just like old times. When Patrick and Bowman were done, the Penguins' defence had been completely overhauled, the only significant holdover being DeBartolo's box-office star, Paul Coffey.

And then there was Ron Francis. A play-making centre who was almost as big as Jagr, Francis had been taken fourth overall as Hartford's first pick in the 1981 draft after starring for the Greyhounds in his home town of Sault Ste. Marie, Ontario. After playing twenty-five more games with the Greyhounds in 1981/82, Francis had come up to Hartford at age eighteen to contribute sixty-eight points in fifty-nine games. He was a play-making scoring star who had broken through the 100-point barrier (with 101) in 1989/90, his ninth NHL season. A tremendous all-round player with great defensive abilities, Francis had toiled in near anonymity in the league backwater of Hartford. Pittsburgh would change that for him. He would win the Frank Selke Award as the league's top defensive forward, the Lady Byng and two Stanley Cups as a Penguin.

On February 21, about eight weeks after the deal for Brown and less than two weeks before the six-player swap for Samuelsson, Francis and Cullen, another significant event occurred involving the Hartford Whalers and Scotty Bowman. Whalers president Emile Francis wrote Scotty Morrison, president of the Hockey Hall of Fame: "I would like to respectfully submit the name of Scott 'Scotty' Bowman to the Hockey Hall of Fame Board of Directors for consideration [*sic*] to hockey's shrine in the 'Builder's' category."

If Bowman wasn't so plainly deserving, one would have been tempted to view Francis's letter as a sweetener for the six-player deal that was about to unfold. But Bowman's career accomplishments as a coach were indisputable, and probably unassailable by any living coach. He had won five Stanley Cups, and held the league record for most regular-season and playoff wins. In the 1979/80 playoffs, Bowman had eclipsed Dick Irvin's mark of 100 post-season wins when his Sabres defeated Chicago 6–4 in game two of their quarterfinal series. And on December 19, 1984, Bowman had broken Irvin's regular-season win record of 690, with a 6–3 defeat of the Blackhawks.

Bowman was appropriately modest about these records, for they had as much to do with staying power as coaching proficiency. "Look at it this way," he said after surpassing Irvin's playoff total. "In the old days when Dick Irvin coached, they only had two playoff rounds. Now we might play twenty or more games in the playoffs in one season." He graciously did not point out that it had taken Irvin 190 games to reach the 100 plateau, while he had required only 156. Bowman's win percentage stood at .641, compared to Irvin's lifetime .532. He was also outperforming several other NHL greats. Hap Day, who won five Cups for the Leafs, had a .613 win percentage; Tommy Ivan, who won three Cups for the Red Wings, finished at .537. Punch Imlach, who won four Cups for Toronto, trailed at .478. As impressive as Bowman's playoff efficiency was, he still lived in the shadow of Toe Blake, who led them all at .689 in winning 82 of 119.

The men connected by the Hall nomination letter—Francis, Bowman and Morrison—made an intriguing triangle. As coach of the Rangers, Francis had delivered Bowman two of his three playoff defeats in his Canadiens years—in the semifinals in 1971/72 and in the quarterfinals in 1973/74. And while on his way to the third defeat in 1974/75, Bowman had squared off in front of the press with Morrison, who was then the NHL's chief of officiating. Playing in Buffalo, Montreal had just lost, in overtime, game five of the semifinal series against the Sabres, to fall behind three games to two. Bowman complained to the press that a penalty given to Doug Risebrough by referee Lloyd Gilmour early in the third had been the turning point in the game. "We had the game well under control and were getting better," he griped. "Then the crowd yelled and called for a penalty. That's the difference between playing at home and away. Then in overtime [Rick] Martin deserved a penalty when he tripped Roberts, but in overtime they don't call a penalty, I guess."

Bowman was holding court outside the Canadiens' dressing room when he spied Morrison. "Nice call, Scotty," Bowman jabbed, unloading on Morrison over Gilmour's call on Risebrough. Morrison exploded. "Just once, just once I'd like to leave the arena without you blaming the referees for a loss. I don't say anything bad about you, Bowman. You made a statement, now back it up, right now. Back it up. You're always the same."

Bowman turned to reporters, said, "There's your referee in chief, boys," and walked away.

Emile Francis's nomination was duly presented to the Hall of Fame's selection committee. With players, the committee normally waited until their careers were three to five years behind them before considering induction. (There had been a few exceptions, such as Maurice Richard, who was inducted immediately upon retirement, as would be Mario Lemieux.) In the catch-all Builders' category, reserved for coaches, managers, executives and the like, nominees need only have accomplished enough in an ongoing career to warrant induction. Emile Francis, for one, had been inducted in 1982.

Since Francis, eleven men had swelled the Builders' ranks in eight years. The Bruins' Harry Sinden got the nod in 1983; in 1984, Punch Imlach and Jake Milford, who capped a long management career by getting the Canucks into the 1981/82 Cup finals; in 1985, John Mariucci, architect of Minnesota's superb high school programs and an executive with the North Stars, and Rudy Pilous, coach of the 1960/61 Stanley Cup–winning Chicago Blackhawks and the Avco Cup–winning Winnipeg Jets; and in 1986, Bill Hanley, a retired secretary-manager of the Ontario Hockey Association once known as "Mr. OHA." Unfortunately, the Hall was entering a period in which it was becoming known as a private club in which directors and selection committee participants toasted fellow members of the NHL's ruling elite. League president John Ziegler was added to the Builders' category in 1987, and in 1988 Philadelphia franchise chairman Ed Snider joined him. In 1989 it was the turn of players' association president and Ziegler crony Alan Eagleson. When the ruling clique rammed through the induction of Gil Stein, who sat as league president for only four months before Gary Bettman was hired as the NHL's first commissioner in February 1993, the clubbiness had gone too far, and Stein's induction was rescinded in a shake-up at the Hall. In these tainted years, Bowman was a welcome break from the parade of corporate insiders. (Another deserving induction, in 1989, was Father David Bauer, the motivating force behind the Canadian national team program of the 1960s.)

In the months between Francis's nomination letter and Bowman's induction in the fall of 1991, Bowman's career shot forward dramatically as he returned to coaching in the NHL. But first, his name was added to the Stanley Cup for the sixth time, as the overhaul of the Penguins Francis had helped Bowman realize succeeded spectacularly.

Pittsburgh finished the season atop the Patrick division, with eighty-eight points. The performance would have left them no better than third in any of the other three divisions. While they won a respectable forty-one games, Pittsburgh had proved to be an all-or-nothing team; its six ties matched Edmonton for the lowest number in the league that season.

But the team's final position in the standings didn't tell the whole story. Even without Mario Lemieux for most of the season, the Penguins had finished second to Calgary in team scoring, with 342 goals—a 24-goal improvement over 1989/90. Also heartening was their improvement in goals against, which had dropped from 359 to 305, eighteenth in the league. More important, however, was the scoring balance. The Penguins now had a healthy surplus of goals; only nine teams scored more than they allowed. Of those, Pittsburgh's 37-goal margin ranked fifth, behind Los Angeles (86), Calgary (81), Chicago (73), and St. Louis (60), and ahead of Boston (35), the Rangers (32), Montreal (24) and Buffalo (14).

Ultimately, analyzing season statistics failed to capture the true potential of the Penguins as the playoffs began. They had played most of the season without Mario Lemieux, and without newcomers Samuelsson, Francis, Jennings and Murphy. The Penguins team that finished the season was not the same one that started it. And a team with hardly any playoff experience in recent memory was now beginning a Stanley Cup drive with four Stanley Cup veterans. Bryan Trottier had his four with the Islanders, Paul Coffey had his three with the Oilers, and Joey Mullen and Jiri Hrdina had shared in the Calgary Flames' win two seasons earlier. And they had Bowman, with five Cups in Montreal on his resume, in the organization.

Their opening-round opponents in the Patrick division semifinal were the New Jersey Devils, a low-scoring defensive outfit coached by Tom McVie. The Devils had finished nine points behind them, with nine fewer wins (but nine more ties). Beginning April 3, they met every other day to trade wins. New Jersey took a 3–2 series lead with a 4–2 win in Pittsburgh. The Penguins tied the series two days later with a 4–3 win in New Jersey, then won the deciding seventh game at home 4–0.

The Washington Capitals were next in the division finals. The Capitals had the lowest goals-against in the division, 258, but also scored only 258 goals. They had downed the Rangers in six games in the opening round, and after four days' rest defeated the Penguins in Pittsburgh 4–2, two days after Badger Bob's team had rid themselves of the Devils. It took a 7–6 overtime win at home for Pittsburgh to tie the series 1–1, and from there the Penguins were in control, winning in five.

Next up were the Boston Bruins in the conference finals. Boston had struggled with Montreal in their Adams division final, which went all seven games and was decided by a 2–1 Boston win at home. The Penguins started badly, losing 6–3 and 5–4 (in overtime) to the Bruins in Boston, but then dominated the Bruins 4–1, 4–1, 7–2 and 5–3 to reach the finals for the first time in franchise history.

If Pittsburgh was an unlikely finalist in 1990/91, the Minnesota North Stars were even more so, having finished the season with only sixty-eight points and a losing record, to claim the fourth and final playoff spot in the Norris division. The North Stars' twenty-seven wins lagged far behind the forty-nine of the division- and league-leading Blackhawks, but their fourteen ties—third highest in the league—suggested competitive reserves. Matched with the heavily favoured Blackhawks in the opening round, the North Stars scored an overtime upset in game one, fell behind two games to one, then racked up three straight wins to upset the playoff favourites. A six-game defeat of the Blues vaulted them into the finals against the Penguins.

The North Stars' underdog act lost momentum only when it confronted the underdogs of Badger Bob. The teams reached game five with two wins each, but then the Penguins took charge. Their 8–0 victory in game six was the most lopsided Cup-winning game in NHL history. Though he missed one game with back problems, Mario Lemieux produced twelve points in five games to lead the series in scoring and win the Conn Smythe. Only Wayne Gretzky's thirteen-point effort in 1987/88 against Boston surpassed Lemieux's against the North Stars. His sixteen goals and twenty-eight assists in twenty-three games was also the best effort of the playoffs, and second (by three points) to Gretzky's record output in 1984/85.

The win put Bowman's name on the Stanley Cup for the sixth time, but the glory belonged mainly to Craig Patrick, Mario Lemieux and Badger Bob. Johnson had become the first American since the Black-hawks' Bill Stewart in 1937/38 to coach a Stanley Cup winner. Stewart had taken a team with a record of only fourteen wins in forty-eight games to the title. Johnson had accomplished almost as much with the unlikely Penguins. With so many trades having been conducted, the team had been a fragmented collection of individuals and cliques, contained within an organization with no winning track record and a lack of enthusiasm for defensive hockey. Johnson had pulled them together, made them take care of their own end, and above all made them see their own potential. "He made us believe anything was possible," Lemieux would say. "He convinced us we could win the Stanley Cup, and that's what we did."

Owner Ed DeBartolo realized the enhanced value of a Stanley Cup victory by selling the team to Howard Baldwin. But the biggest change faced by the team and its fans was the sudden loss of Badger Bob.

Johnson had been chosen to coach the U.S. team in the Canada Cup tournament that preceded the 1991/92 season. On August 26, two days before his team was scheduled to play its first game in the round-robin series, Johnson collapsed at the dinner table at home in Colorado Springs. As his team played its opening game, surgeons removed a malignant tumor from Johnson's brain, but they were unable to remove a second one and were forced to opt for radiation therapy. The therapy greatly weakened Johnson, who was robbed of his speech. He nonetheless peppered the U.S. team with faxed messages from his bedside, and his inspiration was said to have propelled the Americans into the finals, where they lost to Canada.

Johnson was in no shape to coach the Penguins, and Patrick turned to Bowman to fill in for Johnson on an interim basis. Bowman and Johnson had become close in the previous season. Both had five children, and, as with Bowman, one of Johnson's had a serious disability—his daughter Diane, born with cerebral palsy, was mentally handicapped. "Unless you have a handicapped [child], you're always on the outside looking in," Johnson's wife Martha told *The Edmonton Journal* in 1986. "You always say, 'Oh, that's going to happen to somebody else.' Well, this happened to us and when it happens to you, you have to face it and you find out what you're made of." The challenge Bowman and Johnson shared in their private lives helped forge their friendship, and Johnson extended a welcoming hand to Bowman in his coaching of the team. During the 1990/91 Stanley Cup run, Bowman stepped outside his player development role to travel with Johnson and the Penguins.

It soon became clear that Johnson would not be returning. His condition deteriorated steadily, and he died on November 26, at the age of sixty-one, while the Penguins were on the road under Bowman's direction. The club had won three, lost four and tied three. The night after Johnson's death, the Penguins defeated Philadelphia 5–2.

With the death of Johnson coming on the heels of the sale of the club, Craig Patrick decided that the team had been through more than enough at the beginning of the season and refused to put it through any further changes. Rather than go outside the organization for another head coach, Patrick formally gave Bowman the job.

The return of Bowman to NHL coaching nevertheless posed a coaching culture shock for the Penguins, as a father-figure collegian was replaced by an old-school taskmaster. No league team had ever been through the scale of trauma that beset the 1991/92 Penguins. It was enough that the coach of the defending Stanley Cup champion had died, but the amiable character of Johnson made the loss even more difficult. Craig Patrick wept openly at the press conference announcing Johnson's death.

"He was so upbeat, so positive," said Patrick. "He created such a very family-like atmosphere. He was really like the father to our organization. It takes a special man to take a group of young people and accomplish what he did in such a short period of time." Left-winger Phil Bourque remarked that Johnson was the only coach he'd ever had who could criticize him and make him feel better about himself at the same time.

If Toe Blake had been a hard act for Bowman to follow in Montreal, Bob Johnson was virtually impossible. While Bowman might have been the new coach, the team was still playing for the old one. "Bob wanted us to go on and win another Cup," said Tom Barrasso. "He talked of wanting to be part of a dynasty here. If we go out and do anything but play hard for him, it will be a disservice to Bob." Sensing the difficulty of imposing his will on this shell-shocked team, Bowman withdrew uncharacteristically, leaving the day-to-day management to the assistants he had inherited from Johnson, Barry Smith and Rick Kehoe.

The team played with baffling inconsistency. After losing to Washington 8–0 on October 29, they swamped Minnesota 8–1 two nights later. In the wake of Johnson's death, the team registered a string of lopsided victories: 8–4 over New Jersey on November 27; 9–3 and 5–1 over Philadelphia on November 29 and 30; 8–0 over San Jose on December 5; 10–2 over San Jose on December 17; and 12–1 over Toronto on December 26. Yet the team was also guilty of no-show appearances. The Penguins were trounced by St. Louis 6–1 on December 7 (two nights after trashing San Jose 8–0), and by Washington 7–2 on December 14. A 7–4 New Year's Eve loss to New Jersey was followed by a number of high-scoring setbacks in January, including an 8–5 loss to the Islanders. The Penguins were routinely capable of surrendering five or six goals a game. Plagued by back problems, Lemieux appeared in only sixty-four games, and there was some grumbling that even when he was there in body he was absent in spirit, but his 131 points were still enough to win the scoring title, ahead of teammate Kevin Stevens. Super Mario also had the club's second-best plus-minus record, at 27, while defenceman Larry Murphy led with 33. His Penguins finished the regular season with three games against division rivals that characterized the campaign precisely. After losing to the Rangers 7–1 (the day Bob Johnson was posthumously inducted into the Hockey Hall of Fame in the Builders category), they defeated the Capitals 4–1, only to close out the season with a 5–1 loss to New Jersey.

The only major change in the roster had come in February, with the trade of star defenceman Paul Coffey to Philadelphia for hulking defenceman Kjell Samuelsson and right-winger Rick Tocchet. The Coffey trade was a sign that Bowman was at last ready to step in and assert his presence on the team Johnson had made a winner. Coffey's large salary was one reason he was dispensed with under the new Penguins ownership, but his offence-minded style did not sit well with Bowman, and he had been made expendable by the acquisition of Larry Murphy in December 1990. Murphy played brilliantly at both ends of the rink; in the 1990/91 finals, he was a plus-seventeen, and he contributed 1 goal and 9 assists in the playoffs. In the 1991/92 season, Murphy contributed seventy-seven points while leading the team in plus-minus.

With few changes in the roster, the performance of the 1991/92 Penguins was little changed from 1990/91. They scored 343 goals versus 342, allowed 308 versus 305, won thirty-nine games versus forty-one, and produced eighty-seven points versus eighty-eight. It was as Barrasso had predicted—the Penguins were still playing for Badger Bob.

An important difference between 1990/91 and 1991/92, however, was that in the former season, eighty-eight-points had been enough to secure first in the Patrick division. In 1991/92, eighty-seven points left the Penguins in third, as the Rangers and Capitals had improved considerably. This meant they lost home-ice advantage in the playoffs. Not that it ever seemed to matter much with Pittsburgh—the Penguins were making a habit of losing the opening game no matter where the team played. Under Johnson in 1990/91, they lost every opening game in the playoffs—to New Jersey at home in the opening round, to Washington at home in the division finals, to the Bruins in Boston in the conference finals, and to the North Stars at home in the Stanley Cup finals. The pattern continued in 1991/92 under Bowman, as the Capitals, playing at home, downed the Penguins 3–1; a bruised shoulder had kept Lemieux out of the lineup. Two nights later, with Lemieux back, the Penguins went down 6–2. In the 1990/91 campaign, the Penguins had bounced back from opening defeats with a win of their own in three of four series. Only Boston, in the conference championships, had built a 2–0 series lead against them, and Pittsburgh had responded with four straight wins. After the Penguins got back in the series against Washington with a 6–4 win at home, however, they crumbled in a 7–2 loss at the Igloo. Down three games to one, the Penguins made a rally rare in playoff hockey, taking three straight games from the second-best team in the league with 5–2, 6–4 and 3–1 scores. Lemieux showed the way, setting a club record for a single playoff series with seven goals and ten assists in five appearances.

The division finals brought on the Rangers, the top team in the league. Under coach Roger Neilson, New York had produced 105 points, the first time the club had broken the 100-point mark since 1972/73. Neilson had been named a finalist, along with Pat Burns of Montreal and Pat Quinn of Vancouver, in balloting for the Jack Adams Award; Neilson finished runner-up to Quinn. The Rangers were a typical Neilson outfit, physically tough and defensively stingy. With a pair of American goaltenders, John Vanbiesbrouck and Mike Richter, the Rangers had allowed sixty-two fewer goals than the Penguins in producing the league's third-best goals-against record. Rangers general manager Neil Smith had begun to load up on former Edmonton Oilers. Mark Messier had just played his first season as the Rangers' captain, winning the Hart Trophy, and he had been joined by defenceman Jeff Beukeboom and centre Adam Graves. Over the next two seasons,

Smith would hire on Glenn Anderson, Kevin Lowe, Esa Tikkanen and Craig MacTavish in pursuit of the Cup.

The coaching reunion between Scotty Bowman and Roger Neilson in the 1991/92 division finals produced, physically and stylistically, an ugly series. The games were not especially well played, and the Rangers opened the series at home with an awful effort, surrendering four unanswered goals in the first thirty-three minutes. Vanbiesbrouck was replaced by Richter, and the Rangers rallied for two goals, but Bowman's Penguins protected their lead to win 4–2, their first win in the opening game of a playoff series in seven tries.

In game two at Madison Square Garden, the Rangers got nasty as the Penguin's top producers came under attack. Right-winger Joey Mullen, the team's third-highest scorer, took a heavy hit from left-winger Kris King (who had collected 224 penalty minutes that season) and was lost for the rest of the playoffs with a head injury. The outrage, however, was generated by Adam Graves's slash of Mario Lemieux, which broke a bone in Lemieux's left hand and scratched him from the rest of the series, if not the rest of the playoffs.

Although they were without Messier, who missed the game with back spasms, the Rangers evened the series with a 4–2 win. The Penguins went into game three with four starters lost to injuries: Lemieux, Mullen, Kjell Samuelsson and Rick Tocchet (the team's sixth-highest scorer). Outshooting the Rangers 50 to 32 in the first game in Pittsburgh, the Penguins still lost 6–5 in overtime when a centring pass by Kris King deflected off Barrasso into the net.

It was widely expected that Graves would draw a multi-game suspension for the slash on Lemieux, but the NHL's ponderous review process meant he was able to play in game three, and score the opening goal, while his case waited to be heard. "He got a goal tonight and will be suspended tomorrow," Bowman jibed. "I don't know if there's any irony in that or not."

Whether or not Graves's performance qualified as irony, his slash of Lemieux did qualify him for a four-game suspension. Considering that Lemieux was expected to be lost for six weeks, the Penguins were outraged by the sentence. Howard Baldwin fired off a letter of protest to league president John Ziegler, calling for tougher sanctions against offenders and a quicker review process, and then made his feelings known in a press conference that appeared designed to mollify his injured star, who at twenty-six was talking about retiring. In mid-season, Lemieux had complained in the press about the cheap shots he endured, and called the NHL a "garbage league." In the division finals, the league was living up to Lemieux's pronouncement. A cheap shot had taken the league's leading scorer out of the playoffs.

Without Super Mario, the Penguins' hopes for defending their Cup title were seriously diminished. He had, after all, been involved in more than one-third of the team's regular-season scoring, and in the opening series against Washington, he had almost single-handedly carried the team to victory. His seventeen points in five games had come on twenty-four goals by the entire team. And in game four with the Rangers, the Penguins were again in danger of falling behind 3–1 in a series as Messier gave New York a 4–2 lead early in the third period. But the Penguins came back to force overtime, and when Messier coughed up the puck, on a rare overtime powerplay enjoyed by Pittsburgh, Larry Murphy fed Ron Francis, who scored the goal that won the game, tied the series and probably turned it around.

Lemieux's absence revealed a depth of talent in Pittsburgh that not even the Penguins appeared to appreciate. Francis scored three of the four goals that followed Lemieux's injury, Kevin Stevens and Larry Murphy continued to contribute, and Jaromir Jagr showed flashes of the offensive genius that would soon make him one of the game's great stars. After Jagr scored the winner in game five, a 3–2 effort in New York, the Rangers were through. In game six the Penguins finished off Neilson's league leaders with a 5–1 whitewash. With that victory, every division winner in 1991/92 had been eliminated.

"We're legitimate," Bowman pronounced after the Rangers' defeat. "Realistically, after Mario got hurt, I felt we were in a very tough situation.

But when we came back from being two goals down and won game four in overtime, I figured we had a shot. Then when we won [game five] in New York on Monday, I really liked our chances.

"What happened is that Mario didn't just get hurt. It was an upsetting thing and there was a controversy. I think our people fed off that and just became more and more determined. We made something very bad work in our favour."

Beginning with the overtime win in game four against New York, Bowman's Penguins won eleven consecutive playoff games, rolling over the Bruins in the conference finals and the Blackhawks, coached by Bowman protege Mike Keenan, in the finals. The Blackhawks had mounted eleven straight wins of their own in reaching the finals, and were on their way to a twelfth in game one, enjoying leads of 3–0 and 4–1, before losing 5–4. A petulant Keenan, having lost his third Cup final in three tries, tried to make the point that the series was much closer than the sweep indicated. Certainly there were no blowouts, as Pittsburgh won game two 3–1, game three 1–0 and game four 6–5. But the Blackhawks had not won a game because they could not play consistent defensive hockey. They had fumbled a solid lead in game one, and in game four, the Penguins had scored twice on their first four shots, compelling Keenan to replace Ed Belfour with Dominik Hasek, who gave up four more. The decisive factors in Bowman's favour were the play of his old Buffalo draft pick, Tom Barrasso, whom Lemieux thought should win the Conn Smythe, and Lemieux himself, who did win it after returning to play with his broken hand for the conference finals. In fifteen playoff games, Lemieux had scored 16 goals and contributed 18 assists.

Six months after his induction to the Hockey Hall of Fame, Scotty Bowman's curriculum vitae was undergoing an ambitious rewrite. He had won his seventh Cup, his sixth as a coach, and he appeared perfectly positioned to preside over the play of the NHL's next dynasty. "Dynasty's a strong word," Lemieux said. "I guess we'll have to wait until this time next year. I like our chances.... Our future looks very bright."

A word of caution, however, came from Bryan Trottier, the former Islanders star who had just won his sixth Cup. "I think the ingredients are there, but there are a lot of things that go into winning. You've got to get a lucky break, and bad calls or injuries can go against you."

Bowman knew all about luck. He had been lucky that Craig Patrick, one of his former Junior players and the son of his first NHL boss, had been hired to manage a team with ripening talent. And after being hired by Patrick, he'd experienced tragic good fortune when Bob Johnson died on the eve of the 1991/92 season and forced Patrick to turn to Bowman for coaching.

In January 1991, Bowman had been offered the job of consultant and special adviser to Jim Durrell, the president of the newly awarded Ottawa Senators franchise. Bowman, who was then director of player development and recruitment with Pittsburgh, turned Durrell down, saying, "It wasn't an offer you couldn't refuse." In fact, the offer had almost been an insult. At the time, the Senators hadn't filled the general manager's job, and by not considering offering it to him, the Senators implicitly set a post-Sabres ceiling on Bowman's perceived abilities. Bowman explained that he had made a commitment to the Penguins, which was true, but more important, Bowman was in the midst of building a contender with Craig Patrick. Four months later, the Penguins were Stanley Cup champions; nine months later, Bowman was their coach and on his way to winning still another Cup. Seven years of frustration in Buffalo were rapidly being forgotten. The tragic death of Bob Johnson had placed Bowman in the position to oversee a dynasty that could rival what he had accomplished in Montreal. In 1992/93, the Penguins won more games than any team since the Oilers in 1985/86 and finished first overall. But having won fifty-six of eighty-four regular-season games, and four of five in the opening playoff round, the Penguins couldn't win four of their next seven.

14

✧ JIMMY DEVELLANO WAS A young, single man in Toronto, coaching minor hockey, when Lynn Patrick came along the in the fall of 1967 and hired him as the Ontario amateur scout of the new St. Louis Blues. The Blues had just begun playing their first season, and Patrick was about to relinquish his coaching duties to Scotty Bowman. Patrick had also hired Cliff Fletcher, a ten-year veteran of the Montreal scouting system, as his chief scout. In the team lineup was Al Arbour, who was beginning his first full season on defence in the NHL since 1961/62.

Devellano, Bowman, Fletcher, Arbour: the Blues organization had the seeds of what could have become one of professional hockey's most fruitful operations. Instead, the owners squandered the potential of their start-up operation by discarding this nucleus of management acumen. After the Salomon group began the diaspora, when the Blues failed to make a fourth consecutive appearance in the Cup finals in 1970/71, the team never reached the finals again—not once in the next twenty-seven seasons. Arbour would win his four Cups as a coach with the New York Islanders, Bowman his handful with Montreal, Pittsburgh and Detroit, Fletcher his one as general manager of the Calgary Flames in 1988/89. And Jimmy Devellano, Jimmy D. for short, would win five, with the Islanders and the Red Wings.

Jimmy D. is one of the game's half-hidden front-office figures, his role often easy to overlook, his accomplishments considerable. He has been at the forefront of the Stanley Cup successes of the Islanders and the Red Wings, and as of 1997/98 he had the longest uninterrupted tenure of any manager with any NHL team, a sixteen-season run under the same owner.

Neither Arbour nor Bowman would have been able to bring championships to their teams had Jimmy D. not brought Arbour and Bowman to those teams in the first place. They had come to know each other in St. Louis. Devellano outlasted Bowman by one season there. He continued to scout for the team until Bill McCreary, who had been named the Blues' assistant general manager when Bowman was fired in the spring of 1971, in turn fired Devellano after the 1971/72 season. Devellano shrugs. McCreary probably saw him as a Bowman guy. Such house-cleanings are a fact of life in professional hockey.

Devellano landed in Nassau County, Long Island, where the New York Islanders were preparing to play their first NHL season. Their general manager was Bill Torrey, a native Montrealer who had broken into hockey management with the Pittsburgh Hornets when the AHL franchise was revived in 1961/62. When the NHL reached Oakland in 1967/68, he joined the Seals franchise, rising to executive vice-president in 1968/69. Torrey endured the chaos of revolving ownership in the troubled operation; after nine months under the eccentric "Charlie O" Finley, Torrey quit to run an advertising and PR company out of his old haunt, the Pittsburgh Civic Arena. That kept him busy for about a year, until the Islanders franchise was launched and he was hired to manage it. He in turn hired as his chief scout Devellano, and together they strode forward into what was then the worst season by a team in NHL history.

The Islanders had been rushed into the league in 1972/73 to counter the market ambitions of the new World Hockey Association, which was beginning its first season with a franchise, the Raiders, in New York. At the expansion draft in June 1972, Torrey and Devellano saw their best-laid plans decimated by the lure of the new league, as eight of twenty draftees chose to sign with WHA clubs rather than report to Long Island. In that first season, the Islanders won only twelve of seventy-eight games.

Devellano had dipped into his St. Louis connections to secure a St. Louis alumnus, Phil Goyette, as the team's first coach. After being left unprotected by Bowman in the 1970 expansion draft and chosen by Buffalo, Goyette had ended his playing career back in a Rangers uniform (he had spent six seasons with the club in the 1960s) in 1971/72. But Goyette didn't work out. Even with a team as green and underqualified as the 1972/73 roster, Torrey and Devellano felt they should have won more than a dozen games. Goyette was fired before the season was over, replaced on an interim basis by scout Earl Ingarfield.

Torrey believed firmly in the principle espoused by Patrick and Bowman in St. Louis: you take care of defence first and build from there. By the grace of their wretched freshman season, the Islanders held the first pick in the 1973 entry draft and used it to select defenceman Denis Potvin. They already had a strong goaltender in Billy Smith, the first player they had chosen in the expansion draft, and had purchased another one, Glenn "Chico" Resch, from Sam Pollock's Montreal netminding stable. With Goyette gone and Ingarfield having been strictly a pinch-hitter, Torrey drew up a short list of coaching candidates to run his defensive machine. He wanted either Johnny Wilson, the former NHLer who had taken over the Red Wings' bench in 1972/73, or John McLellan, who had replaced Punch Imlach as Toronto's coach in 1969/70.

Devellano proposed another candidate: Al Arbour, the defenceman's defenceman, who had just been through the strange management shuffle in St. Louis.

Torrey listened to Devellano and hired Arbour for 1973/74. It was the beginning of one of the NHL's rare long and productive relationships between a coach and a team. It would take seven seasons for Arbour to bring the Stanley Cup to Long Island, but once he had, three more would quickly follow. The team steadily evolved through the 1970s, and Arbour moved with it, becoming one of the league's most successful coaches and upholding Scotty Bowman's conviction that he had been the right man for the job in St. Louis.

"Al did many things well," Devellano says. "He had the advantage of having done a lot of different things as a player, under a lot of different coaches. He had won Stanley Cups with Detroit, a powerhouse team. He had won a Stanley Cup in Chicago under Rudy Pilous, a very motivational coach. He had won Stanley Cups in Toronto under Punch Imlach, a tough taskmaster. He had played Junior hockey for the Windsor Spitfires under Jimmy Skinner, who became Detroit's coach. In Rochester, he was captain of the Americans and won the Calder Cup under Joe Crozier.

"He took their best parts and he moulded them into himself. He was a fairly tough taskmaster, like Imlach. Al was also a motivator who would use his temper, like Pilous. He was smart behind the bench as well, and he got some of that from Scotty." ("He got *all* of that from Scotty," says Al MacNeil.)

"With the Islanders," Devellano continues, "he was able to grow with a young team—he had time to grow. There were not immediate expectations. He got respect from the players. He had played in the NHL, knew what it was all about. Nobody could pull the wool over his eyes. He was a bit of a father and a bit of a coach with the young stars."

By the time the Islanders were winning Stanley Cups in the early 1980s, when Scotty Bowman was supposed to be winning Stanley Cups in Buffalo, Arbour's Islanders were a mature team, no longer a group of kids. Devellano had risen to assistant general manager, and after the Islanders' third consecutive Cup win, in 1981/82, opportunity knocked in the form of pizza mogul Mike Ilitch. The owner of the Little Caesar's chain had just bought the ailing Red Wings franchise from the Norris family. Ilitch was offering Devellano "the big job," the general managership. Despite the fact that he would be leaving a dynasty in its prime for an Original Six outfit in serious disrepair, Devellano could not turn aside the opportunity for a promotion and the chance to put his own mark, as Bill Torrey had, on a club with nowhere to go but up.

The management experiences of Devellano in Detroit and Bowman in Buffalo could not have been more different. Bowman had taken over a Stanley Cup contender in 1979/80. The Red Wings Devellano inherited in 1982/83 were a mess, the lone Original Six franchise that had not figured out how to prosper in the expansion years. In the first expansion season, Detroit was the only Original Six team that finished behind any of the new clubs in the overall standings. The Red Wings had missed the playoffs in the last Original Six season, 1966/67, and over the next fifteen seasons they missed the post-season another thirteen times. In Devellano's first season with the club, 1982/83, they missed the playoffs again. While the club would miss the playoffs twice more in the next seven seasons, by 1983/84 they were turning the corner.

"The cupboard was bare," Devellano says of the player roster he inherited. The Red Wings "had eighty-one players under contract, and seventy-five couldn't play." Although the accounting of major-league franchises is notoriously pessimistic, with owners eager to tell a hard-luck story in the face of player salary demands, it seems entirely believable that Bruce Norris with the Red Wings had stumbled upon the magic formula for losing money, to the tune of hundreds of millions. He had taken over one of the league's greatest franchises in 1955, wresting control of it from his sister Marguerite. Detroit's Cup-winning years ended the moment he got his hands on the team, and in the 1970s the club went into free-fall. Maple Leafs fans who bemoan the Harold Ballard years can barely imagine the despair die-hard Red Wings fans suffered for more than fifteen years. Many fans stayed away altogether, renaming the Red Wings the "Dead Things." It would take fifteen more years for the Red Wings to complete their recovery program and at last win another Stanley Cup.

Devellano's initial moves to staunch the hemorrhaging of money and recover the disappearing fan base were much like those of the expansion franchise owners in 1967—get some name-brand players into the building to make people happy. Jimmy D. went shopping for old pros who had marquee value, based on their exploits in the 1970s. It was a bit like attempting to revive a struggling Vegas hotel by booking as dinner shows some old reliables who would play to nostalgic middle America while you plotted the arrival of the real headliners. But these stopgap measures were barely that. Ex-Leaf Darryl Sittler and ex-Ranger and Bruin Brad Park came and went, Park in 1983/84 and 1984/85, Sittler in 1984/85. While Detroit returned to the playoffs in 1983/84 and 1984/85 under coach Nick Polano (who had worked for a spell as an assistant coach under Bowman in Buffalo), the experiences were short-lived. St. Louis used back-to-back overtime wins to eliminate them in four games in the 1983/84 opening round; in 1984/85, the Blackhawks did their duty, crushing them 9–5, 6–1 and 8–2. After missing the playoffs in 1985/86, having been coached by Harry Neale and then Brad Park that season, Devellano made Detroit's first stable coaching hiring since Tommy Ivan's seven-season run in the late 1940s and early 1950s. Jacques Demers, who had coached St. Louis for the previous three seasons, was installed for 1986/87.

It was the beginning of the return to glory in Hockeytown, as Detroit likes to promote itself. In addition to hiring Demers, Devellano turned a minor-pro goaltending property named Ken Holland into a scout. In time, Holland would become Devellano's heir apparent and a key figure in Scotty Bowman's sometimes troubled relationship with the Red Wings. A native of Vernon, B.C., Holland had been chosen 188th overall by Toronto in the 1975 draft after playing Junior hockey with the Medicine Hat Tigers. A long-shot to begin with, Holland was never able to establish an NHL career. After signing as a free agent with Hartford in 1980, he played one game for them that season. Devellano signed him as a free agent in 1983, and while he spent the majority of his career in the AHL, Detroit did put him into a couple of games in 1983/84. In 1985, Holland began scouting for Detroit in western Canada, then was elevated by Devellano to director of amateur scouting. Holland became the Red Wings' chief talent-picker at the annual entry draft.

Having finished last in 1985/86, the Red Wings had plenty of room for improvement, and under Demers the team rebounded dramatically. Demers became the first (and thus far the only) person to win the NHL's coaching honour, the Jack Adams Award, in back-to-back seasons (1986/87 and 1987/88). After winning only seventeen games in 1985/86 and missing the playoffs, the Red Wings won thirty-four and forty-one games in the next two seasons, and reached the conference championships. They were the last team eliminated by Edmonton in both seasons before the Oilers went on to win the Stanley Cup.

In 1988/89, the Red Wings faltered. Wins slipped from forty-one back to thirty-four, although the team won its second straight Norris division title. In the playoffs' opening round, they faced the Blackhawks, who, under new coach Mike Keenan, had finished fourth in the Norris, fourteen points back. The Blackhawks capped a six-game upset of Detroit with a 7–1 rout. In 1989/90, Detroit faded badly, winning only twenty-eight games and missing the playoffs. Demers's four-season coaching run was over.

The Ilitch family responded to the backsliding season with a re-engineering of Red Wings management. Their new employee was Bryan Murray, who had parlayed a one-season stint as a Junior hockey coach into one of the lengthiest and most successful coaching appointments in the modern NHL. It had been a spectacular season in the Junior ranks, with a spectacular finish. Murray had taken over the Regina Pats for 1979/80, after the club had finished last in the western Junior league. Under Murray, the Pats won the WHL title and advanced to the Memorial Cup round-robin against the Cornwall Royals and the Peterborough Petes. The Petes were in the care of rookie coach Mike Keenan. Due to the round-robin format, with one game to play the Petes had a berth secured in the championship game. If they beat the Royals in the round-robin's final game, Murray's Pats would finish second and meet the Petes in the final. If, however, the Petes lost the game to the Royals, the Royals would advance. With the Pats considered the better team (having beaten the Royals 11–2 in their last meeting of the round-robin), it was in Peterborough's best interests to lose the game to the Royals and meet the weaker team in the finals. The Pats suspected that this would be Keenan's game plan. Regina star Pat Blaisdill predicted that the Petes could win by five to eight goals. "If they don't win," he said, "it's because they don't want to win."

The Petes took a 4–2 lead into the third period, then conspicuously collapsed. Outshot 21–6 in the final period, the Petes gave up three unanswered goals to lose the game and deny Murray's Pats a berth in the finals. If Keenan's plan indeed had been to secure an easy victory in the finals, it backfired. The Royals won 3–2 in overtime.

Murray was outraged by Keenan's loss in the final game of the round-robin. "The Peterborough coach should be suspended, put out of hockey for a year," he charged. Keenan wasn't, and eight years passed before these two adversaries again met in a playoff series.

Murray went directly from the Memorial Cup disappointment with Regina to the head coaching job of the Hershey Bears, Washington's AHL farm team in 1980/81. The previous season, the team had finished second in the Southern division with thirty-five wins, and coach Gary Green had taken the team to a Calder Cup victory. Green was promoted to coach the Capitals, and under Murray, Hershey had its best regular season since 1972/73, leading the league with forty-seven wins. But Murray could not match Green's playoff success as Hershey was stopped in the quarterfinals by Adirondack, which went on to win the championship. Murray began the 1981/82 season assigned to Hershey; he was quickly called up to Washington to replace Green.

Mike Keenan was also on his way up. After apprenticing under Bowman as Rochester's coach and spending a season with the University of Toronto Blues, he gained his first NHL head-coaching job in Philadelphia in 1984/85, and reached the Cup finals against Edmonton that spring. His Flyers lost in five, but were back in 1986/87, challenging the Oilers in a rematch that saw the Oilers win game seven 3–1. In 1987/88, Keenan's Flyers and Murray's Capitals met in the playoffs for the first time, paired in the opening round's division semifinals. Washington won the series at home with an overtime win in game seven, then lost the division finals to New Jersey by one goal in game seven.

It was Keenan's last season in Philadelphia, as he moved to Chicago in 1988/89. Washington finished third overall in the league that season, only to have the Flyers, who had been coached to a .500 record by Paul Holmgren, upset them in the opening round of the playoffs. The fact that the Flyers progressed all the way to the conference finals before losing to Montreal, the eventual Cup-winners, took some of the sting out of the Washington loss, but for the Capitals' general manager, David Poile, an unsettling pattern was taking shape with Murray's Capitals. Perennially strong seasons were ending with playoff disappointments—just as Murray's efforts with the Regina Pats and the Hershey Bears had come up short. In the middle of the 1989/90 season, Bryan Murray was replaced as Washington's coach by his former assistant, brother Terry Murray.

Detroit, meanwhile, was on its way to missing the playoffs under its once-beloved Demers. Ilitch and Devellano saw an opportunity in the ousted Murray. With Demers fired, Devellano was elevated to senior vice-president and Murray was hired to serve as both coach and general manager.

In 1990/91, Detroit took a 3–1 game lead in its division semifinal series against St. Louis. The Blues rallied to win three straight and eliminate the Red Wings.

In 1991/92, Detroit scraped past the North Stars with a 5–2 game-seven win in the division semifinals, then lost in four straight to Mike Keenan's Blackhawks in the division finals.

In 1992/93, Detroit was eliminated by the Maple Leafs with a 4–3 overtime loss in game seven in the division semifinals.

The Red Wings' ownership watched with creeping horror as Murray's playoff curse continued to haunt him. "It was almost like a sickness for Bryan," is how Devellano puts it. The Red Wings were underachieving. Murray would stay with the team, as general manager, but Ilitch wanted a new coach. The Red Wings had been developing an excellent prospect in Adirondack, Barry Melrose, who had brought the AHL affiliate a Calder Cup win in 1991/92. But after that win, Melrose had been hired away by the Los Angeles Kings, and he took them to their first Stanley Cup final in 1992/93. To replace Murray, Ilitch wanted Murray's old Memorial Cup nemesis: Mike Keenan.

The Blackhawks and Red Wings had been in a neck-and-neck race for the Norris division lead in 1992/93, with Chicago finally prevailing by three points. They had the best- and second-best records in the league, and both teams failed to deliver on their regular-season promise. Keenan's Blackhawks had lost the Cup finals in 1991/92 to Bowman's Penguins, and in the 1992/93 playoffs, the St. Louis Blues, fourth in the Norris with ten fewer wins than Chicago, knocked out the Blackhawks with a four-game sweep in the opening round. Toronto, which had finished only four points behind the Red Wings, in third, did the damage to Detroit.

Devellano was unequivocally unenthusiastic about having Iron Mike aboard. Ilitch had already spoken with Keenan about the possibility of coming to the Red Wings when Devellano voiced his objections. "I was opposed to it and let him know. I wasn't threatened by Mike Keenan. I just didn't think that it was the proper direction for this organization to go." Scotty Bowman, he elaborates, "is the only coach today who gets away with an authoritarian style. Keenan tries, but can't."

Devellano suggested two other candidates, both of whom he knew very well. His first choice was Al Arbour. His second choice was Scotty Bowman. Ilitch gave his blessing, and Devellano approached Arbour.

Bowman and Arbour had staged one of the finest set pieces of the 1992/93 playoffs. Those playoffs followed a season in which overall team performances were somewhat skewed by the presence of a handful of very weak teams. Lack of parity in a league can take two extreme forms. A few clubs can run away with the season, leaving a disproportionately large number with poor records. Or most of the teams can have winning records as they collectively beat up on a few weak operations. In 1992/93, the latter was the case. Sixteen of twenty-four teams had records of at least .500, with two more teams within two points of the mark. In comparison, thirteen of twenty-two teams had .500 records in 1991/92. (In 1990/91, eleven of twenty-one teams were .500 or better.) The addition of two teams in 1992/93, the Ottawa Senators and the Tampa Bay Lightning, had helped boost three more teams into the .500 club than had belonged in 1991/92, with two more close behind. The lame ducks in the eighty-game season were the new franchises in Tampa Bay (23 wins) and Ottawa (10 wins), the 1991/92 newcomer San Jose (11 wins), a struggling young Oilers team (26 wins) and the sinking Hartford Whalers (26 wins).

Thus, while Scotty Bowman's Pittsburgh Penguins were the undisputed champions of the regular season, with 119 points and a win percentage of .708, the league was crowded with clubs on the up side of the win-loss register. Al Arbour's Islanders, who trailed Pittsburgh by thirty-two points in the Patrick division, still had a winning record, with forty wins and seven ties in eighty-four starts. The Islanders were thin on scoring stars of the stature of Mario Lemieux, Ron Francis or Jaromir Jagr, but they still scored a healthy 335 goals, thanks to the efforts of players like centre Pierre Turgeon and left-wingers Derek King and Steve Thomas. The defence featured Tom Kurvers, chosen 145th by Montreal back in 1981, who had blossomed into a points-producer, and Scotty Bowman's great find down at 214th in the 1983 draft, Uwe Krupp. A respectable pair of netminders, Glenn Healy and Mark Fitzpatrick, kept the Islanders in the game.

And there was Al Arbour behind the bench. After winning four Stanley Cups in a row, from 1979/80 to 1982/83, and losing to Edmonton in the finals in 1983/84, Arbour had stayed for two more seasons before attempting to escape the bench by moving up to vice-president of player development in 1986. The Islanders won the Patrick division in 1987/88 in a tight race that saw seven points separate six teams. The New Jersey Devils, in fourth, dropped them in six in the opening play-off round, and in 1988/89 both New Jersey and the Islanders fell badly behind division rivals Washington, Pittsburgh, Philadelphia and the Rangers. After twenty-seven games, Terry Simpson, who had taken over the coaching job from Arbour in 1986/87, was replaced by Arbour himself as the vice-president came back down to rinkside. The Islanders still missed the playoffs, but that June, Arbour was formally named the team's coach for the second time.

He still had Bill Torrey with him, but not for long. Before the 1992/93 season, Torrey left the organization he had been with since the dawn of the franchise for another start-up operation, the Florida Panthers, which would begin play in 1993/94. Former New York Ranger Don Maloney took over as general manager, and that season Arbour followed Scotty Bowman into the record book by becoming the second coach in NHL history to win 700 regular-season games. The 1992/93 playoffs put these two old associates back together again, squaring off from opposite benches.

The Bowman of Pittsburgh was supposed to be a retooled Bowman, a team-spirit Bowman who had learned from the late Bob Johnson's example, that browbeating players didn't work anymore. "I have more experience, more patience," Bowman told *Sports Illustrated* as the play-offs began. "Players are much more sensitive today. It used to be, if a guy's unhappy, so what? Now it might disturb the chemistry of the team. You take players off the ice, and you see they have a big lip on. So you have to explain they missed a few shifts because we needed more offense. You hope they accept it. Ten years ago I wouldn't have bothered. That's the reality of team sports today."

It was a revealing observation, underlining the vast gap between the personalities of Bowman and Johnson. Badger Bob didn't relate to and inspire players just because they had a big lip on. He did it

because it was in his nature. A player like Frank Mahovlich will readily argue that players have always been sensitive, and that it has been
up to coaches to attune themselves to this and not waste talent by
steam-rollering it emotionally. Bowman's comments to the magazine
suggested that he considered modern players juvenile and in need of
stroking. Bowman had been forced to change by the unique circumstances of Johnson's death. The Penguins were a successful team that
had become accustomed to having a positive personal bond with the
coach, and they weren't interested in reverting to a Machiavellian
motivational mode. Bowman changed for the team because he had
to—not because, like the Grinch, his heart grew three sizes the day
Bob Johnson died.

Bowman opened his campaign for a third consecutive Penguins Stanley Cup with a fairly routine elimination of New Jersey in the division
semifinals, a series Pittsburgh won in five games. Arbour's opening
match-up with Washington was more of a struggle, with three consecutive overtime games. The Islanders won two of them to take a 3–1
series lead, and won in six games, but in the deciding game they lost
scoring star Pierre Turgeon with a separated shoulder.

The division finals threw Arbour and Bowman together in a true
seesaw playoff battle. Neither team could win two games in a row.
Arbour won the opener 3–2 in Pittsburgh, and the trading of wins culminated in a game-seven showdown twelve nights later, in the Igloo
in Pittsburgh.

In a way, Bowman was playing his own past. He was back in the
1967/68 finals between St. Louis and Montreal, only now the roles
were reversed. He was the one with the juggernaut team, while his
old Blues defenceman, Arbour, had the tramp steamer. As Glenn Hall
did in 1967/68, Glenn Healy gave the Islanders outstanding goaltending, and Arbour had his team play the old Blues game, clearing
their zone quickly, making sure there were no rebounds to capitalize
on, despite a fusillade of initial shots (forty-five against Healy in the
deciding game).

Early in game seven, Bowman lost Kevin Stevens when a hit by Rich Pilon delivered a broken nose, facial cuts and a concussion. With four minutes to play, the Islanders were winning 3–1. A remarkable rally by the Penguins tied the game, but at 5:16 of overtime Bowman's brilliant season was ended by a journeyman winger from Prague named David Volek, whom the Islanders had drafted 208th overall in 1984.

The Islanders advanced into the conference finals against Montreal and lost in five as the Canadiens moved on to win the finals against Los Angeles. For a team that hadn't even made the playoffs the previous season, the Islanders had done admirably well. Pittsburgh, on the other hand, was left to contemplate the irony of its failure. The team's first two Cups had come after what, for a championship team, would have to be considered mediocre regular-season performances. But when the Penguins put together the season of a true champion in 1992/93, they were rewarded with elimination in the second round.

Jimmy Devellano had watched the two winningest coaches active in the game go toe to toe in the division semifinals, and decided that either would be a worthy replacement for Bryan Murray. It's not hard to see why, however, his first choice would be Arbour. The former skipper of a modern dynasty had demonstrated against Bowman and the Penguins that he was capable not just of achieving, but of overachieving. And as a coaching personality, Arbour had a comprehensive breadth and depth. Bowman's complexity was contradictory and sometimes maddening; players and management were polarized in their opinions of him. Bowman was a character of extremes. Coaching, it is true, is not a popularity contest, but a team cannot achieve if it does not accept a coach's authority. Bowman would be more successful with a team that universally despised him, but accepted his playing system, than with a team that was divided between friends and enemies, confused in its respect for his authority and methods.

Jimmy Devellano pitched Al Arbour on coming to Detroit to coach the Red Wings. Arbour turned him down. He wanted to finish his career on Long Island. He wasn't interested in starting over. So Jimmy D. went after Scotty Bowman.

Bowman was far from a consolation prize. Bowman had failed in Buffalo with a team full of youngsters, but in Pittsburgh he had once again demonstrated the ability first shown in St. Louis and Montreal to goad exceptional performances from mature players. No one else, aside from Arbour, could have merited the salary package Ilitch and Devellano presented to him. At the time, Bowman was making about $300,000 as the Penguins' coach and director of player development. Just to coach the Red Wings, Bowman was offered a $100,000 signing bonus and a two-year contract at $800,000 per season.

Bowman would reflect on how fortunate he was to last long enough in the business to make big money. In four seasons in Detroit, he would make more money than he had in the rest of his career. But Bowman wasn't the only beneficiary. Without Bowman around, the great leap forward in coaching salaries would not have occurred. Overnight, Bowman's hiring by Detroit changed the financial landscape for coaches. Mike Keenan, who had been hired as coach and general manager of the New York Rangers, would be scheming to find some exit from his contract at the end of 1993/94 to land a more lucrative package in St. Louis.

Why did Bowman accept the Red Wings' offer? The money, to be sure, but Bowman had been offered generous packages before—notably the minority ownership with Washington in 1979—and turned them down. Bowman had again shown his knack for choosing his opportunities carefully. Pittsburgh was a powerful team, but with two Cups behind him and a disappointing conclusion to the latest season, perhaps it was time to move on. Bowman had ruffled the usual dressing-room feathers with the Penguins, and after the early exit from the latest playoffs, it was debatable how long Craig Patrick would be able to shield him, or endure him. He had almost not returned after the 1991/92 season when he and Patrick were deadlocked in contract negotiations; in early August 1992, Bowman had even announced that he wouldn't be coming back as coach, and would revert instead to his player-development role. There were also rumours that Bowman's imperial style was not meeting with approval. Leaving practices to assistant coaches, he was sometimes back home in Buffalo when the team was working out.

It turned out that Bowman had chosen his move with precision timing. Pittsburgh's movement was horizontal, while Detroit's was vertical. Mario Lemieux had turned in another superb regular season, and had scored eight goals in eleven playoff games, but persistent back problems would limit him to twenty-two games in 1993/94. The Penguins would continue to turn in solid regular seasons, but not of the league-crushing dimension of the 1992/93 campaign. And no Stanley Cup lay in their immediate future.

The Red Wings, on the other hand, were a team that had produced fine regular seasons and were capable of much more. The team was still in the building stage, with an emphasis on developing new talent through draft picks, not trades. "Don't trade draft picks," had been Devellano's mantra through many lean seasons. He might trade the players he'd drafted, but not the picks themselves. From 1983 to 1991, Detroit had never picked lower than eleventh.

Sixteen of the players who would win a Stanley Cup under Bowman in 1996/97 were in the Detroit system when he arrived in 1993, a year before he had any control over player development. The longest serving (and suffering) member of the championship team was captain Steve Yzerman, the high-scoring centre selected fourth overall in the 1983 draft by Detroit at the beginning of Devellano's career with the Red Wings. No one else who came to the team over the next five years would be part of the championship lineup. The new team had begun to form at the 1989 entry draft, when Ken Holland had taken glasnost and perestroika as a sign that it was time to test the Russian waters.

✧　✧　✧

At 1:45 of the first period in a game in Calgary against the Flames on October 27, 1995, Scotty Bowman made a historic line change. Three days earlier, Bowman had traded Ray Sheppard to San Jose to acquire Igor Larionov. Sheppard was a right-winger Bowman had drafted as Buffalo's general manager in 1984; the Red Wings had signed him as a free agent in 1991. Larionov was beginning his sixth NHL season and was eager to get out of San Jose. By acquiring Larionov, Bowman had five former Central Red Army teammates in Red Wings uniforms. The potential existed to put them all on the ice at the same time, and he did it in Calgary, all five leaping over the boards in unison: Viacheslav Fetisov and Vladimir Konstantinov on defence, with a forward line of centre Larionov, right wing Sergei Fedorov and left wing Vyacheslav Kozlov.

On their second shift of the game, Kozlov whacked his own rebound past Flames goaltender Trevor Kidd at 10:06 of the first period. Detroit went on to win 3–0 and Bowman had made NHL history. No team had ever flooded the ice with Russian skaters before.

"I wasn't thinking about it, really," Bowman told the *Detroit Free Press*. "I don't know how long I'll use it.... They would play as a unit as much as possible in some cases, the power play, too. It might give a different flavour to the team."

Bowman would receive much ink for icing the first all-Russian unit with the Red Wings in 1995/96, but the move toward Russian players in Detroit long preceded him, and it had begun in the NHL overall without his participation.

Throughout the 1980s, some NHL teams devoted late draft picks to the long-shot possibility of Russian stars one day joining the professional ranks. When the Soviet counter-revolution did take hold in 1989, a stream of old warriors, such as Sergei Makarov, Alexei Kasatonov, Igor Larionov, Viacheslav (Slava) Fetisov and Vladimir Krutov, whose careers stretched back into the 1970s, would make their belated NHL debuts, paying dividends to the general managers (or their fortunate successors) who had demonstrated the foresight to devote what was often a throwaway pick to securing their playing rights. Kasatonov, Larionov and Makarov had formed the devastating KLM line of the Soviet national team; Larionov had scored twice in the series-clinching 8–1 drubbing of the NHL All Stars coached by Scotty Bowman in the 1979 Challenge Cup. Vancouver had drafted Larionov 214th in 1985, Krutov 238th in 1986, while in 1983 Fetisov and Kasatonov had been selected 150th and 225th respectively by New Jersey, and Makarov 231st by Calgary. (Fetisov had originally been drafted by Montreal 201st overall in 1978, but the Canadiens' rights had expired.)

Bowman, running the Sabres in these years, didn't bother joining in on the Russian late-pick strategy. And having been fired by Buffalo in 1986, Bowman was left on the sidelines as the next revolution in the entry draft unfolded. In 1988, eight Russians were chosen in the NHL entry draft, as many as were selected in the previous five drafts combined. Buffalo used its fourth choice, eighty-ninth overall, to select Alexander Mogilny. After the nineteen-year-old right-winger completed his second season with Central Red Army, he began his career with the Sabres in the fall of 1989, placing him in the first wave of Russian stars to break into the NHL. Joining him in the league that fall were thirty-one-year-old Makarov, with Calgary, thirty-year-old Kasatonov and thirty-one year-old Fetisov, with New Jersey, and twenty-nine-year-olds Larionov and Krutov, with Vancouver.

The arrival of the pioneer draftees in the NHL, coincident with a new generation of Russian stars, clouded the issue of the adaptability of such enigmatic talents to the North American professional game. Had the talent surge been in the opposite direction across the Atlantic, it would have been like Bobby Clarke, Guy Lafleur and Lanny McDonald showing up as rookies in the Soviet Elite League at the same time as Joe Sakic, Brett Hull and Mario Lemieux.

Before coming to the Sabres, Mogilny participated in the 1989 World Junior Championships in Anchorage, Alaska. The victorious Russians iced the dazzling line of centre Sergei Fedorov, left-winger Pavel Bure (a left-handed shot who would play right wing in the NHL) and right-winger Mogilny. Detroit's Ken Holland, choosing 74th overall in the 1989 draft, took Fedorov; Vancouver claimed Bure with the 113th pick. Down at 221st, Holland made defenceman Vladimir Konstantinov the Red Wings' property. Though only two years older than Fedorov, Konstantinov was practically of a different generation of Russian player. The "Monster of Murmansk" was seventeen when he joined Central Red Army in 1984, and had completed his fifth season on Russia's most celebrated league team when Holland devoted a late pick to him.

Before getting to Fedorov and Konstantinov, Holland had used his third pick, fifty-third overall, to select Sweden's Niklas Lidstrom. The nineteen-year-old defenceman with Vasteras in the Swedish Elite League skated for his country at the 1990 World Junior Championships. These three Europeans proved to be Detroit's best picks of 1989, and some of the team's best for years to come. Fedorov joined the Red Wings in 1990/91 after four seasons with Central Red Army; Konstantinov followed in 1991/92, after seven seasons with Central Red Army, while Lidstrom joined Konstantinov on the Red Wings' defence that season. Even before Fedorov and Konstantinov had arrived, Holland had gone back to the Russian talent pool to select Vyacheslav Kozlov forty-fifth overall with his second choice in 1990. The eighteen-year-old centre had been playing with Khimik Novopolotsk since he was fifteen; after eleven games with Central Red Army in 1991/92, Kozlov had joined the Red Wings.

After not bothering to make the long-shot Russian picks with Buffalo in the 1980s, Bowman showed no interest in Russians when he became director of player development with Pittsburgh in 1989. His overseas focus remained on Czechs and Scandinavians. When he came to Detroit in 1993, he reaped the benefit of the pioneering work performed by Holland under Devellano and Murray. Waiting for Bowman in Red Wings uniforms were Fedorov, Konstantinov and Kozlov, as well as Sweden's Lidstrom. Many other key players were also in place. Martin Lapointe was Detroit's first choice, tenth overall, in the

1991 draft. (Detroit's fourth pick in 1991, right-winger Mike Knuble, would play nine games during the Red Wings' 1996/97 Stanley Cup season.) Detroit's second choice (forty-sixth overall) in the 1992 draft was Darren McCarty. Lapointe and McCarty, both right-wingers, became Detroit starters with Bowman's arrival in 1993/94. Also chosen in the 1991 draft were defenceman Jamie Pushor (second pick, thirty-second overall) and goaltender Chris Osgood (third pick, fifty-fourth overall). One acquisition, made two weeks after Bowman was hired in the summer of 1993, also improved the breadth of players from which he had to select, as centre Kris Draper was acquired from Winnipeg. And in May 1993, backup goaltender Kevin Hodson was signed as a free agent out of the Ontario Junior league.

And so, when Bowman began his fifth NHL coaching job, in Detroit on June 15, 1993, most of the team he would use to win the Stanley Cup, four seasons later, was waiting for him. The situation was not unlike Pittsburgh's when he arrived in 1989. Much of the team-building had already been performed, but there was plenty of opportunity for improvement. In Pittsburgh, Bowman had worked a one-season re-engineering of the team with Craig Patrick that culminated in the Penguins' Cup win under Bob Johnson. In Detroit, the process would be more drawn out, as Bowman and the team in general grappled with meeting the highest expectations to be attached to a club since the 1970s and Bowman's Canadiens. The Red Wings of the 1990s were Bowman's Waterloo. Whether he would prove to be Wellington or Napoleon became the central issue of his years in Hockeytown.

In Bowman's first season as Detroit's coach, there was little to choose between in the Red Wings' performance under him and under Bryan Murray the previous season. Under Murray, the team won 47, lost 28 and tied 9; under Bowman, the team won 46, lost 30 and tied 10. Under Murray, the team scored 369 and allowed 280; under Bowman, the team scored 356 and allowed 275. Murray's Red Wings finished with 103 points, second in the Norris division behind Mike Keenan's Blackhawks, fifth overall. Bowman's Red Wings finished with 100 points, first in the Norris and fourth overall.

In the playoffs, Bowman's Red Wings also performed much the way Murray's Red Wings had. In 1992/93, Murray's Red Wings had outscored the Toronto Maple Leafs 30–24 in the opening round and lost in seven. In 1993/94, Bowman's Red Wings outscored the San Jose Sharks 27–21 in the opening round and lost in seven. While the 1992/93 loss had been a letdown, the 1993/94 loss was truly staggering. In 1992/93 Murray's Red Wings had been facing the Leafs, their Central division rivals, who had finished only four points behind them. In 1993/94, an intra-conference format was used for the opening round, which brought on the Pacific division's Sharks. An expansion team in its third season, San Jose had won only eleven games in 1992/93 and had finished 1993/94 with thirteen fewer wins and eighteen fewer points than Detroit, and a losing record.

The series provided an unsettling flashback to Bowman's experience in 1992/93 against Arbour's Islanders. He could not solve these pesky upstarts. The Red Wings took a 2–1 series lead, then fell behind 3–2. Facing elimination, Detroit pounded San Jose 7–1 in game six. Game seven went awry, and the fans at the Joe Louis Arena were witness to yet another early playoff exit as the Sharks won 3–2.

Prophetically, in commenting on his decision to leave Montreal in 1979, Bowman had said that he could have stuck with the Canadiens and tried to win a power struggle, but that he chose not to. After the 1993/94 season, Bowman chose to play the game. Unlike the Canadiens, which had been owned by a corporation, the Red Wings were the property of the Ilitch family. It made power struggles that much simpler. He who could bend the ear of Mike Ilitch could carry the day. The behind-the-scenes manoeuvring for the favours of the ownership were said to be ruthless, and were ultimately fatal for Bryan Murray, who was fired as general manager. Jimmy Devellano would run the team from his senior vice-president's post, while Scotty Bowman continued as coach, and took on the director of player personnel duties as well. As in Pittsburgh, he could now run the bench and oversee the drafting and trading of players in Detroit, subject to Devellano's approval.

Murray was hired as general manager of the Florida Panthers in August. His protege, Doug Maclean, who had come with him from the Capitals and served as his assistant coach and then assistant general manager in Detroit, stayed on for another year after relinquishing his player development responsibilities to Bowman. He joined Murray in Florida in 1994/95, in the process bumping two former Bowman subalterns from his Buffalo days, Roger Neilson and Craig Ramsay, out of the coaching ranks.

Some of the blame for the loss to San Jose was deflected from Bowman onto Sergei Fedorov. The 1989 draftee had left the Russian team during the Goodwill Games in Portland, Oregon, in October 1990 to join the Red Wings. A defensive forward who adjusted quickly to the NHL, he was a runner-up to Chicago goaltender Ed Belfour in 1990/91 Calder voting. In 1991/92 he narrowly missed another league award, finishing second to Guy Carbonneau of the Canadiens in voting for the Frank Selke Award as the top defensive forward (even though he had polled more first-place votes among the professional hockey writers who determined the winner). In 1993/94, Fedorov had become a complete superstar: he won the Selke, finished second to Wayne Gretzky in the scoring race and captured both of the league's MVP awards, the Hart (the player most valuable to his team, according to the hockey writers) and the Pearson (the league's most valuable player, according to his fellow players).

But the recipient of so many accolades had fizzled in the playoffs, managing only one of Detroit's twenty-seven goals against the Sharks. Fedorov's performance raised the usual cloud of nagging doubts about Russians being able to perform in the NHL. They had to prove that they could play the physical game on a smaller ice surface; that they could cope with a playing schedule that was heavily weighted toward games rather than practices; that they could stand the pressure of regularly playing very good clubs, rather than attending international tournaments filled with second-rate national teams. Finally, they had to demonstrate that a Stanley Cup win truly mattered to them, that they had the desire to play to win in the post-season when they came from a sporting culture that had set within them the goals of Olympic and world championship gold medals.

All these criticisms would be swept aside—eventually. But for the Red Wings, handing the team over to Bowman had not removed the stigma, formerly identified with Murray, of being a regular-season wonder that could not win playoff hockey.

The root of Murray's downfall (aside from the Night of the Long Knives manoeuvring that saw him removed from Detroit and Bowman promoted) may have lain in the Red Wings' continued difficulties with playoff goaltending. Division rivals Chicago, Toronto and St. Louis had found clutch goaltending in Ed Belfour, Felix Potvin and Curtis Joseph. Bryan Murray had placed his faith in Tim Cheveldae, drafted by the Red Wings out of Saskatoon in 1986 sixty-fourth overall as their fourth pick. In 1990/91, Cheveldae had been rewarded with the starter's job by the newly arrived Murray; in 1991/92 he led the league with seventy-two starts and thirty-eight wins. But despite the fact that Murray stuck with him, he was not considered the equal of his division rivals, as the Detroit playoff efforts came up short. At the 1991 draft, Detroit had selected Chris Osgood with its third choice, fifty-fourth overall. The Medicine Hat Tiger still had another season of Junior hockey to go, and graduated to Detroit's Adirondack farm club in 1992/93. In 1993/94 under Bowman, Osgood wrested the starter's job from Cheveldae. Murray traded his former playoff fixture, now made expendable, to the Winnipeg Jets in March, packaging him with centre Dallas Drake in return for netminder Bob Essensa and defenceman Sergei Bautin. Bautin had been Winnipeg's first choice in the 1992 draft, going seventeenth overall. The twenty-

seven-year-old product of Moscow Dynamo proved not to be a factor in the Red Wings' ongoing overhaul: he played one game with
Detroit that season, was sent to Adirondack and was then allowed to
go to San Jose as a free agent in 1995. Nor, for that matter, did
Essensa represent a Bowman goaltending hope of the dimension of
Glenn Hall, Ken Dryden or Tom Barrasso. He played thirteen games
for Detroit at the end of the season, with a 2.62 average, but in two
games against San Jose, Essensa surrendered nine goals. They were
his last games as a Red Wing, and the Cheveldae-Essensa deal was
the last influence Bryan Murray would have on Scotty Bowman's
choice of a starting goaltender.

Bowman officially got the director of player personnel job on June 15
as Murray was ousted from Detroit. Two weeks later, Bowman was
cutting a deal for a heavyweight netminder. In a straight swap, Detroit
sent the Calgary Flames defenceman Steve Chiasson, an eight-season
Red Wings veteran, for local Calgary hero Mike Vernon.

Thirty-one years old, Vernon was born in Calgary and played his
Junior hockey there. In the 1983 Memorial Cup, he was called up in
an injury substitution to play for the Portland Winter Hawks, and he
won the tournament's top goaltender award as the Hawks took the
championship (the first win by an American-based team in the Canadian Junior system).

Vernon had a two-game call-up with the Flames that same season—
he had been chosen by Calgary with its second pick, fifty-sixth overall, in the 1981 draft. He made his first strong impression on the NHL
in 1985/86. After starting only eighteen regular-season games under
coach Bob Johnson, Vernon appeared in twenty-one playoff games for
the Flames, more than any other NHL goaltender in that post-season,
as the Flames upset Edmonton in a seven-game division final and outlasted St. Louis in a seven-game conference final before bowing to
Montreal in five in the Stanley Cup finals.

From that playoff run forward, Vernon was Calgary's main netminder, never starting fewer than forty-seven games, and he always

carried the Flames through the playoffs. In 1988/89, while Scotty Bowman was working his last season providing colour commentary for
"Hockey Night in Canada," he had watched from the broadcast booth
as Vernon compiled his signature season. He led the league with thirty-
seven wins and outshone all rivals in the playoffs. He played more
games (twenty-two), won more games (sixteen) and recorded more
shutouts (three) than any other goaltender as the Flames used a game-
seven overtime win to defeat Vancouver in the division semifinals,
swept the Kings in four in the division finals, and avenged their 1986
loss by defeating Montreal in six in the finals. Vernon's effort, which
produced a 2.26 average, brought him the Conn Smythe Trophy as
playoff MVP.

When Scotty Bowman searched out a new goaltender to comple-
ment or replace Osgood after Detroit's 1993/94 playoff upset, Calgary's general manager was Doug Risebrough, who had won four
Stanley Cups playing for Bowman before ending his playing career in
Calgary in 1986/87. His willingness to deal away Vernon to Bowman
in exchange for Chiasson had seismic consequences in Calgary. Vernon, the hometown boy who, since his Junior days in town, had never
not played for Calgary, was the closest thing there was to a franchise
player. Risebrough was taking a considerable gamble in letting Vernon go and promoting in his stead backup Trevor Kidd, Calgary's top
draft pick in 1990. Scotty Bowman had pulled an inside job, using
his familiarity with Risebrough to make off with the heart and soul
of the team. Or so the theory went. Dealing away Vernon was said
to be one of the reasons Risebrough lost his job as the Flames' general manager in 1995. (Risebrough later returned to work for the
Flames under new ownership.)

With Vernon, Bowman had a money goaltender, a veteran of almost
nine NHL seasons, who had twice gone the distance to a Stanley Cup
final. But he also still had Osgood, not yet twenty-two, some nine
years younger than Vernon, still to be proven or disproven. In one
sense, Bowman had solved his netminding problems in Detroit within

two weeks of gaining the power to do so. On the other hand, he hadn't, not in the traditional Bowman sense, for Bowman had almost always enjoyed one main starter. Glenn Hall had shared the limelight with Jacques Plante for one season in St. Louis, but otherwise had been Bowman's defensive anchor with the Blues. With Montreal, Bowman had depended utterly on Dryden. In Buffalo, he had inherited the team of Sauve and Edwards, but ended up trading them away and banking on his own draft pick, Barrasso, who carried over into Pittsburgh. For the next three seasons, Bowman would have two solid goaltenders from which to choose, and no clear choice between them.

15

⬥ IN 1994/95, THE PROBLEM of Winning it All deepened for the Red Wings in a season that almost had to be scrubbed because of the first major labour dispute between the NHL and the players' association. When the lockout ended, a forty-eight-game schedule was shoehorned between January 20 and May 3. To accomplish this scheduling feat, interconference play was scrapped. And so it happened that Scotty Bowman's Red Wings went the entire season without meeting Jacques Lemaire's New Jersey Devils, until they confronted each other in the Stanley Cup finals. Not only had the Red Wings not played the Devils that season, the two teams had never met before in the playoffs.

The Wings had produced the league's best record, nine points better than St. Louis in the west, five points better than Quebec in the east. In the playoffs they ripped through their conference rivals, losing only two of fourteen games in three quick series. In avenging its loss to San Jose in 1993/94, Detroit outscored the Sharks 24–6 in a four-game sweep.

The Stanley Cup series provided Bowman with another reunion of sorts. He had been in the game so long that encounters with his own past were around every corner. Bob Gainey had coached against the Penguins in the 1990/91 finals when Bowman was Pittsburgh's director of player development. In 1991/92, Bowman's Penguins had clashed with Roger Neilson's Rangers in the division finals and Mike Keenan's Blackhawks in the finals. In 1992/93, Al Arbour's Islanders had ended Bowman's playoff run in the division finals. Detroit's quick exit in 1993/94 spared Bowman another reunion, but in 1994/95 the familiar faces returned. Bob Gainey's Dallas Stars were downed in five in the conference quarterfinals, and in the finals he met his match in Jacques Lemaire.

After his retirement following Montreal's 1978/79 win, when Bowman departed for Buffalo, Lemaire had begun a steady rise in the coaching ranks, first in Switzerland, then in the Quebec Major Junior A, bringing him finally to run the Canadiens' bench in 1983/84 and 1984/85. He then left coaching to become a managing director of the Canadiens; seven seasons in Montreal's front office ended when he was hired to coach New Jersey in 1993/94. In his first season, the Devils achieved a franchise-record 106 points as Lemaire won the Jack Adams Award. The Devils were the last team eliminated (in a seven-game struggle) by the Rangers before New York reached the finals and won the franchise's first Stanley Cup since 1939/40.

When he arrived in the NHL as a player, Lemaire was criticized for being too offence-minded. As a coach, he came to espouse a strict defensive style, and gained fame (and notoriety) for employing the neutral-zone trap, a forechecking style that smothered wide-open offence. In 1994/95, the Red Wings had produced the third-highest number of goals in the league, 180, while the Devils scored only 136. Both teams allowed a minimum of goals—Detroit 117, New Jersey 121, just behind the league-leading Blackhawks, at 115. Bowman had bolstered his defence with two new signings since the early exit from the 1993/94 playoffs. Bob Rouse had been signed as a free agent in the off-season, and a late-season deal, on April 3, secured from the Devils Viacheslav Fetisov, in exchange for Detroit's third-round pick in the upcoming entry draft. Both finalists enjoyed first-rate goaltending: Bowman used Mike Vernon as his main starter, and Lemaire received outstanding service from the 1993/94 Calder winner, Martin Brodeur.

With such a disparity in their offensive styles, however, it was inevitable that, to win, one team would have to get its way most of the time. Detroit was accustomed to scoring 3.75 goals per game that season; the Devils were accustomed to allowing 2.44. During the first three playoff series, Detroit had been able to play the game their way, scoring an average 3.86. Against the Devils, the Red Wings could not mount any kind of offence. Checked assiduously, the Red Wings scored only seven times as they went down in four straight. Scotty Bowman, the master of line matching, had not been able to spring loose his scorers from Lemaire's efficient if dull defensive style. Worse, Lemaire's low-scoring team managed a solid offensive effort against the Red Wings' supposedly stingy defence in winning 2–1, 4–2, 5–2 and 5–2.

When the league returned to a regular schedule in 1995/96, the Red Wings stormed through eighty-two games without any suggestion that their greatness had been dented by the loss to New Jersey. Bowman achieved his five-man Russian unit with the trade of Ray Sheppard to San Jose for Igor Larionov in late October, and he broke his own record of sixty regular-season wins, set by the Canadiens in 1976/77, when the Red Wings defeated the Blackhawks at the Joe Louis Arena on April 12 in the second-last game of the season. A 5–1 defeat of the Stars in Dallas on April 14 set the new regular-season standard of sixty-two wins. The Wings had earned their third consecutive Central division and Western conference titles, with the third-highest number of goals in the league and the fewest goals against, as Chris Osgood and Mike Vernon shared the Jennings Trophy.

The history of the NHL is littered with teams who saw outstanding regular seasons crumble in the playoffs. The Boston Bruins of 1929/30 and 1970/71, the Blackhawks of 1966/67, the Montreal Canadiens of 1944/45, and Bowman's own Pittsburgh Penguins of 1992/93 were some of the more spectacular playoff flameouts. But the NHL had also been marked by a peculiar trend since 1989/90: only the New York Rangers of 1993/94 had been able to win both the regular season and the Stanley Cup. The regular season had proved to be a numbers game, a matter of clubs rotating through twenty-six different arenas, adding up the accumulated points and seeing who had the most. The Red Wings certainly had math on their side. In addition to their record number of wins, strong offensive output and league-leading goals-against average, the Red Wings had led the NHL in penalty-killing and had the third-best power play. Detroit had twice gone nine games without losing, and it was the only NHL club with a winning record in the games in which it trailed after the first period—winning six, losing four, tying three. The Red Wings were also unmatched at protecting a lead. Of fifty-four games in which they were leading after two periods, they lost only two and settled for a tie once.

But the regular season was nothing like playoff hockey, which entailed a series played at a higher tempo against one other team— a team that might be statistically inferior, but that could also play a particular style that exploited a top club's weaknesses. Clubs that have been seemingly all-powerful in the regular season have been undone by playoff opponents who reined in their opponent's scoring stars, came up with clutch goaltending and made the most of their scoring opportunities.

In the 1995/96 playoffs, the Red Wings were burdened by high expectations, weighed down by their own regular-season accomplishments. The hype in Hockeytown ("We want Stanley!") was deafening. Bowman had been in this situation before, with the Penguins of 1992/93. Now his 1995/96 Red Wings could not even manage the confident run through the opening rounds that had prefaced their loss to New Jersey in 1994/95. Winnipeg took them to six games in the conference quarterfinal, and in the conference semifinals the St. Louis Blues nearly ended the triumphal march, with a game-seven overtime goal by captain Steve Yzerman required for Detroit to advance to the conference finals.

There the march came to a sad end after six games against the Colorado Avalanche, the new incarnation of the Quebec Nordiques. A promising Nordiques team, with skilled forwards like Peter Forsberg and Joe Sakic, had been bolstered by the addition of Patrick Roy in goal and Claude Lemieux on right wing. Bowman's Wings had already been vexed by Lemieux when, as captain of the Devils, he had led New Jersey to their 1994/95 Stanley Cup win and won the Conn Smythe. Lemieux was the kind of player it is said teams hate to play against but wish they had on their side, a scorer who checks, who raises the intensity of his game in the playoffs, and who gets in opponents' faces. He was considered dirty by many, and he had been traded to New Jersey by Montreal after a falling out with coach Pat Burns, who could not abide his diving act in search of penalties. In one of his last acts as Lemieux's coach, Burns humiliated him by leaving him writhing on the ice, refusing to send out the trainer. Lemieux was forced to pick himself up and head for the bench under his own power.

Lemieux became the focal point of the conference championship series between the Red Wings and the Avalanche because of two nasty incidents. The first, in game three, was a sucker-punch of Vyacheslav Kozlov that earned Lemieux a game misconduct and a one-game suspension. Lemieux had nailed Kozlov in retaliation for a bit of stick-work that cut Avalanche defenceman Adam Foote for twenty stitches. After the game, the Red Wings' bus was moving through the parking lot of Denver's McNichols Arena when Bowman spotted Lemieux. He ordered the driver to stop the bus and open the door. Lemieux, walking with his wife and young daughter, was confronted by an obscenity-spewing Bowman, loudly promising him that he would be suspended.

The league had changed its review and suspension process in the wake of Adam Graves's slash of Mario Lemieux in 1992. In the second-last game of the season, Detroit's Dino Ciccarelli had popped Chicago's Enrico Ciccone and earned a three-game suspension, causing him to miss the first two games of the playoffs. Claude Lemieux (no relation to Mario) was also suspended immediately, for game four. It was suspected that Bowman's seniority and influence in the league had helped secure a favourable ruling, when Colorado coach Marc Crawford's complaints earlier in the series about a Keith Primeau slash to the back of Peter Forsberg had brought no result. "I had nothing to do with his suspension," Bowman said. "The league was going to review three incidents, which they did. I didn't punch Kozlov. And I didn't make the decision. The league did."

While few were prepared to defend Lemieux's punch, fewer still were prepared to defend Bowman's verbal assault on Lemieux. He had gone too far, stepping outside the time and space of the game to crudely berate Lemieux in front of his family. Marc Crawford dismissed Bowman's histrionics as typical mind games, an attempt to distract the Avalanche. "Scotty Bowman is notorious for taking an incidental factor in a game and trying to create a lot of focus around that," he said. "He does it by planting questions in the media. He does it by trying to create an awful lot of controversy due to a non-fact. He's a great thinker, but he thinks so much that you even get the plate in his head causing interference on our headsets during the game." Asked to characterize his relationship with Bowman, Crawford said, "Diminishing."

"Games are won on the ice," Bowman responded in the media. "That was my favourite quote when I was a young coach. Games are won on the ice, not on the dance floor."

The Kozlov incident was overshadowed entirely by Lemieux's vicious hit on Kris Draper in game six. At 14:07 of the first period, Lemieux drove Draper from behind into the boards in front of the Detroit bench. Draper's upper jaw, cheekbone and nose were fractured and several teeth were knocked out of line. With his jaw wired shut, Draper was on a liquid diet for a month. The two-game suspension handed down to Lemieux outraged Draper and the rest of the Red Wings, and set the stage for a blood feud between the clubs to follow in the new season. "Two games," muttered Bowman. "That was a pretty serious injury. I don't know how long Kris would have been out if we were playing. He'd have been out a couple of months. I really thought [Lemieux] would get ten games."

Ultimately, Lemieux's misbehaviour was a sideshow, an ugly distraction from the larger of issue of Bowman's handling of the Red Wings that season. The verdict was that Bowman bore the bulk of responsibility for the playoff failure. Chasing new horizons in the record book, he had driven a maturing team hard in pursuit of regular-season glory, as he had with Buffalo in 1979/80 and Pittsburgh in 1992/93. After Detroit lost the first two games at home to the Avalanche, *Detroit News* columnist Bob Wojnowski, accurately sensing another playoff collapse, wrote: "The Wings are a thoroughbred that has spent too long leading the pack. All season, Scotty Bowman went to the whip with a 30-length lead. All the Wings could do was look back to see who was gaining. Colorado has gained and passed them."

The team did not play with the energy of its playoff opponents; it was outhustled, outhit and outscored. By the time the Red Wings reached the conference finals, they had already endured thirteen tense playoff games in the first two rounds, including two overtime contests against St. Louis. In 1994/95, they had only played fourteen games in the first three rounds, and had preceded them with a lockout-shortened season.

While Osgood had played well in net, the team had been particularly weak in its own end as an aging defence corps showed the strain of the long campaign. Bob Rouse, Paul Coffey and Viacheslav Fetisov were approaching thirty-two, thirty-five and thirty-eight respectively, while Mike Ramsey was thirty-five. The youngsters were Vladimir Konstantinov, twenty-nine, and Nicklas Lidstrom, twenty-six. Bowman had neither addressed the age issue with trades nor given sufficient rest down the stretch to the veterans. Coffey, for one, had played almost every game in the last half of the season, then had problems with back spasms. Bowman had left defensive prospect Jamie Pushor (Detroit's second-round pick, 32nd overall, in 1991) down in Adirondack for all but five regular-season games, rather than use him to spell off the regulars, and he had been unable to cut an end-of-season deal that would have given his wearying defencemen extra help. He was said to have been after former Oiler Marty McSorley, but on March 14 McSorley was part of a massive deal between his Kings and the Rangers involving seven players and a draft pick. Four days later, Bowman sent defensive prospect Dan McGillis to Edmonton for Kirk Maltby, but dressed Maltby in only nine playoff games and used him little after the opening series against Winnipeg. Another prospect, Anders Eriksson, was called in to spell off Paul Coffey when his back was injured in the Colorado series.

The Avalanche advanced to defeat the Florida Panthers in four straight. Bowman, despite being castigated in the press for having chased regular-season records at the expense of playoff readiness, was not on the list of Detroit personnel requiring replacement after yet another disappointing post-season. He signed a new one-year coaching contract, with a further two years as director of player personnel. The team, however, required an overhaul. Bowman had made few changes from the lineup that had lost to the Devils in 1994/95. After being buried by the Avalanche, though, he had to rethink the lineup. There was no need for a major rebuild, but it was clear that the Red Wings as configured could not win it all.

Mike Vernon, who had become the number-two goaltender behind Osgood, was considered expendable, with twenty-four-year-old Kevin Hodson awaiting call-up in Adirondack. But Bowman did not deal him, and instead extended the tag team into a third season. In August, Dino Ciccarelli was sent to Tampa Bay for a conditional pick in the 1998 draft. At thirty-six, Ciccarelli had performed well in the playoffs, with nine goals in sixteen games, but he had been used sparingly by Bowman in the regular season. Ciccarelli's trade was more of a house-cleaning than a re-engineering move. Bowman needed speed and strength up forward to play with a team like Colorado, and a younger defence. He addressed both issues by putting Paul Coffey on the trading block.

Paul Coffey's talent defied the conventions of the game. No one else skated like him; swift and powerful, he moved up ice on blades sharpened flat, like a goaltender's. He had been an obvious talent as a Junior, at first with the Sault Ste. Marie Greyhounds, for whom he played just after Wayne Gretzky left them to turn pro, then with the Kitchener Rangers. In 1979/80, his last Junior season, which was split between the Greyhounds and the Rangers, he accumulated twenty-nine goals and seventy-three assists in seventy-five games. The Edmonton Oilers used their first pick to choose the nineteen-year-old sixth overall in the 1980 draft, and he had an NHL starting job that fall, joining a young team that was initially mostly offence and not much defence. Coffey became a second-team All Star in his second season, 1981/82, and broke the 100-point barrier in 1983/84, finishing a distant second to Gretzky in the scoring race, when the Oilers won their first Stanley Cup.

His career peaked in 1984/85 and 1985/86, when he was a first-team All Star and the Norris Trophy winner as the league's top defenceman. In the course of Edmonton winning its second consecutive Cup in 1984/85, Coffey contributed twelve goals and twenty-five assists in eighteen games; he tied a record for points production by a defenceman in one playoff game when he produced three goals and two assists against Winnipeg in the division finals. While Wayne Gretzky won the Conn Smythe, Oilers defensive coach Ted Green politely suggested it should have gone to Coffey. "I've never seen anyone play any better, including Himself," Green said, 'Himself' being his former Bruins teammate Bobby Orr.

Coffey's career in Edmonton soured after 1985/86, when the Oilers' quest for a third consecutive Cup ended in the dying moments of game seven of the division finals against Calgary. Oilers defenceman Steve Smith ended a tied game by accidentally banking the puck into his own net off Grant Fuhr's skate. At the beginning of the 1986/87 season, Glen Sather chose to single out Coffey for criticism. Sather had studied psychology in the 1960s, and he was exercising an old-fashioned right (which coaches of the 1950s and 1960s routinely employed) to publicly castigate a player in hopes of getting a performance-enhancing rise out of him. Coffey, however, could not turn his cheek away from the public slap. He played a more defensive game in 1986/87, and after the 1986/87 Cup win, he made it known that he wanted a raise or a trade. He was making $320,000 (Canadian) while Rod Langway of the Capitals, for example, was commanding $500,000 (U.S.). Edmonton owner Peter Pocklington came up with one package that included a chunk of land, but the gap between Coffey and "Peter Puck" could not be bridged. On November 24, 1987, a seven-player deal was swung with the Pittsburgh Penguins that set Coffey on a collision course with Scotty Bowman.

Coffey was back on the first All Star team in 1988/89, and made the second team in 1989/90. Under Badger Bob Johnson, Coffey won his fourth Stanley Cup. Then came Johnson's sudden death and Scotty Bowman's promotion to coach.

It was a strained relationship. Bowman was not a fan of Coffey's end-to-end style, and with a new Pittsburgh owner wanting to trim the payroll, Bowman decided to get rid of him. On February 19, 1992, Coffey was sent to Los Angeles to play with his former Oilers teammates Wayne Gretzky, Jari Kurri, Charlie Huddy, Pat Conacher and Marty McSorley. He lasted sixty games as a King; on January 29, 1993, Bryan Murray acquired him for the Red Wings in a six-player deal. That spring, the Kings reached the Cup finals. Detroit lost to Toronto in the opening round and Murray lost his coaching job. Two months later, Scotty Bowman was back haunting Paul Coffey as the newly-hired coach of the Wings. A year after that, Bowman had control of player personnel as well.

The two men co-existed for three seasons in Detroit, and in the lockout-shortened 1994/95 season, Coffey returned to the peak of his profession, winning the Norris and making the first All Star team. But after the 1995/96 campaign, in which Coffey accidentally scored on his own team in the opening game of the Colorado series, Scotty Bowman wanted nothing more to do with him.

As Jimmy Devellano puts it, Scotty Bowman is the last of a dying breed of coach, the Controller of Fate who once ruled the destiny of players through fear and a pocket full of train tickets that could send them down to the minors, burying them alive. It is regularly noted that Bowman has managed to succeed as a coach in three different eras of the game: the Original Six days, when he coached Juniors and the NHL teams ran the amateur development systems and owned the playing rights of teenagers; the expansion years of the 1970s, when players first gained strength relative to the teams through the players' association and the employment option of the WHA; and the modern free-agency era of the high-paid superstar, who could make known whom he wished to play for and for how much, and who could get a coach hired or fired.

Much of the reason for Bowman's staying power seems to rest in the fact that his own behaviour changed little in the face of these snowballing labour-management events. Bowman retained the power and demeanor of a Controller of Fate from the Original Six, refusing to behave as if the landscape had changed. He was able to get away with it because he had shown himself able to get the most out of the teams he was given to run, and because he had general managers like Sam Pollock and Jimmy Devellano, who were prepared to put out the fires he ignited. With Paul Coffey in Detroit, Bowman was ultimately triumphant, but it was far messier than Bowman or anyone else would have liked.

Before the start of the 1996/97 season, Bowman was trying to swing a deal with the Hartford Whalers. There was a strong Detroit connection to the Hartford operation, whose general manager was former Red Wings goaltender Jim Rutherford. After his playing career ended in 1982/83, Rutherford went to work for Detroit computer millionaire Peter Karmonos, who wanted an NHL franchise and identified Rutherford as the man who could lead the charge. While both searching for a franchise to purchase and waiting for the opportunity to bid on a new one, Karmanos's new Compuware Sports Corporation acquired the Windsor Spitfires of the Ontario Junior league, in April

1984, and it was given to Rutherford to run. The team won the Memorial Cup in 1988, and in 1989 Compuware relocated the team to Detroit. Rutherford was running the Junior Red Wings, who had no connection with Mike Ilitch's NHL Red Wings, in 1993/94, when Scotty Bowman got the Detroit coaching job. In the summer of 1994, Karmanos was able to purchase the Whalers, and he installed Rutherford as his general manager. In 1997/98, the Whalers would move to Morrisville, North Carolina, and become the Carolina Hurricanes.

Hartford had been a strong WHA franchise, but since joining the NHL in 1979, the team had mostly struggled. After a few promising seasons in the late 1980s under Larry Pleau, the Whalers floundered, and after 1991/92 they failed to make the playoffs. It was the NHL's Dead Zone, a poor-cousin franchise with an eroding fan base and an uncertain future. Players wanted out of Hartford. They dreaded being traded there or drafted by them.

Scotty Bowman had already sprung some great players from professional limbo in Hartford when he had acquired Ron Francis, Ulf Samuelsson and Grant Jennings in March 1991 for the Penguins. As the 1996/97 season approached, Bowman had his eye on Brendan Shanahan. Had he not been fired by Buffalo in the fall of 1986, Bowman might have had Shanahan long ago. By virtue of its last-place performance in 1986/87, the Sabres had the first pick in the 1987 draft. Bowman's successor, Gerry Meehan, used it to select Pierre Turgeon. The New Jersey Devils, picking second, took Shanahan.

Shanahan was smart and likeable, with a quick and irreverent sense of humour. More important than his locker-room bonhomie was his presence. A prototype for the modern Canadian hockey player, Shanahan was a big left-winger, standing six-foot three and weighing over 200 pounds, who could score, make plays, check and hit. He was exactly the kind of player Bowman could have used in the previous spring's playoffs against Colorado.

Shanahan had seen his own success deliver him to the cul de sac of Hartford. After four seasons in New Jersey, Shanahan had earned the right to test his worth through free agency. The St. Louis Blues came up with a two-year, $1.6-million deal, but under the league's punitive compensation rules they were forced to give up in return defenceman Scott Stevens (a free-agency signing the previous season, which had required them to surrender five first-round draft picks to Washington). After the 1994/95 season, Shanahan had been traded to Hartford for defenceman Chris Pronger, whom Hartford had chosen second over-all in the 1993 draft. The trade left Shanahan unhappy and wanting out of suburban Connecticut.

As Detroit's season-opener approached, a road game against New Jersey on Saturday, October 5, Bowman also had the problematic Keith Primeau to deal with. A letdown in the playoffs in the past season, Primeau had been a contract holdout, skipping training camp. At the eleventh hour, the Red Wings got his signature on a new contract. Bowman then dealt him and Coffey to Hartford for Shanahan. Although none of the same management was involved, the Primeau move bore an uncanny resemblance to the way Detroit had signed and then shipped Dale McCourt to Los Angeles as compensation for free agent Rogie Vachon in 1978.

What happened next is a matter of who you believe, and how much you believe Bowman would relish washing his hands, again, of Paul Coffey. One account has Bowman approaching Coffey at a practice in New Jersey prior to the season-opener and, by way of telling him he was no longer a Red Wing, brusquely informing him to "find his own way home."

This sounds just like the man who asked John McLennan how much bus fare was from Peterborough back to Ottawa as his way of telling the youngster he was no longer a Peterborough Pete. Bowman, how-ever, would say that he simply told Coffey he could make his own travel arrangements to get back to Detroit, since he was officially no longer with the Red Wings, or stick around and hop a lift with the team. But if Bowman was trying to blow off Coffey (and Primeau), he was a bit premature. Neither player wanted to go to Hartford, and Primeau's agent especially was intransigent about refusing to accept the deal, claiming that Primeau had signed the contract that permitted his trade under duress. The Hartford deal could not be closed.

Bowman was left with an entire omelette on his face. He was stuck with two players he very evidently no longer wanted. Back in Detroit after the New Jersey game, both Coffey and Bowman were asked how they were going to co-exist without the Shanahan deal.

"It'll be like it's always been," said Coffey. "We have a business relationship." He added, "There's really nothing for me to say. I'll be fine. I know this whole thing can still go down. I don't know if this thing is dead or not. I'm just happy to be here now."

"I just want to play hockey," Coffey explained. "I have enjoyed playing hockey since I was five years old and I want to continue playing hockey."

Bowman tried to cast the trade misfire as a positive turn. "It's a cliche, but some of the best trades are the ones that are not made," he suggested.

But this trade was going to be made, one way or another. And in the meantime, Bowman's handling of Coffey cast a pall over many team members.

"I look at that," Chris Osgood said to a *Detroit News* reporter as the team prepared for its home-opener on Wednesday, October 9, against Edmonton. "I know that one day I'll be in Coff's situation."

Mike Vernon, who had landed in Bowman's doghouse with disparaging remarks about trades during the summer, waited for the axe to fall on him next. "I am just a player. I am not the general manager. I am surprised I have not been traded," he said.

The Coffey mess made Sergei Fedorov, whose performance in the 1995/96 playoffs had also disappointed, prepare himself for the day when he too could be dealt away. "It's not a wish, believe me. It's more of a concern. If you look at the business side, it's not like it used to be. It's not just how you play on the ice, but how you talk to the media, the coach, what you do off the ice, everything. Sometimes it's personal between a coach and the player. In the last six years, I've learned that it can turn very ugly. When you play for a team, you work your heart out for yourself, your coach, the franchise. It's a piece of your heart. I've seen people who have been around become bitter and never open their mind or heart again. I don't want that."

Months later, with the 1996/97 playoffs beginning, Bowman told the press that Coffey had been destined to be moved, even if the deal didn't involve Shanahan. "You can't win playing like that."

The deal did come, on the day of Detroit's home-opener, though how many times this trade was vetoed by players unhappy with the deal and management unwilling to give up a draft pick cannot be counted. Bowman convinced Rutherford to accept Primeau with the fat new contract Detroit had signed him to, and threw in his first-round pick for 1997—along with Coffey, of course. In return, Bowman received Shanahan, as well as a veteran defenceman he had no use for, Brian Glynn. The gracelessness of the deal persisted to the end. Coffey found about the trade from Detroit's equipment manager. Glynn heard about it on the car radio.

Primeau stayed put in Hartford for the season, but Coffey made it clear that he didn't want to hang around. A ricochet deal resulted on December 15, sending Coffey to the Philadelphia Flyers.

The Coffey trade was the largest deal Bowman made in revamping the roster that had confounded fans and critics in the 1995/96 playoffs. While the Coffey move could have been handled with far more basic human decency, re-engineering talented lineups that can't win requires some daring and brute strength. Al Arbour would confess to having cried when he traded away Denis Potvin's older brother, Jean, in 1977/78, as he tried to shape a lineup that could win a Stanley Cup. Scotty Bowman wasn't the crying type. Ciccarelli, Primeau and Coffey were gone—with the trades of Ciccarelli and Primeau, the entire line of Ciccarelli-Primeau-Burr from the 1994/95 Stanley Cup defeat had vanished. Soon Bowman would let Bob Errey go. The left-winger had been bounced in and out of Bowman's life more than most mortals ever live to tell about. A career Penguin, the ten-season veteran was shipped to Buffalo by Bowman just before the trading deadline in 1992/93 so Bowman could acquire Mike Ramsey, who had been Bowman's first draft choice in 1979 when he took over the Sabres. Errey had then been collected by Bowman from San Jose for a late trade pick in February 1995. In February 1997, Errey was placed on waivers by Bowman and was retrieved by San Diego.

Errey did not have fun playing for Bowman in Detroit. "A man that doesn't respect people should not be given any respect," he said. Others who left also voiced their disdain. "He's the most disrespectful person I've ever met," said Shawn Burr, a left-winger traded to Tampa Bay after the 1994/95 Stanley Cup finals. Bowman had accused him of handing a lost stick back to New Jersey's Scott Niedermayer in game two of the finals, which allowed Niedermayer to score the tying goal in a game New Jersey went on to win. Burr was benched for the last two games, and Bowman later conceded that the return of Niedermayer's stick was accidental. "He's just a mean man with no social skills," Burr said. "You can't argue with his success as a hockey coach, but the way he treats people? That's not right. There's a difference between not getting close to a guy and treating him like scum. And Scotty, as far as I know, treats everybody like scum." On another occasion, Burr offered, "Trying to understand Scotty is like trying to explain abstract painting,"

Dino Ciccarelli's feelings were equally warm-hearted. "Obviously as a hockey coach, he is the best ever. But as a person? He's a jerk. I hate to even talk about the guy. I mean, I don't want to sound like a crybaby or that I'm whining. But ask anyone who has ever played for him and they'll tell you the same thing."

Success, however, tends to compromise some people's animosity toward Bowman. Bowman's greatest success as a coach, from the perspective of moulding the performance of an individual player, is Steve Yzerman. At twenty-one, he had become the youngest captain in the NHL with the Red Wings in 1986/87, but his stellar career resisted unfolding as planned. Despite great improvements in the club, the Red Wings kept stalling in the playoffs, and Yzerman met personal humiliation when cut from the Team Canada training camps for the 1987 and 1991 Canada Cup teams. A serious challenge to a long career surfaced in 1988 when a knee injury forced major surgery. He was once discussed in the same breath as Wayne Gretzky and Mario Lemieux, but he was consistently shut out of All Star voting. When Lemieux or Gretzky weren't making the first or second team, it was Mark Messier, Adam Oates, Pat Lafontaine or teammate Sergei Fedorov. Beginning in 1991, the captain was regularly the subject of trade rumours the Red Wings made no effort to deny. After the 1990/91 season, Yzerman was offered to the New York Islanders in a package that would land Lafontaine; that same summer, he was on the block as part of a possible deal to land Eric Lindros, who was refusing to report to the Quebec Nordiques. Yzerman publicly declared his unwillingness to report to either team—the Islanders were in poor financial shape and he empathized with Lindros's aversion to the Nordiques. It wasn't cultural, Yzerman emphasized—it was those terrible taxes you had to pay in Quebec and in Canada in general on everything from income to gasoline.

In October 1993, Yzerman was again being shopped around, as Bryan Murray sought a Cup-winning goaltender. There was no deal, and that season Yzerman suffered a herniated disk in his neck, which required off-season surgery. In the 1994/95 conference semifinals against San Jose, Yzerman's knee locked up, and he had to be helped off the ice. He returned for the finals against New Jersey but was ineffective against the Devils. In August 1995, it was whispered that the Red Wings were going to send him to New York to land a brawnier star at centre, Mark Messier. That deal didn't happen, but another one very nearly did, with the Ottawa Senators. Unhappy with his contract, centre Alexei Yashin was holding out for a new deal. Bowman was presented with the opportunity to increase his stable of Russian stars, and Ottawa general manager Randy Sexton flew to Colorado to meet with Bowman before Detroit's season-opener against the Avalanche on October 6. It was one more deal that Detroit would not make for its long-standing captain.

It was also the last time Yzerman would be the subject of a trade rumour. Eighteen days into the new season, Bowman picked up Igor Larionov from San Jose. He now had four strong talents at centre ice: Yzerman, Fedorov, Larionov and Draper. The depth the team now enjoyed spread the workload around and gave some relief to Yzerman, who, at five feet, ten inches, absorbed a lot of punishment. At the same time, Bowman was working to turn Yzerman into a solid two-way player. He tried him for a spell on left wing, and Yzerman drew penalty-killing duties with Fedorov. In November 1996, Yzerman received a four-year contract that ensured he could finish his playing career in Detroit, with a front-office role envisioned for him once he retired. Yzerman was a shining example of two-way dedication in the 1995/96 playoffs against Colorado, and he became a true team leader. After the 1996/97 Stanley Cup win, Yzerman would be one of the players arguing for Bowman's rehiring.

"Not everybody is going to be able to deal with what Scotty has to offer," says Craig Ramsay. "Steve Yzerman was a great player, but a great player on a bad team for a few years, and then a great player on a good team that couldn't win. And now, everybody has to love to watch Steve Yzerman play. He dives to block shots, he backchecks, he wins faceoffs. This guy does absolutely everything for his team, while still being a great offensive player.

"Scotty wants a complete player. In Buffalo, he wouldn't put up with a purely checking guy who had no offensive skills. He couldn't understand why guys couldn't make great plays. He wants a guy who can legitimately play in both ends of the rink. He doesn't want a one-dimensional player. He admires talent, and determination, guys that will fight through.

"If you're willing at some point to put up with Scotty and work at it, you'll find out that, hey, I can do a lot of great things, and win.

Instead of just trying to score goals, I can do more than that, and be a better player. I don't think anybody in the game today can look at Yzerman and not say, 'This guy is a top-notch, two-way, dedicated and determined hockey player.' He's learned how to be a winner."

Asked after he had won a Stanley Cup about Bowman's reputation, Brendan Shanahan, the man Bowman had rescued from Hartford, said, "People say they hate Scotty Bowman. So what."

16

✧ "PAPER" TEAMS—THE TEAMS that exist in statistics, and not in flesh and blood—are deceptive creatures. No two teams better demonstrate the gulf between one that wins statistical battles and one that wins championships than the Red Wings of 1995/96 and the Red Wings of 1996/97.

The 1995/96 team won a league-record sixty-two games and finished first overall; the 1996/97 team won thirty-eight games, finished second in its division, third in its conference and fifth overall. It was the worst finish by the Red Wings since 1990/91. The 1995/96 Red Wings finished third in scoring, with 326; the 1996/97 Red Wings finished sixth in scoring, with 253. The 1995/96 Red Wings had the best defensive effort, with 181 goals against; the 1996/97 Red Wings were second, with 197. The 1995/96 Red Wings had the best penalty-killing record and the third-best powerplay; the 1996/97 Red Wings had the fourth-best penalty-killing record and the seventh-best powerplay. In 1995/96, Chris Osgood and Mike Vernon tied for first and third respectively in goals against as they won the Jennings. In 1996/97, neither Detroit netminder cracked the league's top five. In 1995/96, four of the five leading players in plus-minus—Vladimir Konstantinov, Sergei Fedorov, Viacheslav Fetisov and Vyacheslav Kozlov—were Red Wings. In 1996/97, only one Red Wing, Konstantinov, made the top five.

And yet, the 1996/97 Red Wings were clearly a superior team to the 1995/96 edition. After his relentless pursuit of regular-season greatness in 1995/96, Scotty Bowman backed off in 1996/97. The team was keeping pace with the best teams in the league, and doing no more, while Bowman made further adjustments to the lineup. Having turned Steve Yzerman into one of the game's greatest two-way players, Bowman engaged in a perplexing experiment to turn Sergei Fedorov, one of the most celebrated centres, a Hart and Selke winner, into a defenceman. The move left Fedorov baffled and frustrated, and when the playoffs arrived he returned to regular duties. "It's like they tell you to write a story and tie your hands behind a chair," Fedorov told the Associated Press after the six-week defensive experiment at season's end. "How are you going to write it?"

Although the Fedorov experiment was a flop, Bowman's ability to shape a championship team would shortly prove outstanding. The skill, which seemed so alien to him in Buffalo, was half hidden beneath Craig Patrick's general managership and Bob Johnson's coaching in Pittsburgh. When Bowman was hired in Detroit, the Red Wings had what they thought was a championship team that needed the playoff breakthrough Bryan Murray was unable to provide. The Red Wings were wrong. Over the course of four seasons, Bowman had steadily overhauled the team, promoting some from within the organization, but finding others outside it, through trades and free agency. Only five players who had starting jobs in 1992/93 when Bowman arrived were still with the club as the 1996/97 playoffs approached: Fedorov, Kozlov, Konstantinov, Lidstrom and Yzerman. Four more—Lapointe, McCarty, Pushor and Osgood—were in the development system. No one drafted by the Red Wings after Bowman arrived made the team he had reshaped for 1996/97.

Bowman's trades and free-agency acquisitions turned out almost unerringly in Detroit's favour. His refusal to rid the club of Vernon, despite Vernon's unhappiness at playing second-fiddle to Osgood and his own expectation that he would be unloaded, proved fundamental to the team's eventual success. The deal that surrendered Coffey and Primeau for Brendan Shanahan was one of the most important in the retooling of the Wings, as Shanahan became the team's leading scorer while recording the second-highest plus-minus record.

As the midway point of the 1996/97 season approached, Bowman made an inspired signing. Joe Kocur had been Detroit's sixth pick (eighty-eighth overall) back in 1983, and the right-winger had led the league in penalty minutes, with 377 in 1985/86. A five-player deal sent him to New York in March 1991, where he shed the enforcer's role and played a tough checking game. After being traded to Vancouver in March 1996, Kocur played his last eight NHL games. He was staying in shape in a Detroit recreational "beer" league when Bowman made him a Red Wing on December 28, a week after his thirty-second birthday. Kocur delivered some of the strength and tenacity on the forward lines that Detroit had lacked against Colorado the previous spring. A month later Bowman was picking up veteran right-winger Tomas Sandstrom from Pittsburgh for spare centre Greg Johnson, a promising former first-pick by the Flyers in 1989 who had come to Detroit in 1993.

Another coaching milestone fell to Bowman as he won his one thousandth game on February 8, a 6–5 victory against the Penguins in Pittsburgh. From that point on, most every longevity record was his to set. Al Arbour, with 781 wins, was the only other person alive with a hope of reaching the mark, and he had retired after the 1993/94 season.

"I've been anxious [about] it for a long time," Bowman confessed on February 4. "I don't really want to talk about it because everything is day by day at my age and with my kind of job." That night, the record eluded him as the Red Wings tied St. Louis 1–1; a 7–4 loss to Vancouver postponed the celebrations another two nights.

"Scotty still must love the game," noted his former Canadiens star, Larry Robinson, as the 1,000-win milestone approached. Having assisted Jacques Lemaire in the defeat of Bowman's Red Wings in the

1994/95 finals, Robinson had become the coach of the Los Angeles Kings. "I never realized how tough a job this is when I played," he confessed. "Then, I'd finish a game, go home and relax. Now, it's a twenty-four hour life of preparation. For Scotty to do it this long, this well . . ." "Bowman was," he offered, "a pretty amazing man. What really impresses me is that the kids still listen to him. Our business, after all, is built on repetition, systems and all that crap. After three or four years, you've pretty well said everything you've got to say. And that's when players start to tune you out. It's time to get a new record, right? But Scotty continues to coach, and get results."

When his Red Wings defeated the Penguins, Bowman also held the record for coaching the most regular-season games, 1,706, one hundred more than Arbour. No one had coached in or won more regular-season and playoff games combined. The only record left was Toe Blake's eight career Stanley Cup wins. By leaving Montreal after the 1978/79 win, Bowman had denied himself the opportunity to match Blake's record of five consecutive wins. Al Arbour had the chance to match it in 1983/84, but lost the fifth series to the Oilers. That record, for the foreseeable future, was untouchable, and Blake's eight wins was also relatively secure. Bowman would have to win two more, and at sixty-three he was not expected to continue coaching past this season, whether the Red Wings won or not. His relationship with Jim Devellano had become increasingly difficult, as Bowman bruised player egos and pushed the organization into deviating from its traditional development path of trading neither draft picks nor young prospects for short-term gain.

Now in his fourth season as Detroit's coach, Bowman was enjoying his longest streak behind the bench with one team since the Canadiens, and Terry Crisp in Tampa Bay was the only working coach who had a longer tenure with his current team. He had been allowed to overhaul one of the best NHL lineups and experiment with the role of Fedorov, one of the game's great stars. There was no danger of a recurrence of the Buffalo experience—Bowman was not trading away stars to get draft picks. The value of top draft picks in team-building had diminished in his eyes, so much so that he was surrendering draft picks and young players to get older players—experienced players and role players. Bowman was back at the start of his career in St. Louis, valuing experience over raw potential. And after the dramatic but ultimately fruitless 1995/96 season, Bowman was using the 1996/97 season as a long-running lab experiment. The team, as a result, was not performing at the level it had in 1995/96, and Bowman would have to prove his wisdom with unequivocal success in the playoffs. The organization could not tolerate playoff elimination on top of the turmoil of the Coffey trade and the diminished regular-season performance. There was no enthusiasm for accepting 1996/97 as a rebuilding year. It was Bowman's last chance to deliver Stanley to Detroit. Anything less than a Stanley Cup win in the spring of 1997 would certainly lead to his replacement as coach, and not even the first Red Wings victory since 1954/55 would be enough to ensure his return.

Bowman's roster tinkering resurfaced on the season's trade deadline, March 18. Teams were making last-minute adjustments for the playoffs, and in some cases writing off the playoffs altogether, agreeing to hand over valued veterans in exchange for draft picks or younger prospects. The 1996/97 Toronto Maple Leafs were one such outfit cleaning house of high-paid veterans. With his team on its way to missing the playoffs, general manager Cliff Fletcher had traded captain Doug Gilmour and defenceman Dave Ellett to New Jersey in a five-player deal on February 25. On the trade deadline, Fletcher offloaded two more expensive veterans. Centre Kirk Muller went to Florida, and Fletcher's old St. Louis confrere, Scotty Bowman, helped himself to defenceman Larry Murphy in a "future considerations" deal that rid Fletcher of a large salary and a costly acquisition who had proved unpopular with the fans.

Murphy, who had starred for Bowman in Pittsburgh, had been traded to Toronto by the Penguins in July 1995. The deal cost Fletcher Toronto's second-round pick in the 1996 draft and defenceman Dmitri

Mironov. Murphy produced sixty-one points in his first Leaf season but had not been able to buoy the performance of a sinking club in 1996/97. With only thirty-nine points in sixty-nine games, Toronto fans criticized his every move and treated Murphy as an overpaid, over-the-hill burden; they booed him enthusiastically. Murphy was also being heckled by Washington fans when Bowman made him a Penguin. His second rescue by Bowman as the playoffs approached did not go unrewarded, as Murphy produced nine points in twenty playoff games and the team-leading plus-minus of +16.

With the addition of Murphy, Bowman had seven defencemen to choose from in the playoffs. Murphy, Niklas Lidstrom, Bob Rouse, Viacheslav Fetisov and Vladimir Konstantinov formed the defensive core, with Aaron Ward and Jamie Pushor available to spell them off. Ward, who had been acquired from Winnipeg in 1993, had seen his first significant spell of duty with Detroit in 1996/97; Pushor, Detroit's second choice in the 1991 draft, had come up from Adirondack to play regularly in 1996/97.

Bowman had also developed considerable depth in his forward ranks. Since 1995/96 he had been able to dress four lines, centred by Fedorov, Larionov, Yzerman and Draper, and the addition of Shanahan gave him more size and skill up front. Bowman's team-focused strategy called for a two-way effort which, combined with regular ice time for all lines, cut down the potential for points production by individual stars. Although his experiments with Fedorov provoked frustration, overall Bowman was able to get his forwards to buy into the all-for-one concept.

What remained to be decided was who would tend net in the playoffs. Chris Osgood had been Detroit's lead netminder in 1993/94 and 1995/96, and in 1996/97 again played more often than Vernon. But the starting pattern in the new year left observers guessing as to which had Bowman's favour. Beginning January 8 in Dallas, Osgood played four games in a row. Vernon got the next five games, and on February 2 (with Dallas again the opponent), Bowman began a nineteen-game stretch in which he alternated Vernon and Osgood every other game. The Red Wings were hot, losing only three games—two with Vernon, one with Osgood. The neck-and-neck race was interrupted by a knee injury to Vernon, and on March 16 Osgood played a second consecutive game for the first time since January 14. The new pattern, of Osgood alternating with third-stringer Kevin Hodson, was interrupted on March 23, when Hodson was pulled at 7:19 of the first period and replaced by Vernon in a losing effort against Chicago. It was the first time Bowman had pulled the goaltender all season, and Vernon started the next four games.

As speculation grew that Bowman's favour was shifting to Vernon, Bowman brushed it off, casting Vernon's extra playing time as rehabilitation for his knee. "I just want to make sure I get everybody ready. I may not have a decision if I don't get guys ready."

After beating Buffalo 2–1 in overtime with Vernon—the goaltender's second consecutive start—on March 28, Bowman suggested he wanted to settle the question of a starting goaltender for the playoffs before the Red Wings left Detroit on April 7 for a pair of road games, against Calgary and Edmonton. But the next day, March 29, he wasn't sure. "I probably wouldn't have it set in my mind until we finish the season, the last two home games," he said, and he also professed not to be sure if he would stick with one starting goaltender in the playoffs.

Bowman had never been successful in the playoffs without having one hot goaltender, and it was difficult to imagine him changing now. The pattern most every coach followed, Bowman included, was to start the goaltender who he thought could play every game, and not change him unless his play was in serious doubt. Outstanding goaltending is elemental to playoff success; it is why about one third of all Conn Smythe winners (including three on the losing team) have been netminders. Even with the greatly increased playoff season of the expansion years, successful teams generally found a starting netminder and stuck with him. Ken Dryden carried the Canadiens to five Cups; Billy Smith did the job for the Islanders in four Cups, and Grant Fuhr for the Oilers in five. In Bowman's first season coaching Detroit, 1993/94, Osgood started six of seven playoff games. In 1994/95, Bowman went with Vernon for all eighteen. In 1995/96, Osgood started fifteen of nineteen. There was no reason to believe the pattern of one main starter was about to change. While confidant Al Strachan was writing at the beginning of Vernon's recent streak on March 23 that Bowman considered Vernon his "ace in the hole" and would use him as his playoff starter, Bowman backed away from Strachan's confidence. "I said he *could* be our ace in the hole," he responded.

And after four consecutive starts for Vernon, Bowman switched back to Osgood for Detroit's seventy-seventh game of the season, a 2–2 tie at home against Toronto. Then came the two-game swing through Alberta. Bowman picked Osgood again as his starter, for a 3–2 win over Calgary. But for the Edmonton game he reverted to Vernon, and after a 3–3 tie he started Vernon again in the second-last game of the season, a home match against Ottawa. The Senators won 3–2.

The last game of the season, on April 13, was at home against their division rivals, the St. Louis Blues. Detroit, in second, had thirty-eight wins. St. Louis, in fourth, had thirty-five. If the Blues won, they would tie Phoenix on points but still finish fourth, with fewer wins. Thus, with Detroit secure in second and St. Louis a hair's-breadth ahead of Chicago in fourth, the result of the final game would not change the fact that the Red Wings and the Blues were set to meet each other in the opening playoff round. It seemed significant, then, that Bowman opted to start Osgood.

The Red Wings lost, 3–1. Three nights later, Detroit and St. Louis were playing again, in game one of the Western conference quarterfinal series "G," and Mike Vernon was in goal.

Had Osgood's loss in the last game of the season changed Bowman's mind? Or had he had Vernon in mind for more than two weeks, and was just keeping both goaltenders sharp? "The truth about Vernon is that as soon as we drew St. Louis in the first round, we felt it would be hard for Chris to go against Grant Fuhr in the opposite net," Bowman later explained. "It's tough for a young goalie to go against a Hall of Famer, and our conference is full of them. If it wasn't Fuhr, it might have been Curtis Joseph in Edmonton, or eventually, Patrick Roy." Bowman stuck with Vernon after an opening 2–0 loss and, most significantly, after pulling him in favour of Osgood in a 4–0 loss in game four that tied the series at two games apiece. Vernon started all twenty games of Detroit's Stanley Cup run. Bowman played him like an ace in the hole.

There was an important difference in the Red Wings' level of preparedness in 1996/97 over 1995/96. Detroit's must-win games had been few and far between in their runaway season. In 1996/97, however, they played more overtime games than any other team, twenty-seven in all, and lost only two. They also had a captain whose game had been transformed by Bowman, who had been with the Red Wings since 1983, whose desire and dedication in the 1995/96 playoff shortfall verged on poignant, and who wasn't going to stand for another post-season collapse.

In 1994/95, when the Red Wings fared so poorly against New Jersey in the finals, it was Bowman who turned his wrath on the team. Trailing three games to none, he made his players turn out en masse for a press conference to explain their failure in what was described as "humiliation by inquisition." In the 1996/97 St. Louis series, Yzerman instead took the leader's role after a 4–0 rout allowed the Blues to tie the series. The captain jump-started the roster with a team-meeting speech that precipitated a 5–2 win at Joe Louis Arena. After finishing off the Blues 3–1 in game six in St. Louis, the Red Wings returned home to sweep Anaheim in the conference semifinals.

The conference finals provided another showcase for the NHL's most heated rivalries. Genuine blood feuds were rare in the modern game. There were too many teams and they played each other too seldom to allow institutional hatred to build, the way it had between the Red

Wings and Canadiens of the 1950s. But Claude Lemieux's sucker-punch of Vyacheslav Kozlov and (more important) his vicious hit on Kris Draper in the 1995/96 conference finals had left the Red Wings with a powerful desire for vengeance in the new season. The teams were under the watchful eyes of officials, and the Avalanche won their first three regular-season meetings. The fourth and final meeting, on March 26 at Joe Louis Arena, was treated by the Red Wings as their chance to settle the score. En route to a 6–5 Red Wings win, the teams engaged in an old-fashioned brawl instigated by Darren McCarty's thrashing of Lemieux. Even the goaltenders paired off for the free-for-all, and Mike Vernon scored an unofficial decision over Patrick Roy.

As defending Cup champions, the Avalanche were favoured to move aside the Red Wings. Colorado had won three of four regular-season meetings and had finished first overall, with forty-nine wins. The teams split the opening games of the conference finals in Colorado, however, and a 2–1 Red Wings win in game three in Detroit was followed by a 6–0 blowout that left the Avalanche one game away from elimination. As the game wound down, discipline eroded. Colorado's Mike Keane raised an enormous welt on Igor Larionov's calf with a slash; Kris Draper delivered a charley horse to Peter Forsberg with a hit that outraged Marc Crawford, who claimed it was low and illegal. Claude Lemieux spoiled for a fight, seeking a Red Wing he was sure of thrashing. Crawford would admit that his team was looking to get its licks in. "It was a deliberate effort on our part to show we didn't like what happened in the game."

With his team losing the game and control of the series, Colorado coach Marc Crawford lost all composure. The carefully coiffed former journeyman player appeared to descend into a primeval rage with about two minutes left to play as his spittle-flecked mouth spewed insults in Bowman's direction. Crawford had crudely tossed off the "platehead" barb to the media during the 1995/96 playoffs, and in his maniacal attack on Bowman he offered this and more. Security was required to separate the occupants of the team benches.

With Crawford being restrained by his players, Bowman calmly delivered a devastating retort. "I knew your father before you did, and I don't think he'd be too proud of what you're doing right now."

Marc was one of nine children of Floyd Crawford, born and raised in Cornwall, Ontario; Floyd had played Junior hockey while Bowman was coaching the Peterborough Petes. "His father was an ultra-competitor," Bowman recalled. "He played a lot like Konstantinov. He just hated to lose, and he didn't give an inch."

Crawford's tantrum earned him a $10,000 fine from the NHL for dis-honourable conduct. The morning after, Crawford was humbled and contrite. "I embarrassed the league, and more important I embarrassed my team," he said. "And for that, I am sorry. There's no way you can justify anything like that. If you try to, it's wrong. I was wrong."

Bowman declined to score any psychological points from Crawford's shameful episode. He had drawn his own $10,000 fine from the league that season, for alleging that referee Terry Gregson was anti-Russian. Bowman respected the family (Marc's brother Lou had played in the Buffalo minor system when Bowman was general manager), and when asked if he still felt Crawford's father would not be proud of him, Bowman sought a graceful escape for his coaching rival. "Maybe he would be [proud]," Bowman suggested, "because he's a competitor . . . The Crawfords are tough people. Emotions go, and sometimes they just snap." Forty-five years had passed since a berserk Bowman had to be restrained from going after the referee in the Memorial Cup playoffs. That was nine years before Crawford was born. Bowman was not that teenager any more. Nor was he the dressing-room screamer or the bed-check detective. This was not so much a kinder, gentler Bowman as it was a steely, less theatrical Bowman— a Bowman who didn't appear to really care what people thought of him, but cared enough about Crawford to allow him to escape from his own ignominy.

Crawford responded by inflicting the worst beating the Red Wings had suffered all season, a reciprocating 6–0 loss during which Bowman replaced Vernon with Osgood. Colorado's win put the series at three games to two in favour of Detroit. But the conference finals melodrama ended prematurely in game six. With Vernon back in goal, the Red Wings won 3–1 at home to reach the finals.

The night before the Red Wings' game-six victory, the Philadelphia Flyers had defeated the Rangers 4–2 to win their conference series in five. After the exciting copy generated by Crawford and Bowman in the conference finals, journalists were eager to capitalize on the next clash of wills and personalities as the series reunited Bowman with Paul Coffey, who had been traded to Philadelphia by Hartford in December.

But neither party was interested in reducing the series to a one-on-one showdown between the crusty coach and the jilted superstar. "I'm not going to talk about it," Bowman stated, and he didn't. "I'm not going against Scotty," Coffey said. "It is Philadelphia against Detroit, plain and simple. . . . I want to win another Cup, that's all."

As it happened, Coffey was never a factor. After a fine playoff run, the injured Coffey was dressed for only two games; he finished the series—as did fellow stars John LeClair and Eric Lindros—with a plus-minus of –5 as the Flyers went down in four straight, outscored 16–6. The story of the series was not Bowman and Coffey, but Bowman and Terry Murray, the Flyers' coach. The master of line-matching had played a close-checking game that delivered absolute control. Murray's Flyers never found the escape hatch. The series epitomized Bowman's abilities, his experience, his seniority. The Flyers were portrayed as a team of the future, and Bowman denied them any success in the present. He had succeeded in one important category, where the Flyers failed utterly. Bowman had weighed his two starting goaltenders and settled on Vernon for the playoff run, and Vernon had turned in a performance that earned him his second Conn Smythe Trophy. Murray had never made up his mind between Garth Snow, acquired from Colorado in 1995/96, and the veteran Ron Hextall. Snow played twelve playoff games, Hextall eight. After using Snow in the first game of the finals, Murray switched to Hextall, and the flip-flopping played poorly against Bowman's commitment to Vernon as his starter, even after pulling him twice in favour of Osgood. Bowman gave Vernon his vote of confidence and removed goaltending from the team's concerns. The Flyers' goaltending problems were not entirely Murray's fault, even though general manager Bob Clarke sacked Murray after the series, essentially for the way he had bobbled the goaltending issue. It was Clarke's job to get the team championship netminding, which Bowman had, and he hadn't.

While Murray struggled to avoid a sweep, Bowman stood behind the bench like an imperious guardian of his own reputation. He produced Detroit's win over Philadelphia in 1996/97 even more convincingly than he had Montreal's defeat of New York in 1978/79.

He came to game four with a plan to make history, if fate should be kind that night. When Darren McCarty scored on a spectacular solo effort to give the Red Wings a 2–0 lead (a late Philadelphia goal made for a 2–1 win), the game and the series was in hand. As the Cup made its way onto the Joe Louis ice, Bowman followed—not shuffling in dress shoes like Toe Blake and every other victorious coach before him, but skating like a player. He hadn't had a playing career, and he had brought his skates to the game so he could find out what it felt like to skate with the trophy—the way, in effect, Blake had before turning to the bench. (His ambition produced a moment of crisis on the Detroit bench. When Philadelphia scored its late goal, Detroit's associate coaches turned to Bowman for tactical guidance and discovered he'd vanished to lace up his skates.) He intended to wait until all the Red Wings' players had taken their turn before making his own tour of the rink, but after Yzerman, Larionov and Fetisov had their turns, the team hustled him to the front of the queue and sent him on his victory parade.

"Sometimes," he said afterward with a smile, "you have to listen to your players."

17

✧ IN A LEAGUE IN WHICH new faces ricocheted through coaching and management positions, the Detroit Red Wings were a model of employment stability. When the Red Wings won the 1996/97 Stanley Cup, Jimmy Devellano, general manager and senior vice-president, was completing his fourteenth season in the top hockey operations job. His assistant general manager, Ken Holland, also marked his fourteenth season with the organization. Both, in short, had been around for as long as Mike and Marian Ilitch had owned the team. The team's NHL scout, Dan Belisle, had also come to the organization as an assistant coach in 1982/83, the season Ilitch made his purchase. Scotty Bowman, whom Devellano had lobbied for with Mike Ilitch in 1993, had enjoyed the longest tenure of any active NHL coach, with four seasons behind the Detroit bench under his belt. And his associate coaches could also boast of lengthy tenures. Dave Lewis had been with Detroit since 1986 (a member of the coaching staff since 1987/88), while Barry Smith had four seasons with the Detroit organization.

While personnel elsewhere were playing musical chairs at a thrash-metal pace, Detroit felt more like an old-school, blue-chip corporation than a 1990s professional sports franchise. Employees were recruited, groomed and kept waiting patiently for their chance at promotion.

The organization was inwardly focused, waiting for the rollover in senior positions that would inevitably come.

At the head of the queue for rollover opportunities was Ken Holland. He had proved his worth as a candidate for general manager after three seasons as Jimmy Devellano's assistant. A former goaltender, at the age of forty-two, he had spent all of his management days as a Red Wings employee. In an expanding league littered with job opportunities, Holland had chosen to stake his professional future in Detroit, brought along by Devellano, the man who had started him on his white-collar career.

Devellano was fifty-three—not yet retirement age, in the way Frank Selke, Sr., had been when he was moved aside for Sam Pollock in 1964. But in an industry accustomed to fast-track management careers, Jimmy D's protege, Holland, could not be expected to wait indefinitely for a promotion. Devellano was set to withdraw from the day-to-day hockey operations; he would maintain the senior vice-president's post he had acquired in 1990 and make way for Holland as the club's new general manager.

The scenario, however, had a problem: Scotty Bowman. After the Night of the Long Knives that had dispatched Bryan Murray as general manager in June 1994, Bowman had acquired the position of director of player personnel to go along with his coaching job. Bowman had usurped an important component of the traditional general manager's job: power over which Red Wings players the club drafted, traded and demoted. If Holland were to succeed Devellano in the current management scenario, he would be only half a general manager, bound by Bowman's demands on the player personnel front. And as Devellano's right-hand man, Holland well knew just how difficult the working relationship could be.

Once Bowman had secured the power necessary to rebuild the team according to his own template of a championship club, his personnel decisions had resulted, after three tumultuous seasons, in success. But feuds between Bowman and his players, coming on top of public debacles like the Coffey trade and his experimentation with Sergei Fedorov as a defenceman, made for an increasingly fractious relationship between Bowman and Devellano. The two were on especially thin ice in 1996/97; a month after the Cup was won, they would not even be on speaking terms.

In the 1996/97 Stanley Cup finals, Scotty Bowman deftly moved from one public feud to another. His lengthy spat with Paul Coffey fizzled as game one of the finals was played against the Philadelphia Flyers, with neither man apparently interested in keeping it alive. But scarcely had the Bowman-Coffey feud sunk from sight than the Bowman-Devellano set-to hove spectacularly into view.

Although the animosity would take almost a month to become public, its focal point was a conversation between the two men after game one of the finals, which the Red Wings won 4–2 in Philadelphia on May 31. The Flyers had gone too far too fast in 1996/97, and after only one game of the finals appeared certain to bow to Detroit. With the series being pronounced a foregone conclusion, Bowman and Devellano spoke on the telephone; based on their recollections, they participated in two entirely different conversations. The only thing certain is that Bowman was the one who placed the call.

The Devellano version: Scotty Bowman volunteered that he was ready to retire as coach of the Red Wings and serve out the last two years of his contract as a consultant working out of his Buffalo home, a kind of superscout at large. This was consistent with the organization's intention that Bowman would never be abruptly removed from the Red Wings' payroll, but that he would ease into retirement at the periphery of the organization. Bowman, according to Devellano, was volunteering to shuffle off to Buffalo, but he wanted Barry Smith hired as his replacement. "I said, 'Well, Scotty, what about Dave Lewis?' Scotty just said, 'Barry Smith.'" Devellano says Bowman then told Mike Ilitch the same thing: I retire from the bench, and Barry Smith gets my job. "It's really not up to Scotty to name his successor," Devellano points out.

"It's up to Mike Ilitch. When he was turned down on that request, he said, 'Well, I'm coming back.'"

The Bowman version: He telephoned Devellano to discuss the circumstances of Smith, who coveted a head coaching job of his own. Bowman wanted Devellano's permission for Smith to speak with the Phoenix Coyotes about their vacant head coaching post. Bowman said Devellano then broached the subject of Holland's promotion to general manager, saying that Bowman would be leaving the coaching and director of player personnel positions to assume a consulting role from his home in Buffalo. Holland, with the full powers of a general manager, would then name Bowman's successor as coach.

"I thought, 'Here's a fine kettle of fish,'" Bowman told *The Detroit News* on June 26, when the war of recollections surfaced. "I hadn't even made up my mind yet [about leaving]." Bowman's version flatly contradicted Devellano's own, and the team's general manager had to confront a press buzzing with speculation about a power struggle between him and Bowman as he returned from the NHL's board of governors' meeting. Although Devellano did not discuss Bowman's ambitions for Smith with the press (as he did with this writer), he made it clear that Bowman had told him in their telephone conversation that he was leaving. "He said he wasn't going to come back as coach. He said he was going to go to Buffalo under the final two years of his contract. You usually like to take people at their word." Devellano said that Bowman had also told some team members he was leaving after this season, and had informed Ilitch of his decision at the beginning of the playoffs. A source also told the newspaper that Bowman again informed Ilitch of his decision to step down at a breakfast following the team's victory parade in Detroit on June 12. Devellano was furious that he had to learn from media reports, not from Bowman himself, that Bowman was now thinking about staying on as head coach. "I think everybody is allowed to change their minds, but you should tell the person that you're dealing with about your change of heart." It was a classic Bowman employment derby, with Bowman drawing the media into his negotiating strategy.

Devellano's version in the press and his recollection for this writer have shone a light on a horse-race to succeed Bowman between Barry Smith and Dave Lewis, with Smith backed by Bowman, and Lewis, if not explicitly backed, then at least felt worthy of equal consideration by Devellano. There appeared to be no animosity within the coaching staff. They all worked well together, with Smith in charge of offence and special teams and Lewis minding the defence. But it should come as no surprise that the forty-six year-old Smith would be Bowman's first choice as his successor, if he was given the power to choose. While Lewis has publicly avowed that he considers Bowman a true friend, Bowman and Smith are particularly close; their professional relation- ship began during Bowman's tenure as general manager of the Buffalo Sabres. Smith was a Buffalo native who had earned his degree in phys- ical education at Ithaca College in upstate New York. While he'd played hockey at Ithaca, his future in the sport, as Bowman's had, lay in coach- ing. He'd gained his first coaching job at another upstate college, Elmira, in 1975, where he'd earned his master's degree in education. He found success as an NCAA Division III coach, then headed to Europe early in Scotty Bowman's spell in Buffalo. Coaching in Sweden and then in Norway from 1981 to 1986, Smith did some scouting work for Bowman, who was keen on European talent at the draft. In March 1986, Bowman hired Smith as his assistant coach, after taking the head coaching job back from Jim Schoenfeld. Thus, Smith was on hand for the bleakest period of Bowman's NHL career, missing the playoffs with him in the spring of 1986, and working as an assistant to Bowman and then Craig Ramsay in the short run of games in the fall of 1986 that led to Bowman's firing.

Smith survived Bowman's dismissal and stayed through 1989/90 under coach Ted Sator. When Sator gave way to Rick Dudley, Smith went overseas again, to coach in Italy in a one-season stint that included duties as coach of the country's national team. While Smith was away,

Bowman was hired as Pittsburgh's director of player development; they were reunited in 1990/91, when Smith was hired to serve as an assistant coach to Bob Johnson. After Johnson's death, Smith continued in his assistant's role, now working directly for Bowman. When Bowman was hired by the Red Wings in the summer of 1993, Smith followed him. He kept his hand in the international game, serving as assistant coach of Team Sweden at the 1996 World Cup, and just before Christmas 1996, Smith took a three-month leave of absence from the Red Wings to coach Malmo in Sweden's Elite League, returning in time to join the Red Wings for the playoff run that brought the Stanley Cup to Detroit.

Devellano's association with Lewis was even longer than Bowman's association with Smith. At the 1973 amateur draft, Devellano, as the New York Islanders' chief scout, had made Lewis his second pick, thirty-third overall (after taking Denis Potvin first overall) at the beginning of the third round. The Islanders, coming off their twelve-win opening season, were hungry for defence, and Devellano had delivered it to coach Al Arbour in spades with Potvin and Lewis. They were the opposing ends of the defensive spectrum. Potvin was the dazzling defensive scorer and play-maker; Lewis, standing six-feet, two inches and weighing over two hundred pounds, was the reliable blueliner. In ninety-one career NHL playoff games, Lewis scored once.

At twenty, Lewis had moved directly from Saskatoon in the Western Junior League to a starting position with the Islanders. He came heartbreakingly close to participating in the Islanders' run of four straight Stanley Cups. In March 1980, while Devellano was away serving as general manager of the Islanders' Central Hockey League farm club in Indianapolis, Islanders general manager Bill Torrey made a trade-deadline deal to secure from Los Angeles an experienced centre, Butch Goring. In return Torrey gave up Lewis and right-winger Billy Harris. Lewis was in Los Angeles for the next three seasons while the Islanders piled up their Cup streak, then spent three seasons in New Jersey. In July 1986, Devellano, preparing for his fifth season as general manager in Detroit, signed Lewis as a free agent. Lewis played one more full season, appearing in his one-thousandth regular-season game on April 1, 1987. He had 1,002 NHL games to his credit when he finished the 1986/87 season; after appearing in six more at the start of 1987/88, Lewis retired to join the Detroit coaching staff. As an assistant coach, he was emphatically Devellano's hiring, surviving the departures of Jacques Demers and Bryan Murray as head coach before Bowman arrived.

Smith's and Lewis's stature as associate—rather than assistant—coaches underlined their special role in Detroit. They played a major role in shaping the team Bowman coached, generally overseeing practices and developing game systems. Smith, for example, inspired by his experiences in the European game, garnered the lion's share of the credit for coming up with Detroit's "left wing lock" forechecking system, which had stymied the Flyers in the 1996/97 finals. Even if he wasn't a personal friend of Bowman, Barry Smith would likely stand as the more likely of the two associate coaches to succeed Bowman. While he has never played in the NHL like Lewis, he has broader experience and has coached teams of his own, the last assignment having come in Malmo just before the 1996/97 Stanley Cup win.

Bowman had never said publicly that he wouldn't be returning as coach, but neither did he explicitly say that he would be. The Cup was won at Joe Louis Arena on Saturday, June 7. After crossing the Detroit River to Windsor on Monday, June 9, to visit Jimmy Skinner, the last coach to win a Stanley Cup for Detroit in 1954/55, Bowman hedged on his future. "There is no suspense," Bowman told *The Detroit News*. "I haven't decided yet." That night, at a rally for season-ticket holders, Bowman dangled further uncertainty before the public. "In closing, I have this to say to everybody. I'll be a part of the Detroit organization. Let's go back and do it again." Bowman still had to have a formal meeting with Mike Ilitch, and he noted that it wouldn't happen until the week of June 16, which led into the NHL draft, scheduled for Saturday, June 21, in Pittsburgh. "I haven't even thought about [the

decision] yet," he professed to the *News*. "I'm just trying to enjoy this."
He also regretted having said he would make up his mind by the draft.
"I've put a timetable on myself now. Maybe I shouldn't have . . . but I
only think it's fair to the organization that they know soon."

The organization, according to Devellano, was under the impression that he wasn't coming back as coach. In Bowman's first meeting
with Ilitch, his bid to retire from coaching to make way for Barry
Smith apparently failed. At the draft, the buzz among Bowman associates was that he was going to hang on to the coaching job.

Between the victory parade on Thursday, June 12 (at which he was
alleged to have told Ilitch he wasn't coming back), and the draft on Saturday, June 21, the Red Wings organization was rocked by tragedy. On
the portentous night of Friday the thirteenth, a limousine carrying three
Russian members of the Red Wings organization—defencemen Vladimir
Konstantinov and Viacheslav Fetisov, and trainer Sergei Mnatsakanov—
left a Detroit country club after a team golf outing. At the wheel was
a limousine driver who was under the influence of alcohol and defying
a licence suspension. The vehicle suddenly careened across Woodward
Avenue and slammed into a tree. Fetisov suffered a bruised lung and a
serious knee laceration; Konstantinov and Mnatsakanov were felled
by severe head injuries. Fetisov would return to the ice that fall; the
comatose Konstantinov and Mnatsakanov embarked on a therapeutic
struggle to recover, to at least a modest degree, their faculties.

One year later, Bowman would avow that his decision to return as
coach was influenced by the limousine tragedy—the team needed continuity in the face of this catastrophe. It certainly echoed his (and
Barry Smith's) experience in Pittsburgh after the 1990/91 Stanley Cup
win, when coach Bob Johnson died suddenly and general manager
Craig Patrick moved to promote Bowman from within rather than
subject the team to further change. But in Detroit in the summer of
1997, general manager Jim Devellano was not trying to steady the
organization in the wake of the limousine crash by retaining Bowman
as head coach.

By the time the Bowman-Devellano feud broke open on June 26, Bowman's unresolved future and the apparent reversal concerning his own intentions was creating a logjam of personnel decisions. The roles of Lewis and Smith could not be addressed—nor could that of Mike Krushelnyski, who had filled in for Smith while he was in Malmo and stayed on the coaching staff through the playoffs. The general manager's job was Holland's for the asking, but he was reluctant to accept it without Bowman's role first being settled. The draft and the league board of governors' meeting had slipped by without a resolution. The organization, though, was operating as though Bowman were no longer director of player personnel. Devellano and Holland had decided on their own that free agent Tomas Sandstrom would not be re-signed. (Anaheim would acquire him on August 1.)

Devellano was baffled by a reporter's suggestion that Bowman, in looking to clarify his role for 1997/98, wanted more control over the team. "He has had very good authority," Devellano told *The Detroit News* on June 27. "He was able to acquire the players he wanted to have. No one ever interfered with his coaching the team. He knows it. I know it. Mr. Ilitch knows it." Devellano couldn't help but point out that when Bryan Murray was fired in June 1994, the general manager's job was open, but Bowman had declined to fill it, opting for the lesser, more specific role of director of player personnel. "He didn't want to involve himself in agents, contracts and summertime work. That's in effect how I got to do what I am doing. He's done a magnificent job, but that doesn't mean I haven't put out umpteen player fires over the last three years. I don't know that I want to be a firefighter much longer."

By June 27, Bowman was saying that he was "leaning towards" remaining as coach. Certainly he had supporters. Captain Steve Yzerman felt strongly that Bowman should continue, and fan support was also high. It would have seemed churlish of Ilitch and Devellano not to renew the coaching contract of the man who had ended the forty-two-year Stanley Cup drought in Hockeytown. And there was no questioning the fact that Bowman was a great coach. Personality conflicts aside,

Devellano was not going to do any better than Bowman in choosing a coach for the Red Wings for 1997/98.

But Bowman's continuing employment would have to be on Detroit's, not Bowman's terms. Giving Holland the full powers of a general manager was a priority. If Bowman was going to carry on behind the bench, he would have to surrender the director of player personnel role. Bowman would have to come back to the organization with less power, not more.

The planned announcement of Holland as new general manager did not come to pass on July 1 as planned. Holland and Bowman met the next day for several hours, trying to resolve their differences. Bowman was determined to hang onto the director of player personnel role, which included control of the coaching staff. No solution was found, and Bowman was rumoured to be preparing to leave the Red Wings altogether to jump to the Maple Leafs, where his former netminding star, Ken Dryden, was the new team president. Dryden was in the market for a general manager after the firing of Bowman's former assistant in St. Louis, Cliff Fletcher, and probably would dump coach Mike Murphy as well. Bowman brushed aside the rumour. "I'm not interested in going to Toronto," Bowman insisted.

Two weeks later, Ilitch, Holland and Bowman came to a basic agreement as Devellano withdrew from his day-to-day duties with the hockey operation to make way for Holland. Bowman would get a salary package of about $950,000, for which he would coach, and only coach. His director of player personnel powers were granted to Holland, who would report directly to Ilitch as Devellano was sent off on "special assignment" for the owner. On July 18, Bowman's signing was formally announced: he had agreed to a two-year contract. Lewis and Smith also signed two-year contracts as associate coaches. Mike Krushelnyski was announced to have signed a two-year deal, but there was no real room for him in the organization, and in December he was hired to coach the Fort Worth Fire, the worst-performing team in the Central Hockey League.

While there had been friction between Holland and Bowman in the past, Bowman claimed they would get along fine, saying he had never made a deal while director of player personnel without involving Holland and Devellano. Bowman as much as admitted that he had reversed himself on not returning as coach. "I was starting to think about what I would do if I didn't coach," he told *The Detroit News* on July 23. "I didn't like the alternative. I didn't think I was ready for retirement."

That summer, Bowman read basketball coach Pat Riley's *The Winner Within : A Life Plan for Team Players*. Anyone wishing to fathom Bowman's approach to a repeat championship season—"the year of more," as Riley put it—could do worse than to study what Bowman was absorbing during the off-season. When the original edition of Riley's book was published in 1993, *Kirkus Reviews* gave it this summary: "By his anecdotal account, achievement is more reliant on cooperation, diligence, positive thinking, preparation, resilience, respect for authority, and other bedrock virtues than on tricks of the trade. Not too surprisingly (in light of his vocation), the author puts a premium on teamwork, notably on its highest manifestation— unselfish willingness to subordinate individual goals to the good of a group.... Riley provides cautionary insights on withstanding pressure, the perils of complacency, the frustrations of playing not to lose, and the roles to be played by superstars and lesser lights.... He also endorses occasional, calculated outbursts of 'temporary insanity' as an effective means of jolting sports or other organizations in need of wake-up calls." Much of Riley's philosophy affirmed what Bowman had been up to in his drive to create a Stanley Cup winner in Detroit in 1996/97.

For Detroit to repeat in 1997/98, it seemed Holland had to do little more than keep intact the team that Scotty had rebuilt and let him run it. Unfortunately, an auto accident had removed a key component, as the absence of Konstantinov, runner-up for the Norris Trophy, left

Niklas Lidstrom without his outstanding defensive partner. It would be well into the 1997/98 season before the gap at the blueline would be addressed to Bowman's satisfaction.

One change Holland was determined to make was in goaltending. Though Mike Vernon had won the Conn Smythe Trophy, at thirty-four he was an aging and expensive property. Holland, the former goaltender, wanted to give Chris Osgood, not yet twenty-five, the starting job, with twenty-five-year-old Kevin Hodson serving as his backup. The move would save the Red Wings some money, as Vernon, traded to San Jose in mid-August for a third-round pick in the 1998 draft and a second-round pick in 1999, would make $2.75 million that season, compared with Osgood's $1.6 million. But having shaved about $1 million off the starting goaltender's salary, Holland faced what would prove to be a horrendously expensive re-signing in Sergei Fedorov.

The summer of 1997 was a bonanza for free-agent players, both restricted and unrestricted. Owners loosened the purse strings, and grinders and stars alike cashed in. Mark Messier made his three-year, $20 million move from the New York Rangers to the Vancouver Canucks, forcing the Rangers to go shopping for another star center. New York almost signed away from Colorado Joe Sakic, as the Avalanche were forced to match New York's three-year, $21-million package to keep him. Paul Kariya was a holdout in Anaheim, as was Mike Modano in Dallas. Modano didn't want to leave Dallas, but also didn't want to settle for a longterm package when the free agency market was proving so heated. He accepted a $3.5 million one-year extension on his contract, gambling he could do better before the next season. In Kariya's case, Anaheim's owners, the Disney Corporation, wanted to lock him up for the next seven years, but Kariya wanted a shorter term, and declined to report. Having been paid about $4.2 million in 1996/97, Fedorov was turning his nose up at a multi-year package from Detroit that would be worth about $4.5 million for 1997/98. (Some reports suggest Detroit went as high as $5.5 million a season.) Like Sakic and Kariya, Fedorov was a restricted free agent, meaning Detroit had the right to match whatever offer another team put on the table. And if they declined to match it, they were entitled to hefty compensation in the form of multiple first round draft picks. The Red Wings made it clear they would match whatever was dangled before Fedorov by rival clubs, and the former Hart winner was left without any offers from the rest of the league.

And so the season began with Fedorov and Kariya as high-priced holdouts. Kariya came to terms with Anaheim in December with a two-year-deal that was worth $5.5 million in year one and $8.5 million in year two. But because Kariya had sat out almost half the 1997/98 season, the first-year payout was pro-rated to $3.5 million, with Anaheim agreeing to donate the $2 million balance to charity. That month, Eric Lindros signed a two-year, $18-million deal with Philadelphia. As the break for the Olympic tournament in February approached, it seemed likely that Fedorov wouldn't play at all in 1997/98. The reasons Fedorov wouldn't come to terms with Detroit were seemingly endless. He was supposed to be angry with Bowman for subjecting him to his defensive experiment. The four-line, two way system cut down on his ice time and impinged on his ability to be an offensive star with big numbers. He had to play second fiddle to Steve Yzerman. And there was supposedly friction between him and fellow Russians on the team over his failure to travel with them back to the motherland with the Stanley Cup in the summer. Meanwhile, the fat contracts continued to be inked. Just before the break, Mats Sundin signed a four-year package with Toronto worth $22.8 million.

Back in the summer of 1997, Jim Rutherford had been one of the general managers caught up in bidding for free agent Mike Keane, a veteran defensive forward who had played the last two seasons with Colorado for about $750,000 a season. Rutherford's Hartford Whalers were about to begin their first season as the Carolina Hurricanes, but they would have to do so without Keane, who ended up signing for $2.5 million with the Rangers on July 30. "There are other ways of bettering your team than just going out and spending foolishly," Rutherford sniffed. Less than six months later, Rutherford was offering to spend money not merely foolishly, in some observers' eyes, but insanely.

Fedorov was back on skates with the Russian team at the Olympics when Rutherford made Carolina's astounding bid for his services. The offer sheet presented a six-year, $38-million deal with a most unusual structure. Fedorov would get a $14-million signing bonus, a $2-million salary for the remainder of 1997/98, and a $12-million bonus if he got the Hurricanes to the conference championships. If they didn't get there, Fedorov would still get the money during the remainder of his contract. But if the Hurricanes did pull off the feat, Fedorov would collect $28 million for a few months' work. Not surprisingly, Fedorov signed the offer sheet. Detroit had seven days in which to match the offer. If it didn't, Fedorov was a Hurricane, and Detroit would hold Carolina's next five first-round picks.

With the Hurricanes seven points out of the last playoff berth, Fedorov's chances of collecting a $12-million bonus from Carolina were remote. But if Detroit, the defending Cup champions, ventured to match the deal, it was entirely possible Fedorov would have the greatest payday in NHL history, eclipsing the $5 million being earned that season by his captain, Steve Yzerman.

Detroit's first reaction to the offer sheet was to challenge its legality, alleging that the playoff bonus violated the NHL's collective bargaining agreement with the players' association. On Monday, February 23, the league agreed and ruled against the offer sheet. Carolina, however, objected, and on February 25 the offer was put before an arbitrator, John Sands. When Sands ruled that the offer was in fact kosher, Red Wings owner Mike Ilitch was faced with a quick decision—Fedorov, or five first-round draft picks?

Ilitch consulted with Bowman, who told him: skip the draft picks and give me Fedorov. Bowman wasn't planning to hang around Detroit while five years' worth of draft picks were called; he wanted to win in the here and now. He had also come to devalue draft picks in general, regarding the process as a crapshoot. Bowman had created a veteran team through trades, free agency and promotions from within the organization. Though Devellano and Holland had used the draft to lay the team's foundations in the 1980s, it had now become a low priority. (In 1997, Detroit didn't even pick until forty-ninth, late in the second round, taking Russian centre Yuri Butsayev; at seventy-sixth, in the third round, the Red Wings went back to eastern Europe to select Czech centre Peter Sykora.)

Ilitch heeded Bowman's advice, and Holland re-signed Fedorov on February 27. Bowman tore strips off Hurricanes owner Peter Karmanos and general manager Jim Rutherford as the Red Wings matched the Hurricanes' offer sheet. "They haven't improved their team for three years," he told ABC Radio. "There's not a lot of damage done them. It doesn't cost them anything to make the offer, just guys like me say[ing] that they don't know how to run the team." It was a deliciously wicked shot, as Bowman had pried loose Brendan Shanahan from their club eighteen months earlier in a trade that helped Detroit win the Stanley Cup, while Karmanos and Rutherford missed the playoffs.

The Fedorov deal seemed outlandishly rich, but was widely misunderstood, particularly because of the bonus structure. Should Fedorov collect the $12 million bonus if Detroit won the conference championship (which he did), it meant that he would be making money now that he otherwise would be collecting later in the contract's life. Aggressively front-loading a contract was not unique to the league. When Colorado matched the Rangers' offer and re-signed Sakic, the previous summer, his three-year, $21 million deal actually paid him $17 million in the first season—a $15 million signing bonus and a $2 million salary. Nor was the overall package out of sync with salaries elsewhere in the league. Amortized over six years, the Fedorov contract was worth a little more than $6 million per season, and by the time he signed it, the short-term salary market for the top handful of players was in the $8 million range. And on April 13, Fedorov's deal was topped in total value by the rich package Mike Modano at last agreed to, as Dallas signed him for $43.5 million over six years.

With the season winding down, Holland addressed the hole left on defence by the loss of Konstantinov by looking without rather than within. On March 24, Holland brushed against the trade deadline with two deals. Jamie Pushor, a defenceman who had been Holland's second choice in the 1991 draft, had played his first full NHL season in 1996/97, but had appeared in only five playoff games. Packaging him with Detroit's fourth-round pick in the 1998 draft, Holland received thirty-two-year-old Dmitri Mironov from Anaheim. And from Toronto another veteran defenceman was secured that day as thirty-six-year-old Jamie Macoun was swapped for a fourth-round pick in the 1998 draft, which Detroit had received from Tampa Bay in return for Dino Ciccarelli in August 1996.

Detroit was showing a knack for gathering players abandoned by the Leafs' defence corps. They now had four: Bob Rouse, Larry Murphy (who coincidentally had been traded to Toronto by Pittsburgh for Mironov in July 1995), and Mironov and Macoun. Mironov had scoring ability—he was the sixth-best points-producing defencemen in the 1996/97 regular season—while Macoun was an old-fashioned plodder who had been around the league since 1982/83 and had participated in Calgary's 1988/89 Stanley Cup win.

With Fedorov back, with Osgood the main netminder, with new faces on defence, Detroit finished the 1997/98 season strongly, third overall—better than it had in 1996/97. Even without Fedorov for most of the season, Detroit boasted the second-best offensive team, while still ranking a respectable seventh in goals-against. Eleven different players scored at least ten goals, and the breadth of the team's offence included defencemen Niklas Lidstrom, the top-scoring blueliner in the league, and Larry Murphy, who had finished fifth in scoring among defencemen.

The trend of the past few seasons continued, with the bulk of the league's best teams crowded into the West division's Central conference, making Detroit's path to a repeat championship particularly challenging. Dallas had finished first overall in the regular season, under general manager Bob Gainey, and after Detroit in third came St. Louis in fourth, playing under another former Bowman player, new general manager Larry Pleau.

Over in the West division's Pacific conference was Colorado, which had finished seventh. Detroit likely would have to move aside St. Louis and Dallas before again meeting Colorado in the conference finals... provided the Red Wings could make it past the preliminary quarterfinal series against Phoenix. While the Coyotes ranked only fourteenth in overall league standings, this club of veterans had gone on a tear at the end of the season, winning seven of its last ten games. Of its final five contests, the Coyotes had won four, including victories over division rivals Dallas, Detroit and St. Louis.

Detroit was neither an overwhelming favourite to repeat nor easy to dismiss. What remained to be seen was whether the Red Wings could get the job done again without Konstantinov on defence and Vernon in goal. The replacement of Vernon by Osgood, advocated by Holland and approved by Bowman, became the focal point of much naysaying and fan anxiety. Just one year earlier, Bowman had been unwilling to start Osgood against Grant Fuhr in the opening round of the playoffs. In the one-on-one line matching of goaltenders, Bowman had decided a five-time Stanley Cup winner like Fuhr had to be countered with Vernon, who had the confidence of his own 1988/89 Stanley Cup win (and Conn Smythe performance) to draw on. In the ensuing year, Osgood had started sixty-four games and compiled a respectable 2.21 goals-against average, with a save percentage of .913. But Osgood had posted strong seasons before and still left management wanting when it came to a playoff starter. Having watched most of the 1996/97 playoffs from the bench, it was now up to the twenty-five-year-old "Ozzie" to prove that he had absorbed enough winning experience, indirectly at least, to carry the club to another championship.

In the final game of the season, against Colorado on April 18, the teams' rivalry had boiled over into another season-ending brawl, and Osgood had made a move to become that year's version of Vernon by getting into a fistfight with Patrick Roy. Like Vernon in 1997, Osgood was judged to have gotten the better of the scuffle, conducted right in front of Bowman on the Red Wings' bench. The warm-up for another heated playoff meeting between the Red Wings and the Avalanche, however, was all for naught, as Colorado was upset by Edmonton in their quarterfinal series. It was left to Osgood and the rest of Bowman's Wings to chart a slightly different path to the Cup finals.

The playoff drive opened shakily for the Red Wings and Osgood in the Western conference quarterfinals against Phoenix, which was coached by former Bowman bench man Jim Schoenfeld. Detroit took the first game with a 6–3 win, but then faltered with a 7–4 loss in which two short-handed goals by Jeremy Roenick were surrendered. Moving to Phoenix for game three, Sergei Fedorov and Brendan Shanahan scored in the opening sixty-one seconds to give Detroit a 2–0 lead that it carried into the third period. But as the power play for Phoenix came to life, the Coyotes scored three goals on six shots to take the series lead. Only once in thirty-five regular-season games had the Red Wings failed to win a game after carrying a two-goal lead into the third period.

The Red Wings, once haunted by reversals of playoff fortune, had learned to turn bitter experience in their favour. They could deal with setbacks as part of the process of winning and not allow them to be portents of failure. It didn't hurt to have a coach who had been turning losing playoff causes into winning ones since the late 1950s. Just as the Avalanche's 3–1 series lead against Edmonton collapsed into a 4–3 elimination, Detroit rebounded to win three straight and advance to the conference semifinals against St. Louis. They did so partly because Brendan Shanahan overcame the pain of a herniated disk in his back, which had kept him out of the first two games, to contribute three goals and three assists in four games. At the same time, Fedorov produced six goals and Yzerman contributed seven points. Lidstrom demonstrated what Detroit's defence could contribute to offence over the playoffs by leading all league defencemen in the opening round, with eight points.

The road to a repeat victory should have become harder after the Phoenix series, but in fact it became easier. Neither St. Louis, in the conference semifinals, nor Dallas, in the conference finals (judged to be the true Cup series), gave Bowman the battle widely forecast. St. Louis was a strong club that had won three and tied one in six meetings with Detroit during the season, and had a history of tough playoff series against the Red Wings—including the 1995/96 marathon that was ended by Steve Yzerman with a game-seven overtime goal. The Blues were the only team in the conference to have swept their opening playoff series, moving aside Los Angeles in four, and Grant Fuhr was outstanding, with a 2.00 goals-against average and a save percentage of .929. The goaltending match-up Bowman had avoided between Fuhr and Osgood the previous season was now before him, and Osgood had not produced impressive numbers in the Phoenix series: a 3.02 goals-against average and a save percentage of .885.

After losing the opening game 4–2 at home, Detroit ran up three straight wins, conceded game five at home 3–1, then polished off the Blues with a 6–1 win in St. Louis, in which Fuhr failed to provide the giant-killing goaltending expected of him. The St. Louis series was a blueprint for the conference finals that followed against Dallas. In both series, Detroit's opponents lacked the stonewalling goaltending required (in the Stars' case, from Ed Belfour), and Bowman's checking game shut down the opposing top guns. In the Phoenix series, Jeremy Roenick had been allowed to score four times in the first two games. Bowman was not going to let such a performance happen again. Neither Brett Hull of the Blues nor Mike Modano of the Stars was able break loose against Detroit.

The Red Wings entered the Cup finals as the overwhelming favourites. A quarterfinals upset of the league's second-best team, the New Jersey

Devils, had thrown the Eastern conference playoffs into a battle of middling clubs. In the conference finals, two opportunistic teams— eighth-ranked Washington and tenth-ranked Buffalo—converged in a goaltending war. Buffalo had Dominik Hasek, who was about to win his second consecutive Hart Trophy (unprecedented for a goaltender), and had led the Czech Republic to an Olympic gold medal in February. Washington had Olaf Kolzig, who had turned into a classic hot playoff goaltender. Washington survived the closely played series, winning game six in overtime. As the Capitals prepared to play the defending champions in their first final-series appearance, it seemed the only advantage they might have was in the goal crease. Kolzig had carried the Capitals with an extraordinary save percentage of .946, while the Red Wings were still battling the perception that Osgood was not the equal of Vernon and might in fact represent their ultimate downfall.

Too much was made of Osgood's youth—he was no rookie. At twenty-five, he was older than many previous Cup-winning netminders, among them Patrick Roy (twenty in 1985/86), Grant Fuhr (twenty-one in 1983/84), Rogie Vachon (twenty-two in 1967/68), Terry Sawchuk (twenty-two in 1951/52), Ken Dryden (twenty-three in 1970/71) and Bill Ranford (twenty-three in 1989/90). But on a team in which raw youth was in short supply, Osgood was easy to cast as a kid.

Technically, Osgood had the stuff. A strong positional goaltender, he played his angles carefully and showed quick reflexes. He was also one of the better puck-handlers in the trade, playing it behind the net confidently and firing precise clearing passes. In this regard, he contrasted considerably with Colorado's Roy, a star netminder who nonetheless turned many forays from the crease into grand adventures. In the course of the 1997/98 playoffs, however, Osgood had demonstrated an unfortunate knack for punctuating first-class performances with screwball goals, the worst of which came in overtime in game five against Dallas. Facing elimination, Dallas's Guy Carbonneau had come up with the tying goal with 1:25 to play on a sprawling shot from the left faceoff circle. Osgood appeared to drop to his knees early, leaving the upper dimensions of the net unguarded; the shot was deflected over his shoulder. Then, only forty-six seconds into overtime, Dallas's Jamie Langenbrunner took a stride across centre ice, fired a dump shot into the Detroit end and turned to the bench for a line change. The puck bounced once in front of Osgood, who kicked out his right leg and turned the paddle of his stick outward. The puck, which was on its way to missing the net entirely, deflected off the stick and behind Osgood to force game six.

Already, in the Phoenix series, Osgood had surrendered a goal to Roenick that was shot from outside the blueline, and Al MacInnis of the Blues had scored from centre ice in the conference semifinals. A solitary Bowman, hands thrust in his pockets, could be seen striding briskly toward the dressing room moments after Langenbrunner scored his first goal in fifteen playoff games.

And yet Bowman had no goaltending changes in store. Belfour hadn't been sharp at the other end of the rink, and Bowman regretted that his team hadn't fired more shots at him after he gave up a weak goal to Igor Larionov that put Detroit in the lead 2–1. "We lose as a team," Bowman explained after the game. Osgood was not the goat. They still led the series, 3–2, and as Yzerman ventured, now they could win it at home. And they did, on an outstanding performance from Osgood that produced a 2–0 shut-out.

The game-five overtime goal was the last flutter from Osgood in the conference playoffs. The Red Wings could well have quoted Harry Sinden, who, as coach of the Bruins when they defeated Bowman's Blues in the 1969/70 finals, observed of his unorthodox netminder, Gerry Cheevers: "He'll let in the odd softie, but he gets the big ones. You'd prefer that to having a guy who gets all the softies and misses the big ones."

On the eve of the final series, Bowman offered as strong an endorsement of Osgood as his goaltender could ask for. "His record speaks for itself," Bowman told the press. "His winning percentage is in a class with a guy like Dryden. I think he is right beside Dryden all-time." There was more than a little hyperbole in Bowman's praise. Osgood had yet to win any championship, while Dryden had backstopped five Stanley Cups in Detroit, won the Vezina Trophy five times, plus the Conn Smythe and the Calder, was voted to the first All Star team five times and the second team once in just eight seasons, and had been in the crease when Team Canada rallied to beat the Soviets in game eight of the 1972 Summit Series. But Bowman had overwhelmingly placed his faith in Osgood to see the club through to another championship. And in the finals, Osgood got all the big ones, and the softies, too.

The finals had none of the melodrama of the earlier series, when Detroit had locked horns with a bitter rival in St. Louis and confronted the best team in the league that season in Dallas. Detroit and Washington had no playoff history, and no skeletons in the closet of their regular seasons to make for a blood feud. They had played each other only twice in 1997/98, and Detroit had long dominated play between the two clubs. The Capitals hadn't beaten Detroit since January 30, 1994; the Red Wings had won nine and tied one since then. Washington coach Ron Wilson, a former journeyman player, had no extensive history with Bowman that might spice the confrontation, even though, as coach of Anaheim in 1996/97, he had been steamrollered by Bowman's Red Wings in four straight in the conference semifinals and consequently lost his job. But there were other links to Bowman's past in the final series that were easily overlooked. Three of the Capitals—Phil Housley, Joe Reekie and Calle Johansson—had been drafted by Bowman while he was general manager in Buffalo. As well, Scotty's nephew David, son of his brother Jack, was on Washington's scouting staff.

Still, these connections provided a thin grid on which to build dramatic tension, and Washington was unable to compensate by providing sporting excitement. A starstruck Capitals roster never put together a complete game and compounded its problems with dumb penalties. The Detroit power play, ineffective earlier in the playoffs, began to do damage. Dangerous only in fits and starts, Washington came awake too late in game one to avoid a 2–1 loss, then blew a 4–2 lead to lose 5–4 in overtime in game two, the most entertaining game of the series. Wins of 2–1 and 4–1 in Washington gave Detroit its second consecutive Cup sweep; it was also the fourth Cup series in a row to end so punctually.

As the Red Wings' playoff run unfolded, it was clear that, should another championship come, captain Steve Yzerman would be the clear choice for the Conn Smythe Trophy. Bowman's "total player" project was leading the team to victory with an effort that covered every corner of the rink. Only a wild-card performance, such as a brilliant stand by Kolzig, could deny Yzerman his first individual trophy in the league. Kolzig did not turn in the kind of losing effort that had won the Conn Smythe for Roger Crozier in 1965/66, Glenn Hall in 1967/68 or Ron Hextall in 1986/87. And Yzerman did it all, leading the team with twenty-four points in twenty-two games while killing penalties and blocking shots.

As the Red Wings rolled toward victory, Bowman's impending tie of Toe Blake's Stanley Cup coaching record of eight victories was a narrative hook that begged to be set. But the 1997/98 Stanley Cup was not primarily about Bowman. Vladimir Konstantinov, wheelchair-bound and showing flashes of comprehension, was at the core of the team's spirited play. With Konstantinov installed prominently on view by the Red Wings in game four at Washington's new MCI Center in Landover, Maryland, sporting a Red Wings jersey and occasionally grinning and waving to his teammates, it was difficult to imagine how the Capitals could bring themselves to spoil the party the Red Wings had planned. Every Red Wing had worn a patch on his jersey that season commemorating Konstantinov's therapeutic struggle, with the word "believe" spelled in Russian. The season had been dedicated to Konstantinov, not to getting Bowman into the record book next to

Blake. The Capitals played a few minutes of Cup-paced hockey at the beginning of game four, surrendered a power-play goal and never threatened again. When the game was over and the series won, Konstantinov was the focus of the emotional celebrations. Bowman was not going to be lacing on skates again and taking centre stage. He tugged on a championship T-shirt over his game suit, donned a newly minted Red Wings baseball cap and stepped to the side—as moved as anyone as Konstantinov was wheeled onto the ice to become the first Red Wing to hold the Cup.

Though the Red Wings' victory had placed Bowman on the same line of the record book as his mentor, Toe Blake, Bowman persisted in his long-standing humility on the subject of his mentor. "He was a real good influence on me, and to be thought of in the same breath is a big honour for me, obviously," Bowman commented. "I don't put numbers on the Cups. I just know he did it with a lot of grace and I hope I can do the same thing. It's not been easy. I was very pleased that I could at least come even with him and let it go at that."

As Bowman had already observed, Blake still stood alone, his eight wins having come in thirteen seasons, and all with the same team. Bowman had tacked back and forth through the league, in and out of favour, compiling his wins with four different teams over twenty-two seasons. It was a remarkable accomplishment, but an entirely different one from Blake's. All the same, Bowman could claim his own special place, even in Blake's shadow. He was the king of sweeps. In five of his Cup wins, Bowman had won in four games (he had also lost three Cups, in St. Louis, in four). Blake, by contrast, had produced three sweeps in eight victories, two of them coming against Bowman in St. Louis. In the course of winning his eight Cups, Bowman had lost five final-series games. Blake had lost ten.

But as Bowman himself would assert, these were just numbers. He came closer to Blake's essential success not in any tally of victories but in reasserting the team-focused nature of a championship club with dynastic aspirations—a principle embodied in Yzerman's individual effort. And in the Blakean mould, Bowman, as coach, was the core of the team, the figurehead as well as the final authority. Bowman had not been able to achieve this august status in the course of winning five Stanley Cups in Montreal. Bob Johnson in Pittsburgh had come close—as had Al Arbour in Long Island and Glenn Sather in Edmonton—but when Bowman took over the Penguins from Badger Bob, he could not supplant the status Johnson enjoyed with the team. In Detroit, Bowman initially was as much a source of controversy as an inspiration, but now that he had led the team to a second consecutive Cup, he was rising to match Blake's stature. He had sold the players on the commitment required to win, on the sacrifices to be made for the greater good (no individual award, apart from the Conn Smythe Trophy, had been won by a Red Wing in the past two championship seasons), and he had done it in a peerless fashion. Other coaches in 1997/98 were having fine seasons—among them rookie strategist Lindy Ruff in Buffalo, who took the Sabres to the conference championship, and Washington's Ron Wilson—but no one else was close to accumulating Bowman's career successes and garnering such widely held respect from within his own profession.

Bowman's stature was as much deserved recognition of his accomplishments as it was a sad testament to the state of the professional coaching ranks. Owners and managers had downgraded the job, often with the approval of the players, to a glorified consultant's role. The coach was deposited in the midst of the team, ordered to bring about some quick results and coldly cast aside when a scapegoat was needed for an organization's overall shortcomings, or when another hyped bench talent became available.

Coaching had become the domain of shooting stars, talents that burned brightly and briefly. Scarcely anyone was accumulating successes. There were men who had managed to find regular employment, but with different teams, never staying in one place long enough to add even one Stanley Cup win to their resumes. At the end of the 1997/98 season, Bowman was the only coach actively employed in the league, other than Mike Keenan, to have won a Cup. Keenan had won his in 1993/94 with New York, and after being turfed out in St. Louis in 1996/97, waited until November 1997 to be hired by Vancouver. Marc Crawford, winner in 1995/96, was out of work, having either quit or been fired by Colorado (depending on which report you chose to believe) after the early playoff exit in 1997/98. Jacques Lemaire, winner with New Jersey in 1994/95, was also left unemployed after the Devils made their quick playoff exit that spring. Crawford and Lemaire had earlier delivered defeats to Bowman that might have crippled the career of any other coach, but Bowman had shrugged them off and outlasted these bench opponents, as he had already outlasted his bench opponents of the 1960s, 1970s and 1980s.

Only a year earlier, Bowman had been at the centre of a transitional management struggle, a winning coach who could have greatly simplified a front-office logjam by getting out of the way entirely. After a second consecutive Cup victory, Bowman was being treated unequivocally as a vital component of the team's future.

Bowman was facing a variety of issues in deciding whether or not to return to the bench for another season, some of them left over from 1997. He would be sixty-five in September; even though his load was lightened by two capable associates, Dave Lewis and Barry Smith, perhaps the time had come for him to step back from the daily grind. Toe Blake, after all, had been a comparatively spry fifty-five when he decided, after winning his eighth Cup in 1967/68, that it was time to quit on his own terms. Bowman, of course, had lost that Cup series to Blake, as the coach of the Blues, and he had long admired Blake's ability to end his career on a winning note. Blake, in fact, had won his first four games as an NHL coach in 1955/56 and then won his last five in the 1967/68 playoffs. The temptation was before Bowman to follow another cue from Blake and quit while he was ahead.

Bowman declined to address his future for the media as he and the Red Wings celebrated their sweep of Washington. Six days later, though, Bowman's future was influenced by yet another post-victory tragedy. In 1992, it had been the death of Bob Johnson. In 1997, it was the limousine accident, six days post-victory. Once again, Bowman had only six days in which to savour the championship before calamity struck. But where the accident that crippled Konstantinov came without warning, the death of Bowman's brother Jack had been lying in wait for the family.

Jack had dabbled in scouting amateur hockey players while making his living as an accountant. When Scotty Bowman arrived in Buffalo in 1979, as the new general manager he gave his brother some scouting assignments but was reluctant to hire him for fear of being charged with nepotism. Finally, with the Knoxes' blessing, Scotty put Jack on the Buffalo payroll in 1982. Jack was good at what he did, and when his older brother was fired by the Knoxes in 1986, Jack stayed on. After Rudy Migay retired as Buffalo's long-standing director of scouting in 1996, general manager John Muckler promoted Jack as his replacement. And after Muckler was fired, Jack deservedly hung in. A career highlight was approaching in the weeks following the Red Wings' second Cup victory: the annual NHL entry draft would be held at Buffalo's Marine Midland Arena, and Jack Bowman would enjoy overseeing the Sabres' draft efforts on his own turf.

But his heart was failing. Five years earlier, at fifty-six, Jack Bowman had undergone bypass surgery. By the time the draft was approaching, his condition had deteriorated to such an extent that he could not postpone more surgery. He was scheduled to go under the knife in London, Ontario, on Thursday, June 11.

Only a few hours before the procedure, Scotty Bowman used a cellular phone to call his brother from the Red Wings' team bus as it headed for Detroit's victory parade. Jack congratulated Scotty on the Wings' victory; Scotty tried to persuade Jack, and himself, that the surgery was no big deal. They never spoke again. After complications arose on the operating table, Jack Bowman died the following Monday morning. When the draft was held in Buffalo the next Saturday, a special video commemoration was presented for Jack. Scotty Bowman attended, and appeared drained of any enthusiasm for either the Cup victory or another year of coaching. Asked where the Cup was, he said he thought Barry Smith had it, didn't think he would get it until later in the summer, and didn't seem to care whether he did or not.

Ken Holland and Mike Ilitch made it plain that they wanted Bowman back; so did Steve Yzerman. Even before his brother's death, Bowman had said he didn't want to make a decision based on emotion. After the death, he tried to remove his emotions entirely from the decision by turning it over to medical authorities. As Blake had, Bowman customarily underwent a medical examination before deciding to coach for another year. This time he was undergoing a full battery of heart tests and leaving it in the doctors' hands as to whether he was fit enough to coach. Bowman had no history of heart trouble, but his brother's death warranted his caution. The heart issue aside, Bowman was also battling a deteriorating knee, and was facing replacement surgery in August. If the surgery proceeded, he might be out of action for several months. Bowman was confident that Barry Smith and Dave Lewis could run the team in his absence, but he didn't think it fair to the Red Wings that he commit to coaching if he couldn't be there in person for the entire season.

Holland responded to Bowman's public concerns with what was, for the coaching profession, extraordinary assuagement. Scotty had the whole summer to make up his mind, Holland said. He didn't need to come up with an answer right away.

Holland was striving to keep the championship lineup intact. When Doug Brown, a second-string winger who had come through with two goals in the finals, was lost to the Nashville Predators in the expansion draft, he cut a trade deal to get him back again. The defence corps, however, presented some difficult personnel decisions. Slava Fetisov, Bob Rouse and Dmitri Mironov all became unrestricted free agents on July 1, and Holland allowed Rouse and Mironov to move on, leaving the forty-year-old Fetisov dangling while signing on Jamie Macoun, who was about to turn thirty-seven, for another year. Important to speculation over the possibility of Bowman returning was Holland's signing of thirty-three-year-old free agent Uwe Krupp to a four-year, $16.4-million deal. The former Colorado defenceman had been one of the most inspired draft picks during Bowman's years in Buffalo, as he chose the West German youth 214th overall in 1983. Krupp was eager to come to Detroit to play for Bowman, and Bowman was eager to have him. "Coming to a team like ours, he'll do really well," said Bowman, forgetting for a moment whether or not he was actually going to be its coach. "He's a right defenceman, so I could see him paired with a guy like Anders Eriksson or Jamie Macoun."

Clearly Bowman had the desire to try for three consecutive Cup wins, and Holland genuinely wanted him back. Their partnership in 1997/98, which had begun with the condition that Bowman not get in Holland's way as the new general manager, had proved surprisingly free of aggravation, an about-face from the brittle partnership between Bowman and Devellano. With the most trying roster shuffles having taken place during Devellano's tenure as general manager, Bowman, the notorious managerial lone wolf, had been able to work with the rookie GM profitably and respectfully. It had taken Bowman twenty years, but he appeared to have found his way back into the coaching role he'd had in Montreal, under a general manager who could give him what he wanted, without personal fireworks, on a long-term basis. All that remained to be resolved was whether Bowman was physically capable of making even a short-term commitment to Holland.

Bowman seemed a prime candidate for a life-threatening heart condition: he was approaching sixty-five, heavy-set and employed in a high-stress business. Initial tests suggested no problems, but on Thursday, July 17, an examination at William Beaumont Hospital in Royal Oak, a suburb of Detroit, revealed that a coronary artery was 70 percent blocked. A ninety-minute angioplasty procedure cleared the blockage. He was pronounced 100 percent recovered, but the seriousness of the discovery lingered. Had it not been detected, it might have killed him on the operating table during knee replacement surgery later in

the summer. But within days, hia health status became more complicated. He had high blood pressure, high cholesterol, and signs of the
onset of adult diabetes.

The Red Wings continued to expect him back, even if he didn't show
up on time for training camp in Traverse City, Michigan, in mid-
September. Dave Lewis and Barry Smith pretty well ran that show,
anyway. When Bowman was ready to run the Red Wings, the Red Wings
were ready to run for him. For once, there was something uncomplicated about Scotty Bowman's relationship with a team, its management
and its ownership.

Bowman's essential relationship with the sport he had come to dom-
inate, however, remained inscrutable. During the latest playoff run,
Bowman had reacted to a flurry of penalty calls by referee Bill
McCreary with a piece of advice that either broadcast the arrival of a
New Bowman or set a new standard in disingenuity. "Relax," Bowman
counselled McCreary from the Red Wings' bench. "It's just a game."

Maybe it was just a game, but, as Scotty Bowman's mother had told
him, if you're good at it, why would you want to lose? Indeed, why
would you ever want to quit? It was the one accomplishment of Toe
Blake's that Bowman appeared unable to achieve. Of course, Blake
had had Bowman, giving him fits from the Blues bench in the 1967/68
Stanley Cup finals, to help him conclude it was time to get out of the
game. Thirty years later, Scotty Bowman was in a strangely lonely
position at the pinnacle of his profession. He could look down from
the summit and not see a soul approaching who was capable of moving
him aside. He was the only NHL coach whose future lay entirely within
his own hands.

"Scotty is our coach, and we want him to remain our coach," Ken
Holland said in the midst of the health tests. "That's all there is to it."

ACKNOWLEDGMENTS

The following people (in alphabetical order) granted interviews for this book, and I am grateful for their assistance and insight: Carl Brewer, Jim Devellano, Denis DeJordy, Glenn Hall, Larry Keenan, Al MacNeil, Senator Frank Mahovlich, Larry Pleau, Sam Pollock, Craig Ramsay, Ken Reardon, Jimmy Roberts, Jean-Guy Talbot, Rogie Vachon. Scotty Bowman declined to be interviewed.

Michael Clarkson of *The Toronto Star* also shared insight and information, and is to be thanked.

Writing about a career that has spanned more than forty years would not have been possible without the reportage of daily sportswriters. I am indebted to the legwork and quote-collecting of scribes past and present from the *Winnipeg Free Press*, *Regina Leader-Post*, *The Toronto Star*, *The Globe & Mail*, the *Toronto Telegram*, the *Toronto Sun*, the *Ottawa Citizen*, the *Montreal Gazette*, *The Buffalo News*, *The Detroit News*, and the *Washington Post*, as well as Canadian Press, United Press Canada, Associated Press, and *Sports Illustrated*. Special mention goes to *The Hockey News* and its many writers over the years—back issues are thankfully available on microfiche at the Hockey Hall of Fame and the Metropolitan Toronto Reference Library.

A book with such a lengthy timeline in the sport demands much in the way of context, and I have drawn on resources already detailed in my other books, *Open Ice*, *War Games*, *A Breed Apart*, and *Champions*.

Numerous books were referred to in fact-checking, but four stand out for special mention as sources of information: *The Memorial Cup*, by Richard M. Lapp and Alec Macaulay; *Jean Beliveau*, by Jean Beliveau, with Chrys Goyens and Allan Turowetz; *Lions in Winter*, by Chrys Goyens and Allan Turowetz; and *Game Misconduct*, by Russ Conway.

The Hockey Hall of Fame was its customary font of primary and reference materials, and I thank Craig Campbell, Jane Rodney, and the rest of the staff in the resource centre for their assistance.

Finally, my thanks to two editors, Meg Master and Scott Sellers, as well as copy editor Catherine Marjoriebanks, for back-checking through the prose. And as always, a tip of the hat to Penguin publisher Cynthia Good, for thinking of me when something compelling needs to be written.

INDEX

Jones, Jim, 211
Jonsson, Tomas, 227
Joseph, Curtis, 306, 337
Jutila, Timo, 236

Kannegiesser, Gord, 105
Kariya, Paul, 353–54
Karmonos, Peter, 320–21, 356
Kasatonov, Alexei, 300–01
Keane, Mike, 338, 354
Keenan, Larry, 54, 99, 110, 120–22, 128–29
Keenan, Mike, 182, 244–45, 282, 290–93, 298, 304, 311, 367
Kehoe, Rick, 277
Kelley, Jim, 208
Kelly, Red, 92, 98
Kennedy, Ted, 1, 52
Keon, Dave, 54–55
Ketter, Kerry, 154
Kidd, Trevor, 300, 308
King, Derek, 294
King, Kris, 280
Kirk, Bob, 41–42
Klima, Petr, 234–35
Knox, Northrup and Semour III, 137, 205–09, 212, 220, 240, 249–50, 368
Knuble, Mike, 303
Kocur, Joe, 331
Kolzig, Olaf, 361, 364
Konstantinov, Vladimir, 4, 300, 302, 316, 329–30, 334, 339, 349, 352, 357–58, 364–65, 368
Korab, Jerry, 216–17, 220, 243
Kozlov, Vyacheslav, 4, 300, 302, 314–15, 329–30, 338
Kromm, Bobby, 180
Krupp, Uwe, 237–38, 294, 370
Krushelnyski, Mike, 350–51
Krutov, Vladimir, 300–01
Kurvers, Tom, 294
Kurri, Jari, 231, 319
Kurtenbach, Orland, 44, 186
Kyte, Jim, 267

Labatt's (John Labatt Ltd.), 190–91
Lach, Elmer, 11, 13–14, 37
LaCombe, Normand, 225, 238
Lacroix, Andre, 68

Lafleur, Guy, 140, 146, 150, 153–54, 167–68, 172–73, 179–81, 183, 196–97, 214, 231, 301
Lafontaine, Pat, 254, 326
Lagace, Mike, 46
Lambert, Yvon, 183, 197
Langenbrunner, Jamie, 362
Langway, Rod, 8, 202, 223, 319
Laperriere, Jacques, 8, 56, 63, 82, 139, 150, 163, 169
Lapointe, Guy, 8, 145, 150, 153, 166, 179–80, 183, 197
Lapointe, Martin, 302–03, 330
Larionov, Igor, 4, 300–01, 312, 327, 334, 338, 341, 362
Larocque, Michel "Bunny", 172, 180, 183
Larose, Claude, 100, 139, 153
Larose, Guy, 239
Larouche, Pierre, 183, 203
Larson, Reed, 223
Laufman, Ken, 25
Lawton, Brian, 225, 254
LeClair, John, 340
Leach, Jamie, 265
Lee, Peter, 183
Leime, Keikki, 236
Lemaire, Jacques, 8, 68, 75, 113, 148, 150, 167, 171, 174, 183, 199, 204, 310–12, 331, 367
Lemieux, Claude, 314–16, 338
Lemieux, Mario, 254–56, 260–61, 263–64, 268, 272–75, 277–82, 294, 299, 301, 314, 326
Lepine, Pit, 139
Levinsky, Alex, 12
Lewis, Dave, 342, 344, 346–48, 350–51, 367, 369, 371
Libbey, Bill, 163
Lidstrom, Niklas, 302, 316, 330, 334, 353, 357, 360
Lilley, Les, 28
Lindbergh, Pelle, 227
Lindros, Eric, 326, 340, 354
Lindsay, Ted, 81, 102, 219–20
Linseman, 224–25
Litzenberger, Eddie, 16, 37
Loney, Troy, 264
Lowe, Kevin, 280
Lowe, Mike, 124

Murray, Terry, 7, 292, 340–41
Murray, Ross, 24
Musil, Frantisek (Frank), 234–35
Myre, Phil, 9

Nadon, Yves, 68, 93
Nanne, lou, 234–35
Naslund, Mats, 227
Naylor, Ken, 24, 28
Neale, Harry, 188, 260, 289
Nedomansky, Vaclav, 228
Neely, Bob, 211
Neilson, Roger, 7, 196, 209–18, 241,
    245–46, 279–80, 305, 311
Nevin, Bob, 38, 62, 99
Niedermayer, Scott, 325
Nilan, Chris, 223, 239
Nilsson, Ulf, 227–28
Nolan, Ted, 7
Norris, Bruce, 288
Norris, Jimmy, 4, 87–89
Norris, Marguerite, 288
Novy, Milan, 234
Nykoluk, Mike, 212

Oates, Adam, 326
O'Connor, Buddy, 18
Olczyk, Ed, 255
Olmstead, Bert, 14, 37, 92–93
Orlinski, Jerry, 27–28
Orr, Bobby, 77, 126, 179, 318
Osgood, Chris, 303, 306, 308, 312,
    316, 323, 329–30, 334–37,
    340–41, 353, 357–63
Ouimet, Ted, 76

Paek, Jim, 265
Paille, Marcel, 24
Parent, Bernie, 126, 168, 176–77, 170
Park, Brad, 289
Parker, Jeff, 238, 268
Patrick, Craig, 72–75, 84, 94,
    257–61, 263–69, 275–77, 283,
    298, 303, 330, 349
Patrick, Frank, 89–90
Patrick, Lester, 89–91, 258
Patrick, Lynn, 19, 41, 72–74, 84,
    89–102, 105–07, 111, 116, 124,
    126, 136–37, 141, 158, 176, 201,
    248, 257–58, 269, 284, 286

Patrick, Murray "Muzz", 90–92, 98
Patrick, Steve, 217, 247
Pederson, Barry, 261
Perreault, Gilbert, 201, 214, 216, 220,
    231, 240, 249–50
Perron, Jean, 204
Peterson, Brent, 219–20
Petrie, Jerry, 199–200
Picard, Noel, 100, 105, 110–11,
    130, 176
Pike, Alf, 25–26, 29, 67
Pilous, Rudy, 27, 67, 77, 92, 272, 287
Pivonka, Michal, 235
Plager, Barclay, 53–55, 64, 107–08,
    113, 136, 176
Plager, Billy, 72, 123
Plager, Bob, 9, 105, 130, 176
Plante, Jacques, 1, 14, 80, 82,
    118–19, 121, 123–24, 126,
    129–30, 139, 160, 208, 233–34,
    309
Playfair, Larry, 218
Pleau, Larry, 8, 69, 71, 75, 77–79,
    154–56, 164, 167, 321, 358
Plumb, Ron, 211
Pocklington, Peter, 319
Poile, Bud, 92
Poile, David, 292
Polano, Nick, 289
Pollin, Abe, 201
Pollock, Sam, 10, 15–18, 20, 23–29,
    31, 33, 34, 36–48, 52, 57, 59–60,
    62–65, 67–70, 74–75, 82–84,
    93–94, 96, 100–01, 105, 108, 114,
    116–17, 137–53, 158, 162–65,
    167–74, 178, 180, 183, 185–97,
    201, 204, 206, 217, 222–23,
    227–28, 239, 257, 266, 286,
    320, 343
Potvin, Denis, 286, 324, 347
Potvin, Felix, 306
Potvin, Jean, 324
Pouzar, Jaroslav, 234
Pratt, Stan, 27
Prentice, Dean, 25
Price, Noel, 153
Primeau, Joe, 1–3, 66, 68
Primeau, Keith, 315, 322–24, 331
Pronger, Chris, 322
Pronovost, Marcel, 212